CORNING AND THE CRAFT OF INNOVATION

Dear Fellow Employees,

As we reflect on the rich content of this book, we are—perhaps surprisingly—astonished all over again. We talk so much here at Corning about *innovation*. *Innovation* is one of our seven core values. *Innovation* touches every dimension of our Operating Environment. We have defined our *innovation process* not once, but twice. We attribute so much of our success in the marketplace to our unique inventions of materials and process—our *innovations*. Our new positioning statement, "Discovering Beyond Imagination" implies our continuous stretching of knowledge—*innovation*.

This is heady stuff. But in the end, it all comes down to one critical concept: *the sole source of our innovation is people . . . you*. Imagining, discovering, inventing, innovating—these are human endeavors.

As we read and remember these Corning stories of innovation, we think of our people. We think of scientists whose patents make headlines and of engineers who translate concepts into products. We think about commercial people who creatively connect us with our customers. We think about people on the factory floor who make our processes more efficient and our products more consistently excellent. We think about people in supporting roles throughout the company whose daily contributions to our operations add untold value. We think about people who push and pull and tug at this company to make us better. All of you own a piece of this innovation story.

So please read this book with pride. Know that, even though only a few are mentioned by name, this is your story. Innovation: it's all yours.

With profound thanks,

Roger G. Ackerman, Chairman   John W. Loose, CEO
Board of Directors
June 2001

CORNING

AND THE CRAFT OF
INNOVATION

MARGARET B.W. GRAHAM

ALEC T. SHULDINER

OXFORD
UNIVERSITY PRESS

2001

OXFORD
UNIVERSITY PRESS

Oxford New York
Athens Auckland Bangkok Bogotá Buenos Aires Calcutta
Cape Town Chennai Dar es Salaam Delhi Florence Hong Kong Istanbul
Karachi Kuala Lumpur Madrid Melbourne Mexico City Mumbai
Nairobi Paris São Paulo Shanghai Singapore Taipei Tokyo Toronto Warsaw

and associated companies in
Berlin Ibadan

Published by Oxford University Press, Inc.
198 Madison Avenue, New York, New York 10016

Oxford is a registered trademark of Oxford University Press

Library of Congress Cataloging-in-Publication Data
Graham, Margaret B. W.
Corning and the craft of innovation / Margaret B. W. Graham, Alec T. Shuldiner.
p. cm.   Includes bibliographical references and index.
ISBN 0-19-514097-4
1. Materials science.   2. Corning incorporated.   I. Shuldiner, Alec T.   II. Title.
TA403 G66 2001   607'.73—dc21   00–068466

ILLUSTRATION CREDITS: Page 129, photograph courtesy of Mary Purcell Roche; page 251, photograph
by Weisman; page 373, photograph by Elliott Erwitt; page 397, photograph by Jamey Stillings;
page 444, photograph by Steven Myers.

Book design and composition by Mark McGarry, Texas Type & Book Works
Set in Monotype Dante

9 8 7 6 5 4 3 2 1
Printed in the United States of America
on acid-free paper

*Dedicated to all the employees of Corning
who have contributed to the success of the company
and made the world a better place to live.*

CONTENTS

FOREWORD

Corning and the Craft of Innovation offers an inside account of the investment that Corning has made throughout its history to bring to society innovations that have been life-changing and life-enhancing. It portrays not only our pioneering and sustained investment in R&D, but also the strenuous efforts we have made to ensure that the entire company has been prepared to capitalize on this investment.

As a member of the Houghton Family, when I was growing up, I was taught that investing in R&D was like a "religion." It was something you did on faith, in good times and in bad, whether you could see the immediate fruits of it or whether you couldn't. It was not only a way of preparing for the future, but a way of safeguarding our employees against the sudden disappearance of major businesses. My great grandfather and his brother, followed by my grandfather and his brother were true believers. My father and his cousin supported the practice of this "religion" during the hard time of the Depression and it paid off in Corning's huge television bulb business after World War II. My brother Amo and his colleagues kept this faith alive during some of the darkest days of the company, in the 1970s when many other companies curtailed their investments in R&D; their perseverance paid off in huge growth businesses such as catalytic convertor substrates and, of course, the explosive optical communications industry, that we, in a sense, invented and in which we have a strong leadership role today.

When I was Chairman, we sustained the investment in R&D. Happily, as in other periods, some of the investments we made then, for which we saw no return for many years, like fusion glass for flat panel computer displays, have turned out to be large, high growth businesses.

But we worried that Science and Technology alone would not keep us growing and changing. Thus, we broadened the definition of "Innovation" to include the systematic efforts in all parts of the company to make sure that what we invested in R&D could be harvested. We insisted upon Innovation in everything we did as a company.

This is the first time Corning has had a history written about the company for outside consumption. We have always assumed that our record would speak for itself. But this is certainly not the first time our history has been recorded for inside consumption. Judging from the number of historical documents of all kinds that have contributed to this book, the recording of history at Corning has been almost as steady and pervasive over the years as our investment in R&D—and, as this book points out, this too has been an investment in the future.

We intend this volume, *The Generations of Corning*, to serve as reminders of the forward looking traditions that have made Corning the company that it is. We also intend it to celebrate the lives and contributions of the thousands of employees and outside business associates, past and present, who have enabled the company to achieve what it has. As we come to our sesquicentennial as an enterprise we are welcoming into the company many new employees, some of whom also come from companies with proud traditions. As in former times when we acquired or merged with other companies, we want to share our history with them, and we know that their stories will enrich ours.

Corning and the Craft of Innovation, in particular, is also intended to contribute to the scholarly literature on innovation. It offers to the world of scholarship—to historians of technology and R&D, and to students of innovation—an inside picture of a company that has taken an uncluttered path. Corning has made a practice of innovating in anticipation of opportunity in emerging industries, rather than taking the more common approach of investing when the need is clearer and the payoff easier to measure. For this reason we have had the chance, not once but many times, to help shape new industries in ways that have given us the chance to profit from their most rapid period of growth. As this book demonstrates, there have been reasons that Corning has so often been in the right place at the right time, and I believe that account is worth sharing with others.

JAMES R. HOUGHTON

PREFACE

The Ise shrine, one of the most important in Japan, dates back to the 7th century AD but is rebuilt every twenty years.* Though believed by archeologists to be faithful to its original design, the fragrant cypress materials from which it is constructed are always fresh, and its lines—verticals and horizontals only, to make it earthquake tolerant—are never allowed to go out of alignment. The shrine is rebuilt in each generation for aesthetic and spiritual reasons, but the process has the side benefit of keeping in constant use crafts that might otherwise have been lost centuries ago. Because it goes through a public ceremony of renewal each time it is rebuilt, it has continued to influence styles of Japanese building, so much so that it has been called the "prototype of Japanese architecture."

By Ise standards Corning Incorporated is a recent creation, but at 150 years old it is one of the oldest North American enterprises, and among its

* KenzoTange and Noboru Kawazoe, *Ise: Prototype of Japanese Architecture* (Cambridge, MIT Press, 1965).

most successful innovators. Corning, too, has kept alive a central craft, passing it along from generation to generation. This is the craft of innovation, a
set of skills and sensibilities that cannot be reduced to a science, and that is
motivated by purposes that go beyond simple materialism. Shared through
time, the craft is renewed and reinvented in each era in accordance with its
peculiar circumstances.

Less by design than by habit, each Corning generation has contrived to
pass on its stories of invention and renewal to the next—in earlier times in
the form of brown leatherbound notebooks, at other times in the form of
published accounts, or slide presentations, or videotaped discussions, and
once in the form of a two-day conference on innovation. We have had the
good fortune to play a role in the current generation's effort to capture its
account of Corning's craft of innovation for the next. It is a story that contains much of interest to other innovative companies too, as well as to companies that face the need to become more innovative, indeed to all who
want to understand the history of innovation in the United States.

Just as at Ise, new shrine buildings begin to be erected on an alternative
site as soon as the old ones have been torn down, so Corning's new generation is already reinventing its own approach to innovation. Their approach
is being shaped by the vast opportunities presented by the telecommunications revolution at the beginning of the twenty-first century, amidst pressures that attend the most explosive period of technological change in 100
years. Appropriately focused on the present and the future—on photonics
and optical systems components, on next generation catalytic converters
and advanced LCD screens, they are likely to regard stories of the development of Pyrex glasses and glass ceramics, of fusion glasses and funnel spin-
ners and tubing draw processes as little more than quaint curiosities. Yet it is
likely that some of what they reinvent will echo the essential human and
organizational themes that we recount here, just as previous Corning generations have found themselves rediscovering some of the approaches that
they inherited, often unaware of any similarities. Reinvention is sometimes
mistakenly taken to be a sign of cultural inefficiency. In fact, it is the truest
way for each new group to discover its own powerful tools and approaches
that are needed to tackle an ever-changing environment.

In any case, Corning's history of technology-based innovation over 150 years is a remarkable part of the history of American business. At the same time, it is also far more representative than has generally been realized of a whole side of American business that has been portrayed as out of the mainstream. This side of American business, where specialty materials and manufacturing companies are likely to be found, has relied on knowledge and wit rather than scale, on flexibility and relationship rather than managerial hierarchy and control, to make its way in the world. In this sense, we think of Corning as a prototype of technology-based innovation at the turn of the twenty-first century.

For the ability to pursue our own craft in writing this history we have many people to thank. First, those who conceived the project and gave it their strong support, Eve Menger and Augustus Filbert; secondly, the Advisory Committee to the Corporate History Project, who, in addition to Eve Menger and Augustus Filbert, included from inside Corning, Rob Cassetti, Cindy Demers, Jack Holliday, Jamie Houghton, Al Michaelsen, Meleny Peacock, and Stuart Sammis; and from outside Corning, Peter Bridenbaugh, Bernard Carlson, and unofficial member and honorary advisor on matters chemical, George Hammond. Special mention needs also to be made of Stuart Sammis, who bore the burdens of several years of coordination and did the closest reading of all. All members of this committee met many times at Corning, offering their local knowledge, advice and encouragement, and, above all, reading several drafts. Other vital contributors were those in previous eras who recorded their own stories, kept Corning's archives supplied with fresh documents, and in some cases collected their own private stores of records. Otto Hilbert, in particular, by sending out persistent letters of reminder and putting together historical notebooks in the 1970s, ensured that the accounts of his own generation and previous ones, would not be forgotten*. Equally important to the project were the many members of the Corning community, far too numerous to name here, but noted in the endnotes, who gave interviews to Corning's history project. In many cases, these vital sources not only reviewed the drafts of

---

* How persistent these efforts were is suggested by a note written by Eddy Leibig about a top secret radar meeting he attended during World War II. "That's all I can remember," he wrote to Hilbert with feeling. "Now leave me alone."

their own interviews but read drafts of book chapters for accuracy. We thank them not only for their attention, but for the great enjoyment speaking with them afforded us. To Thomas MacAvoy and Marie McKee, in particular, for calling attention to innovation as one of Corning's most enduring capabilities, we owe a profound debt of gratitude. Other members of the Corning community who contributed materially to this work, in archival research, graphics, picture research, meeting support, videotaping and index preparation, included Michelle Cotton, Nancy Foster, Rich Dreyfuss, Kris Gable, Tony Midey, Gerry Orr, Cheryl Quinn, Tim Shadduck, and Marianna Stewart. In addition, we wish to acknowledge the efforts of archivists and editors, especially Rachel Maines and Gerrol Pottinger of Maines and Associates, Martha Nichols, and at Oxford University Press, Herbert Addison and Helen Mules. We are also grateful to the rest of the Oxford team, Ellen Chodosh, Chris Critelli, Peter Ginna, Liz Hartman, Brian Hughes, Ben Lee, Ruth Mannes, and Amy White. We are grateful to our colleagues at Winthrop Group, Inc., especially Davis Dyer and Dan Gross, whose parallel work on a history of Corning, benefited ours in many ways and whose fine interviews were an invaluable resource, and Suzanne Spellman who with her colleagues transcribed and kept track of hundreds of tapes. Finally, to those who have borne most of the personal burdens of our authorial process with little of the enjoyment, especially Peter Brown, our appreciation for forbearance. With so many sources to consult and so much material to master we have undoubtedly made mistakes, but we cannot claim to have lacked for informed support in our efforts to get it right. Thank you, one and all.

1

INTRODUCTION

I N J U N E 1999, *Wired* magazine, chronicler of the world as seen from Silicon Valley, proposed several new candidates for its forty-stock Wired Index, a list of companies that its experts believe have the most to gain from the meteoric rise of the Internet. It must have surprised many readers to find Corning Incorporated (once Corning Glass Works) among the contenders. Isn't this the company that produced the Corning Ware given to newlyweds at practically every baby boomer wedding and the Corelle dinnerware found on millions of dining room tables? How can the manufacturer of Pyrex, that down-to-earth staple of kitchen and laboratory alike, be among the top few business beneficiaries of the most ethereal of computer technologies?

The answer is that this is not your father's—or grandmother's—Corning. Although the public still generally thinks of the company in terms of household products, it has become a leading global supplier of optical fiber and photonics to the telecommunications industry and of screen glass for state-of-the-art laptop displays; Corning is also a major producer of ultraclear lens components to manufacturers of stepper cameras used in the semiconductor industry. In fact, Corning Ware, Corelle, and Pyrex are all brands of a consumer division that is no longer even part of the company. At present, this once and future glassmaker would be more accurately labeled as the foremost supplier of ceramic substrates for catalytic converters to the worldwide automobile industry or even as a leading maker of a range of *plastic* tools used by pharmaceutical companies for genomics research. And a business observer in the mid-1980s, if asked to predict Corning's future a decade or two hence, might reasonably have identified even more surprising identities: biomedical conglomerate, major provider of medical services, holding company, or one of the world's largest venture capital organizations.

Companies that are a century or more old have experimented with different business lines and developed new competencies over the course of time. Corning's creation and re-creation of its identity has not evolved haphazardly but through a pattern of deliberate, regular, and profitable innovation that has extended over nearly the entirety of the company's 150-year history. Corning has explicitly relied on knowledge as its foremost asset, has acquired that knowledge in accordance with long-held values, and has exploited it with the help of a remarkable series of partnerships with other organizations. In the process, it has changed its product mix, the nature of its manufacturing, and its location within a wide range of industries.

In the pages that follow, we address themes common to the study of any technology-driven company: the role of craft versus science, the complicated interaction between process and product, and the difficulties inherent in managing an R&D organization that produces both "home runs" and "base hits," depending on competitive circumstances. But the central question, and the greatest point of interest in Corning's case, is not so much how it has dealt with these challenges in any given instance but how such a venerable company has done so over the long run. The drive to sustain and remain innovative is at the crux of Corning's identity and has been since Amory Houghton founded the company in the 1850s. Yet in many respects, Corning does not fit the mold for corporate success as it has traditionally been understood.

The dominant narrative of the second Industrial Revolution, as related by Alfred Chandler and others, depicts the main engine of the capitalist economy as the giant bureaucratic corporation that pursues a strategy of uniformity and standardization in an attempt to secure market control.[1]

However, business commentators and academics have noted that the examples best known to students of such corporations—such as General Motors or U.S. Steel—have never been a good fit for large specialty manufacturers and are even less so for companies in the high-tech and information industries. Historian Philip Scranton, in his recent work on the history of specialty manufacturers, notes that focusing on the giants ignores the bulk of capitalist enterprise. He has called companies like Corning "the great uninterrogated stories" of U.S. industrial history.[2]

Corning's progress since the mid-nineteenth century represents a counternarrative that may well apply to many more companies than is generally realized. Its story suggests that what really matters for innovators, especially technology-based innovators, is less economies of scale and distribution— or standardized activity and managerial hierarchy—than the need to foster independent thinkers who are also team players, creative relationship building via joint ventures and strategic partnerships, and, perhaps most important, the continuous generation, management, and deployment of intellectual property as a strategic asset. This last point is of particular interest in light of the growing role of intellectual property in high technology and Internet businesses. For decades, Corning has yoked individual efforts to large project goals, through various institutions and disciplines, without sacrificing its unusual climate for creativity. This struggle holds many lessons, as does the history of the company's attempts to manage intellectual property for the strategic benefit of possible future product lines without compromising the current needs of its existing businesses.

These characteristics are hardly unique to Corning; nor are stories of organizations meeting these challenges rare. But while many commentators have pointed to knowledge creation and knowledge workers as the keys to generating innovation, few have offered a richly detailed account that reflects the odd rhythms, the sheer quirkiness, of such activities and people in a technology-based company. Fewer still have explored the efforts of those who manage innovation and innovative workers not just in one product generation or technological era but over the very long term.[3]

Similarly, tracing one company's struggle to manage its intellectual property over many decades clearly shows that the purposeful handling of invisible, hard-to-control yet crucial assets in a knowledge-driven company inevitably produces tensions among different interests, both internal and external. When does patenting confer advantage? Who gets access to trade secrets? Who is granted a license, on what terms? When do equity partnerships make sense? When does openness engender too much competition, and when does it fuel the flow of creative ideas? What access should government have to internally developed technologies, and on what basis? How is it possible to navigate the shoals of shifting antitrust policy when variously applied to evolving technologies? Corning's approach to these complicated issues will not necessarily match another firm's. Every company is a unique blend of culture, historical circumstance, embedded expertise, and individual talent. Individual employees have certainly played key roles at Corning, as have a powerful corporate identity and an intermittently successful growth strategy. But it is the company's ability to harness its collective ingenuity across all aspects of its business without resorting to excessive bureaucracy—a practice with managerial and cultural roots reaching back to Corning's earliest days— that provides the most striking insights for managers in other businesses.

FOCUS ON INNOVATION?

Students of innovation at the beginning of the twentieth-first century are likely to conceive of this critical activity rather differently than did scholars some thirty years ago. At that time, innovation was seen as essentially synonymous with the linear progression that was thought to characterize R&D. Today we are apt to recognize that successful innovators—whether individuals, teams, or companies—are engaged in a sequence that is highly variable and iterative rather than linear.[4] It is important to mark this change, for the models that frame our thinking guide our attention accordingly, both as a society and as a managerial culture. Such models also influence our expectations of what can be accomplished and how. Organizations, as well as the systems of record keeping and accountability that fuel historical analyses and official stories, are shaped by such expectations.

Another aspect of innovation that has yet to receive the attention it deserves, and which the history of Corning richly illustrates, is the importance of key people at all points along the way, not just at the "point" of invention. Most people at Corning are likely to know the name of Don Stookey, the pioneering inventor who developed Corning's first family of glass ceramics, called Pyroceram, but few would recognize that of Ed Grainger, the production engineer at the Martinsburg, West Virginia, plant who conducted some of the first efforts to chemically strengthen Pyroceram to improve Corning Ware. Everyone in the small world of fiber optics can recite the trio of names on Corning's early fiber-optics patents—Bob Maurer, Don Keck, and Pete Schultz—but far fewer recall their technicians, Fran Voorhees and Jerry Burke, whose clever process experimentation made those patents feasible. Indeed, the development of Corning's optical waveguide business, a history replete with innovation, was dependent on far more than a handful of scientists. Who can recount the career risks taken by project manager Dave Duke in commercializing waveguides or the tireless efforts of engineers like Git Kar and his group who sorted out fiber-optic production—or the years spent by patent attorney Al Michaelsen prosecuting patent infringers—or the miles of international travel Chuck Lucy devoted to the joint development alliances? Yet all were part of the ultimate success of fiber optics for the company.

As economist Lester Thurow has recently observed, having inventive product technologies is no longer enough in a world of stiff global competition, if it ever was: leadership in process technologies is as at least as crucial an element for companies creating new products and industries. Thurow notes that the nature of process technology, especially, requires a rejection of the simplistic linear model of innovation:

> To be masters of process technologies a successful business must be managed so that there is a seamless web among invention, design, manufacturing, sales logistics, and services that competitors cannot match. The secret of being best [lies] in having the skills base throughout the organization that allows it to be the low-cost integrator of all of these activities.[5]

Corning's mastery of process technology, fed by the same inventive ingenuity as its product technology, was for many years directed mainly at keeping it ahead of the field in terms of performance. But when its domestic picture tube customers lost first their lead and then the entire television business to foreign competitors in the 1970s, Corning recognized the need to refocus its efforts on achieving cost leadership as well. That only proved possible because managers paid close attention to innovation in all parts of the company.

The linear model also underrates the importance of serendipity and the power of "failed" projects to produce success. Corning's experience offers countless examples in which innovative activities aimed at one objective have borne fruit in many different arenas. Glass strengthening research first aimed at improving the properties of glass insulators for high-tension wires in the 1920s made it possible to produce new sorts of cookware in the 1930s. The "fusion" process developed for safety windshield production in the 1960s, a project that ended in total failure for Corning, found application twenty and thirty years later in products as diverse as photochromic lenses, mirrors for spy satellites, and notebook computer displays.

Perhaps the greatest example of serendipitous payoff resulted from the work of organic chemist Franklin Hyde, who was hired by Corning to explore the chemical no-man's-land between glass and plastic in a general attempt to push its technical boundaries. In 1932, though temporarily stymied in his efforts to develop what would eventually become silicone cements and other silicone products, Hyde invented and patented the flame hydrolysis technique for producing high-purity silica. Decades later, this was adapted as a vapor deposition process used to produce radar delay lines, the first of many Corning products made in this fashion out of high-purity silica. Today this same process is key to many of the glasses the company makes, often superceding the basic hot glass processes that were Corning's area of process mastery for over a century. Even Corning's pioneering forays into immobilized enzymes, which seemed from the standpoint of the early 1990s to have led the company down a blind, if profitable, alley, have reemerged in recent years to combine with a new foray into polymer research and laboratory ware for the life sciences.

Specialty Materials and Knowledge Work

Corning, then, provides a particularly vital context in which to study innovation. It is a specialty materials company whose products are almost always subsumed within other goods; as a result, it is the sort of enterprise that is easily overlooked and therefore not well understood. Specialty materials companies—others include producers of exotic steels and aluminum or high-tech plastics—are rarely confined to one market. Instead they make a basic contribution to the overall economy by helping to create new markets and by transferring the technical knowledge acquired in one market to others.[6] Corning's products have made indispensable but largely invisible contributions to many of the most potent emerging markets in U.S. history— lighting, radio, television, radar, and telecommunications in particular—and yet the company's ability to reinvent itself by moving deliberately from developing market to developing market has often been dismissed as merely confusing to financial analysts who want companies and technologies they can easily categorize.

Specialty materials companies might be called the original knowledge work companies because so much about their product remains mysterious and depends on human ingenuity. And for most of the industrial era, specialty materials companies have violated generally accepted management norms in order to be successful. Corning has been no exception to this rule. One hundred thirty years ago, soon after our story begins, the company settled in a small town in upstate New York. By the 1960s, many similarly located companies had moved their headquarters to financial centers or other, trendier locations. But Corning's management reaffirmed its odd choice of location then and continues to reaffirm it today: it remains headquartered in the same town in upstate New York, though it has long since extended its operations reach and its vital network of relationships around the world. At the same time Corning has branched out well beyond glass as its material of choice, becoming a specialty materials company in a much broader sense. In these choices and many others, its leaders have displayed the same stubborn refusal to accept prevailing orthodoxies that made the company embrace a knowledge-based strategy from the start.

Family controlled and family owned for most of its history, Corning has nevertheless attracted and retained professional managers of very high caliber, and it has consistently offered them a large degree of autonomy in their decision making. It has worked closely with much larger customers in many different markets (lightbulb blanks, television tubes, optical fiber), outlasting quite a few of them by never allowing itself to be defined by any single set of customers or any single set of analysts. It has also served as a bridge company for processes, transferring the benefits of new technologies from one industry to another. A vital problem solver for the U.S. military in areas as diverse as metallized electronic components, silicones, ceramic nosecones, and mirrors for spy satellites, Corning has never been a typical member of the "military-industrial complex." On some occasions, the company has even gone so far as to invest its own development money in projects that had only military use rather than risk having to give up any rights to its intellectual property.

Steadily profitable for most of its history, Corning has prided itself not on gaining quick returns but on supplying "patient money." It pursued fiber optics, for instance, for sixteen years before even breaking even, and many more before gaining a return on that investment. More recently, its liquid crystal display business has finally gone into the black after consuming an investment almost as large as that of optical fiber before it turned profitable. Yet the company has proved capable of turning on a dime, beating far larger and better-known competitors in highly visible contests, such as the production of the telescope mirror for Mount Palomar in 1932, a feat General Electric had attempted and failed to accomplish, or inventing the ceramic substrates for catalytic converters in a race against 3M in the 1970s. Finally, as one of the best-known participants in highly profitable alliances, Corning often chooses to venture with, rather than absorb or otherwise closely control, many companies around the world, even if leading industrial economists call this a losing strategy.[7] Equally unorthodox, its alliances have often been created as fifty-fifty joint ventures, despite the conventional wisdom that insists one partner or the other should have the majority share and final say.

HISTORICAL OVERVIEW: THE HOUGHTON IMPRIMATUR

For Corning's first 150 years one family had both the controlling interest and the guiding influence over its fortunes. This was the Houghtons, an American family with many similarities to European business dynasties. One

authority on the history of family companies, economic historian David
Landes, maintains that American business families differ from European
business families: they tend to use their companies, and the fortunes they
make from them when they go public, as springboards to other pursuits
rather than remain involved in the business.[8] For several generations the
Houghtons were an exception to this rule. Family members who took leadership positions with Corning certainly pursued serious outside interests—
often second careers—in politics, diplomacy, and the arts.[9] But because of
the family's commitment to the company, generation to generation, these
interests often complemented their involvement with the company instead
of detracting from it. James R. Houghton, known to all as Jamie Houghton,
possibly the last in his family to serve as Corning's chief executive retired in
April 1996 and remained on the board of directors into the twenty-first century. Because of this element of continuity, much of this history of Corning
and innovation is about the Houghtons and their inherited commitment to
what they have often called "the uncluttered path."[10] How much the company's ability to innovate depended on this continuity of purpose handed
down through the family, or the relative independence it was able to give

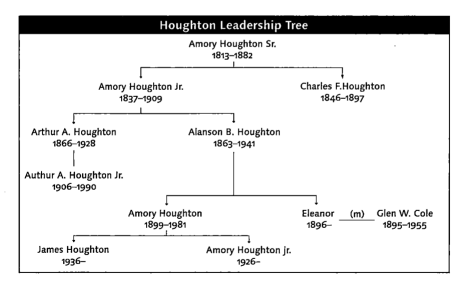

*From the first Houghton investment in the Union Glass Company in 1851 there would be a
Houghton family member in the leadership of the enterprise nearly continuously until 1996.*

the company from the day-to-day pressures of the financial markets, remains for the reader to judge.

The Formative Era, 1851–1907

The Houghton stake in the glass industry began with Amory Houghton Sr.'s investment in the Bay State Glass Company of Somerville, Massachusetts, in 1851. Until 1875, when it was incorporated as Corning Glass Works, this family enterprise consisted mainly of a growing knowledge base, acquired in the first instance from the English glassmaker known as "Gaffer" Teasdale. While still small enough to be loaded onto a few barges, the company moved twice in search of better conditions. In the end, settling for receptive customers, a willing workforce, and good transportation as the decisive criteria, the company responded to an invitation from a group of local businessmen to set up shop in Corning, New York. This move was not an immediate success: a downturn in the company's fortunes temporarily cost the family its control of the enterprise, which was only restored in 1872 when Amory Junior and his brother Charles managed to buy the company back. This experience appears to have been traumatic for the Houghtons; the family's determination never again to lose control probably drove them to invest aggressively in R&D. The desire to remain in control of their own destiny also meant the Houghtons were willing to take substantial risks with new products rather than face the prospect of innovating from a defensive position.

In Corning's formative era—from 1851 to 1909—the paramount obsessions of the family controlling it were acquiring knowledge and know-how about glass and the processes used to make it, often from distant or unlikely quarters, ranging from German glassmakers to the U.S. Geological Survey. Post-Civil War developments in the domestic glass industry had ensured that knowledge was the sole advantage Corning Glass Works could hope to have, given its chosen location. Companies across the Alleghenies in the Ohio Valley enjoyed an ideal resource base, both in raw materials and a readily available immigrant workforce, and the best geographical position for supplying the exploding western markets. When the high volume segments of the emerging industry—flat glass and containers—both fell to western producers, the Houghtons' company was left with little choice but to find a niche in specialty glass or go out of business.

Fortunately, Corning's employees displayed a talent for the kind of problem solving and flexible production that specialty glass required, and they demonstrated these qualities with a succession of powerful customers— connections that were an essential ingredient in its early success. Corning's work on optical design and color for railroad signal glasses from the 1870s forward gave it the opportunity to set color standards not only for the railroads but, in time, for most other branches of the transportation industry as well. In 1880, the chance to supply Thomas Edison with glass tubing for his lighting experiments soon led Corning to that most fortuitous of all combinations—a technically demanding customer in a high-growth industry. As a supplier of lightbulb enclosures to Edison's electrical enterprises, Corning not only secured a steady stream of orders from the two leading electrical manufacturers, General Electric and Westinghouse, but also eventually found itself able to control, via licensing, the mechanical processes by which all kinds of glassware, including containers, were manufactured.

In-House R&D and Its Consequences, 1908–1941

Corning's first step toward institutionalizing its collective ingenuity came in 1908, when it set up one of the earliest corporate research laboratories in the United States. Though established to address serious process problems, such as temperature control in its furnaces, this investment produced a key breakthrough on the product front: a better glass composition for railroad lanterns. This led to Corning's development of its own version of the German-invented borosilicate glass, which, in 1912, gave the company its first patented family of glasses, trademarked "Pyrex." Pyrex glass lent itself to products as varied as thermometer tubing, ovenware, and glass for architectural purposes. Soon, powered by a huge increase in commercial activity caused by the outbreak of World War I, demand for tubing, laboratory ware, and lightbulbs became so great that Corning had a "growth problem" to address. The process changes, such as tank melting and mechanized bulb production, that Corning adopted to meet this problem and to cope with raw material shortages caused by the war led to its second major investment in research infrastructure, the machine research laboratory set up in 1917.

Together with several other companies in its industry, and along with key customers like General Electric, Corning also developed a new generation of mechanized technologies for glass forming in the years directly before and after World War I. The machines invented at that time revolutionized glassmaking in general far beyond Corning's specialty glass segment. This level of mechanization had no parallel in Europe. Arrangements were made to fund and license these technologies through a holding company called Hartford Empire, jointly owned by the Houghton family, General Electric, and others. Meanwhile, unknown to the rest of the industry, Corning leapfrogged its collaborators by inventing the most advanced glass forming machine of all, definitively solving its first major growth problem. The ribbon machine, unveiled in 1926, turned out not only lightbulb blanks but vacuum tube blanks as well in the unheard of quantities of thousands per hour.[11] It remains the state of the art machine for incandescent light bulbs seventy-four years later.

Almost immediately after it patented the ribbon machine, Corning demonstrated its talents once again by taking on a challenge that had already defeated its long-time collaborator, General Electric. In a feat that raised the spirits and caught the imagination of the many astronomy buffs during the Depression, Corning managed to pour and form out of Pyrex the largest single piece of glass ever produced until that time, the 200-inch mirror for the Hale telescope at the Mount Palomar observatory. This achievement propelled the company, still a small enterprise, onto the national stage in 1935, a high-profile position it would maintain, thanks to events that occurred before and during World War II.

Despite its achievements in developing Pyrex into a genuine engineered material, as well as real advances in mechanization that improved its costs, Corning was running scared in the 1930s. Its patents protecting Pyrex were due to expire in the middle of the decade, and DuPont and other chemical companies were experimenting with transparent plastics that offered an obvious threat to glass. Corning headed off competition for Pyrex ovenware by introducing new lines of cookware based on strengthened glass. By the fateful year 1936 it had also merged with MacBeth Evans (another force in domestic glassware), invested seriously in exploratory research to find new proprietary materials, and positioned itself to exploit its findings by forming the first of three new "associations," a form of equity venture that would later be called a "joint venture." The merger and all three of the new organizations, founded in partnership with larger enterprises (Pittsburgh Plate Glass, Dow Chemical, and Owens-Illinois), endured, Owens-Corning growing larger than Corning itself. By the end of the 1930s "Corning means research in glass," the most frequently used company slogan for several decades, had become at once a statement of identity and a corporate insurance policy. The commitment it implied was that Corning's route to growth would continue to be through technology-based innovation related to one versatile material, generated in part by its own research efforts.

War, Television, Corning Ware, and the Triumph of R&D: 1941–1968

World War II was a tremendous watershed for Corning, as it was for many companies. In Corning's case, its efforts to solve all sorts of technical problems for the military led the company to develop many new postwar product opportunities, some of which, like metallized electronic components, its researchers had not previously imagined. Along with this broadening of product lines, Corning took on more of the characteristics of a mainstream company, certifying the Flint Glass Workers as a union in 1943, and issuing stock on the stock exchange in 1945.

Furthermore, the end of the war saw the ultimate resolution of a series of antitrust actions against Corning and its collaborators. Their activities, centered around the Hartford-Empire Company, had been designed to create order in the glass industry through the control of key production technologies. Although cooperative business activities, particularly those in support of research, had been encouraged by Republican administrations in the 1920s, the New Deal's activist Justice Department saw things otherwise, and the Hartford-Empire network, denigrated as the "Glass Trust," was quickly seized upon as an egregious example of illegal collusion. Corning executives were hauled into court to testify, and both Corning and its new young president, the second Amory Houghton Sr. (a major private investor in Hartford-Empire) were severely penalized. Like the temporary loss of family control in an earlier generation, this experience scarred the company's collective psyche. To a large extent this helps to explain why an adversarial relationship arose between Corning and the government during World War II, despite the company's numerous military research successes and role as lead supplier of strategically important items such as vacuum tube bulbs and radar. Corning's temporary abandonment of such practices as the formation of equity ventures can also be attributed to this experience.

Soon after the war, Bill Decker, Corning's president at the time, committed the company to the television bulb business a direct outgrowth of its work on radar. This move involved turning off or deemphasizing (though not killing) a number of other promising product programs, ranging from optical glass to new multiform technologies. Even before black-and-white television was fully launched, Corning threw itself into an aggressive R&D program to develop cathode ray tube bulbs for color television, a preemptive move that would set the pattern for many of its most successful innovations for the rest of the century. With this experience as a model, Corning would try wherever possible to have its technology ready and its capacity on line in advance of demand.

The extremely profitable position that Corning occupied in television tubes in the 1950s and 1960s provided a financial umbrella for a string of other high-tech innovations, some of which were directed at markets that were decidedly not high-tech. Corning Ware, for the consumer market, for instance, incorporated Corning's second major proprietary family of glasses—the glass ceramics dubbed "Pyroceram"—which were initially used for missile nosecones. It made Corning a household name for the first time and led to a string of technology-based innovations for the consumer market, exploiting not only the superior properties of glass but also the popularity in the consumer mind of space-age technology in all aspects of life. Because of major successes with lines like television glass and Corning Ware, the company restructured itself with the goal of churning out major product innovations on demand. But the results of this approach, consistent with the linear model of innovation that industry adopted in the aftermath of the "scientists' war" and the H-bomb, were decidedly mixed.

Beyond Glass, 1968–2001

The extraordinary profitability of Corning's television glass business began to unravel in the late 1960s when its leading customer, RCA, built its own plant capable of manufacturing the most profitable tube blanks. While Corning suffered a major setback here, it fortunately did not have all its eggs in one basket. Although morale and profits inevitably suffered, the company was able to draw on a store of partially developed technologies and techniques—what some called its "technology till"—to formulate new product opportunities. Determined not to be so dependent on one product again, it pushed ahead with several of them. Corelle dishes reinvigorated Corning's consumer division, and Celcor, a ceramic destined to become a part of millions of car mufflers, provided earning streams during the 1970s and beyond. Corning also established a presence in other explosive technology-based markets, like electronic components and medical electronics. In these latter instances, however, the company lacked both the firm proprietary research base and the necessary connections to the scientific (and military) networks required to succeed.

The 1970s were a very rough period for the company. A flood in 1972 nearly destroyed the Corning headquarters complex and wiped out much of the surrounding town. The company struggled to maintain its fundamental identity—diluted by forays down such odd alleys as medical services—while negotiating tensions, heightened by financial difficulties, between the short-term imperative of productivity and the long-term need to maintain an environment conducive to creativity. The linear model of innovation fell into disrepute with industry, and Corning fought to hold on to the fiber-optics technology that would eventually revolutionize its business. The company's adoption of a number of industrial disciplines, most notably its embrace of the total quality movement, helped to resolve these tensions and led to the restoration of its former identity, with a few contemporary twists. Stripped of its consumer division and of distracting ventures into medical services early in 1998, Corning is once again a manufacturer of specialty materials, with a very large stake in fiber optics and photonics, and is a central player in several other high-growth technology-driven markets. Meanwhile, globalization of both Corning's markets and its R&D infrastructure has increased the opportunity to profit from collective ingenuity, but also the attendant coordination issues. Corning was one of the earliest companies to give its international research sites their own independent mission: as the twenty-first century begins, it is increasingly allocating its most urgent research tasks across a global network that extends to laboratories across the United States to France, Russia, the UK and Japan. Now Corning "means" research in optical communications and photonics and in all glass-related specialty materials, conducted and applied in an international complex.

FROM 1851 TO 2001: ALWAYS UNORTHODOX

Corning and the Craft of Innovation is roughly organized in chronological order, but each chapter focuses on a particular topic relevant to a given time period. After an overview of Corning technology in chapter 2, chapters 3 to 5 describe the first ninety years of Corning's existence, ending with World War II; topically, this section concerns itself with three important aspects of the company's formation and its pursuit of a knowledge-based strategy during this time. Chapter 3 deals with the early institutionalization of research and the role of leading-edge customers in helping shape Corning's strategy by example and through knowledge sharing. Chapter 4 covers the challenging and generative nature of Corning's process technology, propelled in its first century less by science than by craftsmanship and artisanry supported by science. Chapter 5 recounts the company's largely successful attempts to capitalize on its knowledge beyond its own immediate sales channels through alliances with other more powerful companies in other markets.

The next two chapters cover the 1940s and 1950s. Chapter 6 addresses the complicated question of Corning's relationship with the government in general and with the military in particular. Chapter 7 focuses on the postwar period, when Corning was consumed by its television business. It emphasizes the evolving institutionalization of research, which had been thrown off track by the war but was now looked upon as a way to start other like businesses on demand.

The last three chapters focus on the 1960s up to the present day. Chapter 8 is concerned with intellectual property and the tightrope that had to be walked between staking out a protected patent position and avoiding antitrust violations. Chapter 9 focuses on the deeply troubled post-TV era and Corning's various attempts to reestablish its identity even as it expanded beyond glass. Chapter 10 details the company's most recent quest to institutionalize innovation in every department and at every level of the organization. The book concludes with an epilogue that catches up with Corning's most recent developments.

"Always unorthodox," Corning once again offers an alternative to the high-tech orthodoxy centered in Silicon Valley that has been magnified by the Internet. Whereas the Silicon Valley model suggests that skilled and knowledgeable researchers and technologists will produce their most creative work only if rewarded with the chance to become individually wealthy through stock options, Corning still attracts men and women who want to be part of an innovating community that pursues "life-changing and life-enhancing" technologies as its primary reason for being.[12]

Another powerful motivator for Corning's innovation must not be overlooked: for a century and a half Corning's identity has been tied to its technology. Most of the time this has been recognized as a major strategic advantage; occasionally it has been viewed as a burden, or at least a constraint, but in either case the technology involved in solving problems with (and creating products of) glass and other specialty materials has been a source of intrinsic appeal to glassworkers, technologists and managers alike. A brief overview of Corning's technology follows in chapter 2.

THE MYSTERY

AT THE HEART OF IT ALL

AN OVERVIEW OF

CORNING TECHNOLOGY

N O BOOK ABOUT Corning would be complete without an overview of the technology at the heart of its business as a specialty glassmaker. This chapter deals with glass as a material and the various processes that Corning used to create it.

"THE MYSTERY AND MASTERY OF GLASS"

This advertising slogan, which appeared in the *Saturday Evening Post*, 3 November 1917, as part of Corning's first national advertising campaign, conveys something important about the company and its technology that has endured to this day. Though intangible, the mysteries of glass composition and the way the material behaves in melting, cooling, and forming were in a sense some of the company's most vital assets.[1]

The mystery of glass was not just the source of a seemingly endless array of problems and obstacles; it was part of the allure of working with

This ad, celebrating what Corning's knowledge of glass was making possible, kicked off its first national advertising campaign in 1917.

glass and the various materials that related to it. In the early days of the twentieth century, the appeal of glass, an often beautiful material with a long and romantic past, was an attraction to craftsmen and scientists alike. The sight of molten glass, being poured out of a ladle or drawn in a long thread at the end of an iron or running in a continuous red-hot ribbon, inspired both awe and fascination. For glassmakers the appeal was strong enough to counteract the hardships of working under hot, dirty, ill-equipped, and sometimes hazardous conditions. Until research laboratories were separated from the glassworks themselves (after 1940), even research on glass was hardly a white-collar job, though professionals wore collars and ties to work at all times. On the other hand, to be a glass technologist—an all-purpose term applied to scientists who pooled their knowledge from several disciplines to form a new industrial scientific discipline—was to have a special calling. Glass technologists aimed to master the secrets of this material, to discover its many surprising properties, and to find commercial applications for them.[2]

   As the advertisement suggests, the mystery of glass was alluring to customers as well. The material, traditionally considered too fragile for anything but objets d'arts, lightbulbs and transparent containers, had already been shown to have a variety of unexpected practical applications. By 1917, readers of the *Post* were reminded, Corning had reason to be proud of what it had accomplished in glass technology. This "scientific glassmaker" had produced railway lanterns, incandescent lightbulbs, and laboratory ware for the chemical and pharmaceutical industries that was far more durable than any previously manufactured, as well as entirely novel glasses capable of selectively transmitting X-ray glasses and ultraviolet light, colored glasses that established standards for signal lights in a variety of industries, bakeware that resisted extremes of heat and cold without breaking, and automobile headlight covers that used advanced optical principles to reduce glare and to deflect headlight beams so that they illuminated road surfaces without blinding oncoming drivers. A great deal more was to come.

THE COMPOSITION PROBLEM

The source of much of the mystery of glass lies in its unstable chemical structure: it is a supercooled liquid that behaves like a solid. Glass by definition is always in a noncrystalline state, and when it is cooled from the molten state must therefore be prevented from taking on the crystalline structure characteristic of more common solids such as metals. The basic formula for glass consists of sand (silica, which melts only at extremely high temperatures) and some fluxing agent, like soda or lead, which allows it to melt and fuse with other ingredients at more workable temperatures. The advantage of its chemistry is that it combines readily with an almost endless array of different chemicals, yielding a virtually infinite variety of properties. Before high-temperature furnaces could be developed, however, glasses were vulnerable to chemical attack. The most basic types would even dissolve in water unless a stabilizing element was added to counteract this vulnerability.

The first fundamental mystery, then, was that of composition: what elements added to a basic glass mixture would produce which properties? In these early days, the mystery lay in the endless possibilities, not in the techniques of mixing and melting the glass; Corning's first researcher, Amory

Houghton Jr., demonstrated that finding plausible combinations and measuring and defining their outputs was essentially a matter of persistence.
What made understanding composition most difficult at first was that raw
materials, though abundant, typically contained unknown contaminants
that significantly affected the properties of the glass. Ridding glass of these
imperfections, which could undermine its strength, alter its color, or otherwise affect it, was another major challenge.

Experimentation with compositions and the properties they yielded
became far more precise as knowledge accumulated and as instrumentation
and measuring devices improved. When both compositions and processes
were better understood, it became possible not just to achieve certain properties but to manipulate them—to get glass that was much stronger or
much more resistant to chemical attack, that admitted some kinds of light
and not others, and so on. By World War I, Corning scientists had developed low-expansion borosilicate glasses that required much higher temperatures than common glasses to melt. These glasses offered high resistance
to heat, good chemical durability, and excellent electrical characteristics.
Based mainly on the borosilicate family of glasses, during the 1920s Corning
developed its philosophy of glass as an engineered material, one that was
produced to meet the precise requirements of customers or to provide
them with functionality and performance far beyond what had been previously dreamed possible with any material. In the 1950s it would produce an
even stronger family of materials, the glass ceramics, which were produced
by causing specially formulated glass to partially crystallize under controlled conditions.

WORKING WITH GLASS

When Corning set up shop on the banks of the Chemung River, its production process would have been intelligible to glassmakers as far back as
Roman times. For thousands of years glasswork had been a craft cloaked in
secrecy, and craftsmen and factory owners alike were content to keep it that
way, changing their ways only to accommodate the occasional new source
of raw materials. Craftsmen with thousands of years of craft behind them,

each having learned from previous generations, saw little reason to change their ways. Then in the late nineteenth century, scientific pioneer Otto Schott, a German glassmaker who undertook the first large study of glass formulas, upset the craft equilibrium. The young Alanson Houghton, who was studying in Germany at the time, recognized in this development the opportunity and the inevitability of introducing science to glassmaking.

The glass that Corning made to supply its early customers—glass engravers, lantern makers, and later railways—was lead-alkali (or flint) glass, consisting of silica and lead oxide along with the fluxing alkali, potash. Heavy and expensive, this glass was used primarily for articles that required cutting or engraving for decorative purposes. Other uses were for items that needed to be chemically durable and were important enough to justify the expense of shipping, such as railway lanterns and lightbulb enclosures. Later neon lights and bulbs for vacuum tubes were also made from this type of glass. Cheaper, less durable items were made of soda-lime glass, which substituted lime for lead and used soda as the fluxing agent. Mass producers of containers and window glass made their glass from this material. Corning would turn to this cheaper glass too when World War I reduced supplies of both potash and lead and when tank melting changed the way glass had to be made.

The Pot Furnace of 1910

As can be seen in the picture of a pre-World War I pot furnace, lead glasses were melted in beehive-shaped pot furnaces, fired first by coal and later by producer gas. Inside each pot furnace was a set of clay pots (in this case sixteen in one furnace), each reached through an opening called a "glory hole." Each pot in this type of furnace could hold up to two tons of molten glass, which was mixed and melted at temperatures in excess of 1,200°F. A gob of glass was taken from the pot on a gathering iron and brought by a boy to the glassblower, or "gaffer," whose job it was to form the gob, either by molding it or by blowing it into a shape, often aided by a wooden mold (seen in the picture). Corning employed this type of furnace to melt glass for thousands of glassblowers making lightbulb blanks. At the time this pic-

A Corning pot furnace, c. 1910, with "gaffer"—or glassblower—and his helper.

ture was taken, Corning had a rabbit warren of nearly 200 of these small blowing shops, each employing a crew of men and boys headed by a gaffer. This pot melting process reached its limits, however, when it could no longer keep up with the volume of bulbs required and the ingredients needed in new glass compositions required heat too high to make pot melting feasible. It continued to be used for certain kinds of glass, including the decorative art glass made by Corning's art glass subsidiary, Steuben. Smaller pot furnaces also provided melts for specialty products and research quantities of glass until World War II.

By improving the understanding of the ingredients to be melted, scientific research contributed to pot melting as a production process. Just as important, research led to improvements in the behavior of the refractory materials that made up the furnace itself, allowing the creation of more durable refractories that did not pollute the molten glass even as they decayed. Scientific methods also helped establish more precise temperature controls for the furnaces. In this early period, however, science contributed little to the later steps of the process: the forming of the glass and its later annealing or cooling remained largely in the hands of craftsmen and their tradition.

This too slowly changed as researchers shifted their attention to annealing, tempering, and novel methods of glass forming. Their developments in turn gave fresh impetus to glass composition research as they raised new problems demanding new characteristics from the glass. The adoption of tank melting had a similar impact: science was called on to find compositions that would not quickly destroy the refractory linings of what had become a very expensive item to build and maintain. The interaction between material and process was an ongoing matter, itself a major source of innovation.

TANK MELTING: THE CONQUEST OF SIZE

By the 1930s, when demand for traditional products had fallen off with the general slowdown of economic activity, Corning had reached the stage of being able to tackle problems of great size and difficulty with a highly integrated process built around a large melting tank. One such problem, representative of the state of the art of tank melting at Corning at the time, was the twenty-ton piece of borosilicate glass cast for the Hale telescope on Mount Palomar. The process used to achieve this feat is depicted in the following drawing, published in *Popular Science Monthly Magazine* in 1934.

The 200-inch Mirror Process

Glass tanks like the one used for the mirror project were "continuous" in the sense that ingredients fed into one end of the tank were stirred and melted as they passed through the tank and could be drawn off at the other end in a more or less steady molten stream. Such tanks could not initially be used for all glasses. Optical glass, for example, required the development of new stirring processes and better feeders before it could be satisfactorily produced via tank melting. For Corning's common glasses, however, which by the 1930s included the borosilicates, the big tanks made it possible to melt many thousands of pounds of glass per tank. Even the smallest "day" tanks (batch tanks meant to be emptied by a day's work) contained as much as ten tons of glass.

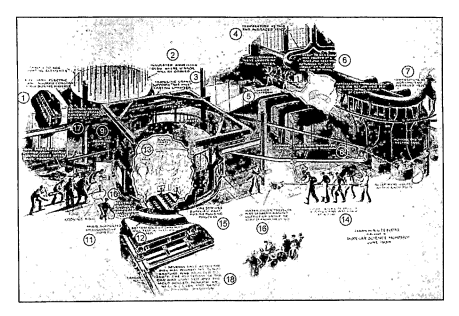

*A 1930s drawing showing the scale and complexity of producing the
200-inch mirror.*

Although they had many advantages over pot furnaces, tank furnaces
were expensive to build and to operate. Because of their size, they lacked
the flexibility of pots. A single melting tank could only produce one sort of
glass at a time, and switching a tank from one formulation to another took
days. Because refractories tend to break down under the immense heat and
pressure of the glass, furnaces had to be rebuilt periodically. Until well after
World War II it was not uncommon for tanks to be rebuilt every eighteen
months, and the best that could be hoped for was a "campaign" (the period
between first firing and tearing down to rebuild) of perhaps three years
total. Although improvements in refractories have lengthened tank campaigns and the method of firing tanks has changed for environmental reasons from the more caustic gas firing to electric melting in many cases, all
tanks require periodic, and expensive, rebuilding.

As the *Popular Science* magazine diagram shows, the 200-inch mirror
blank required that two tanks of borosilicate glass be melted and kept at
pouring temperature for many hours. All the while glassworkers were guiding three giant ladles along an overhead track, filling them from the tanks,

and pouring a third of each into the huge specially constructed mold. The temperature at the front end of the process had to be maintained at over 1,500°F. Although the glass did cool down during the pouring process, gas-fired torches ensured that it maintained an appropriate pouring temperature. The glassworkers were protected by heat shields and by constant streams of water directed at the surfaces they had to handle. When the giant mold had been filled, it went into a huge annealing oven that used over 300 electrodes, automatically temperature controlled, to keep the glass cooling at a steady rate. The mirror blank required many months to cool before it was ready to be crated for transport to the West Coast by custom-built railcar.

Forming

Other types of forming besides the simple molds used for lantern chimneys and bulb blowing seen in the pot furnace picture as well as the casting used for the 200-inch mirror, were the pressing used to form Pyrex ovenware items like pie plates and casseroles, the drawing of thermometer tubing, and the centrifugal spinning used to make larger pieces of glass, such as the glass funnels for television tubes. As already mentioned, Corning's investment in machine research and development resulted in mechanized approaches to all of these processes, large stand-alone machines capable in some cases of producing thousands of formed units an hour (as in the case of the Corning ribbon machine invented to produce lightbulbs) or hundreds of feet per hour (like the Danner machine, which Corning engineers adapted from a European invention to mechanize tube drawing).

Integrated Processes

By the 1960s Corning had invested a generation of effort in manufacturing methods and tooling, devising integrated processes that effectively automated the manufacturing process from beginning to end. By 1961 Corning was producing Corning Ware in a highly automated factory shown in this

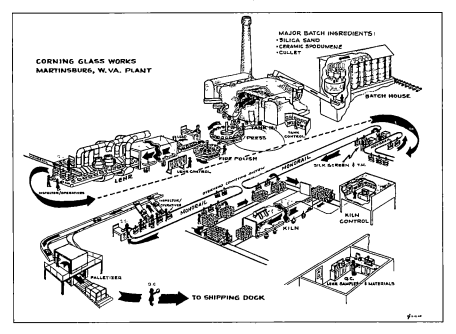

The highly integrated process used to produce Corning Ware at Martinsburg,
West Virginia.

schematic of the Martinsburg, West Virginia, plant. As the glass was drawn off from the tank at a constant rate, the so-called turret machine was turning out casseroles and other forms pressed into molds on an endless chain at a rate carefully matched to the tank's optimal glass draw. They were taken via conveyor belt through the annealing ovens and decorating station to be inspected and boxed at the other end of the line. This integrated process reached its peak with the process for the lightweight laminated dishware, Corelle. Here a much more complicated linear descendant of the turret machine, the "hub machine," made it possible to sandwich together three layers of two different compositions of glass, suck this laminated material into molds, and send the dishes through the remaining stages of an integrated finishing process much like that depicted for Corning Ware.

NEW FORMING PROCESSES: FUSION GLASS AND VAPOR DEPOSITION

During the 1960s Corning was developing two new forms of glassmaking that would come to account for the lion's share of the company's output

The vapor deposition process, here used to produce a telescope mirror blank, and later used to produce optical fiber.

thirty years later. The first, vapor deposition, had been invented and patented in the 1930s and was gradually developed through use on more challenging products, beginning with radar delay lines in the 1940s and 1950s and continuing with telescope and spy satellite mirrors in the 1960s. Here the process is shown being used to make the first fused silica telescope mirror in 1961. These pieces, and even larger ones, could be formed by burning a high-purity vaporized silicon tetrachloride solution to form a very pure silica called soot that was then deposited in layers until the desired mass was achieved. In the 1970s and 1980s it became the basis for making optical waveguides, Corning's most important product by the end of the century. When waveguides finally went into high-volume production in the 1980s, fiber for the product was drawn from vapor-deposited boules held in mammoth towers that were recognizable descendants of the tube drawing towers that had marked the skyline over Corning's Main Plant since the late 1800s.

Meanwhile, Corning's other new process, fusion glass, was developed on the basis of patents filed in 1961. Fusion was also perfected over several decades. It was used in a succession of products like the prototype automo-

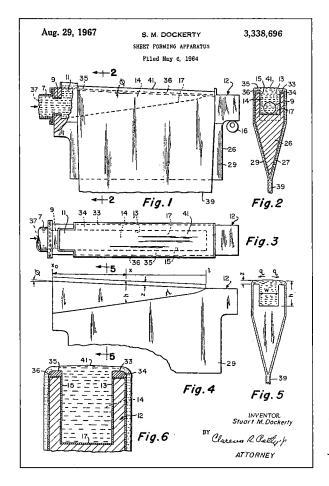

Aug. 29, 1967   S. M. DOCKERTY   3,338,696

SHEET FORMING APPARATUS

Filed May 6, 1964

A drawing of Stuart Dockerty's patent for the fusion glass process.

bile windshields that ended in commercial failure and the more successful, but still low volume, photochromic lenses. By the end of the century fusion glass had become the basis for Corning's highly competitive liquid crystal display glass, produced in Harrodsburg, Kentucky and Japan, and purchased by many Asian manufacturers for notebook computer displays and flat-screen televisions. Crucial to the development of both of these processes was Corning's previous knowledge of glass composition, as well as its ability to do the necessary follow-on composition research to keep its versions of the processes on the leading edge compatible with the fabricators' change processes.

NEW DIRECTIONS

During the 1980s and 1990s Corning's technology extended beyond glass. Research on other materials discovered in the boundary regions of glass, or otherwise bearing on Corning's various existing businesses, took the company into entirely new markets, such as life sciences and photonics. But even as Corning branched out, its leadership was charting a future grounded in glass-related technologies; the possibilities for this material were far from spent. Speaking to the International Congress of Glass on the role of glass in the twenty-first century, Corning chairman Roger Ackerman predicted an accelerating revolution in communications with optical networks, optical computing, optical sensors, and smart glass displays at its heart. In another business to which Corning had made a strategic recommitment (life sciences) he foresaw transformations in medicine, with microglass bubbles carrying radiation directly to the heart of a tumor.

Ackerman left no doubt that the mystery and the mastery involved were still as intrinsic to the innovation process as they had been to Corning's "glass technologists" of the previous century. "We are," he noted with unconcealed pride in the heritage, "an extension of the early artisans of Alexandria and Rome, the cristallo makers of Venice, the cathedral glaziers of Europe, the innovators in sheet glass, fiberglass and containers, and the pioneers of the information age." [3]

FROM LORE TO LEARNING

CORNING FINDS

ITS "FORMULA" FOR SCIENTIFIC

GLASSMAKING

I wish to anticipate the fact that needs are constantly changing, growing if you will, and that the best equipment with which to meet these changes, is a little broader knowledge than your contemporaries happen to possess.... Whether such knowledge is a more valuable asset than the limitation of competition, from the viewpoint of the shareholders, I do not know. In the long run it should be.

—ARTHUR L. DAY TO ALANSON B. HOUGHTON, 1911

CORNING GLASS WORKS first embraced a strategy based explicitly on superior knowledge in 1910. In that year Alanson B. Houghton succeeded his father, Amory Houghton Jr., as president of the company. The son took over a mature enterprise that was facing major shifts in its production practices and new competitive terrain. The "trust system" of combination and cooperation between related companies—the means that large businesses in the United States and Europe had adopted for controlling what they saw as ruinous competition over the course of the nineteenth century—was under attack in U.S. courts. The Sherman Antitrust Act of 1890 had ruled out as illegal "contracts, combinations and conspiracies" in restraint of trade. Corning had benefited from General Electric's stable pricing arrangements. But a new way of negotiating the chaos of the markets had to be found.[1]

The approach that Corning's leadership chose was suggested by Arthur Day, an eminent geophysicist with an international reputation and a close associate of the Houghton family. Day urged the Houghtons to learn from their great electric company customers, General Electric and Westing-house, who were demonstrating the value of having superior knowledge to impose order on their industry. He wanted Corning to compete not on the basis of dominance through size or lower cost but on the strength of supe-rior product performance achieved via closely held information about glass composition and working.

Alanson Houghton and his brother, Arthur, were heirs to what even then was termed a "scientific approach to glassmaking."[2] At a time when glass in general was a wholly craft-dependent business in the United States, Corning's practice already made it an unusually technically oriented organ-ization. This practice extended back through several generations in the immediate Houghton family. Nevertheless, glass was notorious for its mys-terious composition, as well as for the difficulties encountered in melting and working it consistently. By the turn of the century the electrochemical revolution had brought system and mechanization to related industries such as chemicals, explosives, abrasives, and aluminum and other materials; but glass production, even in the most progressive companies, remained imprisoned in its traditions, some of them thousands of years old, and ben-efited little from the application of electricity to industrial production. Most glassmakers producing flat glass (sheet and plate) or containers reveled in this mystery, relying on the difficulty of simply turning out a consistent product to keep competitors at bay.

The Houghtons, who had become specialty glassmakers out of neces-sity, saw their best opportunity in being different from other glassmakers. The first of many in-on-the-ground-floor experiences for the company came with Thomas Edison's 1880 order for lightbulb envelopes. Edison found Corning's lead glass tubing to be a superior envelope for housing his delicate filament.[3] By 1908 lightbulb blanks had become Corning's highest-volume product, exceeding the total value of the rest of its sales combined. Corning enjoyed long-term supply contracts with General Electric (succes-sor to the Edison company) and most of the other big lamp producers, as well as with many smaller ones. While the "obvious" conclusion—that being on the cutting edge of innovation could result in first entry into enor-mous new markets—was there for all to see, it took the outsider, Day, to help the Houghtons see just how far-reaching its implications were. A Corning consultant, as well as the head of geophysical research at the Carnegie Institution in Washington, Day believed that the pursuit of an ever broadening knowledge of materials and processes in glassmaking should be the cornerstone of Corning's strategy as a specialty glass company.

Upon taking the helm, Alanson Houghton made a commitment to push the envelope in glass technology and to make this the rationale for a reorganized company. At this time, he and his brother offered Day the chance to be a full-time participant in that effort. Day's research program on rocks and minerals dealt with naturally occurring phenomena like the melting and cooling of minerals in volcanoes, and thus it offered an emerging body of scientific knowledge that was closely related to the problems of glassmaking.[4] The Houghtons already knew the value of Day's expertise for their business and had demonstrated their acceptance of his ideas by founding one of the first corporate research laboratories in the country. They were now moving toward hiring more full-time scientific personnel while working less with independent consultants. Day applauded their plans but turned down the offer to become a regular Corning employee. Although he was convinced of the wisdom of Corning's knowledge-based philosophy and intrigued by its prospects, he had much to lose if he left his current position at the hub of the burgeoning national scientific community in the United States.[5]

This was not the first time Day had received an offer from the Houghtons, nor was it to be the last. Unaccustomed to taking no for an answer, the brothers periodically reissued their invitation for full-time work. Eventually Day did join Corning, only to find that, as described below, most of his apprehensions and reservations about moving to Corning had been justified. He returned to his job at the Carnegie Institution after less than two years and remained there until he retired. For Corning, Day's help in envisioning and organizing a technical infrastructure centered around corporate research was invaluable. Day remained a Corning vice president and served as a consultant and member of the board even after his departure from the company's regular employ. So important was Day's contribution as an involved outsider that the company found ways to replicate this role after he retired.[6]

That Corning, a relatively small company in what was then an unappealing location, could attract and hold scientists of Day's caliber is remarkable. This ability to attract superior people stemmed in part from the company's already well-established tradition of investing in the development of glass technology both as a craft tradition and a growing body of related scientific knowledge. Over the course of the next several decades Corning would become an environment that supported the development of a group of talented and well-connected people who identified themselves as glass technologists. Its corporate laboratory, which predated those of most other U.S. companies, came to be staffed by scientists from some of the leading institutions in the country. Encouraged in this context to interact with large, leading-edge customers with extremely challenging problems, these researchers accumulated more and deeper knowledge about their field than any other company possessed. Corning had found its competitive edge.

SCIENCE, 1870–1908

Corning's claim to having a scientific tradition in glassmaking before the turn of the century rested first on the combined intellectual curiosity and systematic experimental methods of the company's founding generations, Amory Houghton and his son, Amory Jr. These men bequeathed the rudiments of a scientific approach to their descendants in the form of small brown notebooks filled with formulas and records of batch test results. The notebooks, still extant, attest to the industrious use that Amory Jr. made of his small laboratory at the Union Glass Company in Somerville, Massachusetts. Lacking formal academic training, he nevertheless took a serious experimental approach to the problem of glassmaking.[7]

The melting lore Houghton gathered from his first glassmaking tutor (known as Gaffer Teasdale) and subsequent results from decades of experimentation, were treated as family secrets, handed on exclusively to the son who was most involved with the production side of the business. Amory Jr. was joined in his scientific pursuits by first Charles and then Arthur, who also styled themselves amateur scientists and who both filed their own patents. An understanding of glass composition became essential to Corning as it moved from Somerville to Brooklyn to the Chemung Valley in New York, facing as it did different supplies of raw materials in each area. Indeed, this last move forced the company to switch its basic glass formula from soda-lime to lead-alkali and to style itself a specialty glass company rather than try to compete in the higher volume segments of the industry of flat glass and containers.

For help with certain problems that did not have to do with glass composition and melting per se—the design of lenses for railroad lanterns, the proper construction of furnaces, or the science of color, for example—the Houghtons drew on outside advice. There were no glass scientists as such, but Corning regularly consulted with researchers from Columbia and Cornell and made use of the hodgepodge of independent consultants and small testing laboratories that were springing up throughout the industrial northeast in the last quarter of the nineteenth century. These scientific advisers took on a new level of importance to the company when it attempted to solve the safety problems associated with railroad signaling.

Beginning as early as the 1870s Charles Houghton (one of Amory Houghton Sr.'s three sons) recognized a potential opportunity in the severity of the railroad signal problem and its increasingly serious impact on railroad safety. The railroads were the largest and richest customers it was possible to have, and thousands of people were dying every year in railroad accidents. To help solve their safety problem would be of immense value to the railroads and to their suppliers, to say nothing of their future passengers. Charles Houghton turned his talents to inventing and patenting a superior railroad lantern that would be visible at greater distances and more resistant to fouling by ice and dirt than were other designs.[8]

The problem was this: the railroads used a visual signaling system to inform the train operator of the state of a given stretch of track. Different colors signified different messages (also a problem Corning later addressed), but whatever the color and whatever the message, it was crucial that the conductor see and understand the information it was providing as early as possible so as to have the maximum amount of time to react. Early signal lens covers were designed with a series of concentric bevels on their outside surface, which had the effect of focusing the light. These bevels tended to collect dirt, snow, and other obstructions on the outside of the lens. Charles Houghton's invention avoided this by placing the focusing rings on the inside of the lens. But Houghton did not work alone: he called on Professors William Anthony and George Moler of Cornell University to supply much of the basic optical knowledge that led to his breakthrough. The proper size and placement of the rings was no easy matter. Corning's ability to develop a clearly superior lantern owed much to the services of science.

Charles's nephew Arthur took over the operating side of the business in 1890 and shortly thereafter turned to addressing a related problem, also for the railroads: signal glass color. Again, Corning turned to outside scientific advice, specifically the services of Ph.D. chemist Joseph A. Dughuee of New York City's Health Department. Dughuee worked with Arthur to help him devise and patent a lead-alkali glass called "cerise," which contained the rare element selenium. This new glass was useful for making solid red signal lenses that had better range and uniformity than the old "flashed" (or red-coated) ones had had.

In 1899, Alanson Houghton, Charles's other nephew and successor as Corning's chief marketer, attended a conference of the Railway Signalmen's Association. There he learned of the work of a Yale University professor, Edward Wheeler Scripture, on the "Science of Color." He saw that Corning could tackle a much larger opportunity if it could put together a more comprehensive program to address the whole range of railroad signal colors. Each railroad had its "pet" colors at the time; in fact, there were almost as many different signal color combinations in use as there were railroads. Corning was supplying many of these signals, and it was becoming a "burdensome" matter to keep track of them all.[9] But no standardized scheme existed to determine which colors and shades were most effective in terms of accurate light transmission in various weathers, nor was the human perception of color very well theorized. Without such objective criteria, no railroad was likely to agree to a competitor's signaling scheme.

The Houghtons contracted with William Churchill, one of Professor Scripture's Ph.D. students at Yale (and also a former student of Arthur Day's), to identify the best colors from a luminosity and safety standpoint for distance signaling. For two years Churchill pursued his assignment on a long-distance basis. Churchill had studied briefly in Leipzig, and he traveled

again to Europe to examine signal standards there. He conducted his own
program of testing at Yale's psychological and Kent chemical laboratories
and made frequent visits to Corning. Progress was slow. From Churchill's
correspondence with Alanson Houghton it is evident that Houghton had
not divulged to Churchill what was already known to the company about
color and glass composition. As a result of this insistence on secrecy, some
of what Churchill was "discovering," especially concerning ingredients to
be added to the glass melt to achieve certain color effects, was already
known to Corning. In one letter, for instance, Churchill reported the use of
a selenium additive to achieve solid red glass, evidently unaware that Corning already held a patent for this approach to making red signal glass.[10]

The hiring of William Churchill was the first step toward what the
townspeople at Corning would come to call, derisively at first, the "Smokestack University." Churchill, who began the program to achieve railroad
standards for signal colors, ultimately joined Corning in 1902, and in 1904 he
set up the company's first in-house laboratory. Located in the sales department, this was more than a simple "works laboratory" but considerably less
than a corporate laboratory, for it was narrowly focused on standards, quality, and production control for one particular product and set of customers.

Previously all of the blanks and bulbs Corning produced, whether for
lightbulbs or for railroad signals, had been made out of one all-purpose (and
secret) lead-alkali glass formula using traditional methods. Churchill
attempted to bring Corning's production process for signal glass under the
type of tighter technical control that had recently been applied in the working of iron and steel and concurrently in aluminum and other light metals.
He had his work cut out for him: "achieving the perfect lens color depended
on tight control over numerous factors: the purity of raw materials, the
composition of the batch, the reaction of coloring oxides with the batch,
the precise temperature of the furnace, the duration of the melt, and the
quality of annealing."[11]

This first investment in in-house science paid off handsomely for Corning. Churchill's efforts in following up on Corning's original connections
with the Railroad Signalmen's Association and the various railroad supply
companies not only produced further improvements in lens design but also,
in 1908, led to the adoption of a uniform standard of six basic signal colors

based on Corning Glass Works specifications for roundels and lenses. Throughout this period, Corning's sales increased considerably relative to its competitors selling the same products, namely, MacBeth Evans and Libbey Glass. Both watched their shares of the railroad glass market decline steadily from 1905 to 1910 while Corning's market share expanded from just over one-half to two-thirds. But Churchill's laboratory was not set up to build a knowledge base. It lacked the basic information disciplines and depended largely on Churchill's personal judgment. Under those conditions it was unlikely that what was learned could have general applicability or that it would apply to other products aimed at different markets.

Family Secrets

Meanwhile, Corning hired George Hollister as its first official manufacturing superintendent. Hollister was also the first non-family member to be inducted into the secret art of glass formulation. As an outsider he saw immediately how risky it was for Corning to be relying exclusively on family control and secrecy to maintain its competitive advantage. With more professional chemists, physicists, and engineers becoming involved in industry generally, the defensive posture of relying on closely guarded knowledge made the company vulnerable even to domestic competition at a time when international competition, which relied on more sophisticated methods, was heating up as well.

It was Hollister who first put the Houghtons in touch with his former colleague at the Geological Survey, Arthur Day. He believed that tighter control over high-temperature melting in Corning's ever multiplying pot furnaces would benefit the manufacturing process in a number of ways. Day demonstrated the value of his expertise for Corning in 1905 by doing on a larger scale what he had already accomplished at bench scale on the small experimental furnaces at the U.S. Geological Survey Physical Laboratory. He instructed Hollister to attach platinum rhodium thermocouples in the furnace walls of Corning's glass furnaces, and by using optical pyrometers to check temperatures, he brought melting temperatures under control for the first time. Such control was vital if Corning was to produce more consistent batches of glass, and this consistency was a prerequisite for improving yields in the high-volume incandescent lightbulb business that was straining Corning's production capacity. Equally important in the longer run, better temperature control also made it possible to conceive of experimenting with melting at higher temperatures, which could result in different, perhaps stronger, glass compositions. With this latter prospect in mind, Day recommended that Corning hire another former colleague with specialist knowledge in silicate chemistry, Eugene C. Sullivan, a Ph.D. chemist from the U.S. Geological Survey, who had studied and taught at the University of Michigan. More important for his future career, Sullivan was also an alumnus of German university training. He had worked first at Göttingen before finishing his Ph.D. under Wilhelm Ostwald at Leipzig during the height of his program to reform physical chemistry. Ostwald's group of graduates included over forty Americans, many of whom were to build new laboratories in universities and in industry. Among Ostwald's other students were A. A. Noyes, who promoted physical chemistry at MIT and Cal Tech, J. E. Trevor, who went to Cornell, and Willis Whitney who left MIT to found the first corporate research laboratory in the country at General Electric in 1900.[12]

In 1908 Corning hired Sullivan as its chief chemist with authority to set up the chemical department, its first open-ended research laboratory. The immediate need was a better glass for railroad lanterns to take advantage of the new color standards, but the knowledge gained through Sullivan's efforts would prove more broadly applicable. The Houghtons still hoped to attract Day to Corning, but the returns the company was seeing from Churchill's work and the speed with which science was having an impact in the wider world made it obvious that Corning could not delay.

The move to set up a real in-house corporate laboratory, particularly in the area of melting, caused dissension within the Houghton family. Amory Houghton, father of Alanson and Arthur, opposed spending money on this type of thing in general, but he was especially fearful that bringing scientists in-house would destroy the veil of craft secrecy and thus jeopardize family control of Corning's operations. The younger Houghtons, however, treated the scientists like family members, thereby making them more junior partners than employees.[13] Both Day and Sullivan would become Corning exec-

Arthur L. Day and Eugene D. Sullivan, "architect" and "organizer" respectively of Corning's first corporate research laboratory in 1908.

utives, as well as, eventually, members of the Corning board. In some sense Corning's distinctive research culture began here, for if Amory Jr. had had his way, the entire venture would have taken on a very different cast, one that was less open, less personal, and almost certainly less successful.

SMOKESTACK UNIVERSITY, 1908–1914

The first Corning research laboratory was cramped and rudimentary, but it was a space removed from the factory floor where Sullivan and his associates could work in relative quiet, if not comfort. The facility was tucked away on the second floor of Corning's B Factory, which had only recently been completed and which housed three temperamental sixteen-pot gas-fired furnaces devoted to glass tubing, lantern globes, and railroad signal lenses. This arrangement could hardly be compared to the pioneering industrial research laboratory that had been set up by General Electric in 1900 or to the research facilities that were soon to be organized by Eastman Kodak, DuPont, AT&T, and Westinghouse.[14] When Sullivan was joined by his first lone lab assistant, and then by William C. Taylor, another chemist from MIT, the 1,200-square-foot facility was hardly large enough to accommodate even the necessary test equipment, let alone the sets of *Encyclopedia Britannica* and *Scientific American* that generally had to pass for research libraries in the laboratories of the day.

The first university program to be labeled "glass technology" anywhere in the world would not be set up until World War I (by W. E. S. Turner at Sheffield University in England), but "glass technology" was what the new Corning laboratory was researching soon after it was founded. Sullivan was an organizer and he was excited by the opportunity to pursue physical chemistry in this industrial setting. Glass chemistry, he later pointed out, was an unplowed field: there was no literature and few tools or methods. New laboratory methods and new tests had to be developed, and before much headway could be made, measurements—of strength, clarity, and other properties—had to be devised to measure the lab's progress.

As Corning's chief chemist, Sullivan first had to master melting problems and in particular to establish quality controls for the melt. Nevertheless he and Taylor soon found time to delve into some of the more fundamental work that had been started earlier on Corning's behalf by Arthur Day and continued by consultant Dughuee in cooperation with George Hollister. Day and Hollister had tried to replicate the successes of German researchers from Schott and Zeiss who had already developed a form of "tough" borosilicate glass for thermometerware and laboratory tubing. This glass was known to exhibit much lower thermal expansion than the regular soda-lime glass compositions Corning was using, and it was accordingly much more resistant to thermal shock. Sullivan and Taylor made significant discoveries that led to real improvements in railroad lanterns, which they duly trademarked. But cracking the code for true borosilicate glass would require a more diverse group of scientists and better facilities than they had at their disposal until shortly before World War I, when Sullivan managed to assemble under one roof a centralized and integrated research capability.

Meanwhile more trained scientists, including several Ph.D.s, proliferated throughout Corning works and laboratories in the years after Sullivan's arrival. At first they were dispersed throughout the departments. Just as the sales department wanted Churchill's full-time contribution to make real headway with the railroad signal problem, so other departments recognized the value and the need of having not only a ready source of specialist expertise on hand but also more reliable access to the growing technical community outside the company.

The professional scientific establishment in the country at large was becoming better organized, less fluid, and more in demand in many related industries. The supply of scientists was expanding. In 1890 it was estimated that 1,000 U.S. scientists had graduated from German universities in chemistry, of whom 300 were available to work in industry. But after 1900 U.S. universities had improved to the point that it was no longer considered essential to leave the United States to study in Germany for a good graduate education in science.[15]

Corning's in-house technical community was becoming a microcosm of

Corning's laboratory staff in 1914 still numbered only ten researchers. Shown here are six of them (l. to r.): Donald Sharp; Joe Gregorius; Jesse Littleton, head physicist; William Taylor, chief chemist; William Yung; and James Bailey. Eugene Sullivan, whose formal style as research director bespoke his German research training, did not appear in group photographs.

the broader scientific picture that was developing in the country at large. Eugene Sullivan had imbibed his scientific mentor Ostwald's belief that much value lay on the margins of scientific inquiry, and he soon pushed to add more disciplines to his laboratory. In 1908, Fred Shetterly, a Ph.D. chemist from Cornell, joined Churchill's optical laboratory, and soon after him Emilio Pascucci, a physicist. Lionel Duschak, a Ph.D. chemist from Princeton, came to Corning after a year at the Bureau of Mines, followed closely by James Bailey, a mechanical engineer from Lehigh, who went to work as assistant superintendent in the blowing room.[16]

Such a mix, comprising recent graduates from leading colleges and universities with B.S. degrees and Ph.D.s and more experienced people raided from government agencies like the National Bureau of Standards or the Bureau of Mines, was characteristic of the staffing patterns of most of the industrial research laboratories that were forming at the time. Eastman Kodak, for example, which set up its larger research outfit between 1912 and 1913 under the leadership of the distinguished English organic chemist Edwin Mees, nearly emptied parts of the National Bureau of Standards. It would soon become an explicit part of the mission of these government bureaus, and also of the Geological Survey, to train research talent for industry. This was a pattern that Germany had followed successfully, and though England had chosen a different route, allowing its National Physical Laboratory under Walter Rosenhain to do contract research for individual companies, England's progress had not been as impressive as Germany's in the science-based industries.[17]

In the United States far-sighted individuals, comparing the German and English approaches, had recognized that dedicated scientific research directed toward industrial ends could serve as a booster shot for the country's industry. Andrew Carnegie had endowed the Carnegie Institution in 1902 with $10 million to encourage the study of, among other subjects, the naturally occurring crystallization processes and the silicate materials that were found in a natural state, a mission proposed by Arthur Day and his friends. Carnegie's investment in useful research was imitated a decade later by the Mellon family, also of Pittsburgh. They set up the Mellon Institute, rightly convinced that this would increase the value of their rapidly growing empire of technology-based start-ups in electrochemicals. In return for yearly grants the Mellon Institute performed directed research for specific companies, including some glass companies that did not have their own research capability. One of the companies that took early advantage of this arrangement was Corning's competitor MacBeth Evans. Inventors and industrialists like Thomas Edison, Henry Ford, and Harvey Firestone were also sponsoring systematic studies of naturally occurring substances and processes of all kinds, trying to find substitutes as insurance against supply problems.

It was, in short, an ideal time for young scientists emerging from recently established American Ph.D. programs to enter industrial laboratories, especially if they had an interest in inventing rather than teaching. One such scientist, Henry Phelps Gage, joined Corning in 1911, beginning a career that would span thirty-five years. His broad-ranging interests and connections soon demonstrated the potential that science-based development could have for generating new products for Corning, as well as the advantages that maintaining intimate connections with the scientific community could have strategically.

H. P. Gage: From Measurement to Invention

When Gage joined Corning, the sales department optical laboratory had already played its first important part in the solution of the safety problem that had been plaguing American railroads for years. But railroads and railroad safety were still a matter of intense public scrutiny. Increases in speed and route complexity had led to a further series of spectacular crashes, and the popularity of the railroads in general was further undermined by the cozy relationship they had developed with the monopolist of Standard Oil, John D. Rockefeller Sr. So unpopular was the railroads' cause with the public that in the Eastern Railroad rates case, settled in 1911, Supreme Court Justice Louis Brandeis threatened them with an unprecedented and punitive rollback of fares. Under the circumstances the railroads felt the pressure to make visible progress with safety; once again they looked to Corning for help.

As a newly minted Ph.D. in physics and chemistry from Cornell, Gage brought with him a new level of sophistication in measurement, some pre-existing research, and a set of valuable contacts. His original research on the "radiant efficiency of arc lamps" had given him experience with the latest laboratory equipment and measurement techniques. He was also well con-nected to the powerful informal professional network that had begun to crisscross the country with nodes in universities, companies, and govern-ment agencies.

Gage had grown up in Ithaca, New York, the only child of one of Cor-nell's more distinguished academic families. Both parents were scientists. His father, Simon Henry Gage, in particular, was known for his work in applied optics.[18] In his preprofessional days the elder Gage had been a pho-tographer, a hobby he passed on to his son. Another important influence and set of connections, for young Gage and through him for Corning, was his aunt, Mary Gage Day, an early female graduate of the University of Michigan medical school, who was a leader in the fight to control tubercu-losis. Her credibility with the medical community gave Gage access to research medicine, and its many uses of light, especially ultraviolet, for its health effects, as well as for its research tools.

Gage had worked closely with professors who were consulting with Corning while he was still at Cornell; once at Corning he returned regularly to the university to find out what they were doing and to report anything of interest to the company. Indeed, he completed and published a textbook with his father on projection microscopy (1914) after he joined Corning. He used that connection to communicate with senior technical people at Bausch & Lomb in nearby Rochester, as well as with several members of the scientific establishment who were staffing the young and growing agen-cies in Washington, D.C.

Gage's own publishing career had begun in his last year at Cornell. His first published works on arc lamps for projection appeared in 1910 and 1911 in the *Physical Review* on the academic side and in *Electrical World* a recently established journal of the Illuminating Engineering Society. He and Churchill were both invited to be charter members of the Optical Society of America, devoted to the study and practice of applied optics. Through this society, and particularly through its twenty-four other charter members, they had regular contact with some of the most important optical researchers in the country, both academic and industrial. Organizers of the society included F. E. Ross, professor of optics at Cornell, and P. G. Nutting, optical engineer at Eastman Kodak. Other charter members included C. E. K. Mees, director of the Kodak Laboratories, G. E. Hale, director of solar research at Mount Wilson, F. E. Wright, of the Carnegie Institution in Washington, as well as professors involved with eye research, photography, and optics.

Up-to-date skill with spectrometry was one of the things that made Gage immediately valuable to Churchill. Churchill had already made use of a combination of spectrometry and photometry in his work while at Yale, and he had helped educate the railroad signal engineers in the use of the spectrometer and other related devices for color measurement. But equipment was improving fast, and Churchill's practice for achieving the required consistency in glass color remained a matter of visual inspection, generally performed by Churchill himself. This involved comparing the glass in question with a standard glass in the form of an 8 ¾ inch roundel of the color required and making a judgment based on that comparison. Gage wrote to his parents soon after his arrival, "The whole process was carried out in a location from which Dr. Churchill, who originated the standardization, could be easily reached for consultation and what he said, *went.*"[19] Gage's mission was to achieve reliable measurements that would make such tests reproducible by less experienced personnel, leaving experienced sales and technical people to use their time in more productive ways.

Gage's equally important task was to become acquainted through his mentor Churchill with the various railroad engineers who represented Corning's most important class of customers. Standard setting as an industrial activity was a relative novelty until around the turn of the century outside the machine and mechanical engineering areas.[20] Electrical companies had been among the earliest to seek to set and enforce standards, recognizing that continued differences in switches, wiring, and fixtures could not only be dangerous but also could retard the progress of the industry. Churchill's pioneering approach in working with the railway signalmen to come up with standards had been firmly based on building personal relationships. He had endeared himself to these men by taking what they felt was a constructive approach to the railways' safety problem, in marked contrast to most of the experts involved in the Eastern Railroad rates case. These other experts, who were scientific managers of the Taylorist persuasion, were known for leveling harsh criticisms at the railways for their mismanagement. Unlike Taylor's disciples, Churchill did not try to make the railroad managers look either foolish or criminally negligent. Instead he offered them solutions to their problem, for which generous stance the railroads gratefully credited Churchill, and Corning, with being better than most proponents of system and control.[21]

While Churchill traveled and became increasingly adept at the sales aspects of his business, Gage remained in the optical laboratory. He took care of the technical side of the operation and also began to do his own kind of product development in areas where he detected a need. Churchill especially encouraged Gage to develop his interest in electrical lighting whenever his duties in the signal field allowed. It was obvious that electricity and its applications to lighting were the coming thing. Not only were kerosene-burning railway lanterns a technology facing obsolescence, but volume was declining as the improvements Corning made cut into its sales. In any case the time was foreseeable when railway signals would use electricity, which would mean adapting all of the colors for a different kind of light source. Corning had been trying to improve arc lighting globes with the help of Arthur Day but had not succeeded in getting beyond the technical difficulties of making tough glass. High-quality lights were so expensive to make that the first applications were assumed to be industrial, in situations where artificial light approximating daylight was critical. These included the dye shops of textile manufacturers and laboratories where the accurate use of spectrometry was affected by the distorting color of the ambient artificial light. Gage was soon developing niche products based on filters, which were easier to make, for Corning to offer.

Shortly after he joined Corning, Gage turned his skills at color analysis of the light spectrum to analysis of daylight. Using special daylight filters that he developed, Gage made screens for laboratory lamps, testing them out with his father and some of his father's colleagues at Cornell, and in some of the shops in Ithaca. The owner of the men's clothing store in Ithaca was delighted to discover that Gage's filter attached to a 200-watt Mazda "C" lamp enabled him to sell men's suits on a cloudy day, or even in the hours after darkness. This was no small consideration in a part of the country where cloudy days were the norm.

Soon Corning was making the Daylite roundel for commercial use and selling it in a kit, complete with the attaching band. This Daylite Glass complemented Corning's new Laboratory Glass business, for while they were selling test tubes and other apparatus they could also sell the Daylite units. In 1915, one of Gage's professional acquaintances in the Illuminating Engineering Society, Norman MacBeth, previously an independent illuminating engineer and consultant, started the MacBeth Daylighting Company. He soon became an important customer for Corning's Daylite Filters, turning them into Daylight lamps for commercial uses that sold for $60 each. Simon Gage and his son both invested in MacBeth's company, with the younger Gage regularly attending stockholders' meetings. Gage used his association with MacBeth to stay in close touch with the industrial customers whose needs were shaping Corning's businesses.[22]

Electrical technology was changing every market it touched in the years before World War I. In 1912 electricity was introduced into automobiles. Lighting was an obvious application. Gage worked on headlamp covers that adopted some of the same principles which had been used in lighthouse lighting and railroad signal lighting to concentrate the light beam and direct it to the sides of the road so that ditches could be seen. This work too gradually led to new business for Corning, first in the manufacture of headlamp covers, known as "Gage Covers," based on his patented fish-scale design, and later, in 1935, in the production of sealed beam headlamps. Soon these covers would be required to meet highway safety standards for reduced glare imposed by several different states. New York and Massachusetts were among the pioneers, and Day would be involved in negotiating and influencing their standards.

Gage's salary and work conditions improved quickly during his early years at Corning. Outside the company he soon enjoyed an unusual amount of freedom in the people and institutions he saw—so much so that his mother remarked on it. After receiving an account of his trip to Washington, D.C., discussing his roundels and his methods, she commented:

> It certainly is great to be able to do as many things as you do in the way of seeing people and institutions. That the company gives you your time to go

is doing finely. Everything helps to broaden your outlook on the problems
you have in mind and finally to make you more efficient to the company
and to yourself as well.[23]

Eighteen months after he started with Corning, he reported on taking his
roundels to Washington to give a talk about his methods at the National
Bureau of Standards. Such freedom of movement was common for early
Corning researchers. This was one way the company could overcome the
apparent geographical isolation of its location—to support attendance at
conferences, and frequent travel to customers, and to keep the local hotel,
the Baron Steuben, fully occupied with the meetings of scientific and trade
associations to which Gage and others belonged.

However many products he invented or promoted, Gage's most important personal work for Corning was to turn the art of standard setting into
good business. Gage became one of Corning's leading workers of networks, serving on numerous standard-setting boards. The continuity of his
long career and his long-standing boundary-crossing connections made him
effective at his chosen work.

In the 1920s Gage made the case for his optical laboratory as a way of
identifying early new scientific developments that might offer Corning business opportunities:

> Colored glasses of many kinds are in course of development, and hints of
> great usefullness are continually being received. Some time *the great discov-
> ery* will be made. It may be made in Corning. It may be made elsewhere. If
> made elsewhere, it will be known that Corning is the home of special col-
> ored glasses made in special shapes and because of the constant coopera-
> tion of the Optical Laboratory with many scientist and inventors in
> furnishing any kind of colored glass which can be made, Corning will have
> first news of the discovery.[24]

Over the course of this decade Gage managed and promoted his optical program for the strategic benefit of Corning's business and its growing reputation. As soon as he had the necessary facilities, he made available his
specialized test equipment to customers and to research colleagues in many

universities. Upon request, he supplied color filters for research purposes, both to university programs and to company and government laboratories across the country. Laboratories on his list for receiving color filters in 1921, for example, included Yale's Sloane and Laurens Laboratories, the Universities of Pennsylvania, Illinois, and Toronto, and MIT, industrial laboratories at DuPont and Leeds and Northrup, and, of course, the National Bureau of Standards and other government agencies. A key element in making this program pay off was discipline in maintaining records, a theme that Gage would stress repeatedly both in laboratory methods and in production.

> If the glass which we supply is picked out with sufficient care *and accurate*
> *records are kept*, we are then in a position to take rapid commercial advan-
> tages of any development which would be of commercial use and members
> of our staff have an entree to the laboratories in which this work is being
> done which would be difficult to obtain in any other way.[25]

LABORATORY DEPARTMENT AND A
NEW FAMILY OF GLASSES, 1912–1922

The industrial researcher, Eugene Sullivan said later, should above all be versatile: able to perform three overlapping and inseparable functions: quality control, improvement of manufacturing methods, and the development of new products. To do this he needed to be broadly educated in science but also required intimate exposure to the problems that arose in the industrial heart of the business. In contrast with engineers, who built on the basis of experience, the industrial researcher needed to concern himself with fundamental principles and to conduct experiments to arrive at new facts (or at the very least to demonstrate the creativity to build on less familiar phases of his own science). But this difference in approach did not free him from an obligation to find the problems at their source.[26]

This was the well-articulated ethos that Sullivan espoused by the time he was in a position to concentrate under one roof and one organization a fully integrated research and development organization. Initially, however, the move to centralize was not so much an organizational statement as it was a solution to certain problems: the need for a common location and for making the best use of scarce talents from an all-company perspective.

Lack of space, the perennial problem for all research programs, was temporarily alleviated in 1914. Several years of lobbying on Sullivan's part finally resulted in the enlarged laboratory that he had been promised when he joined Corning six years before. Even before the completion of the new 5,400-square-foot chemical and laboratory building that he designed, he hired Corning's first research physicist, Jesse Littleton (Ph.D., Wisconsin). Tired of trying to get help with measurement problems from the two physicists Corning already employed (located in Churchill's optical laboratory, they were completely occupied with meeting the demands of the sales department), Sullivan got permission to set up a small physics laboratory and to hire Jesse Littleton to head it. Sullivan had convinced the Houghtons that this was one way of attacking the many technical problems associated with finding the right new consumer product for Corning, anxious to make up for the declining sales of its now almost indestructible railway lanterns.[27]

Littleton was to become one of Corning's senior research managers, along with Taylor and Sullivan. Although the first scientists hired had been chemists, it soon became clear that physicists were at least as essential a part of

H. P. Gage, W. Churchill, W. C. Taylor, and E. Pascucci, testing the color of glass roundels with a comptometer in the optical laboratory dark room, c. 1917.

Corning's in-house research capability. Before World War I the researchers located there were joined by Otto Hilbert (a mechanical engineer from MIT), chemist Rowland Smith, George McCauley (a Ph.D. physicist), Glen Cole (a laboratory assistant from Cornell who was later to become a senior executive), and Walter Oakley, a mechanical engineer and furnace expert who would eventually become Corning's chief engineer. Corning's laboratory soon had more trained physicists than chemists, and by World War II it would boast of having a higher percentage of physicists as part of its scientific staff than any other industrial laboratory in the country.

In 1916 Corning brought all its physicists under one roof by moving the optical laboratory out of the sales department into the newly expanded central laboratory. A growing conflict between the demands of "preparedness" work for the military on headlamps, headlight covers, and tank lights, and the work the sales department wanted Gage to do prompted the relocation of the optical laboratory in 1916: it was made a part of Corning's central laboratory. This helped clarify Gage's priorities, providing optical knowledge for the company at large and giving him much needed room to install measurement equipment he had been waiting to use for five years.

The recently hired Littleton was the person who recognized the potential applicability of the properties of the tough glasses developed by Sullivan and Taylor for commercial bakeware. The resulting line of ovenware, the basis for Corning's signature consumer business for the next eighty years, which Corning introduced in 1915, shared the trademark Pyrex with a parallel development of glassware for laboratories: the beginnings of Corning's enduring technical and scientific products line. Both businesses had their origin in a very systematic attempt Sullivan and his colleagues undertook to go beyond mere problem solving, however valuable that might be, to develop a whole new family of glasses.

Borosilicate: The Original Breakthrough

Day, who knew it better than most, referred to it as that "viscous and bubbly Jena borosilicate." Discovered and developed in Germany, borosilicate glass was first used primarily for very precise optical elements, like gun sights and telescope lenses, and for glasses that most needed to resist breakage, like thermometer tubing and laboratory ware. Sullivan and Taylor were determined to crack the secrets of borosilicate glass at Corning: neither its exact composition nor the methods of producing it were known to them when they started. The Germans were the undisputed inventors of borosilicate glasses. Otto Schott, son of a glassmaker, had teamed up with Ernst Abbé, research director of Zeiss Scientific Instruments to develop a tough new family of glasses that had very desirable properties for laboratory glassware: they were hard to break, tolerant of quick changes in temperature, and remarkably nonreactive to chemicals. These glasses, first developed in 1892, entered production in 1894 and gave German glass exporters such a decisive advantage in laboratory ware that American producers did not even try to challenge them until World War I. This was particularly true for university laboratories, which were exempted from the tariff that other customers paid on German glass.

Arthur Day's stay at the Reichanstalt (the German Bureau of Standards) had coincided with Ernst Abbe's time of service on its board. By this time the German standards lab was providing both routine and advanced testing to the government-supported Thuringian glassworks, and Day was familiar with this activity. On his return to the United States Day turned to these glasses made from silica and boric oxide hoping to address on Corning's behalf the problem the railroads were having with its lantern globes. Sullivan and Taylor picked up on this work when they produced the heat resistant or "shatterproof" globes based on the borosilicate formulations. Trademarked Nonex or simply CNX (for Corning Non Expansion), these were produced for stock beginning in 1908 and were marketed in 1909. The demand for such an improved product was never in doubt. Unfortunately this was only the first of a long series of Corning products in which the very superiority of the product ruined demand for it: individual lanterns lasted so long that the replacement market dwindled away.

Mrs. Littleton's Pie Plates

In 1912 Sullivan and Taylor picked up the work on borosilicate glasses again. Corning was looking for new products. When they threw open the search for product ideas to the Corning community at large, they discovered that there was broad agreement as to the potential of the tough new glasses to form a successful housewares product or even a line of products. Suggestions came in for nursing bottles, pots, pans, and griddles. Glass's transparency had instant appeal: middle-class customers were disposed to believe that glass was more hygienic because they could see through it. The problem was once again to select the right mix of borosilicate properties to satisfy the demanding needs of cooking in its varied forms. The lantern glass was low expansion and heat tolerant, but it had the unthinkable defect for a cooking vessel of being too readily soluble in water. Glasses used for regular battery jars were unforgiving as to temperature fluctuation. Sullivan paid a visit to Schott at Jena in eastern Germany, inquiring into a suitable glass for the purpose. He met a welcoming response, but the proposed exchange of information did not actually occur until after the end of World War I.

Although it was Jesse Littleton who had recognized the possibility, it was Mrs. Littleton who performed the first well-documented product feasibility tests by baking a cake in a sawed-off battery jar made of the formulation called NONEX. This was no one-off experiment on her part, though later mythology perpetrated by Corning advertisements made it seem so: she followed up with a whole series of further culinary explorations, which in turn led to a major campaign to develop Pyrex as a suitable material for cookware in general.[28]

Initially called "Py-right" (it was first used for a pie plate), successful development of Pyrex bakeware depended on mobilizing some very sophisticated home economists and early consumer experts.[29] These included Mildred Maddocks, head of New York City's Good Housekeeping Institute and even more prominent editor of the *Ladies' Home Journal*, Sarah Tyson Rorer, who were prepared to attest to the "efficiency" of glass cookware in an age that was suddenly obsessed with efficiency in all walks of life. In an effort to confirm their more authoritative, if subjective, findings by objective measurement, Jesse Littleton, whose wife had started it all, conducted an ingenious and graphically visual experiment. By baking a cake in a dish that was part metal and part glass, he showed conclusively that the cake in the glass half was cooked long before the part exposed to the metal surface. This finding ran counter to all beliefs at the time. As Sullivan noted later,

[O]ne reason for hesitancy in offering glass for oven use was that we thought food would bake very slowly in thick-walled dishes of low heat conductivity, and the first reports of faster baking in glass than in metal were scarcely credited. The fact was soon definitely established, however, and there could be but one explanation—namely that baking is a process of radiation from the oven walls rather than conduction or convection.[30]

These findings led to the patentable discovery that Corning's glassware was indeed more efficient because it absorbed more radiant oven heat than pans made of metal. The head-to-head comparison was but the first of many confrontations between glass and metal, as Corning's new glasses would challenge metal in one product category after another, most famously in radio and television tubes, a story we tell in chapter 7.

As Churchill and Gage had already demonstrated in the case of railroad signals, it was not enough to generate the knowledge, however precise or well substantiated. Information had to be communicated to the right audiences in the right ways. Public relations and advertising—which in these days was more about education than it was about convincing customers to purchase items of questionable utility—were critical to what would become

This early National Geographic advertisement (1916) for Pyrex features Cathryn Huber of Wellsboro, PA. Transparency was the real selling point, as it gave the ware a hygienic appearance. The glass also required lower temperatures and less cooking time, thus conserving on fuel. It sold at the luxury price of $2.00 for a large casserole.

the new Pyrex line of ovenware. Sarah Tyson Rorer, the Martha Stewart of the pre-World War I period, a trusted representative of best middle-class taste and values, demonstrated the new bakeware in department stores and other Corning-arranged venues around the country. The responses she gleaned from her audiences were carefully gathered, compiled, and relayed to Corning's product developers. She not only passed on the observations of crowds of "ladies" in Milwaukee and Chicago and New York, but with Churchill's encouragement she also met with senior Corning executives to propose the most useful sizes and shapes the ovenware might take. Corning's officials found Rorer's feedback persuasive enough to retain her as a consultant.

Other influences on the design of Corning's tough bakeware came from the community of restaurateurs, which Colonel Thompson, a Corning sales representative, managed to tap into through his father-in-law, who managed the Hotel Wolcott in New York. This crowd subjected the bakeware to rough usage and reported their complete satisfaction with its sturdiness, though two pie plate covers used by Thompson's wife cracked owing to annealing flaws. Any flaws that appeared received close scrutiny and testing in Sullivan's laboratory. There was even a proposal in 1918 to start up a test kitchen for testing bakeware under conditions of use, as well as for handling the difficult task of photographing experiments with the ovenware. That proposal was set aside at the time because sales were greater than could be handled by existing capacity, but it was revived in the 1920s when various problems with the ware and the way customers were using it led to a sales decline.

One problem with the original Nonex glass was intolerable. Further laboratory testing of the bakeware in prototype revealed that conventional low-expansion glass released unacceptable quantities of lead into the food when exposed to certain acids during cooking. This disturbing finding pushed Sullivan and Taylor to do more fundamental and systematic work on the composition of low-expansion glass than they had to date. By studying the coefficients of expansion of different glass compositions, they hit upon G 702 EJ. Two patents emerged from this fundamental work, one covering the material and the other the concept of a glass cooking vessel. Both were filed in 1915 and issued four years later.

Laboratory Ware

The other idea that had instant appeal to the researchers in their general search for new product ideas in 1912 was laboratory ware. Few understood better than Sullivan the needs of the laboratory chemist. He focused attention on the properties of low-expansion glass that might contribute to improved laboratory ware, including higher strength and higher chemical resistance. He proposed a borosilicate composition that reduced to four the number of chemical elements in the glass instead of the eight or ten elements common in laboratory ware of the time. He reasoned that limiting the glass to the four elements would reduce the needs for chemical assay to only four tests.

In 1915 and 1916 Corning produced a varied line of hand-made or hand-blown flasks, jars, retorts, and pressed dishes, as well as hand-drawn tubing. These items were sold mostly to dealers and refabricators who remade them into finished laboratory ware. Ph.D. chemist F. F. Shetterly, assistant manager of A Factory and one of Corning's growing number of Ph.D.s in production, oversaw production of the new line to appropriately tight specifications. Frederick Kreisel, acting as Corning's commissioned agent, sold to lamp shops that in turn finished Corning materials to order; he also traveled to institutions across the country, gathering knowledge of the distinctive needs of each group in his travels and bringing it back to Corning.

After the war Corning asked for, and got, reimposition of tariffs on foreign-made laboratory glassware so that the business could become firmly established in the United States. In testimony before the House Ways and Means Committee, Eugene Sullivan noted that American laboratory glass (i.e., Pyrex) had achieved superiority to German glass. Because of its very low coefficient of expansion, Pyrex could be made with thicker walls without developing the strains under heat that German glass developed, and it was thus much less likely to break. Moreover, he claimed, the chemical resistance of American glass was five or six times that of the German glass. But German glass was for the time still unavailable, and very cheap Japanese glass was flooding the market. He was concerned that this Japanese glass, which was coming in at little more than half the price of American glass, would undercut Corning's "infant business" before it had time to achieve the necessary scale and reputation to displace the German glass for good.

To serve the laboratory market, Corning Glass Works set up its own finishing shop inside Building 1. Its lead finisher, a young German-trained craftsman named Herman Schrickel, eventually became one of Corning's most trusted advisers to customer product development. His finishing shop grew into an important new product shop—it was the first place from which Corning supplied early cathode ray tubes for television inventors in the 1920s.[31]

Composition was only part of the problem. A difficult aspect of all Pyrexware, for whatever market, was that it was especially hard to produce and work because of the high temperatures at which it melted and the high viscosity of the borosilicate melt; in fact, Corning's greatest contribution to this family of glasses was its development of refractory materials suitable for melting the German-invented borosilicates.[32] Pyrex tubing was still hand drawn in the early 1920s and was therefore considerably more expensive than regular glass tubing. When Corning agents began receiving requests for Pyrex tubing for laboratory glassblowing, the factory's typical response was to refer customers to manufacturers of lime glass tubing instead. They soon discovered, however, that customers were willing to pay a large premium for Pyrex tubing: less glassblowing skill was required to work it in the lab and less breakage occurred owing to strains introduced during the glass working.

Even after they realized what a desirable product it was, Corning could not produce Pyrex tubing in large quantity. Further expansion of Pyrex-based product lines had to await the tube-drawing improvements that Corning would undertake after World War I, which we describe in chapter 4.

The Prototypical Engineered Material

Over a period of twelve years, by varying the elements that were added to the basic silicate with boric acid compound and by discovering how the compositions were linked to different desirable properties, Sullivan and Taylor laid the foundations for as many as fifteen different glass products in four different Corning businesses: railroad lanterns and battery jars, ovenware, laboratory ware and tubing, and large telescopic mirrors. These products all required interacting with, and learning from, different kinds of customers, and Corning had to devise different methods to work with each of them. This experience formed the practical basis for the technical strategy that Eugene Sullivan would later adopt, "special glasses developed for specific purposes," a concept that would eventually become known as "engineered materials."

Sullivan and his colleagues had to learn for themselves, often painfully, that engineering a material entailed more than hitting upon the right composition to make it a commercial success. It also meant developing a business approach that met the customers' needs in many situations. They also learned that the return from each of these investments in emerging businesses, so costly in time and attention in the early years, was more than the revenue from the sale of products, it was also the growth in Corning's knowledge base—knowledge about glass composition and properties and knowledge about evolving customer needs that could produce further opportunities for new product development when greater understanding about glass technology made that possible.

DAY'S VISION OF MIDDLE WAY RESEARCH, 1917–1923

Meanwhile, having failed in their attempt to attract Arthur Day to Corning for a full-time position in 1911, the Houghtons tried again in 1917. They wanted him to help solve their "growth problem": even though Corning employed nearly 2,000 skilled workmen and had built several new plants, it still could not keep up with demand. The Houghtons hoped Day could help them meet demand for their growing stable of products, lightbulb enclosures, and railroad lanterns, and their new Pyrex-based products, laboratory glassware and consumer cookware, without losing control and without sacrificing profitability. This time Day was interested. "I like your problem," he wrote to A. B. Houghton, "and more bluntly I like you. I can think of no two people I would more like to argue with than the two of you."

But Day worried that full-time employment at Corning would be quite different from the privileged position of an intimately involved but still independent outsider. He rehearsed his dilemma in a letter to Alanson Houghton in the fall of 1917:

> In the face of some uncertainty your suggestion is that I give up a permanently endowed laboratory which I myself founded, my baby if you will, my personal volcano researches which have carried me half around the world, and which might have introduced me to the rest of it; my secretaryship in the National Academy of Sciences which amounts to being the executive officer in a national scientific clearing house, my residence in the center of American scientific activity and in the neighborhood of the Baltimore conservatory, which has hitherto been a special feature of the children's education.[33]

To justify and validate his shift to industry in the eyes of the scientific community, Day wanted the Houghtons to take a big step—to expand their research laboratory to a size and a working philosophy comparable to Eastman Kodak's laboratory, set up in 1912 with a staff of twenty people and a budget of $53,000. For apart from the obvious personal concerns of status in the company, financial compensation, and living conditions in the town of Corning, Day's most important requirement was to have a laboratory of consequence. He wanted a budget large enough to achieve what he regarded as critical mass and to make a serious and sustained contribution both to knowledge about glass and to the strategic direction of the business.

The Houghtons appear to have discussed with Day a much augmented Corning research effort that would have national standing. Corning had a growing business for which a systematically developed knowledge base was essential. Companies all over the country were striking similar deals with senior professional scientists. And the Eastman Kodak model for a laboratory likely appealed to them. It was a middling, moderate approach consistent with theirs, neither as free-form nor as exploratory as General Electric's, which purported to treat researchers like university professors, nor as directive as the gunpowder laboratories, which emphasized tight links between the laboratory and the businesses, enforced by methodical use of such information disciplines as good record keeping and report writing.

The outbreak of war changed things for both parties. Day was caught up in issues of government preparedness. The outbreak of World War I affected the supply of laboratory glassware and optical glasses to the United States, which had long been dominated by the European specialty glass companies. To ensure a supply of precision instruments such as gun sights and telescope lenses to the American military, Arthur Day was asked to visit all domestic glassmakers that might have the capability to produce these products and to assess their available capacity. This gave Day a chance to compare Corning with other better-known companies in the industry. Having visited Bausch & Lomb, Eastman Kodak, American Optical, and the like, he wrote A. B. Houghton in March 1917, "I am fully convinced from such inquiries as I have made, and the information the National Research Council is gathering, that you in Corning know more about glass at this moment than any other firm in this country."[34]

By the time World War I ended in 1918, Day had an even better reason for moving to Corning. Day's wife, Helene Kohlrausch, was the daughter of Friedrich Kohlrausch, head of the German Bureau of Standards. In the bitter aftermath of the war, Washington was no place for those with German sympathies or even German maiden names. The Day family must have found postwar Washington an especially inhospitable place to be and Corning, by contrast, a welcoming one.

But the war, meanwhile, moved the company in a different direction. The heavy demand for lightbulbs, required for round the clock operation in factories across the country, was just one factor pushing Corning to focus on its high-volume businesses. Corning's output expanded steadily until by the end of the war it was eight times greater than at the beginning of the decade. At that point, the company reorganized its entire business, technical departments included. Arthur Houghton, who had headed manufacturing, became Corning's president while Alanson left to make a successful bid for Congress in the election of 1918. Although both brothers remained on the executive committee, their long and solid partnership as Corning's full-time leadership team came to an end.

Whatever the private agreements between Alanson Houghton and Day, they were not fulfilled when Day actually came to work at Corning in 1919. He found that much had changed. Instead of presiding over a significant expansion of Corning's technical effort along the lines of Kodak's new central research department, Day headed the entire operations side of the business (both manufacturing and research departments). Arthur Houghton had fallen ill, and with Alanson out of the picture, his position had devolved on Alexander Falck, the company's attorney. Falck had little interest in sharing power with Day and even less in giving a strategic role to the laboratory or expanding its scope. Instead, Falck contrived to keep Day off the Executive Committee on which he wished to serve with the Houghtons alone. Trapped in a hierarchical box, required to go through Falck to get to the Houghtons, Day found himself cut off from the regular access to power and money he had always enjoyed on the outside.

Day waged a frustrating battle to manage the manufacturing side of the business, to which the existing laboratory reported, without cooperation or budget from Falck. When Day returned to his old position at the Carnegie Institution after just two years, Sullivan, who had been heading the existing laboratory, was drafted into upper management. The laboratory did more hiring, but most of its efforts were directed to addressing the many problems that arose on the production side of the house. The various shifts in the company's production process that had been undertaken in haste during the war now had to be optimized and rationalized in countless ways that required scientific help.

Apart from the growing need to respond to requests for troubleshooting occasioned by the demands of Pyrex production, much of the wartime research program had been occupied with accumulating and systematizing data about the physical and chemical properties of glass. Another important problem, generated by the need to increase lightbulb blank output and the consequent shift from pot melting to the higher volume and more consistent tank melting, was the changeover from lead-alkali glass to some other glass composition. Refractories then in use for tank melting broke down under lead-alkali glass. W. C. Taylor, now chief chemist, invented a soda-lime formulation that could be used for lightbulbs in combination with an improved lead-alkali glass for the lightbulb stems (which required glasses with higher electrical resistance to prevent short circuits in the lead-in wires). This shift in composition, already necessitated by the increasing demands of high-volume bulb production, was also driven by the scarcity of potash—a key ingredient in Corning's lead-alkali formulae—during World War I. The war had made these kinds of demands in many new areas.

Alexander Falck, who remained in charge for most of the 1920s, saw no reason to keep the prickly and thin-skinned Arthur Day around. The Houghtons, however, recognized how important his earlier contribution had been and knew what an opportunity it would be to have a Corning vice president who stood at the crossroads of American science, with strong ties in industry and government. In 1919 Day left the company's employ but retained the title of vice president. Correspondence shows that Day kept Corning posted on strategic developments, from the latest discoveries of important raw materials such as borax mines to the most likely candidates for research posts coming along at different U.S. universities. More important, Day's notion of a laboratory of the middle way—modeled on the Mees conception of researcher freedom and the free flow of information combined with discipline and an awareness of strategic company goals— did shape both Corning's research philosophy and its institutions, although the actual fulfillment of his ideas did not occur until the frenzy of the 1920s had passed.

OPPORTUNISTIC ORGANIZATION, 1919–1931

At the end of the war there were three departments in the laboratory: the optical research department, headed by H. P. Gage, the chemical department, headed by William Taylor, and the physics department, headed by Jesse Littleton. Sullivan became vice president in charge of the laboratory, reporting first to Arthur Houghton and then, for a short time, to Day. The machine development department, which had been set up before the war, reported to manufacturing. A laboratory committee was established and met monthly. It included the heads of the three divisions, as well as Day, Sullivan, and, under the press of activity, an associate Day brought with him from the Geophysical Institute, J. C. Hostetter. This arrangement changed little when Sullivan succeeded Day; Hostetter stayed to become head of the research organization and Sullivan gained control over melting and manufacturing as well.

In fact the entire establishment was still relatively small and informal. Everyone knew what everyone else was working on, and in periods of difficulty it was expected that all hands would jump in. Except for planning and budgeting purposes little attention was paid to the formal program. As Harrison Hood, who arrived from Cornell in the early 1920s, remembered it later, "I was a chemist, but an awful lot of things that I finally got into involved physics and optics and we were all pretty much glass technologists together."[35]

All of Corning's technical departments were understaffed, suffering from both unforeseen competitive developments and greatly increased demand for competent staff across the country. Convinced of the importance of industrial research by the part chemical research had played in World War I, many companies scrambled to open research laboratories of their own in 1919. The gentlemanly and sedate prewar arrangements between government agencies and established research operations were entirely disrupted. Reports of Corning's laboratory committee from 1919 through the early 1920s are filled with complaints about the difficulties of finding and keeping technical personnel of the quality Corning had been accustomed to hiring. The going rate for men, especially physicists, was $3,000 per year, and at that they were hard to find.[36]

Corning was straining for laboratory space. With its factories stretched to capacity to produce lightbulbs, radio tubes (which had seen a surge in demand during the war), and the new Pyrex ovenware line, it became necessary for the laboratory staff to expand into any space at all that could be found and fitted out for laboratory purposes. In 1923 the laboratory added on to its inadequate 9,000 square feet by pushing out the north wall of B Factory to accommodate two furnaces needed for research purposes. It was to be its last expansion until 1940 when the laboratory department moved into its first purpose-built laboratory.

In 1922 Corning's laboratory committee noted with alarm that only 5 percent of the lab's reported time was actually being spent on research. Corning's technical staff was deluged with requests for short-term support from both sales (customer complaints) and manufacturing (testing and troubleshooting). The laboratory department was even engaged in actual production of small-volume products that required high levels of technical skill to produce, such as gauge covers and filters.

Most of the prewar research problems remained on the agenda, unresolved. In addition to a standing order to develop tailored glass compositions with clearly identified properties, there was still the need to understand the working properties of glass and the cooling properties of glass (tempering and annealing), to analyze raw materials to achieve the uniformity necessary to support mechanized production, and to find refractory materials that would not give way under the assault of molten glasses.

This last problem of finding tougher refractory materials was the first to lend itself to a solution, and it led to an important new business for Corning in the 1920s. Chemist Harrison Hood, cooperated with physicist G. S. Fulcher to make electrically molded aluminum silicate refractories called Electrocast. Hood discovered the new refractory when he was asked to troubleshoot a problem that the melting department was having with "stones" in the glass. He reasoned that any particles that were not dissolving at the high temperatures used to melt borosilicate glasses were worth investigating. Not only did the aluminum silicate refractories prove resistant to attack by molten glasses, but they were useful as furnace linings in a variety of other industries as well.[37] This was one of many serendipitous discoveries that turned out to be bigger than the problem researchers had originally been trying to solve. Corning's new refractory business, a joint venture named Corhart with GE's Hartford Machine was launched in Louisville, Kentucky, in 1927, the first of many spin-off businesses that came out of Corning's research. It made refractories not only for use in glass melting but also for use in furnaces for other high-temperature melting jobs such as steel. It was also the first of many successful joint ventures that originated in Corning's research (discussed in more detail in chapter 5).

A listing of major and minor problems that made up the research program of the chemistry department in 1923 gives some idea of the scope of the work going on in the laboratory department—many of these requiring work by both chemists and physicists. Other problems classified as "major" included heat resisting glasses, mechanically strong glasses, and dissolved gases in glass. Many of the so-called minor problems on the list were raised by customers, such as theater operators who were calling for colored glasses that would not develop hot spots and explode when the lights went on or the General Electric Company, which was predicting sales of 5 million

Gordon Fulcher, physicist, c. 1925, tests refractory bricks by the laboratory arc furnace in Building 40, clad in a protective research outfit of asbestos gloves and heavy canvas coat over the obligatory white collar and tie.

radios annually with tremendous requirements for new and replacement radio bulbs.

The physics program was primarily occupied with efforts to devise and implement physical measurements for key glass properties. Littleton and Taylor observed in a 1938 memo to Sullivan, "We believe Corning was the first to recognize the fact that, since glass was made to meet certain physical requirements, a control of batch by means of measuring the significant properties was an advance over a slower, less precise chemical analysis." To this end they devised measurements for softness, electrical conductivity (picked up by the radio companies GE, Westinghouse, and RCA), surface tension, ultraviolet transmission, heat absorption, tensile strength, viscosity (in which they were setting standards for the rest of the world), annealing temperatures, thermal conductivity, strain, and strain distribution.[38]

Littleton's effort to understand the tempering and annealing issues involved in producing the different families of glass that Corning manufactured resulted in controlled annealing, a process soon adopted by the entire glass industry. In this, he and his associates drew on fundamental work performed at the Geophysical Institute in Washington. That this work was conducted at the geophysical laboratory at all was evidence of deliberate efforts being made to support industry: the work had little importance geologically but was crucial for making better refractories and for understanding the devitrification (crystallization) patterns in glasses—matters of considerable interest to the industry.[39]

Under the pressures of customer demand, the chief technical problems that were receiving attention in the 1920s were those that were cost driven and manufacturing related. Corning was not alone in this respect. All over the country new product development was giving way to new process development. Efficiency was the watchword in the postwar era and price competition was fierce. Corning struggled to maintain its competitive position in the rapidly mechanizing business of bulb production, developed a new updraw process for the production of large-diameter glass tubing, and found ways to manufacture its Electrocast refractories in volume.

At the head of the company, Falck was paying hardly any attention to research; his attention turned to licensing Corning's borosilicate glasses overseas, an attempt to gain immediate revenues from technical knowledge without having to grow larger internally or make new investments. When H. P. Gage's assistant, Ernest Ling, was commandeered to oversee quality testing in production, Gage complained that those in charge seemed not to be distinguishing between different types of technical expertise or different levels of competence when they called for help. In the face of such mounting demands for support of the operating divisions, it was hard to devote effort to any new product, even to one for which demand was ready made, such as the government's request for Pyrex spark plugs. And "pure" research, as it was termed in departmental reports, was receiving almost no attention.[40]

In the late 1920s Corning sales leveled off. Demand for expensive middle class ovenware, as a curiosity or gift item had apparently reached its limit, and certain problems had to be addressed if it were to become really useful as a household item. Not only was the pressure of output lessened, and with it the demands for technical support from all hands, but Corning also faced the prospect of the Pyrex patents running out in 1936. Once again Sullivan, who had been pressed into service as Corning's interim president (until Amory Houghton would reach the age of thirty), looked to the research organization for new products. Corning's board was now stacked with men like Day, Sullivan, and Hollister, all of whom had some form of laboratory experience, and the R&D budget, at least as a percentage of sales, began to increase.

To boost slumping Pyrex sales to consumers, Corning revived the idea of setting up a test kitchen and found a remarkable scientist to run it. Lucy Maltby (B.S. Cornell, M.A. Iowa State, and Ph.D. Syracuse in home economics), "with a strong background in physics and chemistry," started the test kitchen in 1929 and remained its head until she retired in 1965.[41] The original idea of the test kitchen had been to educate salespeople on cooking with Pyrex and to field and respond to customer complaints, as well as to provide a good place for advertising photography. In a unique week-long training program, salesmen learned how to "bake a cake, make tea or coffee, or scalloped potatoes," to give them firsthand knowledge of cooking in Pyrex. The point of this was to educate customers, who generally did not

Lucy Maltby, researcher in home economics and organizer of Corning's test kitchen, shown with the staff of the home economics department.

grasp that Pyrex required lower baking temperatures, and to teach them how to avoid unsightly baked-on food. Soon the test kitchen's mission would expand to helping with new product development. From a one-woman show in 1929, the test kitchen would eventually employ as many as thirty-five people, answering customer questions, responding to consumer complaints, sending out recipes, aiding in advertising campaigns, and testing new products.

LIFE RAFT IN THE DEPRESSION, 1931–1940

Pyrex pie plates proved to be a real seller in the early part of the Depression when reduced to a price of twenty-nine cents. Another winner was a steady business in blanks for telescope mirrors, started by George Macaulay, research physicist in Corning's laboratory. Others were headlights, lightbulb blanks, and radio tubes, all recent and rapidly developing products unaffected by the general falloff in business. Though Corning's sales certainly decreased in volume from 1931 to 1937, the drop was not as severe as the plummeting sales experienced by many companies.

Well aware that its life raft in a very troubled economy had been provided in large part by its research discoveries, Corning invested aggressively in research. Now under the leadership of the young Amory Houghton, research budgets went up steadily from around $400,000 in 1928 and 1929 to an average of over $500,000 from 1930 to 1934, roughly 6 percent of sales. In real terms this was a very significant increase, even though sales had dropped well below the plateau of the late 1920s, for the cost of new salaries and plant and equipment for the rest of the company in the 1930s was much reduced.

Amory Houghton, advised by Sullivan, who had returned to the laboratory in 1930, gave his strong support to fundamental research by calling on Corning scientists to overcome some of the deficiencies that limited the utility of glass in major high-volume applications. In this he was influenced by the statesmanlike leadership of major industrial and university scientists such as Karl Compton of MIT and Fred Jewett of AT&T, who maintained that the way to get the staggering U.S. economy back into balance was

through science-based product innovation.[42] Houghton also favored continuing development work in new processes even though process development
was out of favor nationally. The new efficient technologies of the 1920s
were not unreasonably viewed as major culprits in the joblessness of the
1930s. Corning's ability to avoid Luddite attitudes among its own employees, even though many glassblowing jobs had been replaced by machines,
had to do with top managers realizing how much improved glass technology contributed to new products, as well as to the serious efforts they made
to find other jobs for anyone who was displaced.

At a time when many companies were shutting down laboratories established only a decade before, a few large research-intensive companies had the
foresight to invest heavily in research. They were busy laying the research
foundation for decades of future business. Alcoa did the fundamental work
that allowed it to make aluminum into a structural material. DuPont
expanded its artificial fiber business with the dramatic discovery of nylon.
The Radio Corporation of America, one of Corning's largest customers for

Corning's test kitchen was located on the second floor of Building 51. Three research staff
members shown here in 1946 are Helen Martin, Lilla Cortright Halchin, and Mary Alice
Dailey.

radio tubes, poured resources into the development of television. Corning likewise took the opportunity to hire some exceptional graduates of first-rate university programs, among them men like organic chemist J. Franklin Hyde, fresh from a postdoctoral year at Harvard, John Hammond Munier, Ph.D. physicist from Johns Hopkins, and Martin Nordberg, Ph.D. chemist from Cal Tech. By no means as large a company as the others, aided by these new hires, Corning experienced a surge in research productivity during the Depression that prepared the way for several businesses that were to come to fruition in the decades after World War II.

Turning Pyrex into Real Cookware

One of the objectives pushed most vigorously by Corning's top management was stovetop cookware made out of strong Pyrex, which Hood and Nordberg had been working on for some time. This kind of extension to the product line could increase the effective life of the Pyrex patents considerably.[43] Moreover, in the early 1930s stove manufacturers were coming out with new electric ranges. In 1932 market studies suggested that consumers would be especially interested in Pyrex skillets, preferably ten inches in diameter. Even though developers had warned that such a size might not be feasible, management was so intent on this idea that they ordered expensive castings for these new ten-inch molds and "placed them in the machine shop on the finishing lathes ready for immediate production." The problem was that the new rangetop designs had six-and eight-inch rings, with the result that ten-inch skillets placed on these burners would break because of the stresses occasioned by the hot spot in the middle and the cold outer rim.

Physicist William Shaver, who was involved in this development program, later recorded a wry description of seeing Lucy Maltby testing one of the new skillets:

On a visit one afternoon to the test kitchen the household science expert who was in charge of this area was testing Top-of-Stove ware, 10" skillets on the 6" diameter electric heating element. She was encased in asbestos cloth from her shoulders to the floor and was wearing a plastic face mask. This garb would certainly be impractical for every housewife so changes had to be made.

Management pressure to produce the ten-inch skillets was not deterred until the laboratory asked the purchasing department to buy up all the six-inch diameter heating units available in town. Then twenty-one ten-inch skillets were placed on twenty-one burners, all wired together so that one switch would turn them on simultaneously. Within a few minutes of the switch being thrown, three of the frying pans had broken "more or less explosively." Having witnessed this nightmare, the factory manager offered a resounding recommendation that six-inch skillets were the type that should be manufactured. Along with a number of other products such as blown coffee pots and double boilers, the skillets helped to fulfill the objective Lucy Maltby had set for her operation—to make Pyrex into something "basic in cooking and serving rather than more or less a novelty or gift item, as it was at that time."[44]

Research Freedoms and Controls

Among other products that were invented in the 1930s several were discovered in the quest to find strong Pyrex. One was Hood and Nordberg's Vycor, a low-expansion glass that contained 96-percent silica. After leaching with acid, this material became what Sullivan would liken to a "rigid sponge," demonstrating high resistance to heat and temperature change.[45] This was immediately recognized to have important implications for the labware business and for countless other uses in the chemical industry. Later it was also discovered that Vycor was a conductor of infrared light and thus suitable for certain military applications. Another important product development was wide Pyrex tubing that not only led to expanded lines of laboratory and chemical works glass but also made it possible to manufacture fluorescent glass tubing. But there were also products developed, in the effort to defend against other company programs, that bore no relationship to existing Corning products at all. They were motivated by defensive concerns in a research climate where large companies were increasing their investment in fundamental work in order to open whole new markets for their materials. These products were silicone, Franklin Hyde's answer to plastic, which Corning developed with Dow Chemical (Dow-Corning) and fiberglass, which it developed with a direct competitor, Owens-Illinois (Owens-Corning). We pick up the stories of these strategic partnerships in chapter 5.

Asked to compare this period with later ones, researchers were apt to note the small size, the lack of specialization, and the intimacy of the enterprise. They also credited an atmosphere of freedom for the creativity of the outcomes. Harrison Hood, who collected more than forty patents during his active Corning career, said it this way:

> We were given absolute control of what we worked on. We were just there
> and spent the day doing our darnedest to dig up something new and no one
> directed us to what we should be working on and put a time limit or any-
> thing of that nature. So as these problems came up, and mysteries occurred
> we were all extremely anxious to find out why these things happened,
> unusual things, and what good use could we put them to ... there were so
> many obvious things to be working on and so few people to do them.[46]

There was, of course, another side to this research environment. As though to counter any impression that freedom could translate into laxness with information, there was an ironclad rule about information control. No written material containing scientific information of any kind, whether advertisement or conference paper, left the premises without receiving Eugene Sullivan's scrutiny. Sullivan, a no-nonsense man of very few words, was vigilant on this score. Robert Dalton, who joined the laboratory in the early 1930s described the condition of the first paper of his that Eugene Sullivan reviewed. When it came back to him for revision, almost no sentence had escaped either crossing out or serious modification, and there were detailed instructions for cutting and pasting. At the top in small precise writing, Sullivan had written, "A few suggestions."[47]

THE FORMULA

If the Houghtons and other senior Corning executives had not already believed in the commercial value of working the fundamentals, the experience of Sullivan and his associates in cracking the code for borosilicate and producing from it the low-expansion glass that spawned a whole family of glasses and an entire suite of new products, would certainly have convinced them. In 1929 Sullivan published what amounted to his manifesto for glass as an engineered material in an article in *Industrial and Engineering Chemistry*. Entitled "The Many-Sidedness of Glass," the article contained a list of the many properties of glass that had been revealed by Corning's search for new products using Pyrex, as well as Sullivan's reflections on the even greater amount that remained unknown:

> To many people glass is glass, and that's the end of it. Actually glass is a many-sided material. . . . not much more than a beginning has been made on the chemistry and physics of glass. We know practically nothing of the chemical constitution and structure. . . . An abundance of interesting and fundamental work, then, remains to be done in glass, both in pure science and in its application. One of my fellow students in Ostwald's laboratory, in Leipzig, thirty years ago, who was laboring as we all were to give birth to something that might charitably be regarded as a contribution to science, was in the habit of lamenting bitterly that the easy things had all been done. In glass not even the easy things have all been done, and help is needed from those who like to do the hard things.[48]

By the end of the 1930s, Corning's identity was tied to one aspect of its business above all others, "Corning Means Research in Glass," an advertising slogan, that would remain the company's hallmark well into the 1950s. The slogan reflected reality: the Houghtons had developed a very effective formula for scientific glassmaking. The problem came in ensuring that Sullivan's "hard things," once understood, were also possible to make. That had proved extremely difficult with borosilicate glasses, even after their core compositional mysteries were solved; it would prove more difficult still with future materials, since the company would need to strike a creative balance between new materials and processes, allowing each side to challenge but not impede the other.

In Corning's formative era, superior people, including a few redoubtable women, were lured by the qualities of glass as a special and elusive material.

The pipe that can't keep a secret...

"The pipe that can't keep a secret" advertisement is an early version (c. 1932) of the long-running series featuring the slogan—"Corning Means Research in Glass." The picture of piping in a gingerale plant stresses the sanitary aspects of see-through piping for the food and beverage-making industries.

They were received by distinguished and open colleagues, they stayed because of close mentoring relationships, and they were given the freedom to contribute as they saw fit, except in times of urgency or emergency when everyone was expected to chip in. The risk of isolation in a small New York town was great, but they were encouraged to maintain close relations with scientific colleagues and customers and to mine those relationships for news and ideas. Taken by itself, this might have described a number of organizations at the time. What made Corning distinctive was that it not only built the environment for scientific work and collected a solid knowledge base but also continued to draw on and maintain strong craft traditions. This, as Amory Houghton Jr. would say in later years, was truly pursuing "an uncluttered path." By following this path the company avoided some of the worst excesses of "scientific management" and its ensuing labor problems, a theme we expand on in the next chapter.

CRAFT AND SCIENCE

PARTNERS IN PROCESS INVENTION

> *[Corning] population 15,000. Americans. Cannot do things as you
> would in P'gh [Pittsburgh] where there is foreign population. In
> Europe do exactly as your father do. American workmen not afraid
> of new things. 2,000 men, substantially all skilled workmen in Corn-
> ing. Importing of labor from abroad does not result in proportionate
> increase, [if] increase men, could not house. Produced more during
> war with increased effort. If we try to multiply by 5 production, spe-
> cial tools required... cannot hope to do it by multiplying hands by
> 5—or even by better system, but [only by] perfected machinery.*
>
> —H. P. GAGE, HANDWRITTEN NOTES OF A SPEECH
> BY ARTHUR L. DAY, 23 MAY 1923[1]

A RTHUR DAY's brief stint as Corning's vice president in charge of manufacturing and research was unhappy but instructive, and it lasted
long enough to convince him that the approach to manufacturing and R&D
he had long advocated with the Houghtons was correct. A specialty glass
company located in a small town far from any major urban center could not
engage in mass production of the sort that had come to dominate much of
American manufacturing before and during World War I; Corning would
have to find its own way.

In the speech Day gave in 1923 to Corning's newly organized Production
Club, a group of plant foremen and managers, he elaborated on this thinking. Unlike large cities such as Pittsburgh with their crowds of recent European immigrants, Corning inhabited several small towns containing proud
workforces with a strong craft tradition. Its 2,000 workers were open to trying new things, and what they needed were the right "purpose-built"
machines. The history of Corning's policy vis à vis the development of

process machinery was always marked by this fundamental sensitivity. Faced with a surge in demand for its first high-volume business, the production of lightbulb blanks, Corning opted to create and use tools and special purpose machinery to increase the productivity of its skilled workforce, but not to dispense with either jobs or skills.

At Corning it would be as true in the 1930s as it had been in the 1870s: science was useless without craft. In one way this was obvious in most companies before World War II. As long as processes remained poorly understood and methods remained imprecise, craft couldn't be dispensed with entirely, much as scientists and some managers might long for this. But in specialty manufacturing companies like Corning, which lived by their wits and relied on coming up with new ideas for their customers, craft in several forms was not viewed as a necessary evil, best eliminated as soon as possible, but as a source of new ideas. The question was how to balance craft and science, those two sometimes culturally incompatible sources of inspiration and knowledge.

One answer to this problem was to set up shortly before World War I the mechanical development department, Corning's first in-house generator of process inventions. This department became the other half of Corning's central technical infrastructure, and its creation, in terms of the history of innovation at Corning, was second in importance only to the founding of Sullivan's chemical department. The philosophy espoused by its founder, David Gray, reflected his personal views of the way craft and science might coexist and it was also right in step with the views of Corning's leadership team, the Houghton brothers, Alanson and Arthur. These men had already staked not only their company but also their personal fortunes on finding ways to mechanize the high-volume parts of their specialty glass operations without alienating their workforce.

Corning launched its in-house machine development at a time when many large companies in America were striving to limit or do away with the influence of both art and craft on the manufacturing floor. Scientific management, or Taylorism, crudely conceived, was the guiding ethos and tactical cover for a broad attack on craft traditions and worker autonomy in much of American industry. Corning, however, needed a workforce that was constantly improving its skill and building on its experience, and one that was motivated by goodwill toward the company. Consider David Gray's vision of his department, expressed in a 1916 letter to Alanson Houghton:

> The Mechanical Development Department should have full charge of all mechanical experimentation and the design and manufacture of special machinery. It should keep in close touch with the patent situation and, as much as possible, with the work of other concerns. It should not only study the requirements of other departments but should endeavor to anticipate them. It should obtain and work out the feasible ideas of the workmen. It should keep complete records of all work it does, especially that of an inventive nature. It should act in an advisory capacity in routine engineering problems when called upon. Whenever the machine shop or any part of it is not engaged on work of the department itself, it should be used for repairs or similar work for the Works in general.[2]

Gray's clear conception of how the department ought to function, quoted above, indicated his compatibility with the Houghtons' philosophy of knowledge-based competition. It reflected a respect for skilled workmen and their ideas that augured well for the work he would ultimately perform, for several of the most important machines that the new development department introduced were conceived by ingenious skilled glassblowers. Still, his desire to put into practice ideas developed on the shop floor was not necessarily shared by fellow mechanical engineers, who had for some thirty years or more adhered to a strictly utilitarian view of shop management.[3]

The account that follows concerns the nature of process innovation at Corning Glass Works through World War II. It explains how the company, so much a part of its broader industrial culture, managed to keep a stream of process inventions in the works when many other manufacturers chose to stabilize their processes and drive out further innovation in the interests of maximizing efficiency. At a time when American industrial society prided itself on eliminating all "irrational" elements like art and craft from the workbench and the factory floor alike, Corning protected them as key to its fundamental approach to innovation. It also managed to make materials, process, and product innovation work together, each generating opportunities and solving problems for the others. Some of the ways it achieved this feat were to attempt extremely challenging projects, like the 200-inch mirror for the Mount Palomar Observatory, and to maintain as part of Corning's immediate culture elements that were not strictly economic. Neither Steuben art glass, nor the architectural business, which used Corning glass in ways both decorative and structural, made money directly for Corning. They served a different purpose, however: to maintain the highest esthetic standards of the glassmaking craft and the best aspects of American design as guiding elements in Corning's business.

GAFFERS AND GLASSHOUSES, 1880–1910

Until well after the turn of the twentieth century, Corning resembled most other glass companies in physical appearance. Though twice as large as the average U.S. glass company, of which there were more than 150 in 1880, Corning, with its nearly 300 employees, was nevertheless housed in the same structures of brick and wood, located between river and rail line, equally threatened by fire and flood. Corning's first plant (A Factory) and its outbuildings mushroomed by the Chemung River, its hundred foot chimneys belching soot, its furnaces consuming railcar and barge loads of coal for fuel, and its melting pots fed with sand, soda, and other chemical additives temporarily stored in sheds scattered around the factory. Thick black soot from the glass furnaces, and later the furnace that turned coal into producer gas, blanketed the plant and most of the buildings in the area, winter and summer.

One telling physical feature did distinguish the Corning plant from others, a testimony to its pioneering approach to innovation. In the 1890s A factory sprouted a series of very tall towers; looking like oversized chimneys, these towers were used for a new "updraw" method for vertically drawing glass tubing that Arthur Houghton had first observed on a trip to England and later patented in the United States. Before the turn of the century most thermometerware was imported from Germany. By 1900 Corning's tubing tower had reached a height of 187 feet. By 1912 Corning was by far the largest single domestic supplier of thermometerware, though it continued to share the domestic market with German manufacturers.

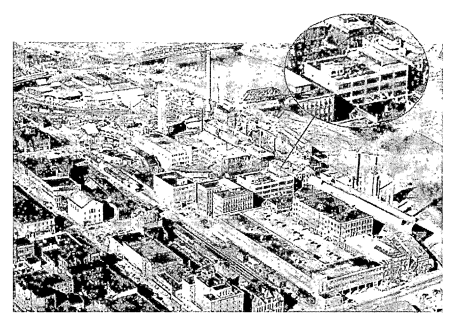

The Corning factory complex in 1946 shows the company between the river and the (Erie and Lakawana) railroad tracks running through the center of town. The Chemung River frequently flooded the entire downtown area engulfing factories and low-lying dwellings. The thermometer tube tower is visible near the central bridge. The enlarged detail is the research laboratory, specially built for research in 1940, but still attached to Corning's Main Plant.

The tubing tower, adorned in later years with a picture of the iconic lightbulb blower, "Little Joe,"[4] symbolized the ability that would eventually become a hallmark of Corning's development as a company: applying and adapting a process developed for one product to the production of others, sometimes many others. Corning's early ability to produce relatively uniform and reliable lantern globes and tubing at a reasonable cost not only earned it the chance to become lead supplier for Thomas Edison's lightbulbs but also led to businesses supplying chemical plants, fluorescent lighting envelopes, and even architectural materials. This one business breakthrough signaled the kind of adaptability that would carry Corning through a transition that put most glass companies out of business by World War I: the shift to mechanization.

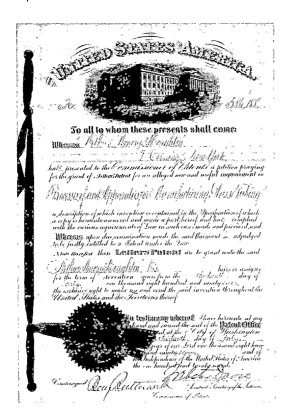

Arthur Houghton's Updraw Patent ("Process of and Apparatus for Manufacturing Glass Tubing") issued in 1897, improved on methods he had observed in Europe.

As at all other glass companies of the time, Corning's operations before World War I were controlled by skilled craftsmen; in glass they are known as gaffers. The gaffer in charge of the shop was paid by the company, and he in turn hired and paid the men and boys who worked for him. It was the gaffer who had the most glassworking know-how in the operation, did the training, and controlled the pace of work. The company owners, and those whom they trusted, controlled the melting operations and the composition of the glass, and also bore the expense of the furnaces and the shops.

With the advent of new sources of fuel—gas and electricity—new kinds of materials, and a dawning understanding of the chemistry and physics of glass, the processes for making specialty glass in particular were poised to change rapidly around the turn of the century. Pressure to capitalize on the availability of new knowledge and resources came from several sources, chief among these increasing competition, more demanding products, and customers of greater sophistication. As a specialty glass producer with a work was 1,440 pieces. When that quantity was completed, the men quit for the day. Rules of thumb were just about all the cost data there were to go on. For the Houghtons, profitability was an even more closely guarded secret than the secrets of glass composition. Few expense records were kept at Corning before 1900, concerning either materials or labor. The contract selling price for Corning bulbs was $21.00 per thousand, rising to $44.44 for blue, purple, and green bulbs, $66.66 for yellow and green, and $88.89 for ruby bulbs. A 1907 cost study of Corning production by the accounting firm of Niles and Niles showed that a turn (or half day's work) of 600 bulbs had a direct labor cost of $1.79, increasing slightly for smaller turns (larger bulbs) to a maximum of $2.04 for a 300-bulb turn. In contrast, tubing, which was also hand blown in 1895, had a contract price of twenty to thirty cents per pound, dropping slightly in price after the turn of the century.

The high cost of labor for lightbulb production was one factor in Corning's subsequent labor troubles. In 1890, the company had suffered a serious and devastating strike, from which it had only recovered by hiring replacement workers. Because the entire town of Corning at the time was filled with small shops (mostly glass cutting concerns) and was heavily craft oriented, those who wanted union representation, and were willing to strike to get it, were very much outweighed by those who opposed it. The dissenters lost their jobs and left town to find work in the "western" glass companies of the Ohio Valley. The incident was, however, embedded in the town memory by one terrible experience: in July 1891, a crowd of these younger glassworkers was killed in a train wreck while returning home for the Fourth of July. A memorial to these workers, all well-known in Corning, was placed in St. Mary's Cemetery to serve as a constant reminder of the painful consequences of labor strife in the Corning community.

This disruption prompted General Electric, which had organized and consolidated the industry a couple of years previously, to look around for new sources of bulb supply. The Libbey Glass Company of Toledo, Ohio, had made progress on a variety of fronts and had even attempted to mechanize bulb production. Michael Owens, an ingenious inventor employed by Libbey and later a president of that company, had developed the first successful bottle-making machine. Libbey's blowing machine, only economical at first for bottles, took the place of the glassblower with his molds. Though it was a huge, cumbersome device, expensive to build and maintain, the bot-tle machine concept was adapted for bulb making, producing the widely adopted Westlake machine. At first, production was neither faster nor cheaper than hand labor, but it did offer some insurance against labor actions. The effort must have impressed GE, which was always looking for signs that a supplier was searching for better and cheaper, or safer, produc-tion methods. From then on GE allocated 40 percent of its requirements to Corning, 40 percent to Libbey, and the rest elsewhere. It also moved to make its own glass, while other buyers, chiefly Westinghouse and later Syl-vania, relied solely on suppliers and paid a higher price.

Cost was not the only consideration in the production of lightbulb blanks however. GE itself learned more about making glass, setting up its own glass factory and accompanying laboratory, and it began to demand certain standards of manufacture of its suppliers. Indeed, GE's production of some of its own bulbs gave it the benefit of greater process knowledge in its own plants than Corning itself had accumulated. Arthur Day described to Alanson Houghton a visit to Corning made by Willis Whitney, head of GE's research laboratory, in 1910:

> With regard to Dr. Whitney and his problem, you should know, and no doubt you do, that Dr. Whitney's natural inclination is that of a research student—to go after underlying facts, and [that he] is unwillingly influenced by commercial considerations. He then examined carefully into our ability to control: (1) the chemical composition of the ingredients that go into the pot; (2) possible changes of composition thereafter; (3) the temperature of the glass in the pots and during working; and finally (4) the ability of hand workers to put the glass through uniform process in bulbmaking. He did not intimate a shade of doubt upon any of these points save the last.[6]

Day (as noted in chapter 3) had been instrumental in bringing Corning's melting process under some degree of control, but his ambitions went far beyond that. He believed that there were inherent limits to the craft system and that it was time to stop relying solely on the handworker to control the process of bulb making. He dreamed of devising a self-contained, fully automated bulb-making process where even the gathering step was automated. Whatever his dreams, the transition to bulb-making machines turned out to be very gradual at Corning. In the end it occupied the best part of three decades, not only because of the lack of capable machines but also because the company lacked all but the most rudimentary system in manufacture.

The Case for Special Machines

Specialized machinery to extend the skills of the American worker was an old and often tried idea by 1900. The "American system of manufacture" as it was known in Europe, combined specialized equipment and uniformity of product. In the metal trades this latter characteristic meant interchangeable parts and required, first of all, reliable methods of gauging and, more gradually, harder metal alloys for machine tools that could in turn make precise cuts in softer metals. By the late 1880s these developments had created the necessary conditions for industrial America to take another major step. This step was masterminded by Frederick Winslow Taylor, the father of scientific management, who reasoned that once machines were consistently capable of precision, rules could be made to govern how operators used them. A given job was no longer to be left to the discretion of the skilled workman but embedded instead in the machines and fixtures designed to do that job, and encoded in the process instructions written by process engineers. From there it was, for Taylor, only a short step to measuring the human part of the job as well, so that the operator became just an extension of the machine, and all of the critical knowledge associated with the job became the province of management.

In the decade between 1900 and 1910 companies all over the U.S. industrial heartland were using Taylorist consultants to perform "time and motion studies" on skilled and semiskilled jobs. The results of such studies were used to determine how much time it ought to take a worker to perform his job with the minimum amount of excess motion and the maximum amount of output. According to Taylor's philosophy, the appropriate way to compensate a skilled worker was to offer a higher wage after a given optimum output level was reached. Similar developments in the organization of work were taking place in the fast-growing automobile industry, where Henry Ford had combined the moving assembly line with the comparatively high wage of $5 a day to attract unskilled workers to his rapidly expanding automobile factories. The American system had also given way in the metal trades, and in many associated manufacturing processes, to the mass production philosophy, which rested crucially on the assumption that only management should have the right to control process knowledge and that operators were to serve their machines, rather than the other way around.[7]

As we have noted, the glass industry was late in coming to these ideas about mechanization. What Corning was doing just after the turn of the century resembled the American system of specialized machines and uniformity of product rather more than its descendant, mass production. But Corning was attempting these first-order process changes at just the time when mass production was in the air and when the skilled American workforce, and the labor movement that proposed to organize the glass industry, reacted with fear and hostility to the loss of its former prerogatives in the workplace. Consequently, Corning executives felt the need to tread very softly in the area of labor relations.

The Flint Glass Workers Union, the craft union that organized the glass industry by region beginning in the 1880s, attempted to organize Corning and other glassworking establishments. In this early period of union activity it had been a fairly easy matter for employers in the town of Corning to fire the handful of troublemaking union organizers and thereby quell the union's activities. But by 1890, the situation had changed, partly because specialized machines had made further inroads.

As we have already noted, the 1890 strike against Corning created an opening in the bulb market for the Libbey Glass Company and its blowing machines. Fortunately, relations between Corning and Libbey were cordial, and Corning was able to track Libbey's mechanical progress fairly closely. Nevertheless, unless Corning wished to pay royalties to Libbey for every bulb it made, it needed to undertake its own machine development.

Corning did belatedly respond, though its answer was delayed by Amory Houghton Jr.'s staunch opposition to putting money into mechanical development. Finally, research into a bulb machine was funded by his sons Alanson and Arthur and a few other interested parties contributing their own money.[8] The Houghton brothers consulted Arthur Day and in 1906 started the effort with a machine inventor named William Chamberlin, whom Day initially oversaw at the Carnegie Institution. They even went so far as to establish a separate research corporation to do this work. This organization, the Empire Machine Company, was started in 1909 by the younger Houghtons, along with Corning treasurer William Sinclaire, Day, and the machines' inventors, Chamberlin and Corning machine builder Charles Githler. This enterprise came to hold patents associated with its various machines valued at several million dollars. Corning itself owned none of Empire's stock and in fact paid licensing fees for its technology. Though financially and legally separate from Corning, Empire came to be physically located in the Corning plant, specifically in A Factory.

Mechanizing Bulb Production

The Empire Machine effort produced four different successive models of lightbulb-blowing machine before the fifth-generation machine, called the E machine, finally made it to the factory floor. All of the development work for the E Machine, including the prototype installation, had been conducted in secret, that is, behind doors closed to Corning's workforce. While experimenting with these early machines, the researchers were even careful to break up the cullet, or waste glass, produced by their experiments, and when the time came in 1913 to attempt the first full production run, the machines were installed not in a Corning plant but in the Central Falls, Rhode Island, glass factory that belonged to GE. Corning did not acquire a significant number of the E Machines until sometime after 1915, when it decided to equip its Wellsboro plant with a battery of these devices.[9]

Throughout this period, Corning's research efforts were driven by the Westlake threat. The Westlake machine, after some further modification, brought Libbey's bulb costs below Corning's (which in 1914 was still producing its sale bulbs entirely by hand) and provided the necessary proof that an automated process could work and, at least in one instance, offered a relatively cheap alternative to hand production. At Corning the E Machine yielded to the F; this latter proved only marginally better than its predecessor, though the two together produced hundreds of millions of bulbs for Corning between 1915 and 1927.

A second Empire development effort, this time funded and organized entirely by Corning, began in 1922 and, four years later, produced the famous Ribbon Machine, a device that was, and remains, the most cost-effective way to produce lightbulb blanks. Both of these efforts owed much to two legendary men: William Woods and David Gray. Woods was a talented inventor with no engineering training, while Gray, a mechanical engineer from MIT, headed the mechanical development department; the two naturally complemented one another.

Gray first became involved in 1916. Before installing the machine in a new plant, the Houghtons hired him as an independent consulting engineer to evaluate the E Machine. His assessment was that, with a few minor adjustments and modifications, the E Machine under development at Empire had gone about as far as it could unless they intended to make it fully automatic. "I wish to repeat, that I consider the conception of the device as a whole, very ingenious, and I believe that with the few changes I have suggested you will have a very serviceable semiautomatic machine," he wrote.[10]

Meanwhile Woods was a young glassblower who had come to Corning from Pittsburgh in 1898. In 1916, he accepted the challenge of serving as plant manager of a new Corning plant in Wellsboro, Pennsylvania, which used the E Machine to produce lightbulbs. Woods was authorized to take with him a small core group of experienced lampworkers but had to recruit most of his workforce from the local area. Woods himself had previously been only peripherally involved in blowing machine development but nevertheless managed to transform local farmboys (his idea) into skilled operators of the E Machine. He was aided in this by the fact that many such farmers were reasonably good mechanics by the standards of the day and by the fact that the Wellsboro E Machine was fed by a melting tank rather than the traditional pot furnace. Under Woods's direction the machines were up and running in time to take over half of the surge in demand for lightbulbs that Corning faced with the onset of World War I.

The first Amory Houghton Jr. having died in 1909, there was nothing preventing Alanson and Arthur from using company resources directly to further develop these machines; Corning and GE together took over Empire's experimental work in the early 1920s, working to perfect the E Machine in particular. The Westlake machine, however, continued to serve as a benchmark against which successive generations of Corning technology were measured. Neither the E nor the F Machine ever clearly surpassed it as a production technology. That honor would be left to the Corning Ribbon Machine.

1,000 Bulbs per Minute

In 1924 Corning bought GE's Central Falls plant, which contained three Westlake machines. The company purchased three more Westlakes immediately thereafter, and used the six, as well as a limited number of its own E and F Machines, in its bulb production until as late as 1949. GE also acquired some Westlake machines and used them in production for many years. Both companies were aware of the Westlake's shortcomings, and both knew that neither of Corning's other bulb-production technologies were likely to rise much above them. Another machine was needed.

Fortunately, it was in the works, kept secret even from GE. Called "Problem 399" while under development, the new design was the brainchild of Woods. An operations supervisor with the company at the time, he might have been expected to base his design on analogies to hand blowing, but his work at the Wellsboro plant also contributed to his understanding of the problem. It is likely that this experience, though on the whole positive, impressed on the inventor a sense of the limitations of the E Machine; it was shortly thereafter, in any case, that he came up with the basic idea of a Ribbon Machine, which he conceived of as a machine process from beginning to end.

The Westlake machine had been adapted from an already extant bulb-blowing machine, the Owens-Libbey bottle machine. The E Machine line was also an adaptation of sorts: it was inspired by the relatively primitive technology of the gathering iron and blowpipe. The first Corning bulb-blowing machine—the A Machine—was exactly that: a machine that directed bursts of air down a preloaded blowpipe. All of the subsequent machines in this line were essentially variations on this theme: semiautomatic, hand-loaded blowers.

The Ribbon Machine, on the other hand, represented one of the first glass processes ever to be developed not as an imitation of a long-standing craft method but as a machine-centered answer to a given production problem. In Day's words,

> Success was finally attained by a process not usual in the development of automatic machinery, namely, by completely abandoning all of these details developed out of the experience of the hand-worker, and basing all operations upon the measured mechanical properties of molten glass at the various stages and temperatures through which it must pass. Briefly described, the machine in use today is a 'theoretical' development and not an embodiment of the hand-worker's skill.[11]

This distinction should not be overemphasized: Woods was, after all, a skilled glassblower in his own right, and he worked closely with handworkers. Nevertheless, the history of the Ribbon Machine development was a turning point in the way Corning had previously thought about glass and glass knowledge. As Day had predicted, the company was no longer confined merely to capturing and codifying the glass secrets of its craftsmen. For certain key process technologies craftsmen would increasingly be asked to take their cues and their assignments from the engineers, researchers, and designers who would try, and often succeed, to do with glass things that the craft tradition had never dreamed of.

The key to the development of the Ribbon Machine was not only abandoning the idea of mimicking human practice but also starting with the goal of developing a fully automated, continuous process (the E and F Machines were only semiautomated, though the latter, with the addition of certain ancillary technology, could be almost fully automated). Such a process itself had to begin with a constant flow of glass, and for this Woods's inspiration was almost certainly the Danner machine, a continuous-process device that utilized a ribbon of glass for tubing production. Developed by Libbey Glass, this device relied, as the Ribbon Machine would, on a continuous flow of glass, in this instance one guided by a hollow mandrel mounted on a hollow shaft. The shaft channeled a constant flow of air to keep the tubing open as it was seized upon and lengthened by a pair of conveyors.

Woods himself had little education, and while he claimed to be able to translate his ideas into practice, he had no way of translating that practice into the sort of dollars-and-cents figures the company needed to make a rational choice as to whether or not to proceed with development. This was where David Gray came in. Gray's assessment accurately predicted that the Ribbon Machine, though a costly investment, would repay that money many times over if brought to fruition.

Though Gray saw the value of Woods's idea more or less immediately, it had, in its early stages, been rejected by Woods's peers: "the idea was so new and revolutionary that when it was presented to older and experienced glassworkers, it was immediately pronounced unworkable and was even received with ridicule."[12] The concept of a ribbon of molten glass laid atop an endless chain of linked forms was ingenious in itself; the combination of this with air plungers above and paste molds below was perhaps a bit less inspired but certainly no less challenging to imagine, much less develop. The bulb was formed, and others, numbering thousands per hour, came after it in a fully automated, continuous process. This was all accomplished over the course of a few feet, as the Ribbon Machine, unlike the Westlake Machine, was relatively small.

The Ribbon Machine cost approximately $200,000 to develop, with highest expenditures rising to $90,000 in 1926, the year it was introduced.[13] Though by no means cheap, the machine returned Corning to its position of dominance in this market and allowed the company to break free of hand production for most bulb types. Corning appears to have made this transition with remarkably little fuss. One author offered the following description:

> It is easy to see that in so radical a change in methods as would be involved
> in abandoning hand production, dislocations in labor relations might result
> in serious trouble. But throughout the entire period of change the matter
> was so discreetly handled by the management that no labor difficulties

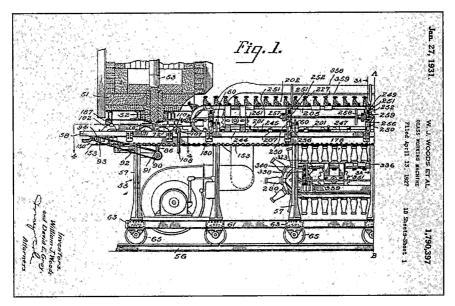

The Ribbon Machine schematic is one of several illustrations attached to the Ribbon Machine patent filed in 1927 and issued 1931. Titled simply "Glass Working Machine" and signed by co-inventors William J. Woods and David Gray, the drawing shows the tremendous complexity of this revolutionary machine. Its blowing nozzles, carried on a revolving upper chain, ride above a molten ribbon of glass and produce glass gobs which in turn are clasped inside moving molds carried by a second, lower chain until they are formed into bulb blanks.

arose. Fortunately, the transition was gradual so that it was possible to find work for many of the former bulb men in other departments of the Company or on new products coming into the factory.[14]

The company first introduced the Ribbon Machine into the Wellsboro factory, which had never known hand methods for bulb production.[15] Wellsboro had shut down temporarily when Corning took over GE's Central Falls facility in 1925; when it reopened in 1926, it was running Corning's first production Ribbon Machine. This was joined by a second such machine in 1928. By 1933 it was obvious that the battle against the Westlake machine had been won: GE licensed the technology from Corning, and together the two companies produced an improved version capable of churning out 1,000 bulbs per minute by 1939, dwarfing the Westlake's best efforts. The company was so delighted with its new invention that it called it the Corning machine. GE, nonplussed by this constant reminder of Corning's success, chose to make its own modification both to the machine and to the name, naming its reworked version the Ribbon Machine.

Recall that Corning kept "Problem 399" secret while in development, even though the two companies were supposedly working together on the same problem. Minutes of meetings held between GE and Corning after Corning introduced the machine show that the two companies then shared much technical data and knowledge in their joint quest for ever higher output levels from the renamed Ribbon Machine. But GE's resources dwarfed Corning's; it spent over $100,000 trying to improve on the bulb transfer mechanism that connected the Ribbon Machine with the bulb lehrs, while Corning had had qualms about spending $200,000 for the initial machine development. GE had both the money and the staff necessary to experiment with all available bulb machines, not only Corning's but the Westlake as well. Had the Ribbon Machine not proved such a success, Corning would almost certainly not have held on to its long-lasting business in lightbulbs.[16]

MECHANICAL DEVELOPMENT DEPARTMENT, 1917–1940

Along with assessing the Empire Machine Company's blowing machine efforts in 1916, David Gray had also agreed to sketch out for Alanson Houghton what an in-house mechanical development program might look like for Corning. It was his recommendation that further development should be done by Corning itself, not by Empire Glass, to promote closer cooperation with other departments, simplify accounting, and strengthen Corning's position in patent matters. There were also economic justifications. Such a department would be likely to come up with a "great many minor devices" that would not be of interest to the Empire Machine Company. This was an important insight: small devices were of little interest in the generic sense, for they would generate few patents and little licensing income for Empire's shareholders. But they could make a big competitive difference to the ability of Corning's machines to deliver most effectively and to adapt most closely to local conditions.[17]

Gray's proposal pictured the ideal mechanical development department as consisting of engineering rooms (drafting rooms, file and blueprint rooms, experimental device storage, and compartments for individual men working on individual projects), machine shops (equipped with an "ample variety of machine tools"), and a laboratory (an experimental plant where new processes, machinery, and furnace arrangements could be tested and perfected before they were installed in the works, and a place where the chemistry department could test things that could not be handled in its own experimental facilities). He suggested that such a department should incorporate quarters for routine engineering that were to be centralized under one head. "In my opinion," he wrote, "there is an urgent need for the concentration of routine work on an economical basis." A permanent arrangement for mechanical development, Gray suggested, might be housed in a new two-story building on the southwest corner of the Glass Works property.

The mechanical development department's first efforts revealed that Gray might have underestimated the complexities of his task. His attempts to address a vexing Pyrex dish molding problem used a continuous horizontal chain molding device in which gobs of glass were deposited in little molds and then hit with a plunger. This Cleveland press was an "awkward and clumsy affair [that] did a fairly good job," according to Gray's later account, but by other accounts "never worked properly for Pyrex and had to be scrapped."[18] This effort nevertheless led to later successes with other continuous machines, including the Ribbon Machine and its counterpart for making Pyrex objects, the Turret Machine.

A major problem with all such presses was getting the glass from furnace —pot or tank—to the machine. Feeders were worked on for years; the most successful one came out of work performed by what was then Hartford-Empire, a combination of GE-sponsored Hartford-Fairmont and Empire Glass Company that together held most of the key glass machinery patents that were not already in Corning's possession. Another problem in pressing was the imperfections of the joints that were left after the pieces were removed from the mold. At first these had to be fire polished using a combination of equipment purchased outside and developed inside the company. Later the perfection of the molding technique did away with this expensive finishing step altogether. Only when Corning merged in 1936 with MacBeth Evans, which had a sizable business in consumerware of its own, did it learn how to perfect "free" molding and precision molding of the kind that produced ware that was satisfactory to customers without extra polishing.

Soon after Gray set up his department in 1917, Corning obtained rights to Libbey Glass's Danner machine and made a number of significant modifications of its own to it. This sort of transaction was in keeping with the pre-World War II spirit of the industry. Though companies competed, they shared their different processes, usually by licensing and occasionally by exchanging one valuable tool or concept for another. The creation of the mechanical development department allowed Corning not only to invent its own process equipment but also to monitor effectively what was going on in the rest of the industry, whether in the United States or abroad, and to adapt the best of what it found for its own use. Its closest relationship in mechanical matters continued to be with General Electric (always referred to in the records as "The General"). Until World War II, Corning and GE shared virtually everything each knew about the development of glass machinery.[19]

A second key source of expertise in mechanical development was Mac-Beth Evans. The merger gained Corning far more than consumer product expertise. It also acquired the MacBeth Evans experience with machines made by Westlake and Empire, and a sophisticated cost system for manufacturing that the acquired company understood and applied much better than any Corning had been able to develop on its own. Eventually, by taking advantage of all the improvements made on the Ribbon Machine, both inside and outside Corning, engineers would adapt the machines for producing high-volume ware other than lightbulbs. The device worked not only for bulb blanks but also for radio receiving tubes (for which by the early 1930s there was extremely high-volume demand, despite the Depression) and, later, Christmas tree ornaments.

The same kind of adaptation took place in Corning's tube drawing processes: after modifying the Danner machine, Corning finally adapted it in the mid-1920s to Pyrex tubing. Corning made a crucial contribution to the state of the art in tubing technology by developing automatic gauging equipment, which variously measured and sorted pieces of tubing by weight and diameter at high speeds and to very close tolerances.

In 1933 Corning licensed the Vello tubing machine, which had been invented by an Italian machine designer of that name. Vello was known to St. Gobain, the French glass company with which Corning had close relations in Europe. The story of adapting the Vello machine, later recounted by Corning's creative Austrian tubing expert and engineer, Ed Wellech, shows how deep Corning's mechanical development capability had become by the 1930s, and how important it was for the company. According to Eugene Sullivan's daybook there was even a debate among executives in the 1920s as to whether the mechanical development department ought to receive a bigger budget than the research department.[20]

Wellech later wrote that when Corning learned of the Vello machine from a Mr. Gentil of St. Gobain, Corning executives Glen Cole and William Curtiss went to Europe. There they found a device that needed only one operator to run each installation, a source of pride for its inventor. However, when Wellech examined Vello's blueprints he concluded that he could improve the machine radically. To install the technology according to Vello's specifications would, according to his calculations, cost Corning $125,000. But if he installed it with the modifications he had in mind, it would cost Corning closer to $35,000. Wellech struck a deal with Vello: if his approach worked, Corning would pay Vello the lower amount; if not, they would have to adopt Vello's plans and pay his entire fee.

The inventor and his chief engineer arrived at Corning a week before the machine was to be installed and tested. On inspecting Wellech's setup and proposed modifications, Vello exclaimed that Wellech had ruined him. Wellech wrote later:

> We started the "Vello" one noon and by 8:00 we made salable tubing—#36 gauge at 500 lbs./hr., twice as fast as the Danner process. I called Cole and Curtiss, who came to see it and congratulated Vello and me. Vello kissed me in true French fashion on the cheek. Corning Glass Works bought the process for the 'Americans.'

Corning's improved Vello process was a radical reinvention that allowed Corning to make progressively larger sizes of tubing, eventually achieving diameters as large as 2.25 inches. Among other things, starting in 1939, it

Inventing engineer Edmund Wellech (inset) shown with a picture of the Vello machine he adapted for Corning's use. This vital machine for Corning, when installed at the Fallbrook plant, was used to draw large-sized tubing such as fluorescent light bulb blanks.

enabled the company to make fluorescent lighting tubes for lamp makers like Sylvania.

PRODUCTION CLUB: 1922 AND ON

Machines were not the only answer to the growth problem, however. The press of wartime production, with its demands for overtime work and the difficulties of meeting demand, brought home the need to make other changes in Corning's production capability. Problems with "shrinkage" (i.e., waste) had become quite serious, and there was a long-standing difficulty with information being sequestered within departmental walls. New ideas in general had trouble finding acceptance in production. Renewed efforts to introduce some of the benefits of "system" that H.P. Gage and others had called for as early as 1912 came a decade later, when an executive named William Curtiss, newly hired from the Harvard Business School, convinced Corning that its managers and supervisors would benefit from training in the "science of industrial management."[21]

One hundred fifty of Corning's superintendents, foremen, and administrative staff were given the opportunity to take a course together offered by the Business Training Corporation (BTC) of New York. The course, involving discussion of six different texts and numerous graded problem sets, was held during the winter of 1920–1921. To extend its benefits, top management formed Corning's Production Club, limited in membership to those who had successfully completed the course. Its stated aims were "to conserve and extend interest in the science of industrial management, to apply the principles of this science to the problems of this Company through discussion and practice, to form an active and permanent connecting link between management and men, and to establish an association for enjoyment and recreation."[22]

In later years recreation became the club's primary purpose (including annual performances of a men's and women's glee club, minstrel shows, and dances), and membership grew to more than 400. In this regard, it was a vital way of retaining key trained employees. But in the early years the Production Club was all business. It enforced stringent membership requirements, created a forum for officers of the company to talk about matters as they saw them, and served to bring about serious conversation between managers and floor supervisors. Company officials were invited to speak on production issues; A. D. Falck, for example, lectured on bulb history and the impending changeover to Ribbon Machine production in 1926. The club also sponsored safety campaigns and correspondence courses open to any Corning employee on a voluntary basis.

This effort to educate a senior echelon of managers in systematic techniques for controlling manufacturing, and to adopt and optimize the use of new equipment, improved Corning's production methods considerably in the 1920s. It also served the important purpose of smoothing the transition to new equipment on the plant floor. The introduction of the Ribbon Machine, for instance, could have created much more labor unrest than it did. The balance Corning attempted to maintain between craft traditions and science served it well here and was unusual for the time.

Beyond establishing a club for industrial management, Corning also increased its commitments to its workforce, maintaining harmonious relations during the Depression. Under the leadership of the young Amory Houghton, the company tried to maintain employment levels and improve working conditions even in the face of decreasing sales. It also adopted a set of progressive policies that Corning had begun as early as 1918 when it instituted its first company-wide life insurance policy. This was followed by other benefits such as health insurance and a company sports center. A young designer who arrived in Corning early in the Depression wrote later of life in Corning as he witnessed it:

> The Glass Works appeared to be unusually enlightened in its attitude towards its employees at a time when this could hardly have been said of Corporate America in general. They maintained a company recreation center that included a swimming pool, bowling alleys and badminton courts; a labor-management panel consisting of duly elected representatives from each side of the fence sat in judgment upon corporate proposals that might in any way affect the welfare of the work force, and Corning Glass was among the pioneering firms in the country to provide employees with comprehensive accident, health and life insurance policies... during the '30s Amory Houghton maintained what might be called an 'open door' policy: that is, if any employee of the Glass Works felt that he had a good reason to talk to the president or had something to get off his chest, then he had only to call his secretary and make an appointment.[23]

Another way that Corning's management buffered the worst effects of the Depression era on its workforce was to take low-margin work that it might not ordinarily have accepted. One such project was the casting of the largest piece of glass ever produced until that time, a project that not only gave Corning some important learning opportunities but also involved very direct interaction between research personnel and glassworkers. At Corning during the mid-1930s every worker on the plant floor could see that science created jobs because of the work on the challenging and dramatic telescope mirror for Mount Palomar. The Palomar project, more than any other single event, brought Corning into the public eye as a leading research-performing company. It was an outcome that the whole organization worked hard to achieve.

ORDEAL OF THE 200-INCH MIRROR, 1932–1935

Corning found in the Palomar project a customer more scientifically knowledgeable than the researchers purchasing Pyrex labware and more demanding than the restaurateurs buying its cookware: the trustees of the Mount Wilson Observatory and the Carnegie Institution that helped fund it, as well as the astronomer George Hale and his colleagues. Hale had devoted his entire career to raising the money and designing and building ever larger and more sensitive telescopes. Astronomy was the science that above all had caught the public imagination in the first three decades of the twentieth century, and the effort to build state-of-the-art telescopes was the equivalent of the push to construct ever larger particle accelerators of the second half of the twentieth century. Hale's previous experience with the Hooker telescope on Mount Wilson, which had a 100-inch mirror cast by the French glass company, St. Gobain, before World War I, had convinced him that the critical property of interest in an even larger telescope mirror had to be stability in the face of temperature change. The Hooker telescope had been so sensitive to temperature that it was only usable for a few hours in the middle of the day after the optical elements had stabilized from the overnight changes in temperature.

For this reason designers of the new 200-inch telescope to be located on Mount Palomar had awarded the mirror project to Elihu Thomson's General Electric in 1929. GE proposed to supply a mirror blank made of fused quartz, which was known to have a lower expansion coefficient than Pyrex. But fused quartz had never been fabricated in pieces larger than a few inches, and the process for making it was highly experimental. GE took the project apparently intending to have the trustees of the Mount Wilson Observatory and the Carnegie Institution, who were jointly involved in its funding and assembly, fund a very ambitious and open-ended research project. By 1932 it was clear that GE was nowhere near fulfilling its promise to make a fused quartz mirror blank of the size required: the best they had managed was a blank twenty inches in diameter. By the time their sixty-inch blank ran into trouble, the company had already charged $600,000 to the project, many times what their estimates had suggested. Moreover, they acknowledged that they had almost no idea what the ultimate costs would be. Meanwhile close engineering of the supporting apparatus at the 100-inch Mount Wilson telescope had altered the low expansion levels required of the mirror blank, suggesting that Pyrex might suffice after all. Hale, who knew Corning through many contacts and trusted Arthur Day, decided to transfer the project in 1932.

Corning's research physicist George McCauley had long wanted to pursue telescope mirrors as a product. He knew that low-expansion Pyrex would be a good material for this purpose and that the large size and demanding requirements of the mirror blanks would make them ideal candidates for pursuing research questions on annealing and tempering large masses of glass. In addition to problems with melting and working Pyrex, great uncertainties remained in the areas of annealing it. The strains introduced in cooling were not well understood, and there were serious problems of scale: the patterns of strain that developed in small quantities of glass seemed to have no relationship to the patterns that developed in larger masses.

Corning had supplied small glass disks for the Mount Wilson laboratories as early as 1922 and had experimented with pouring disks as large as twenty-seven inches in diameter. When the 200-inch telescope project was first announced, the publicity had set off a wave of smaller telescope building at universities across the country. But Corning had proved unable to land a large order. Nevertheless, by the time Macauley was invited to make an alternative proposal to GE's foundering project, Corning had accumulated more than a little experience and it had devised an attractive plan.

Unlike GE, which charged the project for a variety of custom-built facilities and equipment as well as labor and profit, Corning used mainly existing equipment, with the exception of one enormous new lehr. Moreover, the company proposed to produce several smaller mirrors that could be used for auxiliary purposes in the observatory before it proceeded to the 2,000-pound, 200-inch mirror. Corning's charge was cost plus 10 percent, estimated to work out at $150,000 to $300,000 for three 60-inch disks, one 60-by 80-inch oval, a 120-inch disk, and the 200-inch disk itself. Both budget and timetable were clearly spelled out. Corning's obvious intention to meet them if at all possible must have been music to the ears of the Mount Wilson staff.

The actual preparation of the 200-inch mirror for the Hale telescope was an important opportunity for the Corning laboratory and plant engineering to work together in a research effort that would ultimately turn into a production process. If the big research question to be resolved was confirmation for large glass structures of the physical laws of annealing, the biggest challenges to overcome were all engineering problems: the design of molds, the effective control of molding and annealing temperatures, the movement and transport of a twenty-ton strong, but easily damaged, piece of glass. This exercise in learning by doing laid the foundation for Corning's business in telescope mirrors, which was to be a significant and highly visible Corning line for the rest of the century.

The Laboratory in Charge

In 1931 Arthur Day promised George Hale that his 200-inch mirror project, if given to Corning, would be run by the laboratory. Such a statement would have seemed less an assurance than a cause for concern if proffered by most other industrial organizations. But coming from Corning in the 1930s, it was meant as the highest form of commitment and was recognized as such. For the Corning scientists this was a chance to be highly visible to funders and opinion leaders in the scientific community; the project was rich with contacts in universities and research institutes all over the country. For the production side of the house it was a chance to gain experience with and help to shape a process which, if successful, would lead to further telescope business that they could handle on their own.

McCauley portrayed the mirror project to the world as an enormous stretch for a "maker of technical glassware." It was typical of Corning to identify itself to its different audiences in this way: mechanized volume manufacturer to lamp makers Westinghouse and GE, small technical glassmaker to the scientific community. In this case Corning's two sides were mutually reinforcing. And McCauley was a master at managing risk. By the time Hale turned to Corning to salvage the mirror project, McCauley had already constructed the necessary knowledge base and reinforced it with the experience base he thought he needed. He had also compared notes with the National Bureau of Standards, the only other maker of large telescope disks in the country, where he had worked before coming to Corning. The NBS had cast the largest domestic disk to date—sixty-seven inches for the Perkins Observatory at Ohio Wesleyan University—and McCauley had concluded that Corning's approaches to pouring and annealing were as good or better. Neither the 100-inch disk used for the Mount Wilson telescope (made by St. Gobain in 1904) nor the 67-inch disk for Perkins had used low-expansion glass, and conventional plate glass would obviously behave differently. But there were lessons to be learned from these projects. The St. Gobain disk, for example, had been marred by layers of bubbles marking each of the layers created when a ladle of glass had been poured, a problem that could be avoided by skimming the surface after each pouring.

McCauley had done his homework on costs and methods by producing, at Corning's expense, a sizable prototype disk. He was not acting alone. In addition to Corning research colleagues who were prepared to do the analytical and measurement work, he had strong support from the production staff under the direction of Alfred Vaksdal. Some of Vaksdal's crews had just about run out of even the deferred maintenance that had been neglected in the boom of the late 1920s, and he would soon have no work for them to do. Since the mirror would employ people who would have been paid anyway, it could be priced accordingly.

As McCauley and his colleagues saw it, they had three areas of strength. First, they understood their material, Pyrex 702EJ, which they had already used for the smaller disk prototype and which was regularly used for ovenware. Second, Corning was already melting tanks containing up to 6,000 pounds of glass at a time for use in the high-volume production of this same Pyrex ovenware. Third, sequencing the project as they had from the 27-inch disk to the 60-inch to the 120-inch to the 200-inch, they expected to work up to whatever problems might develop around size. McCauley chose to do the pouring in the most conservative way possible: he had the molten glass ladled in 300-pound bites from the center of the tank, thus avoiding impurities from the refractories that might collect at the sides and bottom of the tank, and skimmed the surface each time to remove any gases that might have collected there. For this project Corning purchased some huge ladles originally made for pouring steel that had been mothballed a decade earlier. In the average glass company, where only high-volume tank melting was done by the 1930s, the knack for manipulating such ladles would no longer be available, but McCauley could draw on skilled glassworkers who had long experience pouring glass into molds. Problems they had had with the 27-inch disc taught them to be particularly cautious with the material in the bricks used to line the glass melting tank. An accidental triggering of the plant's sprinkler system when they poured the trial disk had made him very aware of the need to protect the surface from any such accidents from above.

There were still some areas of unavoidable uncertainty. Chief among them was the design of the disk. In order to minimize its weight and to make it more maneuverable, Cal Tech designers had chosen a honeycomb structure, ribbed on its back, that would be formed by casting the glass over cores attached to the mold. The cores would have to be strong enough to withstand both the weight of the glass and its intense heat (1,300C) throughout the entire pouring cycle. These cores would only be "knocked out" when the disc had cooled. No one had worked with such a design before, so McCauley brought in Corning's most experienced mold makers from the production side of the house to address this issue.

Crash Composition

A serious unforeseen problem emerged as the project passed through one of its early checkpoints, the pouring of the 60-inch disk. Close testing of material broken off from this disk by research chemist Martin Nordberg revealed that Pyrex 702EJ was behaving in an unexpected way when annealed as slowly as it needed to be for the larger-sized glass structures. Tests showed that the glass was more vulnerable to moisture than anyone had expected. This was a definite setback because the wait for data from the annealed 60-inch disk threatened the schedule of the 120-inch disk.

Harrison Hood, chief chemist, assisted by Nordberg, undertook a crash program to find a version of Pyrex that would be more resistant to moisture attack. In two months they came up with Pyrex 715CF, which had a higher aluminosilicate content. It also had a 25-percent lower expansion rate than the original composition. McCauley only informed his clients at Cal Tech about this potential snafu after he had found his solution—they would be using a different glass, he explained, because it was better. Unfortunately, this new type of Pyrex had to be heated and kept at higher temperatures throughout the pouring cycle. For a large disc using twenty tons of molten glass, the pouring cycle would last as long as twelve hours. McCauley decided to take the precaution of pouring the mold inside a pouring "igloo" that had only three openings in it. This would keep the heat in and extraneous matter out. The igloo was sized for the 200-inch disk so that it could be used for the rest of the project.

Uncomfortable in the Spotlight

The 120-inch disk went without a hitch in early 1934: the lessons of the minor setbacks of the smaller disks had been well learned. McCauley had also taken the opportunity to pour two or three other smaller disks for the universities and observatories that had deserted GE to line up as Corning customers after the fused quartz fiasco. A rapturous telegram from Hale showed how relieved he was that this supplier, unlike GE, was committed to keeping to its schedule.[24] By the time March rolled around, Corning's labo-

This picture was taken during the production of the first 200-inch disc as molten glass was ladled into the specially made mold. It shows the ladlers in their protective shields and clothing closely observed by visitors' galleries on two sides of the work area.

ratory director, J. C. Hostetter, had gained confidence to the point of authorizing a special observation balcony to be built for press and dignitaries in sight of the pouring igloo. To ensure minimal interference with other work in the factory, the pouring was scheduled for a Sunday morning. The chief remaining uncertainties appeared to be crowd control and balcony design, along with some sensitivity to diatribes from conservative newspapers that were predicting certain doom for any project carried out on the Lord's Day.

Scale turned out to make more of a difference than McCauley had anticipated. The weak link was the mold design, though this only became clear well past the point where the 120-inch disk had been completed and had begun its early cooling period. Eight hours into the pouring, the weight of the glass and the prolonged heat destroyed the cores at last. First one core, then another, bobbed slowly to the surface, from which no amount of effort by asbestos-clothed glass ladlers could retrieve them. McCauley's anxiety peaked as twenty-some cores could be counted dotting the surface of the glass. Having abandoned the futile attempts to retrieve the floating cores, he ordered the disc to be treated as though the pour had gone according to plan. None of the onlookers knew for sure, but McCauley's somber demeanor could not have misled anyone into thinking the procedure had gone without a hitch.

When the disk had cooled to 300C, further attempts to remove the cores were made and, for the most part, succeeded. The disk was transferred to the annealing lehr, located a floor below. This was the only other piece of equipment specially constructed for the project: it sat on the ground floor of B Factory and was powered by the two huge, specially built electrical transformers (originally paid for by a grant from the Rockefeller Foundation) that were the only pieces of equipment the Corning effort had salvaged from the entire GE project.

The first cautious look into the lehr came on Memorial Day, when the disk temperature had been lowered from 1,800C to 120C. Arthur Day was on hand to report to Hale himself. So were Amory Houghton, Eugene Sullivan, President Glen Cole, and other senior executives, who had been kept informed of the progress, and the setbacks, of the project throughout. "Henceforth," read the official statement issued at the viewing,

Research physicist George McCauley, project head of the Palomar mirror project, in over-alls, inspects the second successful mirror blank crated for shipment across country in 1935.

two courses of action are possible, in which the economics or cost of the alternate courses will be the determining factors. To drill out the disc, providing certain mounting support cavities required in the telescope and to drill away superficial core fragments is feasible technically and the economic advantage involved in this procedure will be compared with cost of a recasting operation.

As most of the glass to a depth of five inches would be removed in the grinding and polishing anyway, it was conceivable that the original disk could still be used. But here McCauley had a chance to meet both his research objectives and his customers' aims in the best way possible, and he was given the leeway to do so: Amory Houghton himself approved a plan to pour a second disk. There was the chance that the problems would not be solved and that this disk would also run into difficulty, but if not, there would be one dummy disk to play with to aid in logistical preparations like crating and moving, and to test out theories McCauley had about annealing.

Theory held that if the disk was annealed ten times as fast as the calculated optimum time, it would show roughly ten times the strain. He chose to do this with the first disk, thus getting the annealing over more rapidly and freeing up the specially built annealing oven for the second disk, which was poured in December.

Deliverance and Delivery

The first disk emerged from the annealing lehr as predicted: annealing theory confirmed, if not proven. Having been reheated to a temperature of 1,300C, the disk surface had become almost smooth, if somewhat unsightly. The second disk was poured without a hitch, having the benefit of an intense effort to use even stronger heat-resisting materials for the cores and also to make them hollow so that they could be air-cooled during the pouring. Tried with one of the smaller disks, this approach worked admirably.

For the second disk the drama began after the disk had been secured in the annealing lehr. Four months into the cooling cycle, as the disk temperature was still being reduced daily at the theoretical optimum of one-tenth of one degree centigrade, the Chemung River overflowed its banks in one of its worst floods in a century. The rising waters reached the level of the electrical transformers minutes after an exhausted crew of men, in an effort to save the disk, managed to hoist one of the two big transformers to safety. Though the second transformer was put out of commission by the flood waters, the first one was able to keep the annealing cycle going with only a three-day pause.

No other mishaps occurred and the second disc was crated and shipped via special train across country at speeds no greater than twenty-five miles per hour. The route had to avoid all underpasses lower than fifteen feet, which made for a peculiarly circuitous route. This irritant was turned to advantage: wherever the train went during these deepest months of the Depression, it drew crowds. Nowhere were the crowds more dedicated, however, than in Corning itself: there 5,000 chilly onlookers turned out during a blizzard in March 1935, to watch the send-off.

It was fitting that George McCauley, who had borne the most responsibility for the longest period of time and had taken enormous pains to write up the experience in numerous detailed articles and papers, should in the end have received the largest part of the credit for the achievement. But inside Corning it was known to have been a team effort. For that reason McCauley's fullest acknowledgment, recorded at the end of an article in the 1935 *Bulletin of the American Ceramic Society* deserves to be quoted at length:

> May I express here to the executives of the Company through its President Amory Houghton, my sincere thanks. To J. C. Hostetter, Director of Research and Development, I am indebted for the assignment which gave me the responsibility and authority to see the work through, and I desire to express my thanks for his unfailing support day after day. To J. T. Littleton and W. C. Taylor, thanks are due for the facilities of the Physical and Chemical Laboratories, especially of the assistance of H. R. Lillie for measurements of annealing constants, of W. L. Wetmore for measurements of other physical properties of the glass used for control of melting, of W. W. Shaver for assistance in strain measurements, of H. P. Hood for the very remarkable glass composition, of M. E. Nordberg for measurements of chemical stability, and for R. D. Smith and men in his charge for analyses of material. To W. Woods and R. Newman, I am grateful for the help given in carrying out the experimental work involved in ladling and mold construction. To the foremen and men of the Engineering Department and Trades, I owe the realization of all the many ideas put forth to solve the problems presented here. To these men too numerous to give individual mention, for their patience and untiring efforts, and for their fine workmanship I am deeply indebted. To the men of the Mixing and Melting Departments, I wish to state my appreciation for the careful manner in which the glass was prepared. To the Purchasing Department and to the firms with whom they dealt I am grateful for the excellent deliveries and quality of products secured. To the men at the ladles and to those who assisted them in the long arduous task of forming a 200-inch glass disk, I express my appreciation for their willing and determined efforts to succeed and for the fine work accomplished.

The finishing of the disk to its final shape was expected to take years, but World War II delayed it even further. Reflecting telescopes do not require optical quality glass, but the surface of the glass has to be as optically perfect as possible and in this instance was "figured" to within millionths of an inch. This effort consumed thousands of pounds of carborundum and polishing medium, hundreds more than expected because cords and strains were discovered to have penetrated far deeper in the glass than McCauley had supposed. He had already achieved agreement to grind the surface down to three and one-half instead of four inches at its shallowest point, but even he was no longer confident that his reassurances to the men doing the optical polishing were justified. It was not until three years after the war's end that McCauley and the entire Corning effort were completely vindicated: the Pyrex disc was pronounced optically ready, hoisted into its elaborate mechanical harness, and put through its paces for the first time in June 1948.

By that time, Corning had delivered many other lesser mirror blanks to many different prominent observatories; indeed, the entire mirror making process had become routine enough to be taken over by production. But beyond confirmation of scientific laws and increased know-how, the most significant outcome was the recognition of the value of persistence and the importance of managing failure. That this was a lesson consciously learned by the company as a whole could not be in doubt, for the disk that was not shipped to California, its dusky yellow honeycombed side exposed to view, complete with missing and misshapen sections, was placed first in a square in the center of town and later in the Corning Glass Center for all visitors to see. Unlike GE, which had abandoned even the potentially reusable portions of its project, Corning treated its first flawed 200-inch disc as an emblem of the value of patience in adversity, a reminder of the need to stand firm in the face of failure if ultimate success is to be achieved.

In this project as in others, Corning's approach to processes involving a careful balance between craft and science gave it a unique set of capabilities that others proved unable to imitate. The company was capable of radical achievements, and though not all such efforts were completed with speed, they were often accomplished faster than anyone could have anticipated or dared hope. Corning proved able to take advantage of unusual opportunities and overcome unanticipated difficulties because its entire system was prepared for extraordinary events: geared to think in advance, to anticipate general needs before they arose, and socially designed to pull together when the need arose. Yet such capabilities, while important, would likely not have been equal to these various challenges had not the company also maintained wellsprings of creativity well out of proportion to its size.

One of these wellsprings was Steuben, a small art glass house that Corning had acquired in 1918. After the war Corning deliberately restarted its art glass business instead of simply absorbing its plant as additional production capacity. Corning then brought in architects to work between Steuben and Corning, brokering the use and installation of decorative glass panels. The rest of this chapter is concerned with the unusual combination of art, science, and craft tradition that Corning's management chose to maintain within its organizational boundaries. Corning's forays into architectural glass and its adoption of Steuben stretched Corning in ways that complemented the challenges posed by the 200-inch mirror.

ARCHITECTURAL GLASS AND STEUBEN, 1918–1940

Through its contacts with the architectural profession, Corning helped promote experimentation with glass building materials and at the same time tapped into the creativity of some of the profession's more famous adherents, using their vision to help transform parts of its operations. The enormous glass installation designed by Lee Lawrie for the RCA Building, which went up at the heart of the Rockefeller Center complex in 1935, was the most significant Corning success with architectural glasses. Corning's newfound expertise in annealing very thick castings for telescope mirror blanks applied here. The screen was an enormous relief sculpture; made up of some 240 rectangular blocks, the entire piece measured fifty-five by fifteen feet and weighed approximately thirteen tons. The difficulty lay less in its size than in the variation of thickness across its parts. The use of Pyrex and careful annealing appears to have guaranteed the longevity of this installation. David Gray and George McCauley played the lead roles in this project, with Frederick Carder, the founder of Steuben and an expert in art glass, called in to consult on questions of design.

Further up 5th Avenue from the Rockefeller Center stood another testament to the potential of glass in modern construction: the Corning "House of Glass," built in 1937 to house the company's New York sales office, along with Pittsburgh-Corning's offices and a Steuben showroom. This window-less structure used glass blocks in a variety of ways, as well as fiberglass for insulation. In promulgating these uses of glass by architects, Corning was fighting a familiar battle: "The general reluctance to recognize glass as a building material is, no doubt, due very largely to the persistence of ideas about glass that originated before modern scientific manufacture produced glass with new properties, and before new methods of application made glass available for this use."[25] This comment by Eugene Clute, a noted architect, is strongly reminiscent of the laments of various Corning researchers over the years: even among relatively educated populations, glass was considered a fragile material.

The company was not alone in its boosterism. It was a time when new materials of many kinds were being used in buildings. The *Glass Industry* urged its readers to "take our cue from the aluminum metal industry, which is enjoying marked progress with cast aluminum as a building material, and at a selling price far in excess of clay products."[26] And a number of Corning's domestic competitors established operations to produce glass block and other glass pieces for construction purposes; these, along with the flat glass manufacturers, added their voices and advertising materials to the chorus of architectural glass promoters.

However, the most influential advocates of the use of glass in building were unquestionably architects and industrial designers. Walter Dorwin Teague and Frank Lloyd Wright were the most notable proponents of novel uses for glass in construction. Wright in particular was often held up as a champion of the industry who preached a "gospel of light [with] glass as its apostle."[27] Corning boasted of its connection with the famed architect and, not without reason, made much of its contribution to the Wright-designed S. C. Johnson R&D Center built in 1950. This building used some twenty miles of Pyrex tubing (manufactured at Parkersburg) in its interior and exterior construction. As the *Gaffer* described it, "tubing has literally been wound around and around the tower from top to bottom, and made completely weather proof by the research and engineering skill of Corning."[28] The building exemplified Wright's theory that modern architecture should be built around central supports massive enough to relieve most exterior and interior walls of their load-bearing function: the Pyrex tubing was dec-

Interior reception area of the Johnson's Wax Research Building in Racine, Wisconsin, c. 1952. Designed by Frank Lloyd Wright, the building was a showcase for the use of glass in architecture. Wrapped with literally miles of Pyrex tubing, the walls were essentially glass curtains with the weight of the structure itself borne by massive internal supports.

orative and provided shelter from the elements, which was all Wright wanted a wall to do.

Wright's building highlighted Corning's technical expertise. The company had contributed a similar amount of tubing to this same research complex in 1938. The tubing was a relatively standard order: it was similar in size to that used in the chemical process industry and needed only reheating and bending to suit Wright's needs. In this latter case, however, Wright's plans called for extremely long lengths of tubing. This necessitated finding a way to join tubing pieces, as unobtrusively as possible, end to end. The new electroseal process, so effective in vacuum sealing television bulbs, proved adaptable even to a glass that had a much higher softening point; it was used in conjunction with glass couplers designed by Corning's Product Engineering Group.

The S. C. Johnson Center, like the RCA Building in New York City, was a flagship project as far as Corning's architectural products were concerned, but for Corning proper there were relatively few ships in the fleet. Glass blocks were a business success, but that was primarily the result of a joint venture between Corning and Pittsburgh Plate Glass (see chapter 5); architectural glass and glass tubing appealed to a low-volume specialty market

and depended on the often faddish status of glass in the architectural community. Nevertheless, architectural glass gave Corning publicity quite out of
proportion to its sales, and in most such instances this exposure gave Corning much free advertising. Corning's work in architectural photosensitive
glass was an excellent example. An architectural glass product developed by
Corning in the immediate postwar period, this material was first used by
Corning itself in the construction of its Glass Center opened in Corning in
1951. A number of other projects followed, including, most famously, the
north facade of the United Nations General Assembly Building. As one
internal document stated in reference to these projects, "It is doubtful
whether a profit was made on this business, but considerable knowledge
was gained and promotional value attained."[29]

Acquiring Steuben

Though architectural products never became a high-volume market for Corning, architects and industrial designers had a significant impact on the company in one respect: they made an important contribution to the
transformation of the Steuben division from a loss-making embarrassment to
a source of corporate pride, an icon of Corning's ability to combine craft with
science, and a living symbol of the company's respect for creativity at all levels.

The history of the two companies' relationship with each other begins
with a marriage of necessity during World War I. Steuben, at that time producing glass blanks for sale to glass cutters, and lighting fixtures of various
sorts, fell squarely in the category of nonessential producer. As such it could
not obtain fuel for its furnaces. The war was not Steuben's only problem,
however: the advent of cheap pressed glassware had undermined demand
for glass blanks, tastes were changing away from indirect lighting fixtures of
the sort they produced, and competition from Europe continued to offer a
serious threat to the company's profits. Steuben would not have survived
without Corning's deeper pockets; it had been struggling since at least 1915.[30]

Steuben had been founded by Frederick Carder in 1903 and had met with
some initial success, especially in colored glassware, Carder's forte. Though
Corning was sensitive to Carder's pride—again displaying the ability to

value mavericks, or at least tolerate them when necessary—war needs forced the company to move quickly: the majority of Steuben's workers were set to work on Corning's wartime contracts, with only few continuing their work on art glass projects.

The historical record is silent as to exactly why Corning chose to preserve Steuben in its existing form after the war instead of simply turning it into another Corning factory. Carder's reputation—he was regarded as a British national treasure for his wonderful works of glass artistry—had something to do with it, and Carder may have exercised more of a direct influence than that: he was a close friend of Eugene Sullivan. In any case, Steuben, now a division of Corning but still under Carder's leadership, returned to its work producing colored glasses and similar products.

But the war neither ended European competition nor destroyed the pressed glass industry. The division struggled on until the early 1930s, when a number of developments came together. First, Corning moved the Steuben operation to B Factory—closer to the geographical heart of the company—taking the opportunity to modernize the plant and retire the old equipment of coal-fed furnaces and oil-fired glory holes. Second, scientists at Corning developed a crystal glass (code 10–M) that was almost perfectly colorless and transparent (a case of serendipity, since most of the development was accomplished in the process of working on a UV-transmitting glass). Third, motivated by reports of "deficiencies . . . in plant organization, cost planning, cost efficiency, morale, working conditions, sales assistance and general co-operation [of such] a degree as to make it clear that a change must be effected within a comparatively brief time if continued and increasing losses are to be avoided," the Steuben part of Corning's operations was taken over by the young Arthur Houghton, who presided over a long-overdue transformation of the division.[31]

Restructuring Steuben

Arthur Houghton, son of the much-loved Arthur A. Houghton, who had died after a long illness, stopped the Corning board from shutting down what had become a money-losing operation by asking to be allowed to run

Steuben himself. He wanted to use it, he told the board, to produce the finest glass in the world.[32] In 1933, Arthur the younger, in the face of tremendous opposition from Carder (who though well past retirement age was still a force to be reckoned with), put Steuben through a radical and dramatic shift in its product line and marketing channels. Joining him in this bold enterprise were Jack Gates, a young architect, and Sidney Waugh, a prize-winning sculptor, both hired to be designers for Steuben's new line. Working with the brand-new, virtually colorless crystal glass that Corning had recently developed, Steuben adopted a simple modern line that made it something of a trendsetter. Steuben production was transformed in keeping with this approach by Robert J. Leavy, its production manager and the only executive holdover from the old Steuben.

This period was clearly cathartic for Steuben. It conceded its old markets to its competitors and, armed with its new crystal, took the high road. Its new designers learned to create novel patterns completely in ignorance of Steuben's former work or the nature of glassmaking in general. Department store sales channels were mostly closed down in favor of selling via the planned New York City showroom and similar such dedicated venues. Colored glass disappeared from its repertoire: the new Steuben product was to be about shape, pattern, decoration, and the capacity of these elements to emphasize the beauty of the crystal.

These changes were, not surprisingly, initially resisted by Steuben's craftsmen. Fred Schroeder (a Steuben craftsman who worked for the company from 1904 to 1950) observed:

> The workmen themselves at first had difficulty. There was a tendency still to inject their experience, their understanding into these new forms [handed down by the designers]. . . . Gradually and by closer association, this feeling was dissipated and as the years passed, we found a much closer interest on the part of the workmen, striving to do their best, probably because the designers expressions and fancies were a challenge to the workmen's glass making talents.

Schroeder believed that "there is no question of doubt that the entry of the design group in 1933 was one of the most significant factors in my entire experience," and yet he too had his initial concerns: "The thought that some one with no actual experience in the glass industry could or would design anything worthy of merit seemed at the time to me to be really fantastic."[33]

Such skepticism stemmed from Steuben's experience working with Walter Dorwin Teague a few years previously. From the plant floor, the division's work with the famous designer appeared to be "a flat failure."[34] A more removed perspective, however, showed that Teague in many ways masterminded Steuben's new approach to its business. Teague initiated contact with Amory Houghton in November 1931, claiming to be interested in Corning's potential contribution to architectural glass, and specified the possibility of doing something new with Pyrex. Over the course of the next year or so, he parlayed this contact into a consultancy and produced for Corning a line of decorative patterns for Steuben's artware. The shop's perception of failure came from the fact that Teague's designs were abandoned a year later. In fact they disappeared along with virtually everything else of the old Steuben, in a restructuring that Teague himself helped initiate.

Teague's vision of Steuben was of an art glass concern producing professionally designed, ultra-high quality crystal, which was to be marketed to a cognoscenti of collectors but sold primarily to a larger cadre of nouveau riches who took their decorating cues from this smaller elite. In 1932 he wrote,

> Are there enough people in America who sincerely appreciate this value of ours [i.e., Steuben's ultra-high quality], to buy a half-million dollars' worth of Steuben crystal a year? I'd like to think so but I don't. . . . Fortunately for us there is a very large number of people in the country who may not have fine appreciations, but want to be thought to have; who may not possess perfect taste but want to display it; who are, in short, exceedingly eager to do the right things and have the right things. Many of these have plenty of money, because this attitude of mind often comes with the acquisition of money.[35]

Whether or not this perspective on the market was accepted, Teague's specific suggestions were implemented over the course of the following year.

Steuben's works were concurrently transformed by the scientific expertise of Corning's researchers. Evidence shows that not only the new glass crystal formula came from Corning: procedures for mixing, stirring, and feeding the glass were also developed by the parent company. The "let 'er down easy" process, in particular, which was crucial to keeping the crystal free of cords and striations, was invented by the mechanical development department. Where previously gatherers had pulled molten glass directly from the melt, they now sliced a piece out of a continuously falling glass stream and then attached the gob to a blow iron.[36]

Arthur Houghton took his initial cues from Teague and carried them out with the help of Jack Gates. Houghton's authority and flair for show-manship, however, provided the crucial element. His decision to take the collection international, for example, was a typically bold move. Shortly after taking command of the Steuben division, Houghton traveled to Lon-don onboard the SS *Majestic*, carrying with him a variety of the new Steuben ware for display in a Bond Street gallery. Houghton reserved the vessel's Gold Room suite (which was so named because it was often used to transport bullion for financial settlements) and made sure to assemble a crowd of British aristocracy for the exhibition's opening. Then, in a move that guaranteed Steuben intensive press coverage on both sides of the Atlantic, he informed prospective buyers that the various pieces on display were not for sale.

Arthur's charm did not win over everyone; Carder in particular remained staunchly opposed to change at Steuben, and he did not retire until 1959. He had rejected early attempts to employ glass molds in produc-tion on the grounds that it would mean breaking his policy of "no two pieces alike."[37] Carder himself was an amateur chemist and spent a good deal of time tinkering with glass formulas to achieve the colors he wanted for his ware. Despite this appreciation for the experimental method, Carder did not welcome the "School Boys from Smoke Stack University," as he per-sisted in calling them even though he was on good terms with Sullivan. Corning's engineers had to tread softly even as late as 1950 when, as part of Steuben's move to a new location in the Glass Center, they installed first a tank melter (replacing the pot operations used since 1903) and then sophisti-cated mechanical devices for handling the glass stream.[38]

Small and experimental though it was in these early years of its transformation, the presence of Steuben as a highly visible though peripheral part of Corning contributed to the climate of creativity in the company at large. Steuben sales did not exceed $1 million for twenty years and it continued to lose money (though not as previously), but it gave Corning a very distinctive and upscale presence in the world of industrial design and architecture. Furthermore, the presence of the Steuben designers and those from Corning who worked with them had an effect on the life and culture of Corning that went beyond their numbers.[39]

CRAFTSMEN OF INVENTION

Art, craft, and science—these were all sources that fueled Corning's creativity before World War II and continued well past it. They were never easy to keep in balance, however, because Corning could not help being affected by changes in society at large. One of these was the rapid disappearance of craft skills. Not long after perfecting the Corning Machine, William Woods came up with another of his radical process changes. Eugene Sullivan later called it the most remarkable piece of glassworking equipment he had ever seen. The device drew thermometer tubing directly from molten glass (the one sort of tubing neither the Danner machine nor its progeny could produce). This machine proved very difficult to perfect and under other circumstances might have been abandoned, but a new urgency was now driving mechanization at Corning: the company's workforce was gradually losing its handworking skills. Management realized that when the next generation retired, it would no longer be possible to find glassworkers in any numbers who knew how to work tubing by hand to the exacting requirements that Corning's customers now demanded.

In society at large, time was beginning to run out for another group of people prized by Corning—respected mechanical inventors whose genius was in their hands and their intuitions, and not derived from formal training in engineering. Men like Wellech and Woods were members of a sizable fraternity of Corning inventors and developers who made it possible for the company to push the state of the art in machines. Some, like Woods, worked in partnership; some, like Wellech, were capable of reinventing what others had first made; others were extreme individualists like Jim Giffen, the redoubtable inventor of several key inventions for television and consumerware whose story appears in later chapters. All had, in addition to their remarkable intuitions, maverick personalities. In a time when other companies turned to the homogenization of systems, Corning continued to accommodate their quirks and deal with their idiosyncrasies, recognizing the peculiar way such traits were linked to human creativity and recognizing also that these machine inventors were the essential replacements for the original craft workers in the old era of glassmaking—craftsmen of invention.

In contrast to the legendary mass producers of the turn of the century, it was typical of manufacturers like Corning, which were not mass producers, to personalize their dealings with their employees, to value their skills, and to do everything to keep them happy. Few successful business proprietors would have been so foolish as to alienate their most important assets. In other respects, however, Corning was atypical, even among such a heterogeneous multitude as the small and medium-sized manufacturing enterprises of early twentieth-century America. Considering its middling size (twice as large as the average prewar glass company but twenty times smaller than large glassmakers like Libbey and Pittsburgh Plate Glass), it was atypical in making its own equipment when it was not an equipment manufacturer.

Second, it retained an unusual amount of give-and-take among the three variable components of its business—the material/composition, the product/market, and the process/operational. None of the three was allowed to freeze in place, or even to stop evolving, in order to accommodate the others. The research laboratory and the process research laboratory commanded equal respect and seesawing budgets. It was just as likely that a new glass composition would emerge from solving a production problem as it was that a new process would be invented or acquired to produce a new product. However much a new family of glasses might generate new products, a new process concept like the glass ribbon, which later reappeared in one form or another in the Hub and the Turret chain machines, could be just as generative. Invention might be expected to appear in any part of the company, though in later eras there would certainly be parts of the company where it would be very unlikely.

Though openness to serendipity played a large part in Corning's culture, certain aspects of its difference were by design: not only its practices (e.g., the treatment of personnel or the mixing of engineer and craftsman) but also the larger organization of the company and its external relationships. What would appear to be quite eccentric choices had their purpose. For a company that so highly prized mechanical inventiveness, the persistent architectural connection helped to ensure that there was more of an architectural sensibility than a mechanical one. For a company that achieved miracles with mechanized forming of shapes, Steuben's place in the family ensured that the original craft remained an active and visible part of the culture. Finally, the willingness to take on tremendously risky projects like the 200-inch mirror kept alive in the company a sense of adventure that would eventually make it possible to consider without flinching technical risks of even greater magnitude, such as the fiber optics of the 1970s. So much creativity and risk taking could have generated more opportunities than a small company was able to use. But Corning early hit upon a way to share them with larger partners. Chapter 5 covers the first of these novel partnerships, known as associations and later as joint ventures.

LEVERAGING TECHNOLOGY

CORNING AND THE LESSONS OF

STRATEGIC PARTNERSHIPS

Starting from the nebulous idea that because the chemical element, silicon, was responsible for the useful properties of glass, the same chemical element introduced into plastics might improve them, Dr. Hyde succeeded independently in producing for the first time the world's first useful silicones.

—EUGENE SULLIVAN
QUOTED IN THE GAFFER, 1956

B Y 1930 the Houghtons had established two core strategies designed to ensure the long-term success of their company. The first, a decision made at the turn of the century, was not to enter the high-volume areas of glass manufacture—flat glass and containers. These markets were already dominated by very large companies (e.g., Pittsburgh Plate Glass), and Corning's intimate dealings with its electrical company customers had clearly demonstrated the futility of going head-to-head with such larger enterprises. The second strategic decision was to rely on a consistently funded research effort for finding and exploiting new product areas. The wisdom of this second decision had also, by this time, been proven.

These strategies, along with Eugene Sullivan's conception of glass as an engineered material (with Corning as the preeminent glass engineering company), promised to serve as Corning's compass for some time to come. But the 1930s would see new threats: economic upheaval in the form of the Great Depression and the rise of an entirely new class of materials, namely, plastics. Of the two, it was the latter that was most troubling. Bakelite, an early form of plastic invented by the Belgian chemist Leo Baekeland, had first appeared in 1909. During the 1920s it had become a household word, though it was limited at first to small items such as light fixtures and toys. Still, it established a precedent: all sorts of organic (i.e., carbon-based) compounds that had formerly seemed without value might now prove to have commercial utility. Indeed, a new synthetic material could yield any number of surprising properties.[1]

For Corning, plastic's initially amorphous threat became crystal clear when urea formaldehyde and lucite, both hard, transparent substances that looked like possible replacements for glass, appeared. Though these plastics were initially weak and prone to deform and melt at low temperatures, Sullivan, at the time Corning's new vice chairman, had little doubt that further work would produce stronger and more heat-resistant versions. Unwilling to sit by as this nascent challenger grew powerful, Sullivan resolved to seek Corning's defense for glass in a good offense: a move into exploratory applied research.

The problem was not merely a technical one. Plastics had the advantage of novelty, while glass had to overcome existing preconceptions: fragility and rigidity. Furthermore, plastics had powerful industrial backing. Corning had to counter this threat without meeting DuPont and other large concerns head on. Sullivan's answer to the plastics threat was reminiscent of his mentor at Leipzig, Wilhelm Ostwald, who believed in exploring the border regions in physical chemistry.[2] Sullivan decided to invest in exploring the no-man's-land that lay between the inorganic glasses and mineral silicates on the one hand and the organic rubbers and oils on the other. This space between carbon and silicon had been covered in the scientific literature but not commercially exploited; Corning hoped to get there first.

Corning's move into exploratory research turned out to be very successful; perhaps too much so, for it opened a Pandora's box for the company and its owners. After only a decade of research Corning found itself facing a new and troubling question: how could a relatively small enterprise, dependent on family money and very thin in management expertise, control and exploit the numerous significant technological opportunities it was creating for itself? Lacking the capital, the market presence, and the management corps necessary to exploit its multiple opportunities, how could Corning make sure that it was the one to profit from its discoveries?

Ultimately, Corning's response to plastics—an extremely productive research effort led by chemist Franklin Hyde—would lead it into a series of novel relationships with larger companies. Taken together, these ventures constituted a third fundamental strategy, that of association. In the 1920s and 1930s Corning experimented with several new organizational forms, finally settling on the association, which later came to be called a "joint venture."[3] This chapter is about Corning's efforts to leverage its technological opportunities through many different forms of technology-sharing partnership. These included overseas licensing, which ebbed and flowed according to protectionist sentiments internationally, the merger with MacBeth Evans, and technology sharing with major customers like Sylvania, as well as the early associations. We begin with Franklin Hyde's story, which illustrates the risks Corning was willing to take with fundamental research and the mistakes it made in learning how to strategically share information.

HYDE'S "MONKEY BUSINESS," 1930–1940

In the summer of 1930, J. Franklin Hyde, Ph.D. (University of Illinois, a leader in organic chemistry), was nearing the end of two postdoctoral years at Harvard University. In need of a job, he took the suggestion of his major professor, the eminent organic chemist James Conant, to interview with an unlikely employer, the Corning Glass Works. Why, he wanted to know, would a glass company be interested in hiring an organic chemist? The night before his first interview with Corning's chief chemist, W. C. Taylor, Hyde read up on a subject that had first struck him during his studies—the organo-silicon compounds, covered in the literature by the famous English chemist F. S. Kipping of the University of Nottingham. Kipping, who would come to be known as the "father of silicon chemistry," had made no effort to find commercial applications for his discoveries; he was simply dedicated to expanding the theoretical frontiers of organic chemistry. His own test tube version of an organo-silicon concoction he dismissed in his writings as "a sticky mess."[4] Others would see further.

Hyde was, therefore, as well prepared as he could be to discuss Sullivan's idea of working in the area of glasslike substances. In his interviews with Taylor and others, Hyde talked in animated terms about the opportunities that might arise from exploring the notional space between carbon and silicon. Despite his impeccable credentials, Hyde was completely devoid of the sense of entitlement that would accompany many beginning industrial researchers of the next generation. The onset of the Depression was not a time when scientists could afford to overlook any job offer. At Corning he found both people he liked and an atmosphere that suited him. When it was clear to Hyde that this company would give him room to pursue his own interests, he accepted the offer to join Corning's research department. Ordinarily it would have seemed an unlikely choice: Corning had done nothing with organic chemistry. It was, however, very much in touch with the latest developments in the wider scientific world, and there also appeared to be useful contacts with companies like General Electric that did have significant work going on in organic chemistry.

Hyde already had an offer from DuPont, but the large-company atmosphere had not appealed to him. Besides, Corning wanted Hyde enough to outbid DuPont by $200, setting Hyde's starting salary at $3,400 per year. Two hundred dollars was no small difference to a young man who had recently married and was flat broke after graduate school. Yet it was the stylistic difference between the two companies, not the richer offer, that most attracted him. DuPont's experimental station operated via a well-organized hierarchy; there he would be part of a stable of organic chemists working under the direction of such renowned scientists as Wallace Carruthers and James Conant, a DuPont consultant.[5] Corning was smaller and much less hierarchical: it offered Hyde the chance to do exploratory research in a more informal environment. "I felt I was good at doing new things," Hyde said. "Monkeying around," he called it later.[6]

Eugene Sullivan was not a playful man, and in a period that was already looking bleak economically he did not incline toward extravagance. His decision to hire an organic chemist to do exploratory work—the first such work he had authorized—was a calculated gamble: he hoped Corning would learn to synthesize new compounds that would have the best features of both plastics and glass (most obviously, higher melting temperatures than plastics, easier formability than glass). It was the spirit of engineered materials carried to its next logical step: not modifying the properties of existing materials but finding whole new types of materials that matched a desired list of properties and were complementary to the development path he was seeking for glass.

An Introduction to Organo-Silicons

Hyde was made welcome at Corning. Taylor, number two man at Corning's laboratory, expressed a genuine interest in his work. He also made sure that all the equipment and chemicals Hyde needed were there when he arrived. Hyde focused his first efforts on attempting to reproduce Kipping's experiments with organo-silicon compounds, but with a greater interest in finding uses for the substances that resulted. He produced compound after compound incorporating silicon, a witch's brew of hybrid mixtures. But

J. Franklin Hyde, Corning's first organic chemist, and his assistant, biochemist Mary Purcell Roche, working in his laboratory to discover commercial versions of silicon compounds.

where Kipping had been trying to prepare compounds that were analogous to the principal classes of carbon compounds, Hyde realized that there were so few analogies and so many differences with the carbon classes that the matter was best treated as though it were an entirely new field of chemistry.[7]

Learning that there was a need for glass adhesives and having noticed that silicon chloride adhered to the side of a test tube as a thin film, Hyde began investigating its properties. As he wrote later of those first experiments,

> While neither plastics nor organo-silicon materials were immediately forthcoming, which possessed properties in any way comparable to the wide diversity of useful properties of glass, we did learn that polymeric materials with resin-like properties were possible, and that some of the organo-silicon compounds were unusually stable at temperatures which would rapidly destroy the normal organic resins and plastics then available.[8]

Hyde was on the track to synthesizing commercially useful silicone, a term that covers all organo-silicon polymers (large molecule compounds) that have bonds of carbon, silicon, and oxygen. But useful outcomes of these studies proved frustratingly elusive. Nothing that looked like glass emerged from this work, and no promising resins resulted either. Hyde needed a deeper understanding of how useful compounds might be synthesized, as well as more experience of how materials with different properties might interact with glass in use.

At the time, no other Corning researcher had the privilege of monkeying around as Hyde had been invited to do. But while he was caught in the never-never land between original idea and patented reality he decided to help out with a few current problems. He began experimenting with powdered quartz, which GE had been using without much success as part of the 200-inch telescope project. Among other things, he tried melting the powder with a blowtorch. This led him to experiment with vaporized liquids and he hit upon silicon tetrachloride. Passed through a flame, the result of Hyde's efforts was an extremely fine silica soot that could be deposited onto a surface where it would fuse into solid, nearly pure silica. This process for the vapor deposition of silica was patentable; Hyde filed under the title

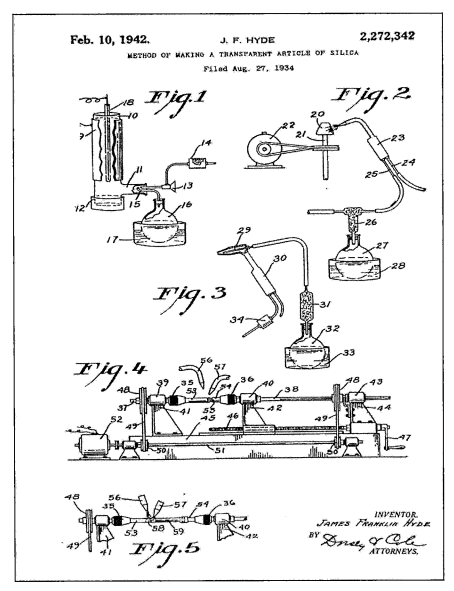

Feb. 10, 1942.

J. F. HYDE

2,272,342

METHOD OF MAKING A TRANSPARENT ARTICLE OF SILICA

Filed Aug. 27, 1934

Illustration from J. F. Hyde Vapor Deposition Patent ("Method of Making a Transparent Article of Silica"), filed in 1934 and issued in 1942, showing method for vaporizing silica. The method was used to produce almost perfectly pure glass. Sprayed through a flame, the liquid turns to soot that is then deposited on a rotating bar or other shape in order to build up the desired form.

"Methods of Making a Transparent Article of Silica" in 1932. The vapor deposition process would come to be used at Corning for everything from telescope mirrors in the 1960s to optical waveguides from the 1970s on. Its first commercial application would arise after World War II, when Corning used it to make electronic delay lines for radar systems under a highly secret contract with the Signal Corps. By this time Hyde would be completely absorbed by other matters, also defense related.

In what might have seemed like a detour, Hyde became involved in the construction of Corning's fifteen- by fifty-foot window at Rockefeller Center. As the one organic chemist around, his general knowledge was of use in any number of ways. In this case he was consulted about the need for a plastic material that would not only act as a cementing agent for the huge engraved glass blocks making up the window but would also fill out the borosilicate glass castings to bring them to accurate dimensions. He identi-

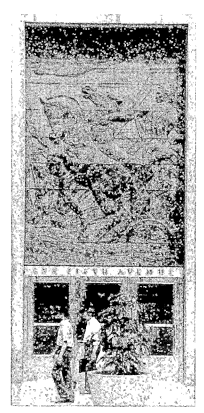

Mural, 15 ft. by 50 ft., constructed from large glass blocks, adorning the Fifth Avenue entrance of the RCA Building at Rockefeller Center in New York City. Franklin Hyde's work to find the right cements made this construction durable, and also contributed to his greater understanding of the nature of cements.

fied "Vinylite," a new plastic cement by Carbide and Carbon Chemical Corporation (later Union Carbide), as having the right combination of adhesion, load-bearing ability, and index of refraction. Later he helped make the right form of Vinylite in the vendor's laboratories. The effort brought him into contact with David Gray of Corning's machine development department, who was making a machine for edging the blocks. Hyde even had the fun of supervising the actual application of the adhesive at Rockefeller Center. Having received a special dispensation from the New York City Glazier's Union in order to work on the glass installation, he was perched on the scaffolding watching when the fuss about the Marxist artist Diego Rivera's socialist mural led to its removal: heady stuff for a bookish young scientist from Syracuse.[9]

Hyde savored all such experiences out in the world; he was gaining a much better sense of how a good adhesive needed to behave and what different properties it might need. He was also becoming better acquainted with the properties and structure of glass, which was the only real ticket to membership in the fraternity of Corning researchers. Nevertheless, his perspective remained unique: to Hyde, glass was, and would always remain, a "very high polymer."[10]

A Detour Through Fiberglass

The next two years were a long, dry period for Hyde. When nothing further of interest seemed to be emerging from his central long-term project to come up with usable glasslike plastic resins, Sullivan authorized Hyde's transfer out of the research department. At this time, the low point of the Depression, all Corning laboratory efforts were focusing on new product development. Hyde willingly accepted the chance in 1936 to give direct technical support to Corning's new fiber products division, where more applied research was needed. Fiberglass was as yet in its commercial infancy, but several important new applications were being experimented with, chief among them insulators and textiles.[11] Corning was making electrical tape, other forms of electrical insulation, and architectural insulation. Problems relating to lubricating, sizing, bonding, and impregnating fiberglass textiles and electrical insulating tapes offered Hyde a chance to focus once again on improving his understanding of organo-silicon cements.

Hyde viewed his transfer as another opportunity to gain hands-on experience with new product problems. But when George MacBeth, who had just joined Corning's executive ranks following the 1936 merger with his family company, MacBeth Evans, visited the fiberglass division, he expressed surprise at finding Hyde working at the new Fallbrook plant. MacBeth, who had begun sponsoring research on silicone cements at the Mellon Institute in Pittsburgh several years before his company merged with Corning, questioned Sullivan about Hyde's presence on the plant floor rather than in the corporate laboratory. MacBeth himself had first taken an interest in silicone cements when word about the glass block problem had circulated around the industry. MacBeth arranged to put Hyde in touch with the work going on at the institute under Rob Roy McGregor, work that was complementary to Hyde's. He knew that the field of organic cements was alive with interest, and he questioned whether Corning could maintain its momentum if Hyde continued to be diverted into product development.[12]

When Owens-Illinois and Corning combined their fiberglass businesses in 1938 to form Owens-Corning Fiberglas (described below), Hyde was transferred to the new Owens-Corning plant in Newark, Ohio. There he found that the laboratory notebooks recording his work on silicones for sizing and fillers for fiberglass, which had been moved to Newark in boxes along with everything else belonging to the fiberglass business, had been pitched onto a garbage heap at the back of the building. They were mostly irretrievable, a fact that harmed Corning in its later patent claims.[13]

The Race for Silicone

Hyde did not remain long with Owens-Corning; due primarily to MacBeth's intervention, he returned to the Corning laboratory to work full-time on his idea for a high-temperature silicone varnish for electrical tape. By this time Hyde was aware that both of the large electrical companies, General Electric and Westinghouse, were interested in high-temperature electrical insulating tapes made of glass fiber. The tapes were needed to replace asbestos, which was in short supply, but they would only be acceptable as a substitute if there were varnishes to go with them. Hyde assured Corning's salesmen that he could prepare a thermally stable, high-temperature varnish. This new compound became Hyde's first practical silicone resin, designated 990A.

But Corning had waited too long: both GE and Westinghouse had learned of Hyde's work on silicones. In January 1938 Les Morrow, manager of the Corning fiberglass division, had been anxious to use any leverage he could to excite GE's interest in his products. He invited some GE researchers to Corning to see what Hyde was doing. GE sent two of its research managers, A. L. Marshall and Winton Patnode. Hyde, hoping to engage them in joint development work, told of his work on ethyl phenyl silicones, starting with Kipping and going through to his latest work on improved binders. Perhaps because GE was already under pressure from the Justice Department for working in combination with the other electrical companies, the visitors evaded the subject of joint work. Upon returning to their laboratory, however, they immediately initiated a similar project of their own, without telling Corning. Corning would only learn of this work two years later when the GE researchers involved informed the company that they were delivering a paper at the American Chemical Society and filing patent applications on their own related formulations.[14]

It was discovered later on that Games Slayter, new head of research for Owens-Corning and a former Owens-Illinois employee, had taken the liberty of furnishing samples from Hyde's work to GE without Corning's knowledge. GE's silicone-related research at its Schenectady laboratories turned on work being done by a young researcher, Eugene Rochow. He wrote later, "I saw no reason to duplicate work that was already in progress in Hyde's capable hands at Corning; besides I was busy with insulation at 1000 degrees and couldn't be bothered with stuff that came apart at a mere 400 degrees."[15] He focused instead on methyl siloxanes, another form of silicone.

Meanwhile, beginning in 1937, Hyde received support to pursue his silicone work vigorously. Hyde and the team now funded by Corning, and also working on silicones at the Mellon Institute, met for the first time and soon charted a new collaborative program for their combined research teams, nominally headed by Hyde. The joint program of research that was worked out in April 1938 covered an ambitious agenda:

> SECTION 1: develop improved plastics with regard to chemical stability, heat resistance, waterproofness, hardness, flexibility, adhesion to glass, electrical properties, and impact resistance of resin-coated glass
>
> SECTION 2: detailed study of the composition and behavior of organic silicon compounds
>
> SECTION 3: study of properties of organo-silicon compounds from the point of view of practical applications, which included protective coatings for plastics and decorative coatings for glass

Although the two-man Mellon team had been reporting to Sullivan monthly for some time, he had not previously revealed the existence of the work of one group to the other. His reasons are not clear. Sullivan appears to have known that the nature of the arrangement with Mellon meant that the rights to discoveries could be somewhat ambiguous. Though support for a fellowship meant that the team working on a particular project considered itself to be something like an employee of the supporting company, there were multiple company sponsors and information naturally flowed between groups. On the other hand, Corning lacked much of the equipment needed and was desperately short of research manpower, so the Mellon option was the only game in town regardless of the risks involved. For Hyde the joint program was a turning point: he had colleagues, he had a focused objective, and he had confidence that the teams best equipped to do the work were now well matched to their respective assignments. For the first time he had the manpower to generate both well-articulated knowledge and reduction to practice.

During 1938 Hyde's group proceeded with the laborious task of turning out a full quart of usable resin in the laboratory. Just this task of "bodying the resin" (i.e., bringing it from a liquid to a resinous state) took weeks of his group's time. Flasks were small and with the primitive equipment available, the critical procedure had to be repeated over and over in the same painstaking way. As word of Hyde's new focus spread in the Corning laboratory, other researchers joined him, including Kenneth Johannson and Richard DeLong, a new graduate of MIT. DeLong helped him develop a Grignard machine to produce larger quantities of starting material. He also characterized the silicon tretrachloride into its various constituents, identifying the unique boiling points of each. This work was key to Hyde's ability to patent the materials later. Evidence of the intensity and productivity of the entire joint program was a long list of key patents awarded to both Hyde and to the Mellon team based on work done from early 1938 to 1940. Unfortunately theirs were not to be the only timely patents filed in this area.

Inevitably, Westinghouse also learned of Hyde's promising discoveries. Their source was the Mellon Institute, where they were sponsoring projects of their own. Westinghouse fellows were asked to synthesize some of the material for the team at Mellon, which, in a departure from its original assignment, had chosen to work on finding industrial applications for silicone fluids. In keeping with the spirit of cooperative work at Mellon, Westinghouse researchers, once involved, continued to work in what they recognized as an exciting and crucial area for any company producing electrical equipment. According to members of the Mellon team, it had been agreed that cooperative work could be done in their branch of the silicone research as long as Corning and Mellon managements were kept informed. In 1940, both Westinghouse and General Electric filed for broad patent coverage in the production and uses of silicones.[16]

For his part, Franklin Hyde applied first for patents on the applications of silicone to cement. His patent applications spelled out both the silicone formulation and the processes by which it was made in the accompanying documentation, but his claims were more modest and focused on more specific uses. He was hampered by the serious limitations of the Corning patent attorneys who were, of course, primarily familiar with glass. The situation improved when Corning hired a new patent attorney who had training as an organic chemist, but this set of transactions took time. When Corning discovered that GE had stolen a march on Hyde, Sullivan contacted his friend Coolidge, head of GE's laboratory, and asked for two concessions, first, that Eugene Rochow's paper not be published before Hyde's paper could also appear in the same issue of the *Journal of the American Chemical*

Society and, second, that Rochow note that GE's work had been stimulated by the GE research visit in 1938. This he did, stating in a published acknowledgment that "our interest in this field was aroused by Dr. J. F. Hyde of the Corning Glass Company who showed Dr. A. L. Marshall of this laboratory some samples of phenyl silicone which he considered promising as impregnants for glass fiber tape."[17]

In the interference proceedings that ensued with both GE and Westinghouse, Corning opposed the rival patents on the grounds of the priority of Hyde's discoveries, but there was little other documented proof that Hyde had understood the fundamental nature of his findings: he could only say that his notebooks had disappeared in the move to the Newark, Ohio, facility. In truth, Corning had failed to recognize the broad applicability of Hyde's work soon enough to file early broad claims or even to give Hyde time to write up his work for scientific publication.[18] Moreover, the fact that it assigned Hyde to a divisional job in 1935 and failed to limit disclosure of the work to third parties made it hard to support the company's claim that it had exercised due diligence in pursuing the work. This naivete ultimately cost Corning what could have been a commanding patent position ensuring broad control of silicones in all their forms. Instead it had to settle for a myriad of lesser patents, specifying applications and the means for producing the material.

It may seem odd after nearly fifty years of emphasis on research that Sullivan and his near associates would have missed the broadest implications of Hyde's early silicone discoveries. But in this very productive period of research before World War II the notion of consistently aiming for broad patent positions and fundamental breakthroughs was still a decade or more away, a future consequence of the new patterns of scientific work that emerged out of wartime experience. Even at GE in the 1930s research was still expected to be primarily a support function for the advanced engineering department, not the originator of fundamental scientific ideas that formed the first step in a process of radical product discovery. Indeed Corning's technical department at this time was termed not coincidentally "development and research," not as later, research and development.

Hyde's experiences held several important lessons for Corning's future behavior. Obviously, as Corning moved out of conventional glass and into the realm of engineered materials, the risks of technical exposure would increase. The company had to develop new information disciplines and new methods for rapidly securing the advantage of a potentially valuable patent position. Unlike Corning's Ribbon Machine or other advanced proprietary processes, fundamental breakthroughs in areas on the periphery of Corning's technological territory could just as easily open up opportunities for others as for Corning, and, unlike process innovation, they were not particularly likely to require significant amounts of glass-related know-how to exploit.

Clearly an exploratory research program could open up a surprising number of new areas, especially if other enterprises got wind of the new developments. There were lessons to be learned, therefore, about the conduct of joint work and joint enterprises of any sort. Understandings had to be clear and communications excellent, if shared work were not going to result in the casual loss of control of valuable information, like the strange case of Owens-Corning's untoward disclosures to GE. In general, Corning's experience with GE and Westinghouse illustrated how quickly and effectively new and useful knowledge could travel in a hot technical field. In this period just before World War II industrial research was becoming a much more competitive arena. Corning's need to share information and its laxness about disclosure to third parties were presumably consequences of its long-standing relationship with GE and also of its traditional, more "gentlemanly" practices of information sharing in the less technically competitive glass industry. These practices would change.

EXPERIMENTING WITH ASSOCIATION, 1920–1940

Even before Hyde joined Corning, the company had looked for ways to gain additional returns from its technical work, over and beyond what it could make via direct sales of its products. Two of its early inventions, Pyrex and alumino-silicate refractories, illustrate the two main options available: licensing and creating a separate company. Both approaches had advantages and disadvantages, and each required new types of investment of management energies. Corning also, in this period, gained experience with mergers, which was a common way of sharing both technologies and markets. Alternatively, one could simply share information about such things, protected by some form of written agreement; Corning did this too.

Licensing

One of the obvious sources of potential revenue for Corning was licensing products for others to sell. The danger here was that one would cannibalize one's own markets; licensees had to be prevented from competing on Corning's home turf. After a fair amount of travel and negotiation on the part of Alexander Falck, Corning moved to set up licensing relationships in Europe for its Pyrex glasses. International licensing agreements seemed ideal in the 1920s because, with the permissive attitudes of Republican administrations toward antitrust, they could be drawn up in such a way that a licensee was forbidden to sell in markets that Corning chose to exclude. Under the New Deal of the 1930s, however, antitrust policy would evolve so as to limit the corporation's ability to control the development of technology in its own interest through restrictive licensing practices of this sort.

Corning's Pyrex licensees in Europe were both subsidiaries of major glassmakers, Pilkington in the United Kingdom and St. Gobain in France. In each case the parent formed a subsidiary (Jobling and Sovirel, respectively) to exploit the license they had purchased from Corning. For nearly fifty years these companies would yield a reasonable return on the initial licenses and, later, dividends from the minority interests Corning acquired in the 1950s.

Furthermore, the relationships with the parent companies were valuable in themselves. For many years, St. Gobain and Corning kept each other apprised of interesting technical developments. This was, for instance, the reason that St. Gobain shared with Corning the knowledge of the updraw process developed by Ed Wellech, as described in chapter 4. Likewise Joblings provided Corning with a reason to stay in touch with Pilkington, a long-established flat glass company. During the 1930s Corning shared regular technical reports with Pilkington, a practice that was modified in 1940 when Corning came under antitrust scrutiny as part of what the Justice

Department called the Glass Trust, the close relationship between Corning, GE, and the other members of the Hartford Empire. When Corning and its relationships came under scrutiny in the 1940s and beyond, licensing became less of a route to new knowledge. Corning no longer felt as free to work through production or marketing problems with licensees that were in the same business.

Merger

By the early 1930s, when Corning's leaders wanted to reposition its Pyrex line, they sought outside sources of expertise to help accomplish this task. MacBeth Evans, a Pittsburgh-based glassmaker with considerable experience in consumer products, was producing lighting using Corning-manufactured lenses and was interested in increasing its own consumer sales. The two companies could both see that the natural direction of their expanding product lines was likely to put them on a collision course, and they decided to merge rather than compete. (Corning came very close to making a similar arrangement with Anchor Hocking, another consumer glass company, before it discovered that Anchor Hocking was losing money on a new glass of its own.) The merger gave Corning not only a decided boost into the consumer business but also a presence in the lively Pittsburgh area, which, with Toledo, still formed the heart of the U.S. glass industry. It was, of course, also through MacBeth Evans that Corning gained access to important research work going on at the Mellon Institute. The great merger movement that had taken place earlier in the century had created a general public bias against big-business mergers, but neither Corning nor MacBeth Evans was a large company. And since both were quite innovative, there was little reason to fear that their combination would stifle innovation.

Technology-Sharing Partnerships

Another common form of organization was a partnership with a major customer that involved neither ownership nor shared revenue but did entail the exchange of technical and market information as well as the joint development of key technologies. Corning established such a partnership with Hygrade Lamp Company, later known as Sylvania, shortly after World War I.

Headquartered in Salem, Massachusetts, Hygrade was one of a number of lamp-making concerns that had long-term contracts with Corning for lightbulb blanks. The particular agreement stipulated that any development that either company made concerning the technology of interest would be shared with the other. Hygrade eventually became Sylvania, and its business grew to encompass fluorescent lighting, radio tubes, and a variety of other product lines, but its deal with Corning remained the same. In return for negotiating a long-term price for a set number of bulbs, Sylvania agreed to keep Corning apprised of any developments and would expect to get the same in return.[19]

By the time Sylvania began making television tubes after World War II, it had been doing business with Corning for over twenty-five years. As the television business exploded in growth, Corning located its plants relatively close to Sylvania's so that this prized customer would feel well served. This closeness did not prevent Sylvania from considering making its own glass from time to time, for reasons that also tempted Westinghouse. (Indeed, Westinghouse would go so far as to build its own southern plant for bulb glass before Corning was able to persuade it to reconsider, based on an adjusted price schedule.) Each time Sylvania raised the subject, Corning rehearsed with it the risks it would be assuming: the considerable costs entailed, the minimum market size needed to make any money, and the management and other differences between the glass business and the lightbulb and television tube businesses; casting glass and assembling cast glass pieces had less in common than one might imagine. Sylvania apparently listened to this advice, for it remained a major customer of Corning's even when others would follow through on their threats and become glassmakers themselves. In the period after World War II the two companies became even more closely involved as they jointly ran a nuclear reactor. As discussed below, together they also formed one of Corning's really disastrous joint ventures, Sylcor.

Corhart

Of course, Corning's preeminent technology-sharing partnership, until the Justice Department put an end to it, was with General Electric. In addition to their direct dealings, Corning and GE both had a stake in Hartford Empire, which not only engaged in machine development but handled the licensing for that technology on behalf of its several corporate owners. Hartford Empire gave Corning its first experiment with association, Corhart, an early form of association that was a valuable learning experience for Corning. Later Corhart would become a wholly owned subsidiary.

Corning moved to form a new business around its innovative Electrocast refractories in the late 1920s. Corning had always made its own clay pots for melting, though it rarely produced more than its own requirements dictated. Following its development of the alumino-silicate refractory invented by Harrison Hood and Gordon Fulcher (discussed in chapter 2), however, Corning decided to get into the business of helping other people build their furnaces. This entailed developing a new manufacturing process and setting up a new organization to sell to a wholly different set of customers, primarily other process companies such as bulk glass and steel companies that used melting furnaces lined with fired bricks. This effort, organized in 1927 around a plant in Kentucky, required all the spare management talent the company had, and then some. Moreover, because some of the key patents overlapped with patents held by Hartford Empire, which had been conducting research of its own on refractories, the company was set up as a joint venture between Corning and Hartford Empire.[20] The Corhart venture, not an altogether happy relationship, was the first and only time Corning chose to put its name first on a joint venture.

Corning's internal operations delayed adopting Corhart refractories for many years. Walter Oakley, who as Corning's chief engineer was responsible for refractory selection and in-house development, always maintained that the refractories he used, developed in practice, were superior to those made by Corhart, though some Corning researchers charged that this was simply a display of not-invented-here bias against Corning's research department, stemming from rivalry between R&D and the production side of the house.[21]

Corhart soon became a sizable business and quickly developed its own roster of international licensees, including the Japanese company Asahi, which signed an agreement with Corhart in 1930. Asahi's agreement, like the earlier Pyrex ones in Europe, initially prevented it from selling back any of its refractories into the United States or other markets that Corning had reserved for itself. Corning agreed to send a qualified engineer to help transfer the technology and to receive engineers from Asahi at its plants in Kentucky. In return, Asahi paid $25,000 up front and a royalty of $8 per ton. The agreement gave Corhart the right to file for and sell products containing Japanese inventions anywhere else in the world.

In 1941 this arrangement changed suddenly and dramatically. Under pressure from the Justice Department, Corhart, as Corning's subsidiary, was forced to retract this provision of its agreement. A terse letter to Asahi dated April 25, 1941, read as follows:

> In order that there may be no claim on the part of anyone that we are preventing the importation of goods which compete with our products manufactured in this country except as we have a right to do so on account of exclusive patent rights in our hands, we enclose to you this unilateral waiver of said covenant in the contract between you and us. We hope that we will be able to discuss this matter with you personally once the international relationship has returned to normal, at which time we may be able to explain more fully the course of developments in this country which has induced us to make this release.[22]

Corhart remained a good investment even in the context of a changing antitrust environment, but the initial strains were costly. Quite aside from the strain on capital, there had been dissension among Corning's senior managers concerning how to staff Corhart, how to provide it with adequate technical support, and who, in general, was and was not doing a good job with it.[23] When Corhart was set up, Corning had been without a Houghton in a direct leadership position for almost a decade, and the real issue was absentee ownership. Nevertheless, the problem was universal for this sort of endeavor: running a joint venture represented an investment of management energies that could always be better used within the parent company.

After Hartford Empire came under antitrust pressure (a story that is recounted in greater detail in chapter 6), Corning took over Corhart as its own wholly owned subsidiary. Though the record does not give direct evidence of cause and effect here, it may well have been the learning from this experience that led to a different, and much smoother, set of relationships in the several associations Corning formed with other companies in the 1930s, all of which lasted much longer in one form or another.

"ASSOCIATIONS" OR JOINT VENTURES, 1937–1950

As useful as other technology-sharing relationships were to Corning, none of them addressed the three technologies the company was most interested in. By the mid-1930s a number of advanced technologies that Corning had developed were coming to fruition. Unfortunately, the company was very lean on resources with which to exploit them, and even leaner on management personnel to assign to build the businesses. The most pressing of these included glass blocks—an architectural product that had originated in Europe as a purely decorative conceit; fiberglass, which Corning had been pursuing as a potential new product since the early 1920s; and, of course, Franklin Hyde's silicone discoveries. For each of these Corning decided to form an association.

Pittsburgh-Corning

Glass blocks began entering the United States from Europe in the reconstruction period following World War I as modernist architecture, with its vertical lines, angular masses, and bright colors, began to sweep all other forms of architecture in front of it.[24] In Europe companies like Siemens in Germany, Pilkington in England, and Leerdam in Holland were all producing glass bricks to meet the modernist-inspired demand, and avant-garde American architects were having to import these products if they wanted to follow the trend.

In America glass bricks were used primarily for nonstructural purposes except in penthouses, which did not require materials that were on an approved list. But the American architectural viewpoint put emphasis on utility as well as appearance, whereas the European idea was centered only on decorative value. Herein lay a potential opportunity for Corning. Glass bricks made out of Pyrex would have a useful degree of fire resistance and might be made tough enough for underwriters' requirements. They would also cater to the increased demand for natural lighting inside buildings.

Two basic developments were needed, one technical and one organizational. The brick itself had to be made of a very low expansion glass so as to minimize material matching concerns. In order to be suitable for architectural use, it also required special waterproof joint cements that did not dry out and that showed a high adherence to glass, which normal cements did not have. Early work in glass blocks had been undertaken by a variety of European manufacturers: Jobling and Pilkington in England, an unnamed producer in Czechoslovakia, and St. Gobain subsidiaries in Italy and Germany. St. Gobain's French effort was the most intensive.[25] Not until 1932 did domestic manufacturers begin to offer products of their own.

Corning used two formulations in its earliest glass block designs: a Pyrex type (code 7740) and a high-alkali "soft" glass called Lumite. The Pyrex block, the first such Corning product, was not resistant enough to abrasion, a serious problem given that these blocks, like common bricks, were generally mortared into place. This discovery came sometime after 1935, the year Corning began production of Pyrex blocks.[26] A hiatus in production followed, which lasted only a year or two before a new formulation was adopted. The lime glass, Lumite, was Pyrex's successor, though it was not particularly low expansion.

After rigorous but insufficient testing, production resumed in 1937, and Corning shipped its first Lumite blocks in January 1938. The following September Corning halted sales of this item: checking followed by fracturing of the blocks was occurring in an unacceptably high number of instances.[27] Corning responded with a battery of engineering and other tests designed to simulate long-term field wear in an accelerated fashion. Not that time compression was required; as one bricklayer said, "If he tapped the mortar surface of a block with the edge of his trowel before assembly, within one week there would be a check in the glass beginning at the point of the trowel impact."[28] The blocks were clearly unfit for the environment in which they were being used. The issue was their formulation. An entirely new glass was eventually developed—code 124 IK—which proved satisfactory.

These failures must have pained Corning's leadership. It took the architectectural market quite seriously and believed that winning the trust of architects was crucial to success. "We need," wrote A. E. Marshall in a memo to Amory Houghton,

> to develop some method of cooperation with architects which will permit us to follow and profit by the working out of new forms of structural assembly.... Such architectural cooperation should also help to keep us in touch with new building projects, and the trend of individual architectural offices toward glass brick structures.[29]

Despite consciousness of the importance of serving architects' needs, when Corning introduced its first Pyrex blocks it also failed to appreciate the need to observe architectural standards: a standard size based on bricks or some other architectural constant. According to a 1934 sales brochure,

> In selecting a size for this unit, it was not felt necessary to conform to any accepted building material size. After long and expensive experiments with smaller units, which were rejected by the building profession, it was decided to adopt a unit which was a logical and economical shape to manufacture and which had inherent esthetic qualities.[30]

Nor did the company pursue a standards-setting program of the sort it had so successfully engaged in under the leadership of Churchill and Gage. As one observer commented in 1935, "A frontal attack must be made on this problem of standardization before individual materials can be used to their fullest advantage." Engineering was vital in getting glass blocks to be considered. As Sullivan summarized later,

> In structural blocks the glassmaker is required, for the first time, to produce an article in which the glass body is under heavy tensile stresses as a permanent condition. Moreover the articles are used as masonry and therefore subject to severe surface scratching by sand and mortar. The shrinkage of

hydraulic-setting mortar, acting through its bond to the glass, induces additional tensile forces, and the effects of sun, rain, and freezing on the mortar-
glass assembly include both chemical and physical reactions.[31]

Organizationally, the effort required "a method of cooperation with architects that would permit Corning to follow and profit by the working out of
new forms of structural assembly." This was the product concept that led
Corning's machine development department to work on machines for making glass blocks. It was thought that the second requirement might be satisfied by Corning's 1936 merger with MacBeth Evans, which had already
invested resources in exploring the potential market for glass blocks.

Even augmented by MacBeth Evans's resources, Corning's were judged
insufficient. The company needed more contact with builders and builder
supply houses in particular. Pittsburgh Plate Glass (PPG), with which Corning was regularly in contact over technical issues in the 1920s, was interested
in promoting glass for architectural uses of all kinds. It was already well positioned in this market, though it lacked Corning's glass block technology.[32]
The two together formed Pittsburgh-Corning, the first of three major associations that Corning entered into in the 1930s and early 1940s.

William Decker, who had been Corning's corporate accountant in the
1930s and became its president in 1946, played a leading role in consummat-
ing the Pittsburgh-Corning deal. Ownership was exactly fifty-fifty between
Corning and PPG, and leadership was as close to evenly balanced as the two
companies could arrange. Both companies purchased 5,000 shares of the
outstanding 10,000 shares of issued stock at a price of $100 per share. Pitts-
burgh-Corning began producing its own glass blocks early in 1938 in its new
factory in Port Allegany, Pennsylvania, a depressed industrial site. The first
product was the one called Lumite.

Because glass blocks were not a product with a wartime market, Pittsburgh-Corning's operations were severely disrupted between 1942 and 1945;
its main factory was converted to handling extra capacity for Pyrex. A venture to produce Foamglas, a flat product used for structural purposes and
insulation, was launched in 1943 but proved difficult to keep moving forward. Immediately after the war, however, demand reversed itself, and for
the next five years Pittsburgh-Corning was in a position to take advantage of

Glass block inspection station at Pittsburgh-Corning Plant in Port Alleghany, PA.

pent-up demand for housing and office buildings. Glass block shipments averaged around 8 million pieces annually in those years, peaking in 1947 (10.6 million pieces) and 1950 (9.7 million pieces). Foamglas shipments averaged around 14 million board feet annually during the same period, peaking during the same years at 16 million board feet.

Over time Pittsburgh-Corning's product lines expanded into insulation, acoustical materials, and even electrically welded double window units. Beginning with exclusive arrangements with PPG and the Armstrong Cork Company, it eventually offered its products through a number of independent distributors. This freedom to do business more broadly brought the company in 1950 to what it saw as "the threshold of a dominant industry position."[33] Eventually it took its entire range of products overseas. Manufacturing had originally been performed by 125 people in one plant, and by 1945 it employed 528. By 1950 it had expanded to employ 751 in several different plants, two of which were located in Sedalia, Missouri. Sales of structural blocks rose from 6 to 12 million units and those for cellular glass products from 13 million to 45 million board feet.

Corning not only provided the initial technology but also continued to provide technical backup through its laboratories, even though Pittsburgh-Corning developed its own in-house R&D as well. The two together tackled the serious problem of chemical attack and wear that forced Pittsburgh-Corning to replace a large number of its blocks in use every few years. In 1950 one report noted that "large sums have been spent for replacements, continuous research and field investigations have been devoted to the determination of service performance, and published claims and specifications for product usage have been kept conservative." Still, the product remained in demand.

PPG provided the lion's share of the management talent as well as the aforementioned marketing know-how and contact. To maintain an even balance of power, Corning usually had one extra director when there was an odd number of directors. In later years, George MacBeth expressed concern that Pittsburgh-Corning might be broken up by the government because of its board structure's interlocking directorships, but in fact this never became an issue. The period in which Pittsburgh-Corning came close to commanding a dominant share of the market for glass blocks was relatively short, and from a broader perspective glass blocks had many competitors in the building materials market after World War II.

Pittsburgh-Corning had to be judged a substantial success as a company. It introduced hundreds of vital new manufacturing jobs to an area that was suffering acutely from a lack of good jobs in the 1930s. In the early years it provided a handsome return to its two corporate parents, which had invested only $500,000 each (though they also advanced significantly more capital in the form of loans to the new company). Eventually the company outlived a change in architectural taste that greatly reduced glass block's popularity as a building material, though a resurgence of architectural interest occurred in the 1980s and improvements to other products (Foamglas in particular) gave the company a new lease on life.

Perhaps most important of all for an understanding of Corning's efforts to build successful partnerships, Pittsburgh-Corning demonstrated Corning's ability to sustain a solid fifty-fifty relationship with a much larger company over a long period of time, one that provided a conduit for cross-learning about markets and technologies. On the other hand, as a strategic matter, the new association may, over the long run, have prevented Corning from making a success of the business in architectural glass that it had intentionally kept for itself. In forming Pittsburgh-Corning, Corning essentially gave away its own chance to develop the ability to deal directly through the builders and building materials channels. Instead it remained tied to the architects, a channel which, though admirably suited to Corning's style and aspirations, did not prove to be the most effective marketing influence for Corning's products.

Corning followed Pittsburgh-Corning with two other domestic associations in quick succession: Owens-Corning (1938) and Dow-Corning (1942). Both of these companies were provided an umbrella during the war by the government, which needed their products as quickly as they could be produced and was trying to speed and rationalize production even to the point of encouraging, as in the case of Owens-Corning, direct combination if necessary. The first of these involved the merging and patent pooling of two different makers of fiberglass; the second was a simpler arrangement between two companies that were not otherwise competitors. In their early days the latter two companies had products that were highly interdependent. Owens-Corning became much larger than Corning and yielded significant returns on the capital and technology invested. In return for fairly modest amounts of money and, in the early years, fairly heavy amounts of technology and technical support, Corning received royalties for its technology and/or half of all the profits declared in each business in the form of dividends on its half of the shares held in the business.

Owens-Corning Fiberglas

Along with several other specialty glass enterprises around the world, Corning had been pursuing the idea of fiberglass since soon after World War I. As noted in chapter 4, Corning had hired Austrian engineer Ed Wellech to pursue commercial production of fiberglass, or glass wool as it was also called, in 1924. But his was a virtually solitary effort, and his superiors became convinced that the path he was on would not result in the low-cost process that would be required to generate a mass market. Wellech was then assigned to other projects, though he rejoined the effort briefly when the Corning Fiberglass Division was formed.

Fiberglass had first become more than a curiosity or luxury good (as in decorative spun glass) during World War I when the supply of asbestos was curtailed. In 1929 an F. Rosengarth associated with the Hager Company in Ohio invented the centrifugal spinning process. But production of fiberglass cheap enough to qualify the material for high-volume markets awaited both better mass production processes and the better plastic fillers that Hyde and others were developing. Then, in 1930, Libbey-Owens-Ford Glass started producing glass fibers by drawing them from melted glass rod. The resulting fibers were used to make a double-paned insulated glass known as Thermolux. Shortly after this development was announced, Owens-Illinois began an intensive program to make fiberglass and Corning revived its own effort. Eventually Corning located a German firm from which it acquired the rights to use a fibrous glass process in the United States; it based the production of its new Fiberglass Division on that process.

At that time fiberglass was made by drawing tiny glass fibers, either from glass marbles or straight from the tank melt, through the small orifices of a round bin. (A direct melt process came into use within a decade.) The fibers were then fluffed with pressurized steam, resulting in a "staple" of fibers that could be formed into either mats or cushions. In its most basic form white wool was used as thermal insulation for temperatures ranging up to 538C. Making products of greater densities and rigidities required the addition of a "thermosetting" resin binder (a key use for the resins Hyde was working on), after which the wool pack was compressed and cured to the desired consistency, which might be a batt, a roll blanket, or a rigid mat as stiff as a board. Further fabrication steps could include coating or painting. Coarse fiber could be used to make filtration products, and fine fiber was exceptionally impervious to sound. Because of its extremely high ratio of surface area to volume, either sort demonstrated a very high dielectric resistance (and, if appropriately treated, that resistance could be preserved even when exposed to moisture and other environmental factors that would normally break it down). The wide range of possible outcomes made this material endlessly customizable to the requirements of a large variety of customers, who might be fabricators themselves or merely distributors.

Alternatively, multistrand fibers could be spun from continuous filament and turned into fiberglass materials or textiles for use in curtains or other kinds of durable fabrics that resisted moisture, fading, or the other forms of attack that degraded more conventional fabrics. Here silicone played a critical role as a lubricant.

Corning produced fiberglass for several years at its new Fallbrook fiberglass plant, its peak output exceeding $800,000 in 1937. The output in that year broke down as follows:

Building insulation	$666,901
Bulk fibers unfabricated	$25,278
Bulk fibers fabricated	$100,006
Textile fibers unfabricated	$1,513
Textile fibers fabricated	$20,990
Total	$814,688

As promising as this was, it was evident that competition between Corning and Owens-Illinois, which had constructed a new plant in Newark, Ohio, was delaying the focus on problem solving needed to tackle the nascent industry's technical problems. The two competitors decided to collaborate: Owens-Corning Fiberglas was formed in November 1938, combining two undersized fiberglass businesses into one that no longer had to worry first about competition. The new business now had support from the combined and collaborative technical efforts of two able development organizations. As with Pittsburgh-Corning, glass formulas were primarily Corning's responsibility.

Owens-Corning was set up as an association very similar in structure to Pittsburgh-Corning. Both parent companies owned equal shares, in this case 45 percent stakes. The new business gained momentum quickly. Sales of the combined operation rose to over $2 million in 1938 and then doubled each succeeding year until the war. Revenues reached the $100 million mark in 1952 and surpassed $200 million in 1959.

Owens-Corning had one thing going for it that the Pittsburgh-Corning venture did not have: a charismatic and inventive leader in the person of its president, Harold Boeschenstein. Boeschenstein came to Owens-Corning from his position as vice president and sales manager of Owens-Illinois. Within a year of the company's formation he articulated the policy by which Owens-Corning products were developed, manufactured, and sold: where fiberglass was not the sole possible material for the application, it must be the best or, failing that, the cheapest.[34] It was Boeschenstein who, armed with a piece of glass tape coated with a varnish made from one of J. Franklin Hyde's earliest specimens of usable 990A resin, sold Commander Hyman Rickover, then head of the electrical section of · the U.S. Navy's Bureau of Ships, on the use of fiberglass insulation for submarines.[35] "I want it tomorrow," Rickover is characteristically supposed to have said, inaugurating a relationship. Certainly the fiberglass insulating tape, varnished with a substance that not only protected wire from abra-

Harold Boeschenstein and Games Slayter, key figures on the Owens-Illinois side in the founding of Corning's most important early joint venture, Owens-Corning. Slayter as head of research participated vigorously in Sullivan's cooperative research meetings; while Boeschenstein was central to the negotiation and start-up of Dow-Corning as well as Owens-Corning and very involved in meeting the needs of the U.S. Navy for new materials made of fiberglass with silicone fillers.

sion but also kept out water, would be a revolutionary development for the Navy.

Another former employee of Owens-Illinois who ultimately contributed to the rapid development of Owens-Corning, and to its extremely innovative progress in developing new products, was Games Slayter—the same vice president of research and development who gave samples of Hyde's early silicone work to GE. Slayter was a chemical engineer and inventor from Purdue who had joined Owens-Illinois when it launched its development effort into glass fiber. He held some of the key patents on manufacturing glass wool and thus contributed technically as well as managerially. Owens-Corning also had the benefit of a close relationship with the consulting firm of Arthur D. Little, a partner it inherited from Owens-Illinois. This firm was located in Cambridge, Massachusetts, and used its contact at the Massachusetts Institute of Technology to help Owens-Corning find research advice. Robert Goddard, an MIT professor better known for his work on rockets, advised Slayter on improving the steam blowers that Owens-Illinois originally had developed for the fiberglass process.

In the early years of its existence Owens-Corning worked closely with its parent companies, with Corning on technology and Owens-Illinois on marketing. One of the problems Corning helped to tackle was the effect of fiberglass melt on refractories. Fiberglass, because of an absence of the usual potash and soda in the melt, was a substantially alkali-free type of glass and interacted very differently with furnace linings than typical lime glass or even borosilicate mixtures. Chromium oxide was proposed as a solution that might make refractories "survive the attack of fiberglass batches." Owens-Corning loaned its parent company the services of a ceramic engineer who helped Corning's ceramic laboratory develop methods for producing chrome oxide shapes by a new form of casting called organic slip casting. Eugene Sullivan's "daybooks" show that Games Slayter made trips of several days' duration to Corning every quarter, meeting with key Corning researchers each time. Owens-Illinois, Owens-Corning, and Corning worked together on a number of important programs, including electric melting, which they agreed to develop "separately, but in consultation." This relationship remained close during the war when collaboration was viewed as vital to the rapid improvement of fiberglass insulation for use in electric motors and many other weapons-related applications.[36]

The fiberglass business had little trouble converting its product line to civilian uses after the war. For one thing, its weapons-related demand remained high: the military continued to push for airplanes with ever lighter components, and fiberglass insulation was essential for high-temperature engines in any case. Paths of product development for civilian use were also easily summarized: "Where heat or cold must be saved or controlled; where sound and noise are to be reduced; where electricity is generated or transmitted; where air is to be cleaned or conditioned; where strong, easily cleanable, enduring, firesafe fabrics are required; where plastics of great strength are needed." In all these places Owens-Corning Fiberglas was a likely candidate for the job. By 1958 the boosters claimed more than 30,000 end use applications for fiberglass; hundreds of fabricators and distributors, big and small, had built their businesses around this new material.

But soon after World War II the government opposed the three-way interlocking relationship that Corning, Owens-Illinois, and Owens-Corning had formed. In a suit filed in 1947 the government maintained that the arrangement was tantamount to one company having a monopoly on a strategic market; at the time Owens-Corning produced 98 percent of all the glass fibers made in the United States. The June 1949 federal court order, contained in a consent decree, prohibited Corning, Owens-Illinois, and Owens-Corning from entering into certain contracts among themselves and foreign companies similar in nature to the contract cited with Asahi and, further, "forbade them from acquiring any glass fiber manufacturing firm or distributor; refused to allow interlocking positions among the companies, and required Owens-Corning to license certain patents on a non-exclusive basis." The companies involved contested the decision, but in effect the relationship between Owens-Corning and Corning was rendered a strictly arm's length one. Corning's holdings in Owens-Corning remained a major asset and a major source of revenue for the company, but Corning ceased to play an active role in the business. The decree was modified in 1978 and at that time required divestiture of 90 percent of Corning's shares in Owens-Corning by 1986.

Dow-Corning

As for silicone, Corning faced even greater technical and managerial challenges. Formidably intricate pilot plant facilities and chemical engineering work were required to exploit Franklin Hyde's discoveries. Corning lacked the necessary engineering ability, as well as the money, to invest in chemical manufacturing of such complexity or likely magnitude. Furthermore Corning was under pressure to produce: word had spread well beyond the Navy's Bureau of Ships about the new silicones, raising urgent demands from all branches of the military. All had reason to be interested in any material that would allow engines to run hotter. Corning's formerly close relationship with GE had been strained by the Hyde/Rochow episode, and cooperation between the two was foreclosed in any case by the antitrust suit that the Justice Department had filed against the electrical companies in 1939; the glass suppliers had been named as parties to the suit. Some correspondence took place with DuPont, but DuPont was heavily engaged in the very work on plastics that had posed a threat to begin with.

It was Hyde himself who suggested contacting Dow Chemical, which was already in the synthetic chemical business. Dow was given access to the pilot plant work at Mellon on a modified form of the "Grignard" reaction, the magnesium-based reaction that both Corning-supported teams were using to obtain silicone compounds. As work proceeded and the government began to limit supplies of essential strategic materials, Dow was also one of the few companies that had access to the magnesium needed to perform the Grignard reaction.

Under the pressure of the wartime need for silicones, Corning and Dow concluded a simple gentleman's agreement to form a joint company for the purposes of exploiting the new substance as rapidly as possible. Five men attended an organizational meeting on April 1, 1942. They included Willard Dow, president of Dow Chemical, Glen Cole, president of Corning Glass Works, Harold Boeschenstein, President of Owens-Corning Fiberglas, William R. Veazey, research coordinator for Dow, and Bill Collings, general manager of Dow's Cellulose Products Group. Boeschenstein expounded at length on the potential uses of silicones, on the need for heat resistant resins to be used with fiberglass yarn and fabrics and on the unusual properties of silicone fluids and their potential uses for defense applications. Then Glen Cole proposed a model, which by this time was a familiar protocol for everyone involved in Corning's "associations:"

> I suggest that Corning Glass Works and The Dow Chemical Company form an equally owned company. We have some inventions and you have chemical know-how. Let's not take stock for these; just consider them of equal value. I propose that we form a new company into which we agree to invest equal amounts of money and then take equal numbers of shares.[37]

Silicone research speeded up at Dow Chemical itself and by mid-1942 its entire Cellulose Products Group had shifted to the new field of silicones. By July 1942, the joint venture effort headed by Collings reported having shipped thirty gallons of Dow Corning 990A additive, which was Hyde's resin. They had also detected strong demand for another commercially feasible compound, first synthesized by the Mellon group. This was Dow Corning 4 compound for use as a spark plug sealant. It would reach 4,000 pounds per month by August 1942.

In September a Dow-Corning division of Dow Chemical Company, an interim arrangement, was formed under a management committee of three senior Corning people and three equally senior Dow people. Each company also agreed to put in $500,000 and up to a maximum of $100,000 per year during the next five years. After the problems Corning had been running into from antitrust investigations, there was some concern that this venture might run into regulatory trouble. But these joint venture plans were blessed by Undersecretary of War Robert Patterson, who sent a letter to Willard Dow from the War Department in January. The formal agreement followed a month later.

The company had already been in operation even before it had been formed as a legal entity. Plant, staff, and equipment for the new company were assembled gradually, with great difficulty given wartime conditions. Fortunately, Commander Rickover again came into the picture, signing an order for twenty-five motors, twenty-five pounds of grease for the bearings, and enough paint to coat the motors. This order carried the priority needed to purchase the essential controlled magnesium, and with that the Dow-Corning board authorized a plant to be built on a lot adjoining one of Dow's plants in Midland, Michigan. Such were the complexities of the required facility that it did not achieve production until January 1945. Nevertheless the new company shipped enough product out of Dow to achieve a profit of $24,000 in its full first year of operation.[38] For the duration of the war at least, Hyde and the rest of the old Corning research team remained with Corning laboratories, while the Dow research group continued its work at Dow, augmented by the Mellon team. All three groups met regularly for research conferences.

Hyde's group grew to about fifteen people, and their wartime work included original research on a variety of critical applications from water-repellant substances to the polymerization of cyclic siloxanes, which later became one of the main methods for forming high polymers. This work eventually led, among many other important outcomes, to the development of silicone rubber. Even by 1946 a staggering number of products critical to the war effort were entirely dependent on the ability to synthesize silicone. These included aircraft ignition insulation allowing for sustained high-altitude flying, electric motor insulation that quadrupled the service life of electric motors even in wet conditions, silicone paints that withstood temperatures exceeding 360C, silicone lubricants used for mold releases, and silicone rubber that retained its flexibility from -21C to 260C and could therefore be used as gaskets in airplanes and as coatings for resistors.

Only in 1951 did Hyde and several of his group move to Dow Corning permanently. Meanwhile the crucial first group of Hyde patents, known collectively as the Hyde 19, emerged from a nine-year limbo to issue on October 25, 1949. Delayed first by the difficulties inside Corning's own legal department, they had then had to undergo several major interference proceedings, only to be classified under government wartime secrecy provisions. The Hyde 19, along with earlier copolymer patents, together covered a large range of organo-silicon compounds (125 different compounds were cited) supporting a wide variety of Dow-Corning products. They also provided the necessary leverage to achieve for Dow-Corning substantial

cross-licensing with General Electric for the silicone substances it controlled. The agreement between the three parties to the Dow-Corning venture provided for Dow and Corning to make their patents available to
Dow-Corning royalty-free until 1958. It would take almost that long for
Dow-Corning to become a viable business.

Unlike Owens-Corning, which had already been in operation before the
war and therefore had a roster of civilian applications to fall back on, Dow-
Corning faced tense times shifting gears to production for civilian markets.
Neither Dow nor Corning had the marketing expertise to develop the kinds
of markets Dow-Corning would need in the near future. Both companies
were primarily used to having customers come to them with their problems. Silicones were such new substances that it was hard to convince customers to try them even when novel uses could be imagined. Marketing of
this type required years of cash infusions from the parent companies and
individual arrangements with other chemical companies, always a dicey
proposition because there was always the chance that the outsiders would
find a way to replicate or improve the product themselves.[39]

The earliest products that provided a base for the company to grow
included mold release products used first by the tire industry, and then anal-
ogously by the baking industry. Next came consumer products—Silly Putty
for children, Sight Savers for eyeglass cleaning—suggested and developed by
the Corning laboratories. These products provided the base and the entree
into different market segments to hold the company together while it
assembled a professional marketing staff, performed the necessary product
development and testing, and worked to convince larger but harder to convince and more cost-conscious customers in industrial markets like electric
motors for civilian uses or in other consumer markets like leather treatment
and furniture polish. By 1950 the company was booking $6 million in annual
revenues, not impressive by Owens-Corning standards but healthy enough
to stay afloat. By the end of the decade Dow-Corning sales in domestic markets had reached nearly $17 million, and small but significant sales were
under way overseas.

As with the other domestic associations Corning realized several benefits from Dow-Corning, only one of which was a healthy revenue stream.
One of the key benefits was an understanding from working with Dow of

how to control issues relating to the protection of intellectual property in an industry that was much more bitterly competitive than glass. As Franklin Hyde wrote to a friend in the late 1940s in some bemusement, "Research has come to be a very competitive business." In the early days of Dow-Corning, for instance, Corning adopted a system of handling samples for outside customers that Dow had developed as a result of its own bitter experience of having to buy up patents obtained by outsiders on the basis of Dow samples. This procedure, copied by Corning, involved sending out samples only through the research director's office, and only after they had been released by the Dow patent department, the research department, and the sales department.[40]

As with the other associations, the nature of the relationship between Corning and Dow-Corning changed over time. As the new company grew and developed its own direction the two gradually grew apart, but the Dow-Corning management openly acknowledged the enlightened treatment it received at the hands of both parent companies. The fifty-fifty structure ensured that no one party had control, but the personalities and the values of the board members were equally contributing factors in the sense of support, combined with encouragement for autonomy, that the board offered the new management.

Taken together, the affiliated companies, as Corning's associations were identified in its annual reports, amounted to nearly $12 million equity in excess of its original investment by 1950. On this the company booked more than $1 million in dividends. In 1952, they realized more than $2 million after tax profits on sale of Owens-Corning stock to get down to a 33.4 percent holding, which was the maximum they were allowed to own. Even so, by 1957 their equity stake in Owens-Corning Fiberglas was over $22.6 million in excess of their original investment. Pittsburgh-Corning and Dow-Corning were much smaller and grew much less rapidly, but by 1957 they were together worth $12 million more than Corning's original investment in them. These were sizable investments for a company that was only worth $137 million in assets and had sales of $163 million in the same year. By comparison, total investments in foreign subsidiaries at that time were running just over $500,000.

Corning's successes with its joint ventures appeared to establish sufficient precedent for further associations of this sort, but the postwar environment, as it turned out, demanded significant modification in Corning's strategy for leveraging its technology. One factor in particular had changed: antitrust. The government was pursuing such cases more aggressively, and the military was no longer able to afford the protection of a hot war's necessity (though the Cold War soon helped it reextend that umbrella of protection). In general, this served to limit Corning's options and to turn Corning's licensing focus more heavily in an international direction toward exporting its technology. However, the mistakes the company made during this period were not always a product of a lack of choices.

Licensees Foregone

Naturally, Corning did not license simply anybody who wanted a license, nor did it enter into associations or joint ventures with everyone who wanted them. They were influenced in this decision by judgments as to how well the enterprise in question could stand on its own feet, how much help it would need to be successful, and how much it was likely to earn. In at least a few cases the judgments made in answering these questions cost Corning business and created more competition.

One notable example involved Philips, a bulb customer and major electronics manufacturer based in Eindhoven, Holland. Glen Cole met with representatives of Philips while in Europe in the early 1950s. Accompanying Cole was the young Pierre Roederer, only recently moved to the international side of the house, having started his career at Corning as a trainee and then as a salesman. Philips received the two men cordially and then presented them with a request to become Corning's licensee in Europe. At that time the other licensees were all glassmakers like Joblings and St. Gobain. "How could we license Philips," Cole asked his hosts. "You're not glassmakers." This response produced an instant and negative change of mood in their hosts, who, like GE did make their own glass bulbs and considered themselves a very competent company technologically, on the order of GE in Europe. Cole and Roederer had to find their own way back to the hotel. Philips went on to expand their own glass production, and although Philips continued to buy certain products from Corning the incident between the two companies came up repeatedly for years wherever their employees ran into each other.

In later years it would be said that the one big mistake Corning's president Bill Decker ever made was in turning down an offer of association with Asahi. As we noted, Asahi had already taken the opportunity to license Corning's refractory technology in 1930. Although this agreement was supposed to end in 1941 when Japan and the United States became locked in mortal combat, immediately after World War II visitors from Asahi showed up at Corning with a check for all the royalty payments it owed Corning since the start of the war. It was the only international Corning licensee to make such a gesture. Impressive as this show of loyalty and good faith was, Bill Decker was not tempted by Asahi's offer to form a joint venture with Corning to produce television CRTs in the early 1950s. He turned Asahi down, reasoning that Japan could not be expected to be either a very large or a very sophisticated market any time soon. Having been intimately involved in the formation of the Pittsburgh-Corning venture, Decker believed that the effort of starting such a venture with a Japanese partner would cause more headaches than it was worth. Furthermore, the Japanese market was in a sorry state and was not expected to recover in the foreseeable future. Asahi licensed Corning television glass technology instead.

But through careful observation and thorough questioning the company proved adept at extracting that technology from Corning's plants and transferring it to their own facilities in Japan. Forrest Behm, a Corning plant manager at the time, described Asahi's methods for replicating Corning's process technology as having a thoroughness and effectiveness that no other Corning licensees achieved:

I can remember clearly standing behind one of these Japanese engineers. He had a pad that was probably smaller than a 9 x 11 . . . and he had an absolutely beautiful drawing of the machine and of the operator. He had a lot of notations, obviously in Japanese, on this sheet. They would get things verbally. They would get measurements. They would get detailed technical. They would get the formulations for the mold. They'd get the formulations for the glass. Then they'd go out and draw things. Then they'd come back and ask it all again.[41]

Asahi soon had as their customers many of the Japanese television makers that would start exporting their televisions to the United States. Those that did not use Asahi glass bulbs used bulbs from NEC, which licensed its technology from Corning's U.S. competitor, Owens-Illinois. In later years Corning's head of international business, Robert Turissini, noted that Corning would have had a much easier time against Japanese competition if it had been part of a joint venture with a Japanese company in the 1950s. "We took," he said, "the no-risk route in Japan when we licensed television technology to Asahi rather than operating a business with them, and by doing that we lost the knowledge we could have had of doing business in Japan directly when that knowledge would have done us some good."

Sylcor

In contrast, the technology-sharing relationship with Sylvania eventually led to a formal association between the two companies. Yet it was the one joint venture in which Corning ended up violating its own unwritten, but nevertheless well-understood, policies about such associations. As such it was the exception that proved the rule; measured in dollars lost, it was one of the company's worst failures. It merits close examination because the experience did as much as any of the successes to embed a "right approach to venturing" deep in the company's collective psyche.

The establishment of a nuclear energy industry in the 1950s and the concomitant growth in nuclear research proved fertile ground for Corning in its postwar search for new commercial opportunities. Edward Condon, Corning's research director in the early 1950s and an important figure in the Manhattan Project, early on recognized the nuclear industry's need for glass products such as radiation-shielding windows, and he led Corning to develop radiation-resistant glasses of a variety of sorts, in particular, an optical glass resistant to gamma ray darkening. The company was also involved in creating equipment for research in high-energy particle physics: its stake in scientific ware had grown along with this new field of research. Corning even contributed, along with seven other companies, to building a research-scale nuclear reactor.[42]

The company had also done some work on ceramics and nuclear fuel. The earliest such studies had been funded initially by the Atomic Energy Commission, and later by the Atomic Power Division of Westinghouse. Practically the only one of Corning's nuclear research projects that was not self-initiated and self-funded, it was this work that was to lead to Corning's most capital-intensive effort along these lines: its multimillion dollar investment in Sylcor.[43] A fifty-fifty venture with a much larger partner that lacked a technology Corning was thought to have mastered, the venture was, in typical Corning fashion, named with "Corning" in the second position: the Sylvania-Corning Nuclear Corporation. It was not, however, Corning's idea.

Sylcor, a nuclear fuels supplier, was formed in April 1957. The rationale for the partnership was a perceived complement in technical abilities related to nuclear fuel production. Sylvania's Atomic Energy Division was already invested in developing reactor components, esoteric metals for use in nuclear environments, and other nuclear materials. Corning's knowledge of ceramics, a high-temperature material, was seen as broadening the range of products a combined corporation could offer. The new company was endowed with approximately $5 million from each parent and established an R&D facility in Bayside and a manufacturing plant in Hicksville, both in New York. The new organization essentially combined Sylvania's Atomic Energy Division and Corning's nascent nuclear research branch. Sylcor was charged, however, to avoid operating in its parents' main spheres of interest: electronics and glassmaking.[44]

In 1954, Hyman Rickover, now an admiral in the U.S. Navy, had approached Corning with a unique materials problem. Rickover's contacts with Owens-Corning and with Corning itself had convinced him that it was the one progressive company in an otherwise backward industry. Early in World War II, Rickover, then a lieutenant commander, had grown frustrated with what he perceived to be the glass industry's generally unprogressive and unhelpful attitude toward Navy problems with ship lighting.

Corning, particularly keen at that juncture to distinguish itself from the rest of the industry, sent William Shaver to the Bureau of Ships to correct this view and did much else to convince the Navy and other military services that it was, on the whole, a competent organization.[45]

The admiral's problem was that metallic fuel elements (i.e., uranium pellets protected by a metal cladding) were insufficiently resistant to the great heat generated inside the Navy's nuclear reactors, and Rickover hoped that applying a ceramic cladding instead might increase the pellets' serviceable life. This was a project of the highest import (the longer the pellets could be made to last, the less time a nuclear submarine would have to spend in dock, the one place, it was thought, where it was vulnerable to attack). As part of the Navy's extremely aggressive building program, the proposed project had the potential to be very lucrative as well. When the proposal was made to respond to Rickover's suggestion through a venture with Sylvania, Eugene Sullivan, who played Cassandra throughout the project, noted, "Admiral Rickover is quoted as having 'thrown Sylvania out' because of unsatisfactory relations" and that "Corning was warned that we must do better than Sylvania."[46] Decker too was lukewarm about the idea from the beginning, though it was difficult for Corning not to accede to Sylvania's requests when the supplicant was such a big customer for its lighting and vacuum tube products. Decker warned in 1956 that "Navy reactors [are] the only large dollar volume market which appears reasonably certain to develop during the next five to ten years" and that "Corning appears to have no place [there]."[47]

In the event, the Navy needed speed and by the time Sylcor had begun research into fuel elements suitable for Navy use, at least five other companies had already started supplying metallic elements for submarine reactors (all of them operating at a loss). Admiral Rickover canceled Sylcor's contract "very suddenly." Without his support the company's chance for Naval work of this sort evaporated.[48]

Decker had foreseen that Corning's ceramic materials might also find uses in land-based nuclear power generating plants, and he indicated that such materials would be of interest in nuclear propulsion systems for aircraft and rockets (Sylcor did, in fact, contribute to this overly ambitious venture). Indeed, Corning and Sylvania were hardly the only companies interested in supplying what was predicted to be an enormous demand for nuclear fuels. But that predicted demand proved to be vastly overestimated. The buyer's market that resulted was a tough one to negotiate, and by the end of the 1950s it was already apparent that, in the words of Sylcor's treasurer, "the main business problem facing companies in the commercial fuel cycle industry is the fact that they entered the business in the first place."[49]

Corning had joined Sylvania in the hopes that its technology would give their corporate child an edge in the nuclear fuels market. Unfortunately, as it turned out (to quote Sylcor's treasurer again), Sylcor's "business problems are in many cases more acute than [its] technical problems" and as a result, Corning's research expertise offered little hope of saving the struggling company. Furthermore, the specific technical abilities that Corning was thought to possess proved to have only one real potential buyer, and the Navy, as it turned out, wasn't buying.

Its technical contributions irrelevant, Corning could do little but watch as Sylcor's losses mounted. No one had expected the company to make profits in the first few years of its operation, but the amount of red ink it was generating was staggering, with losses as follows:[50]

1957:	$299,000
1958:	$1,481,000
1959:	$2,279,000
1960 (1st two months) :	$116,000

Nobody could say when, or if, the cash flow was likely to reverse itself. Like most other entrants in the business, Sylcor had taken its first few contracts at a loss in order to establish a reputation in the field. Just one of those contracts, the supply of fuel elements for the Power Reactor Development Company, was an extraordinary technical challenge which, one Sylvania VP admitted, might well be "the most difficult metallurgical production problem in the world today."[51] This project alone generated over $1 million in losses in the first three years of Sylcor's existence, on a $1.3 million contract.

Both Sylvania and Corning found themselves extending loans to the joint venture in roughly $500,000 increments, and Corning soon lost its taste for such high-stakes poker. When Sylvania finally offered to buy out its partner for $950,000, Corning accepted, even though this meant booking a loss on the project of almost $4 million.[52] Corning removed itself from Sylcor's board and requested that its former partner, now sole owner of Sylcor, change that company's name within the year. Corning wished to disassociate itself from what it viewed as a failed venture. In the press release announcing its decision to abandon the Sylcor project, Corning cited only the fact that the ceramic fuel elements had not proven to be a focus for Sylcor.[53]

Despite the negative numbers, Sylcor had shown some early promise. It supplied product to a variety of foreign programs via the U.S. Atoms for Peace Program and other channels, and sold its goods to a large number and assortment of domestic buyers as well. By the early 1960s, it claimed to have "produced more nuclear fuel elements in its plants than any other commercial supplier in the world" and had a large variety of such elements in its portfolio. But, unable to win profitable business, it was in the impossible position of trying to make up in volume what it lost on each sale.[54]

Was there any justification for Corning's engagement in this venture in the first place? There is some indication that it hoped to learn something about electronics from Sylvania, but the main attraction was probably the allure of the nascent nuclear industry, which looked like just the sort of rapid growth opportunity Amory Houghton Sr. was seeking at the time.[55] It was in keeping with the blockbuster mentality of the postwar era and with Corning's sense of its own history, on a par perhaps with electric lighting and television.

Furthermore, powerful forces, aside from Rickover himself, were working to bring Corning into the industry. The company reportedly acquired a share in a research nuclear reactor in a postwar golf game between Amory Houghton Sr. and his former wartime associate, now a Corning board member, Walter Bedell Smith.[56] A 1956 report by the Batelle Memorial Institute likely served as a catalyst for subsequent decision making. The document, titled "A Survey of Opportunities in the Nuclear-power Industry for the Corning Glass Works," reviewed the state of the industry, presented an optimistic estimate of the future of nuclear power, and appealed to Corning's philosophy of patient money. It suggested two specific undertakings that appeared particularly well suited to Corning: the "development of fuel materials" for reactors and the "processing of nuclear fuels and waste utilization." Then the author concluded that "one of the principal requirements on any company which seeks to enter the field at the present time is that it must have an able and flexible research staff and must be prepared to invest heavily in research activities over this [long] period of time."[57]

However the decision was made, the company took a wrong turn. Though superficially akin to Corning's earlier joint ventures, Sylcor was, in fact, of a very different breed. Despite their history of close collaboration, the corporate parents were culturally ill matched. Sylvania was changing in character, and its culture was becoming considerably less compatible with Corning's as a result. An April 1959 Sylcor's news release announcing the election of two new directors to its board illustrates this well. The first, Robert E. Lewis, president of Sylvania Electric Products, could be called a managerial butterfly: he was a Columbia M.B.A. who had held a variety of upper management positions in three entirely unrelated firms before coming to Sylvania. In contrast, Charles LaFollette (Corning's appointee) had never held a management position outside of the company and had no professional training: he had joined as sales manager of the Pyrex Housewares Division and had worked his way up from there to the position of financial vice president. In short, Corning took on half of the cost and half of the risk for only a small potential percentage of the gain, in the interest of redeeming Sylvania's reputation with the U.S. Navy. It would never mount such a rescue operation again.

VENTURING AS AN ASSET

Despite the Sylcor fiasco, Corning's domestic associations in general had been lucrative for the company as well as valuable in other ways; but after World War II, Corning avoided such arrangements domestically because they raised antitrust suspicions in the Justice Department.[58] Fewer such restrictions applied overseas, and it moved to make similar arrangements internationally. Except when regulations in the home country dictating unequal ownership, for instance, precluded it, Corning's international joint ventures would all follow roughly the model first established by Pittsburgh-Corning. The ownership would be equal with the other partner; Corning would provide both the technology and the technical expertise; there would be very close relationships between Corning executives and the company executives (stemming perhaps in part from the Houghtons' longstanding familiarity with international diplomacy); and in a gesture that no doubt bought the company much goodwill, the Corning name would always come second. In the next few years joint ventures would be established in Latin America, in Asia, and with European companies both at home and abroad. For the next twenty-five years few of them would depart from the model that the early "associations" had established and that Sylcor had reinforced in the breach rather than the observance.

Though profitable, the greatest benefits of these ventures may well have been intangible ones. As we have seen, Corning learned much about the skillful handling of research-generated opportunities from Dow and Owens-Illinois. It also gained access to valuable sources of idea generation in both products and processes. The perspective these companies offered, coming as they did from outside Corning's own industry, could likely have been obtained in no other way. As isolated as Corning was geographically, its isolation within the glass industry mentality could have been far more detrimental had it not been for the leavening influence of the associations. Corning did not immediately adopt this learning model in its arrangements with its international partners. There, high returns on capital invested and technology shared were the main goals. In retrospect, those involved at the time recognized this attitude as an opportunity lost.[59]

As we explain in chapter 7, the postwar era was a time when Corning found itself with more cheap capital for expansion than it knew how to use and its wariness of setting up new domestic associations led to a preference for wholly owned subsidiaries. Having issued public stock in the later 1940s, Corning had a luxury in that period that it had never known before: it could, if it chose, fund multiple subsidiaries (though management was always a limiting factor) or internal product lines, thereby keeping all revenues for itself and maximizing its return on capital invested. Another factor in this change in strategy was the fear of antitrust pressures directed against any domestic joint venturing that was not blessed by the government for its own reasons.

Then, as now, the heart of the decision was always partly one of control. Obviously, to enter into association with another company was to surrender some degree of control over its own technology. But less obvious was that not to do so threatened a loss of control on a considerably greater scale. Had Corning managed to fully exploit silicone or fiberglass by itself, the company would undoubtedly have been transformed beyond all recognition, but part of that transformation would have entailed the Houghtons' surrendering their control of the company far earlier than they did.

In point of fact Corning had a genius for setting up and maintaining productive and largely amicable joint ventures, as well as other technology-sharing partnerships, over a long period of time. Just as the Houghtons had a knack for creating the conditions inside their company for creative and fruitful scientific work, so they had a knack for taking a supportive laissez-faire stance towards managers of new joint ventures. Few other American companies could claim to do this well, and most found it difficult to maintain good joint ventures for more than a few years, if at all.

In time, under the Republican administrations of the 1980s, antitrust pressures would lessen. Corning would tire of acquiring companies which propelled them into markets they had trouble understanding. Joint ventures would become once again a standard way for Corning to realize reliable and cross-fertilizing gains from its technology. When that occurred, the approach to joint venturing did not have to be thought through from scratch. It was as though encoded in the company's genetic material—patterns so deeply embedded that no one knew where they had come from. As one commentator warns, "Corning does *not* offer a model [for others].... It is not the way to learn. It is the way to act once you have already learned. Admire, applaud, and gape in disbelief, but don't copy."[60]

CORNING AND THE MILITARY

INNOVATION IN AN ERA

OF PERMANENT MOBILIZATION

> *Government business is the toughest, most undesirable, highest risk and lowest margin business facing Corning. It is a business within a business, involving its own mores, accounting, legal, selling methods, etc. More and more it is developing political overtones. There is no question that improperly handled it can affect growth, profits and corporate image.*
>
> —"THE UNITED STATES GOVERNMENT AND CORNING"[1]

TECHNOLOGY SHARING with its partners in association was vital both to Corning and to the larger war effort that consumed the American economy in the early 1940s. Ironically, the political climate took a sharp turn in this same period, rendering such associations increasingly suspect. In the wake of the Depression, many believed them to be contributors to undue concentration in the economy. For Corning's leaders World War II thus presented terrible conflicts quite aside from anything encountered on the battlefields. The company and its executives were laboring under a cloud of antitrust accusation that had been stirred up in the late 1930s but had not been resolved. At the same time Corning was being asked to engage in new kinds of activity with the U.S. military, a demanding new customer that would test the company's capacities and raise a perennial question: Was Corning at heart a specialty manufacturer or a mass producer?

World War II transformed both the federal government and the national economy, making the one interventionist and the other consumerist. Known also as the "wizard war" in which allied scientific superiority had played a decisive role, it radically reshaped industrial research to support these changes. Corning, which had previously done little government work, was completely swept up in the war effort. Nor did the war's end allow a return to a state of relative isolation; Corning found itself forced to renegotiate its relationship with Washington and, in particular, with an increasingly powerful defense establishment. The company did this in a typically unorthodox way by carving out a position on what might be termed the "active periphery" of the military-industrial complex. This stance saved it from becoming a creature of defense spending and federal handouts, a not-uncommon fate for many other high-tech companies.

As Washington's influence grew, its patronage became ever more desirable; Corning could have avoided several painful experiences had it maintained a closer relationship with the military services in particular. Its refusal to do this, even though it did make use of some government resources, closed off certain avenues of expansion. This policy was not the product of a single grand strategy but the result of a consistent expression of corporate values that emphasized independence, commercial markets, and the sanctity of Corning's intellectual property.

WORLD WAR I AND OPTICAL GLASS, 1917–1920

Corning's earliest contacts with the federal government had been instrumental in the formation of the company's laboratory. After all, Arthur Day, Eugene Sullivan, and Houghton family member George Hollister had all come to Corning from the U.S. Geological Survey, bringing with them the accumulated expertise developed at the Survey concerning furnace control and silicate sciences. Their continuing association with the Survey resulted in further beneficial exchanges between the company and the agency, including theories and data concerning controlled annealing, measurement techniques, and even instruments.[2]

The company's earliest military contact came somewhat later, when the British naval blockade of World War I stemmed the flow of German glassware into the United States. This gave Corning an opening to begin production of scientific glassware for the American market, but it also cost the

United States its access to the world's foremost producer of high-quality optical glass. Binoculars, fire control equipment, range-finding instruments, and other crucial military goods were all dependent on superior German glass. In order to command sufficient stocks of optical glass during the coming conflict, the U.S. Department of War decided to intervene in domestic production. That effort, which from 1917 to 1919 closely managed upward of 90 percent of America's optical glass production, was led by the same Arthur Day, who by that time had left the USGS to serve as the director of the Geophysical Laboratory at the Carnegie Institution and remained a Corning officer.[3]

Day had very little knowledge of how optical glass was made: "the processes of manufacture had been kept carefully secret [by the European manufacturers that dominated this part of the industry] and were nowhere on record."[4] The challenge posed would require not only manufacturing expertise but significant research capabilities as well. As a Corning intimate, Day called on Eugene Sullivan for help. But Sullivan recommended against it. Corning possessed the necessary scientific expertise for such an undertaking. But the government was not proposing to fund the enterprise, and thus it struck Sullivan as an unprofitable sink for scarce resources. "We are not in a position to spend money on optical glass experimentation at the present time," he wrote to Alanson Houghton, "unless the Government is willing to take its share of the outlay." Patriotic necessity was not the primary issue: as Sullivan argued, "there is little occasion for our going into optical glass on patriotic grounds, for the reason that at least one other firm has the necessary equipment, and is marketing such glass."[5] A commercial justification was even harder to find: high-end optics was a small and highly specialized market, and the major producer, Bausch & Lomb, supplied its own peacetime needs internally. Absent these considerations, Corning chose not to act.

Corning was still small and peripheral enough not to be accused of malingering when it declined involvement in Day's optical glass project. The stance the company took at that time reflected a wary patriotism that would characterize its attitude toward government work through the 1970s, even though much else changed.[6] Company policy would dictate that Corning accept government contracts only if at least one of three conditions were present: Corning was the only possible supplier, and it was therefore a patriotic duty; the government was willing to defray most of the expense; or there was a commercial market in which Corning could participate profitably if it made the requisite investment. In almost no instances in World War I did these conditions apply. Later a further condition would be added: that the company would not have to yield control over its intellectual property.

Off the beaten track, Corning escaped wartime scrutiny. Late in the war, when the U.S. scientific community was bitterly split between internationalists who wanted to welcome German scientists back into the fold and others (the majority) who wished to punish and exclude them, Corning's technical community proved internationalist in sympathy but was not so vocal or large a group as to draw criticism for its minority stance. Rumor had it that there were arrangements of some kind, family to family, between the Houghtons and the family that controlled Germany's leading scientific glass maker, Schott; if so, they were not the subject of public comment, and Corning continued, even in a rather nasty anti-German postwar climate, to honor commitments it wished to maintain with German scientists.

Those relationships, however, did not prevent the company from taking advantage of the opportunity to break into the post-World War I market with materials that had previously been available solely from German suppliers. As discussed in chapter 1, Nonex, the borosilicate glass and forerunner to Pyrex that was invented in 1912, came into its own following the war, benefiting from the fact that previous forms of borosilicate glass had been German.

WAR WORK, 1941–1945

World War II was an entirely different matter. By the time the Lend-Lease program (the U.S. industrial effort to keep England in the war against Germany) commenced in 1941, Corning's involvement was an established fact. Early attempts to remain aloof had cost it dearly. As a supplier that was not at first considered essential to the war effort, the company initially received a low priority ranking and found itself vulnerable to materials shortages and manpower losses. In America's new command economy larger companies in industries that were considered vital to national security—steel, aluminum, or aircraft and tank production—received the best there was to have. Corning, which had long since learned how to leverage much larger companies to its technological and commercial advantage, turned these skills to leveraging its contacts with the U.S. government, itself another large and rapidly growing bureaucratic institution.

At first glass in general was not considered a vital material (except as a potential substitute for materials that *were* vital). Just as bad, the glass industry was early on regarded as uncooperative and unresponsive to military needs. Corning played a large part in changing that assessment by supplying optical glass, and most especially by the development and manufacture of radar bulbs. By 1944 the *Saturday Evening Post* could report that "Corning is tied into war jobs by 75 per cent of its capacity."[7]

The war transformed Corning from a niche player into a major industrial concern over the course of the early 1940s. It was not an easy transition: the company found itself playing a frantic and seemingly endless game of catch-up, unable to draw breath long enough to rationalize its production or even perform necessary maintenance. Eugene Sullivan's research agenda was thrown off course by a constant stream of urgent requests from the military. Yet while time, people, and resources were lost, a great deal was gained and the groundwork laid for an even greater metamorphosis. Corning finished the war with a larger research establishment, additional manufacturing facilities, and a widened worldview.

Personnel Lost and Gained

At the start of the war, Corning was classified as a glass container manufacturer, there being no specialty or technical glass category. It took time and endless petitioning to convince the authorities that its work deserved a separate designation and that awarding it the low industrial priority accorded containers was as detrimental to the war effort as it was to the company. In the meantime Corning lost 3,000 of its employees—many of them technicians, supervisors, and people with special skills—to the military and to industrial concerns with higher priority ratings.[8] When, later in the war, Corning brought new plants on line and production requirements increased at old ones, the company had to find 7,000 new workers, 4,000 to staff new positions and the remainder to replace existing ones. Recruiting trained workers was impossible. Many of the replacements and most of those staffing new plants were women, a necessity that in fact proved a benefit: the women were judged in general better at the assembly tasks than the men they had replaced.[9]

In retrospect it is evident that there were tremendous cross-fertilization benefits to bringing in new people, especially in a company with such employment stability as Corning had enjoyed. Many of the new hires came from organizations with greater or different production experience. Others came from college and university engineering departments. As Chuck Lucy later observed, "A fair number of people were being hired into the company after the War, and there was really quite a generation gap. Not a major one because the thing was all integrated, but there definitely was a larger chunk of younger people who were not . . . in the older tradition of the way the company operated."[10] At the time, though, the loss of know-how at so many levels was keenly felt and even after Corning's priority rating was raised, key personnel continued to be lost to higher priority endeavors, such as those centered around MIT's radiation lab and the Manhattan Project. Corning was involved in several ways in the latter: it devised extensive Pyrex piping systems, special Multiform insulators, and Vycor glass for the manufacture of high-purity materials, and it engaged in a number of major problem-solving exercises. John Hicks, whom Corning recruited from MIT to do advanced work on optics with Eastman Kodak, for instance, was loaned to the Manhattan Project in 1942, and many other disruptions and redeployments occurred as these top-priority efforts moved into high gear.

Last but not least, Corning temporarily lost its chairman, Amory Houghton, who was tapped for the War Production Board (WPB) to serve as one of a growing army of "dollar-a-year" men called to Washington to help the country mobilize quickly. Houghton worked first for former GE chairman Philip Reed in the materials division and was later appointed director of operations directly under the head of the WPB, Donald Nelson. Among other things this gave him access to large amounts of data about his and related industries, as well as knowledge of projected military needs. Perhaps more important, Houghton became the WPB's chief liaison to Lt. General Walter Bedell Smith, chief of staff under General Eisenhower and head of military procurement; this tie, if nothing else, guaranteed Corning a place in the postwar world. But in 1943 Houghton resigned his WPB position to avoid embarrassment when it was determined that he, his company, and the other members of the so-called Glass Trust were in violation of antitrust laws, a story we take up in chapter 8.

Houghton later returned to service in another critical capacity: as deputy chief administrator of the new U.S. Mission for Economic Affairs stationed in London (again, as it happens, serving under Philip Reed). The mission was responsible for lend-lease financial affairs and many other functions of the Anglo-American economic relationship. In some respects this was an even better venue from which to foster Corning's future interests. Not only did this assignment give Houghton continued contact with U.S. Army procurement in England, but the time spent in London allowed him to become better acquainted with the leaders of the British glass industry.

Unplanned Research and Wartime Products

When Corning executives first addressed the question of attaining a higher priority rating, some doubted that a convincing story could be told. It was research that changed this picture. All three services and a number of companies and other organizations, including instrument makers, oil companies, and university research laboratories, approached Corning with research requests. Corning's labs carried out 174 research projects at the government's request over the course of the war. These included work in optical glass, filter glasses, lighting ware, electric lamps, electronic devices, atomic energy, triggering devices, projectiles, landmines and accessories, chemical warfare, jewel bearings, army and navy restaurant ware, precision finished ware, high strength ware, and silicone products, among others.[11]

Unlike most research-performing companies, however, Corning took no money from the federal Office of Scientific Research and Development (OSRD), and very little from the various branches of the military that

requested its help.[12] This was in marked contrast to many of its major customers in the radio industry: Westinghouse, RCA, General Electric, and
Zenith all received many millions of dollars in OSRD funding alone. Some
of that money ultimately passed in one way or another to Corning (a chunk
of the nearly $5 million that Eastman Kodak received went to support
research at Corning, for example), but Corning's lack of direct funding was
considered a precaution against future claims that it had any obligation to
share its proprietary technology with other government suppliers.

Radar posed the greatest test of Corning's ability to respond to a surge
in manufacturing demand. Corning was already a major supplier of glass
blanks for vacuum tubes of all kinds and sizes, particularly to the radio
industry before war broke out. Its role in producing cathode ray tubes
(CRTs) the large vacuum tubes that were essential components in radar,
became nothing short of critical. Over the course of the war a full two-
thirds of the company's production capacity came to be devoted to manufacturing vacuum tubes and display devices for radar sets. Production of
cathode ray tubes had reached 2 million per year by 1944; five years previously it had been a mere 50,000.[13]

A second wartime production role vital to defense needs was the manufacture of optical glass. Though five plants owned by different companies
were producing optical glass domestically after World War I, only two companies remained in the business: Bausch & Lomb and American Optical, to
which Pittsburgh Plate had added some capacity in the late 1930s. The
National Bureau of Standards also produced small amounts of optical glass
for its own use. But after the early 1940s, Corning became not only one of
the two largest producers of optical glass in the country but also the lowest
cost manufacturer.

Even with new wartime facilities, many lines of production had to be
dropped: bakeware, flameware, coffeemakers, pharmaceutical ware, railroad ware, and some lighting products, among others. Other lines of Corning business were maintained, including lightbulb blanks, headlights for
automobiles, ophthalmic glasses for lenses and bombsights, Pyrex for laboratory ware and dinnerware (hardened for use in the field), glass tubing for
thermometers, and piping for many other purposes.

Production targets were not the only thing affected by government demand; Corning's approach to manufacturing itself had to adapt to the military's emphasis on high-volume, on-schedule output to tight specifications. Most importantly, this meant that there was no chance to do the kind of specialty work with new compositions where much of Corning's research expertise had previously focused. New compositions required working with too many uncertainties and too much gradual testing and improvement; government requirements were for predictable quality and predictable cost wherever possible. There were two areas, however, where the military authorities pushed Corning to try new things: replacements for metal (there was a need to minimize inessential uses of critical metals such as aluminum) and products where the special properties of glass offered performance that could be achieved in no other way.

The first of these efforts met with limited success. Corning experimented with a large variety of items, ranging from glass mess kits and glass razor blades to glass-impregnated airplane propellers and, of all things, glass bullets, most of which never made it to market. As a replacement for mica (used in certain electronics applications) an ultrathin glass Corning invented was of particular value, and fiberglass later played an important role in propeller manufacture. It soon became evident to the military that the real utility of specialty glass lay not in mimicking what metals could do better but in its own tremendous versatility.

This characteristic, native to the substance, was enhanced by Corning's Multiform process, which came into its own during the war. At first justified as a better way of forming the glass insulators needed for all types of communications equipment, it was soon used to manufacture heat and moisture-resistant glasses in a variety of new ways. The process proved vital in making insulators for radios, and the newfound ability to mold glass into intricate shapes (even threaded pieces were possible at a level of detail that pressing was unable to mimic) portended a large postwar market as well.

Corning's Vycor glass, the super-Pyrex capable of resisting heat up to 899C and all but chemically inert, proved of special benefit during the war. It found use in radar and other communications applications, as well as chemical warfare activities. Another product with unusual attributes was Pittsburgh-Corning's Foamglas. Said to be one-third lighter than cork and even more buoyant, it was used in life belts, life rafts, submarine gear, and roof sections of war plants, where its low weight allowed speedier assembly.[14]

As difficult as it was to continue producing old products with a diminished workforce, it was that much harder to manufacture new ones. Plants were operating with a mere thread of engineering support and little or no in-house production expertise. Hammond Munier, who, despite having no manufacturing experience at all, was pulled out of his research job to manage the Bradford plant, recalled the entire enterprise as a continual case of inventing on the fly. He found this so stressful that as soon as the opportunity presented he willingly gave up the coveted job of plant manager to return to new product development, where people at least expected not to know what they were doing.[15]

Radar

Though Multiform, Vycor, and other wartime innovations all mattered to the war effort, the main production challenges were meeting military demand for CRT bulbs for radar and supplying optical glass. Both entailed important production innovations: the development of mass production techniques for cathode ray tubes and of continuous melting for optical glass. Although production of both products had begun prior to the war, they became much greater undertakings as the military understood the scope and urgency of its needs. As it turned out, both products could be reliably manufactured using 1930s methods, albeit slowly and inefficiently. For optical glass, prior methods proved sufficient. Though Corning made a huge technical leap forward in its production methods for this product, that innovation came late in the war. Meeting the military's requirements for CRTs, however, pushed the company's production facilities well past their limits and forced the adoption of experimental techniques.

In producing the CRT bulb enclosures for radar, Corning played a central (though still unrecognized) role in the scientific efforts that, together with the better understood atom bomb project, won the war for the Allies and earned it the sobriquet "wizard war." All but two of Corning's plants at the time produced radar parts, Main Plant, Fallbrook, Charleroi, Central

The first radar set installed aboard ship, on the old USS Leary in 1937. This picture and the other radar pictures that follow appeared in Corning's in-house magazine, Gaffer, in an article entitled the "Glass Heart of a Secret Weapon" in 1946. So secret was all of the work associated with radar that this was the first time Corning employees who had been working on radar and optical glass knew what they had been working on during the war.

Falls, Wellsboro, and Parkersburg all contributing. Furthermore, because of patented methods that only Corning possessed, it could boast of being "the only company which produced a complete line of cathode-ray bulbs to meet the government requirements at any time during the war."[16]

Corning's earliest experiences with rudimentary CRTs occurred in the late 1930s. The company was among the first commercial suppliers of CRTs for oscilloscopes and other testing devices, and it was involved even earlier in providing bulb samples for several radio companies and would-be television manufacturers. Vladimir Zworykin, RCA's claimant to the title of the "father of television" for his invention of the iconoscope, had been in touch with Corning in the early 1920s, trying with difficulty to get it to produce experimental envelopes for his invention. A series of broadcasting tests conducted by RCA from the Empire State Building in New York City between 1936 and 1939 used receivers outfitted with a Corning-manufactured nine-inch bulbs. By 1941, regular commercial television broadcasts had begun in New York City and Corning supplied the bulbs for the 5,000-odd sets built to take advantage of it.[17]

While war temporarily halted television testing, it did a great deal to prepare Corning for its later dominance of the television bulb market. The move to wartime CRT production, with its enormous increases in both number and type of units produced, was precipitated by the U.S. Navy's Bureau of Ships's 1941 radar conference. Corning was the only glass manufacturer invited to attend this top-secret event, the rest of the participants being major electronics manufacturers. Ernest Ling, sales manager of the Bulb and Tubing Division, represented Corning. That the navy's interest in CRTs stemmed from its desire for radar was concealed from Corning and the other attendees. Corning received "only suggested designs and quality specifications" to work with in its efforts to gear up for wartime production of CRTs.[18]

CRT bulbs throughout the war were of two basic types: the one-piece blown and the multi-piece sealed. One-piece bulbs were made like light-

C. J. Phillips and Ernest F. Ling of Corning's Bulb and Tubing Division inspect cathode-ray bulbs for use in radar sets.

bulbs, using a highly mechanized sag-and-blow process. They were limited in size to nine inches in diameter, and the quality of the faceplate was likely to be unsatisfactory. Sealed bulbs, which combined a separately formed funnel with a pressed faceplate, could be manufactured in all sizes (3, 5, 8, 9, and 12-inches) produced during the war.[19] But the sealed bulb, covered by a Corning patent issued in 1939, was a more complicated technology, consisting of either two or three pieces (faceplate, funnel, and in some cases, neck). As the name implies, the primary challenge lay in achieving a vacuum-proof seal between the components.

Corning's single most significant development related to CRT production was the invention of a method for the electric sealing of glass. E. M. Guyer, who had joined Corning in 1929, was a key figure in this effort. Arriving shortly after Jesse Littleton and "Sparky" Smith invented an "electric hole punch," a device that could melt a hole in a piece of glass quite rapidly, Guyer extended this work to produce a tool of his own invention that used electricity to melt two pieces of glass together along a seam. This process allowed Corning glasses to match one of metal's great advantages in the radio and electronic tube market, its spot-workability.[20]

Electric sealing was also crucial to the development of large CRTs. Gas-fired welding of the various parts of a multi-piece CRT bulb tended to overheat the surface of the glass before softening its interior. Electric sealing was, by comparison, extremely precise and able to heat the glass throughout. Better seals, made more quickly (though not necessarily more cheaply: the tooling requirements were greater than those of gas-fired welding) were the result. Corning's development of low melting frits (ground glass applied as a paste between two parts to be joined and then melted, thereby cementing them together) also aided the company by offering yet another avenue for the sealing of black-and-white CRTs; they would prove even more crucial in color television production.[21]

The bulk of CRT production was initially located in Main Plant, shifting to Charleroi after 1943. By war's end, Corning was capable of producing 2 million CRTs per year, with the bulk of this capacity having come on line in 1945.[22] CRT production processes prior to the war had been handshop operations, carried out entirely by craftsmen. Although the manufacturing lines had been enlarged and rationalized in some respects, much of the work was

Radar pioneer Robert M. Page examines one of the elemental radio tubes in a set at the Naval Research Laboratory at Anacostia, D.C.

still done by hand. The number of different styles and models in Corning's portfolio limited the company's ability to mechanize production, as did the pace of the work. The shift to production for the television market proved an even greater leap technically and psychologically, and a far longer one in terms of the growth in sheer output. Yet the pressures were similar: Corning needed to manufacture an unprecedented number of this product under tremendous time pressure from its customer, and it was forced to rely on in-house research and production capabilities to do so. It is difficult to imagine the Corning of 1938 summoning sufficient resources and determination to dominate the market for television bulbs had it not been assigned a central role by the military in wartime CRT production and, not incidentally, guaranteed a market for its product.

Optical Glass Revisited

Perhaps the most important similarity between Corning's optical glass and CRT experiences lay in this point. Though the military was not directly responsible for Corning's initial interest in optical glass production, the guaranteed market it provided for the product allowed management to justify a continuing investment in R&D directed toward improvements in optical glass melting and, later, optical glass formulations. As with radar bulbs, wartime optical glass eventually led to a lucrative peacetime product line: in this case ophthalmics (i.e., optical glass for eyeglasses, a specialized subfield of optical glass).

Having forgotten the lessons of World War I, in 1939 the U.S. military found itself once again seriously undersupplied with optical glass as hostilities loomed; domestic suppliers had exited the market after World War I in the face of renewed German competition. This time Corning was eager to help. In fact, the company had begun "a full-scale development program for the melting of optical glass" in 1938. Early in that year, Eastman Kodak, probably prompted by the government, approached Corning to discuss a joint program of research on optical glass production methods. As 70 percent of Kodak's glass supplies came from overseas, its optical glass position was badly threatened, and it was willing to help fund the research effort. Meetings between C. E. K. Mees, Kodak's director of research, and Eugene Sullivan led to approval of a series of experiments to be performed under the direction of J. F. G. Hicks, an MIT physicist Corning hired for this purpose.

Hicks's goal was to create volumes of glass as free as possible from striations, seeds, bubbles, or inhomogeneities of any sort. His work focused on the melting process, leading to the development of a sealable tilting melter that sloshed the molten glass back and forth in a low vacuum. This increased the yield of optically acceptable product from a given batch of glass ingredients, though it did little to accelerate the speed of the overall process of production. For Kodak the tilting melter was good enough and the joint research program came to an end in 1940.[23]

While Hicks was busy with his melter, Charles DeVoe and his group at the research laboratory had been working on melting glass by means of an electric current directed through the glass bath. Originally driven by one of the periodic shortages in natural gas, they realized that this process might have other benefits, aside from allowing one to work off the power grid. Initially used as a sort of preheater for the tilting melter, electric melting showed promise for the production of optical glass since it melted the various ingredients in the bath evenly from the inside out (gas burners, in contrast, could boil some parts of the bath while leaving the rest unheated). DeVoe was also engaged in a series of experiments intended to determine the optimal design for the stirrer that mixed the glass ingredients as they melted.[24]

With such interests already high on the Corning laboratory's research agenda, the government's request for help with optical glass production was more welcome than it had been some twenty years previously. Nevertheless it was George Macbeth (whose company had only recently merged with Corning), not Sullivan, who championed the idea for the pragmatic reason that "if we did not, we might have difficulty getting materials...for the rest of our business."[25] This time the military offered to cover its costs. Recognizing that Corning would have to build production facilities more or less from scratch if it were to supply optical glass in the desired amounts, the Army Ordnance Department offered to pay the construction costs for a plant dedicated to optical glass production. Corning's accountants and researchers alike were happy with the offer.[26]

An improved version of the tilting melter, when combined with DeVoe's stirrer, promised an efficient operation with the desired yield. The proposed plant, built in Parkersburg, West Virginia, in 1942, was designed to use individual pot units. Aside from the improvements in melting, Corning was still relying on the old pot-melting furnace process that was a close cousin to that used in World War I and earlier. Giant clay pots, tilted and stirred for a prescribed length of time, were then allowed to cool. Once solidified, the pot and its contents were broken up, and the pieces were sifted through and tested for their suitability for use in optical instruments. Even with the improved melting and stirring process, little more than 10 percent of each pot's contents was usable. Despite the tremendous inefficiency inherent in this operation, the volumes needed were so small that production goals had been met in the early months of 1944. The military's problem had been solved by the Parkersburg plant, which was twice awarded Army-Navy E awards "for excellence of optical glass production" during the war.[27]

Yet even as Parkersburg was producing optical glass via the pot transfer method, Main Plant was gearing up for a different and much more high-tech approach. This method, called continuous melting, was a direct result of DeVoe's experiments with electric melting and August Erickson's work with platinum-clad stirrers. It was kept carefully segregated from the government-funded plant in order to avoid later claims on the company's intellectual property. If electric melting could produce a homogeneous flow of glass, the flow could be tapped in a "continuous" fashion as was common with less technically demanding glasses. Again, an optimized stirrer design (patented by DeVoe in 1944) made the difference: continuous melting was possible and proved to be a much more efficient way of obtaining large quantities of high-quality optical glass.[28] A pilot plant was first set up in 1943, combining the major developments of Devoe and Erickson and employing 126 people. Their work was supported on the composition side by George Hares, William Armistead, and others. The first fully functional installation was CU-4, a "continuous unit" located in the optical pilot plant in B Factory in Main Plant. Coming on line in January 1945, it produced optical glass for the remaining months of the war.[29]

CORNING DEMOBILIZES, 1945–1954

Corning was one of many research-driven companies that faced uncertain conditions after World War II. No corner of the economy had been untouched by the war, and none could expect to be unaffected by the peace. The postwar economy promised new opportunities, but there were keen memories of the terrible slump that had afflicted the economies of both the United States and Europe after World War I. Then government arsenals became competitors, selling stockpiled goods as a way of defraying national expense budgets. Arsenals had even turned to production of aircraft or other goods that had previously been purchased from outside suppliers. Under such altogether possible scenarios even companies that had had windfall profits could find themselves flirting with bankruptcy.

Numerous companies had acquired the nucleus of their in-house industrial R&D establishments by raiding government agencies and arsenals of their accumulated civilian expertise after World War I. In the interwar years, R&D had remained largely a private sector matter, with some collaboration with small-scale government agencies, while the military's arsenals tended to do much of their own work in-house. During World War II, however, several new approaches had been tried, most notably the funding of R&D through civilian channels rather than exclusively under the tight control of the preexisting military procurement organizations. The OSRD alone had funneled $500 million into weapons research performed by civilians working for civilian institutions.[30] Eventually the piper had to be paid. In areas of strategic importance the government had exercised what amounted to eminent domain over all intellectual property. Key patents previously controlled by one company were shared among competitors. As in the case of Parkersburg, government money also supported the building of defense plants for critical materials like aluminum and ammunition, and for critical weapons like airplanes, tanks, radar, and armaments in many strategically important areas of industry. DuPont, to take just one example, had built fifty-three explosives plants for the government at a cost of $500 million.[31]

Well before the war was over, influential members of the national research community in universities and leading companies, led by men like Karl Compton of MIT, Crawford Greenewalt of DuPont, and Fred Jewett of Bell Telephone, were arguing that the major national scientific assets mobilized during the war must not, in the national interest, be allowed to disperse completely. Among liberal scientists there had been intense admiration for the Soviet technocracy, which treated science as a high priority. At war's end the argument resurfaced. Science, it was said, had won the war and would be key to effective mobilization should that prove necessary again. This was the only strategic advantage the United States was likely to be able to maintain in the face of massed enemies who might once again field superior numbers of troops and weapons.

With the 1948 detonation of an atomic bomb by former ally, now turned enemy, the Soviet Union, this argument came into its own. That same explosion lent the debate an ugly cast. Scientists, who had so recently received credit for winning the war, suddenly found themselves under a cloud of suspicion. Their widely espoused philosophy that science should remain internationally open made them vulnerable to charges of giving away atomic secrets to the enemy.[32] Talk of reproducing in peacetime an arrangement similar to that of the OSRD met with grave opposition. Each military service wanted to control its own weapons development, and each wanted its own research programs not only in its own laboratories but also in industry and the universities.

As it happened, the postwar environment for research proved to be entirely different from the earlier one. Companies owning vital patents and expecting to get them back were likely to discover, as a result of changes in New Deal antitrust policy, that their exclusive control of technological assets could be construed by the courts as monopoly. Many were forced to license their rights, sometimes to direct competitors created by the government, at nominal cost. In the postwar environment competition in R&D increased rapidly. Each branch of the military, and the Department of Defense on behalf of all of them, designated certain high-priority technologies it wanted pursued, including aeronautics, electronics, and communications, along with such related areas as scientific instruments.[33] For industry the consequences of these developments were quickly apparent: the growth in new and extant laboratories quickly outstripped the supply of scientists needed to staff them. The problem was exacerbated by the security issue. While increasing amounts of scientific information were classified as militarily significant, the Washington bureaucracy struggled with the mammoth task of providing security clearances for thousands of scientists. At one point around 1950 as many as 20,000 scientists were said to be awaiting their clearances.[34]

Relatively few other research institutions were doing the kind of work Corning was engaged in, but many relied on a similar scientific base. Moreover, though materials research was not high on the totem pole in terms of direct federal research funding, many of the areas of research that were drew heavily on materials in general, and on glass in particular. The relevance of glass technology, already powerfully demonstrated during the war, would only increase if the added effort was made to do the painstaking work needed to produce suitable glass compositions.

Postwar Planning

Though wartime production was virtually all-consuming, Corning executives began planning for peace as early as November 1941. By then William

Shaver, head of new product development at Corning, had already initiated a continuing dialog concerning the company's place in the postwar world. Otto Hilbert, a senior executive with a background in mechanical engineering, and Tom Waaland of finance focused the debate on practical concerns in 1943 and 1944. Offering the first estimates of the dimensions of the opportunity and the size of the investment that would be required to take advantage of it, Waaland suggested that Corning's planners assume "that the European War will end in the Fall of 1944 and the Pacific War by the end of 1945" and that they conduct their planning within the framework of a top-to-bottom review of markets, products, and the business as a whole.[35] This memo stimulated a series of monthly meetings of senior management beginning in October 1944.

Documents from that period show how much Corning's war work was both broadening its market horizons and deepening its technical capabilities.[36] Shaver's first list of postwar opportunities, assembled in 1941, consisted almost entirely of extensions to the prewar product lines: stovetop Pyrex could enhance Corning's kitchenware line, both glass tubing and scientific glassware could be offered in greater variety, and so on. Opportunity lists from 1944 contained far more exotic items, all direct outgrowths of the company's work supplying wartime needs. Black-and-white television, electronic components, optical and ophthalmic products—some hardly dreamed of before the war—were now considered concrete and feasible new projects.

Even more important was the company's newfound sense of determination and willingness to compete head-on—to carve out new markets or substantially new positions in existing ones. Optical glass, for instance, was deemed to offer "an extremely interesting possibility" even though any entry into that field would bring Corning in direct competition with American Optical and Bausch & Lomb, among others. In view of its new process developments, the company was in a position "to establish a foothold in the postwar market for optical blanks as a result of wartime developments in optical glass manufacture at Corning" and was seriously considering doing just that.[37]

Accompanying this measured approach to planning was a general sense of confidence, bolstered by a new awareness of Corning's relative place in a domain (research and development) that the nation was coming to value as never before. As one executive noted,

> [I]f anyone doubted "Corning Means Research in Glass," such doubt has been erased by the wartime requirements placed on our laboratory and production organizations. Countless projects have been solved for the various agencies of the Government. Corning possessed the largest technical staff of any [glass] company. Corning had built its reputation on doing in glass that which others could not do. Naturally then, in this most scientific of all wars, the Government turned to us for vital and new products.[38]

Despite the heady anticipation, Corning's planners did not pretend that the war experience, and especially the direct and indirect involvement with the government as customer, had been an unalloyed blessing. Sullivan, for example, found himself torn between satisfaction with Corning's accomplishments and resentment at the government's power to disrupt his carefully laid out research program. "Scarcely a day went by," he later reflected, "without our receiving a delegation from the armed forces or from a manufacturer for the armed forces, and this required the time of our top development men. . . . Scarcely a mail went out without a letter answering some inquiry as to the use of glass."[39] Others noted that "war needs have meant . . . that much of our know-how has been given to competitors or to other firms engaged in war activities."[40] Such reluctant technology transfer had included strengthening, sealing, and other techniques, as well as specific formulae, all of which the government, under wartime powers, had ordered to be divulged to other manufacturers.

Back to Business

For Corning's management the prospect of demobilization was daunting but nonetheless eagerly anticipated. Workforce dislocation, supply problems, arrears in maintenance, and gaps in technical capability were all recognized but, it was hoped, balanced by opportunities. Like a select few other companies, Corning had invested heavily in fundamental research before the war, and many wartime projects had served to test the feasibility of this prewar work. Like these companies, Corning sat atop a store of accumulated knowledge that had been significantly augmented by new-found know-how during the war. Furthermore, while Corning's task was great, it was hardly on a par with the about-face that conversion from tanks to automobiles represented for a company like Ford. For Corning, demobilization meant modifying products for civilian markets, not abandoning most of them altogether.

Still, the new environment posed a number of challenges and risks, chief of which was the need to expand even while closing the yawning production gap between where the company was and where it needed to be to compete with low-cost producers in the postwar world. As early as 1943, Corning had made plans to spend more than $6 million on ten different plants. New competition motivated this experience. In areas where Corning had been unable to meet demand, such as scientific apparatus and coffeemakers, new entrants had found a foothold. Where customers or dealers had been disaffected, they had embraced new competitors whether they were glass companies or in competing materials businesses. The new government-created aluminum producers, Reynolds and Kaiser in particular, were busy creating new markets for themselves, and plastics, which had also been given a boost as a wartime substitute material, was a threat of unknown extent.[41]

In order to meet the postwar need for increasing mechanization, Corning had to improve its in-house machine development. Previously the company's most sophisticated equipment had actually been developed in concert with other members of the industry, often under the rubric of the Hartford-Empire Machine Company. The era of such cozy cooperation was clearly at an end, and even before the war was over, a new machine research facility, reporting to research, had been created with Jim Giffen at its head. A man of equal parts mechanical genius and asperity, Giffen would play a crucial role in Corning's push to meet the growth in the postwar television market.

Both of Corning's major wartime efforts, optical glass work and CRT production for radar, led to postwar military contracts, but such projects were not the most important inheritors of their respective technologies in terms of commercial potential: for Corning, radar grew into television, and military optical glass demand was dwarfed by the company's ophthalmic business. These examples point to one of the most important facts about Corning's war effort: while some companies had used the war to transform themselves into permanent defense contractors, Corning had not. Instead it found ways to parlay wartime work into a new source of commercial opportunity in the civilian sector.

The Limits of Foresight

Even the most foresightful planner could not have predicted the course of the Cold War that was coming in the late 1940s and early 1950s. Few but the most diehard cynics would have anticipated another war in less than a decade, and even they would have been hard-pressed to foretell the bomb and the creation of the permanent wartime economy with a voracious appetite for military hardware that marked the new era. The rise of consumerism was seen by some, but no one at Corning supposed that pent-up demand for television could suck black-and-white televisions into households at a rate entirely unprecedented in the history of capitalism.

In fact the size and shape of television demand was particularly uncertain. Though Corning was well aware that it would have to scale up television bulb production facilities, did this mean doubling its current capacity in Charleroi? Or did it perhaps mean combining television with sealed beam headlamps and moving it all into a new facility under the Bulb and Tubing Division? The real fear underlying all these calculations was a concern that the substitution of metal for glass in vacuum tubes, a dangerous postwar trend, would overtake Corning in this market as well.

In a very few years economic developments would undermine some of the basic assumptions upon which Corning's planning had been based. The company's best guess had been that the postwar period would see a shrunken military effort and a consumption pattern for consumer goods that fell somewhere between the boom days of the late 1920s and the terribly depressed demand of the 1930s. Instead, based on a blend of New Deal philosophy and wartime experience, policy makers chose to stimulate demand with a combination of defense spending and mass consumerism.[42] Finally, no one foresaw the effect that a war believed to have been won by scientists could have on virtually every technology-related endeavor in the country for the next quarter century or more.

Focus on Television Bulbs

As the electronics industry emerged from the war, unwelcome attention focused on Corning's ability to produce CRTs as a potential serious bottleneck in the projected television expansion. This threatened to be a black eye for the company, for failure to meet the industry's needs could lead not only to lost sales but to loss of the business altogether. Meeting the challenge, however, would require overcoming significant technical problems and making capital investments so massive that should the venture fail the company's financial viability would be in question. Wartime production of radar bulbs under government contract had given Corning a lead, but it was not the only contestant, and winning was by no means assured.

As shortages of technical manpower became front page news, Corning struggled to dig itself out of a hole. In 1946 A Factory was facing its largest ever backlog, the Bradford factory was coping with conversion from wartime to peacetime electronics orders without adequate engineering support, and production of the new television bulb business, recently moved from Charleroi back to Corning to be near headquarters' concentration of engineering expertise, was having serious problems. Yields of CRTs were very low, as few bulbs manufactured using the current flame sealing method seemed to be able to hold a vacuum.[43]

In the face of this, William Decker, Corning's new president and former head of its electronics business, committed the company to doing whatever it took to move on top in television and to stay there. To some extent he must have been nerved by the collective memory of Corning's previous successes not only with CRTs but also with lightbulbs, which had also experienced spikes in demand. Nevertheless, neither of these experiences required risking the company or putting on the back burner peacetime projects already under way, like optical glass or skillets. Television had not even been on the list of products planned for in late 1944. But Decker took the view that television not only merited but also required investing in advance of demand, and he resolved to throw at it virtually every technical resource Corning had at its disposal, as well as most of its financial ones.

This advertisement showing bell-shaped cathode ray tubes mass-produced by Corning for military radar appeared in major news and business magazines in October and November, 1945. It urged prospective customers to consider glass, this versatile engineering material with "ever increasing possibilities," as a possible missing link in their new production plans. In fact, the impression the advertisement conveyed—of easy links between television and radar—was misleading. Television bulb production involved huge amounts of additional development in manufacturing processes for black and white, and a major research effort on glass compositions and sealing for color.

Decker had good reason to believe his company could rise to this occasion. Where Corning had once been a bit player in an industry dominated by the likes of such giants as RCA and GE, it was now the preeminent producer of CRT enclosures. Furthermore, despite wartime manpower shortages, Corning's R&D staff had grown from 190 to 300 people, and, along with any number of experienced line workers, represented the single greatest concentration of bulb-working expertise in the world. On the other hand, neither Decker nor anyone else could at that time fully appreciate how heavy the challenge would ultimately become.

The problem did not lie in the technical differences between CRTs suitable for radar and those suitable for television but in the problem of adapting the production process to whole new glass compositions. Codes 7720, 7740, and 0120, all leaded glasses, had been utilized for wartime production of radar tubes for the simple reason that "the urgency [of wartime needs] did not permit the luxury of developing a special glass."[44] The company knew full well, however, that the extremely heavy bulbs installed on battleships would not be feasible in a set meant for the average American home. Methods of construction that had produced acceptable volumes and qualities of lead glass for seven-inch radar CRTs would require a significant retooling when applied to a non-leaded CRT with a twelve-inch diameter, not to mention the challenges that would shortly come in transforming the circular radar scope into the rectangular television screen. In short, radically new processes and formulations were required to meet the demands of the postwar economy, and at least part of this Corning knew at the outset.[45]

Yet Corning did not anticipate the problems posed by the sheer quantity of production. Corning had manufactured something over 3 million CRTs between 1938 and 1945; by 1948 black-and-white sets were selling at over a million a year, and by 1953, the year it began production of bulbs for color television, Corning had produced many times that number.[46] The company's bulb production lines were largely mechanized by 1947, but mechanization alone did not allow it to step up production so drastically. An entire series of further technical improvements (described further in chapter 7), had been required, and that, in turn, had meant hiring in one of the most competitive markets for R&D personnel ever.

The Rise and Fall of Edward U. Condon

Decker's bold move made Corning's staffing problems worse in R&D. Jesse Littleton, writing in the first postwar *R&D Annual Report*, lamented the almost total diversion of the research program into television work and highlighted both the numbers of key researchers lost during the war and the likelihood that they would never return. Gone with them was a wealth of accumulated and irreplaceable Corning know-how.

The company made little effort to recruit high-level people immediately following the war, but by the end of the decade a number of key research and engineering posts stood empty. At a time when high-paying jobs in quasi-academic surroundings could be had in some of the most appealing locations in the country, it was hard to get R&D personnel to even consider joining an organization so clearly focused on one major applied program: television bulb development. Then there was the seemingly insuperable problem of Corning itself, with its grimy, generally unattractive location. Decker turned his attention to the latter problem, seeking to clean up the locale and to import cultural events from New York City, as well as arranging educational opportunities at nearby Cornell University. But it was Littleton, Corning's senior physicist who had been holding the fort in the laboratory after the war, who hit on the one factor that could help Corning overcome its handicaps: the reestablishment of outstanding intellectual and organizational leadership. He proposed hiring eminent physicist Edward U. Condon. The company did this as part of its recommitment to a mixed R&D program (25 percent of the research was *labeled* fundamental). Nowhere would the consequences of Corning's independent postwar stance, or the difficulties of maintaining it, be as clearly spelled out as in Corning's experience with its new director of research and development.[47]

Condon was a celebrated but controversial figure in postwar Washington. He had spent the war on loan from Westinghouse to the government, first at the radiation laboratory and then at the Manhattan Project. For a short time he had been Oppenheimer's second in command at Los Alamos. Like his more celebrated colleague, he had later been branded a security threat by rightist elements in the congress. Following the war, Condon became director of the National Bureau of Standards. An outspoken advocate of internationalism and the open sharing of nuclear "secrets," Condon then became the target of the House Un-American Activities Committee, which in 1948 declared him "one of the weakest links in our atomic security." Condon weathered this initial charge, but a second such attack forced him out of public service. He announced both his resignation from the NBS and his intention to join Corning on August 10, 1951. The atmosphere in the nation's capital had grown increasingly ugly since the first Soviet atomic bomb detonation, and Corning's offer of a position represented a welcome change of scene.

Corning, long accustomed to adopting government scientists and more than comfortable with mavericks as long as they were talented, welcomed Condon with open arms. His experiences at the heart of the new military/scientific order, his standing in the research community, and his own scientific abilities as a nuclear physicist all recommended him to the job. It was one he was to perform brilliantly. Condon swiftly demonstrated his ability to articulate a research philosophy to upper management; to represent and link Corning to the broader research environment; to analyze and react to developments in the political, scientific, and industrial spheres; and to monitor and contribute to the day-to-day work of his research colleagues. Corning treasured Condon but lacked the power, in the changed postwar political environment, to provide him with the kind of safe haven that had sheltered Arthur Day after World War I.

Condon had come to Corning with his governmental security clearance intact: the House committee's charges had been mostly innuendo and their "investigations" had never uncovered material sufficient to warrant revocation of Condon's clearance. Condon was a popular figure in the scientific community, even newly elected as head of the American Association for the Advancement of Science, and President Truman had publicly exonerated him, warning of the evil that irresponsible charges could do to a valuable reputation and career.[48] Two years after leaving the NBS, however, Condon lost his cleared status automatically and, as Corning was involved with classified research, applied to have his clearance reinstated. He was cleared for access by the Eastern Industrial Security Board in June 1954, but when news of the board's action reached the Washington papers in October 1954, the

Secretary of the Navy personally revoked Condon's Q clearance. Vice President Richard Nixon claimed credit for the secretary's action, which gives some sense of the forces aligned against Corning's chief scientist. Condon appeared ready to fight these charges as he had the others, but late in the year he declared that he was, after all, "unwilling to continue a potentially indefinite series of reviews and re-reviews," especially with no guarantee of success.

The matter of Condon's revoked security clearance left Corning in an awkward spot: its director of R&D was no longer able to direct, or even to know of, some of his own research projects. Though classified research was a small part of the company's total R&D activity, the position was clearly untenable. The immediate issue was resolved by Condon's resignation—likely his suggestion and decision—late in 1954, but a larger problem remained: Corning, still inclined to think of Washington and its politics as safely distant, was obviously wrong in that assumption, perhaps dangerously so. Sullivan had been distressed at the ability of the federal authorities to alter Corning's research agenda; he must have been even more disturbed to learn that they could determine the company's research leadership.

THE ACTIVE PERIPHERY, 1954–1963

While the Condon incident served as a reminder of Washington's growing power and its interest in Corning's activities, it was just that: a reminder. Corning had had previous notice, during the war and in postwar military contracts, that its mastery of glass technology guaranteed it a place in the looming military-industrial complex. In addition, the authorities could and undoubtedly did speak directly to the uppermost levels of corporate management.

Establishing a position on the periphery of this complex was a matter of trial and error, and some of those errors were significant. At the government's behest, Corning became engaged in more than one multimillion-dollar disaster and not all of the research tasks it accepted advanced it along the paths demarcated by its larger R&D agenda. On the whole, however, it was spared the worst pathologies afflicting some companies engaged in military work. In particular, it managed to avoid one of the biggest pitfalls: the creation of an internal gap between commercial work and government (and in particular, military) projects. This phenomenon, which at some companies resulted in parallel noncommunicating R&D structures, different accounting systems, and even separate assembly lines, was a common result of the military's demand for secrecy, ultra-high performance, and ultra-high reliability, combined with a tolerance for ultra-high costs; commercial work generally operated under a different set of rules.

A number of factors helped Corning avoid these problems, at least in part. First, it never allowed government contracts to grow beyond a small fraction of its sales or even of its R&D funds, and it took the role of prime supplier only where it was in essence the sole feasible source. As a materials company, it rarely found itself with a product or method that was not of some relevance to other company endeavors and to the work of other manufacturers. While materials was not one of the sectors selected for direct intensive federal funding, many of the critical areas that were selected— including electronic devices, communications, instruments, optical components, and nuclear devices—drew on Corning's expertise in some way. The company also remained unfailingly cautious about accepting public money for research and testified against the government's attempts to secure title to patents generated with federal research funds.

Furthermore, Corning's research tradition and its intimate culture had long been opposed to secrecy, increasingly a defining condition of military work. Arthur Day had been an outspoken enemy of craft secrets, noting that they were "generally a cloak to cover ignorance rather than great wisdom." Glassmaking, he declared, had been too long "dominated by secret formulas and tricks of personal experience which followed no law and formed a part of no system of generalization." It was up to science, and Corning's scientists in particular, to make that tacit knowledge explicit.[49]

In terms of Corning's research efforts, perhaps the most important factor working to maintain coherence between military and commercial research was the laboratory's general avoidance of overspecialization among its employees. With so few people covering such a broad spectrum of problems, versatility was a necessity. A firm believer in the importance of a communal approach to research, Condon, while still director of R&D,

reinforced this policy during a period of considerable growth in the number of lab personnel. He initiated regular programs of research presentations "to be attended by the managers and supervisors of the research staff, and such other members of the staff who have a direct interest in the particular topic under discussion that day" and in general worked to prevent excessive specialization among Corning's researchers.[50] A notably accessible manager, he conducted lengthy discussions with junior researchers about the state of their work, whether or not they were fellow physicists, a practice that set a cooperative tone throughout the company's R&D enterprise. His university relations program further contributed to this open atmosphere by bringing scientists from academia to work at Corning and share in its research.

Condon was not, however, trying to build a research structure that could operate in isolation from the growing R&D activities of the federal government. He, perhaps more clearly than anyone else at Corning, recognized the increasing importance of those efforts for the work of private research organizations. While director of the labs, he saw to it that Corning took on several additional projects for the military, including work on ultrasonic delay lines, one of the most sensitive technologies of its time.

Postwar Electronics and the Military

Nowhere was the complexity of Corning's relationship with the military better illustrated than in the company's ultimately unsuccessful attempt to establish itself in the electronics industry. Corning's prewar sales of vacuum tubes had translated into some electronics work during the war, and that, in the immediate postwar period, had led the company to become a supplier of high-performance glass tin oxide resistors and glass dielectric capacitors, in particular. (It also led eventually to a foray into integrated circuits, as recounted in chapter 5.) These devices were fairly exotic: more reliable, more high-performance, and much more expensive than standard resistors and capacitors; in short, of interest to the military and few if any others.

Government contracts also moved Corning into completely new product lines or, in at least one instance, resulted in Corning reviving a dormant technology. This latter example was a result of the military's need for help with the DEW (Distant Early Warning) line, a series of radar installations built across the far northern reaches of Canada as a detection system for incoming Soviet ICBMs. This system relied on ultrasonic delay lines, devices that acted as a sort of crude information storage system, allowing the radar operator to compare sequential scans. The military was performing this trick with mercury-filled tubes, a hazardous and difficult solution (especially given the arctic environment) that, among other things, made it all but impossible to build an airborne system.

Chuck Lucy, then employed by the U.S. Naval Air Development Center, was searching for a better approach, and thought fused silica, which had been brought to his attention in the course of a patent review, might serve.[51] The patent of interest dealt with Franklin Hyde's work on vapor deposition back in the 1930s, and that brought Lucy to Corning. After a short while spent working as the navy's go-between on the project, Corning, which recognized the importance of the project, invited him to reverse positions, offering to hire him as their liaison with the navy. In early 1952 he accepted that offer.

The proposal had originated with John Carter, a former air force procurement officer who was working in Corning's New Products Division. As Lucy recalled, Carter "knew the military game quite well, and also had quite an entrepreneurial outlook towards business."[52] Carter was supported in this by Condon himself, who interviewed Lucy and sponsored the project, assigning him to work with Fred Bickford and George Mann. The work itself involved both materials research and device development. The former was, of course, very much Corning's bailiwick, and, crucially, established the groundwork for optical waveguides. Corning retained the intellectual property rights and then applied that knowledge to the creation of the delay line itself. This, the deliverable part of the project, involved government-purchased electronics facilities and further support, but the device itself, as well as the technology going into its construction, was owned by the military.

This demarcation between material and device appears to have satisfied any qualms Corning may have had about intellectual property, but it had a hidden and ironic cost. While the project on the whole represented a step toward manufacturing complicated devices and was by far the most sophisticated electronics work the company had ever done, the contractual arrangements helped reinforce Corning's bias against producing such devices (much less the systems of which they were a part) by associating them with an area of intellectual property that was harder to protect. As one consultant diagrammed it for the company, Corning concerned itself primarily with the bottom of the manufacturing pyramid, materials, while largely ignoring opportunities to produce components, equipment (or devices), and systems that rested on that base.[53] Electronics was something of an exception—Corning was producing components or even, as was the case with delay lines, devices—but, as Wakeman and others repeatedly asserted, Corning had to "set a goal of moving toward end products [meaning] `systems' as defined in some way."[54] The company resisted this in part because greater military aid was required to develop more sophisticated devices, and that aid represented a threat to Corning's intellectual property.

By the 1960s at least half of Corning's electronics output was purchased by the military or military contractors. Quite aside from any intellectual property issues, as one report noted, "the enormous sums the government is pouring into electronic research" (much of which went to swell competitors' R&D budgets) had the effect of driving the pace of innovation to levels totally unknown within other parts of the company.[55] Although Corning invested significant sums in electronics R&D, it failed to make the wholehearted commitment required to keep up, partly because such a commitment absolutely required a closer relationship with the military, and here, as elsewhere, Corning sought to limit, not enhance, that connection.

Cold War Secrecy

Corning's work on delay lines revived the technology of fused silica and proved again that the company could be counted on to contribute to (if not volunteer itself for) ultra-high priority efforts. Both this reminder and the technology itself led to another top secret project of the Cold War era: the development of U-2 plane and spy satellite optics. These systems were dependent on extremely precise lenses and mirrors, and Corning's capabilities not only with fused silica but with even lower expansion materials in general (not to mention mirrors specifically) meant that it was all but certain to be conscripted for this effort.

Production of the delay lines had ended up in the Bradford plant; manufacturing for satellite optics was lodged there as well. The process, however, was highly polluting: the vapor deposition itself produced hydrochloric acid in gaseous form. Bradford was a rural but by no means unpopulated part of Pennsylvania. Neighbors complained of the damaging effect on surrounding trees and other greenery, and in particular the very visible damage to a nearby cemetery. Furthermore, the government needed quite a lot of mirrors and other parts, more than the Bradford facility could supply. As Tom MacAvoy, later Corning's president and then vice chairman recalled,

> The volume started to build up like crazy because the probability of getting
> the thing off from Vandenberg [Air Force Base, where they were launched]
> was maybe one in four. Once you got it off, the probability of insertion into
> orbit was one in ten. So the demand for mirrors was fantastic. But the first
> couple that they got to work, they were reading Russian newspapers from
> outer space! They were so turned on by the results that they were pushing
> us like crazy.

An unfortunate side effect of the increased activity was an "enormous mushroom cloud" of hydrochloric acid fumes. With no time to rework the process to eliminate the pollutants, Corning dealt with the problem by moving it: "We bought a humongous tract up in the northern woods [of New York State] up in Canton. Canton is totally surrounded by woods, as far as the eye can see. We built the plant up there. We built it there for two reasons: Security, the government was paranoid about security, understandably, and the second was because of the fallout, pollution."[56] Canton is the closest Corning ever came to establishing a secure cell of the sort common among defense contractors, but even on satellite work, as sensitive as any project Corning was ever involved with, the motivation was at best mixed. The company undoubtedly complied with government secrecy requirements (anyone seeking documentation of these matters will be disappointed; there is a lacuna in the record that speaks volumes) but had previously made do with specially secured rooms or areas in otherwise not particularly restricted operations.

Over time, all work of this sort, whether for military or commercial markets, came to be located at Canton. (Mirror work previously done at the Erwin plant, for example, was moved up there when Celcor came in.) Canton's physical isolation near the Canadian border meant that intercourse between it and Corning was naturally limited, and, in a company that enjoyed extraordinary loyalty in its employees, Canton stood out as an enduring subculture of its own. It was not so much classification as this distance, both physical and cultural, that kept Canton separate from the rest of the company. This distance did not, however, prevent all technical flow from one to the other, allowing Canton, even as it focused largely on government work, to serve as a sort of reservoir from which important commercial technologies would later be drawn.

New Uses for Optical

With delay lines, Corning was working from a relatively small and totally unused technical base: the process of vapor deposition. Optical glass, on the other hand, tapped into a large number of crucial Corning technologies. Corning's abilities in continuous melting represented the cutting edge in optical glass production technology in the 1940s. For a short time the company considered a major commercial effort in the field but did not make any overtures to the military for work to replace wartime contracts from Parkersburg. The demands of the CRT market, combined with Decker's strategic assessment of television's importance, forced it to focus on that single obsessive undertaking and the commercial possibilities of optical were dropped. The military, however, was not prepared to see a repeat of the interwar neglect of optical glass, and the air force in particular had plans for Corning's technology.

Optical glass work had in the past largely been a matter of preparing material for the relatively small lenses used in various optical instruments. Aircraft development, however, required optically pure disks several *feet* in diameter for use with aerial camera lenses and as wind tunnel windows. For these early projects, accomplished in the late 1940s, Corning already possessed all of the necessary techniques: "all it took was patience and care" to make very large castings, the largest of which would measure fifty-two inches in diameter and eight inches in thickness.[57] Manufactured at the Corning optical plant in the late 1940s, these enormous pieces of almost perfectly clear glass were installed in wind tunnels.

But air force demands, in keeping with the trend in military hardware, grew more exacting with time, and when it called for help with a second program of massive optical development it was apparent that taking the contract would require research time as well as already extant production expertise. Corning chose to do this work primarily because it was clear no other company could, but also because it saw it as a way to "stretch" technical goals, thereby furthering research programs that would otherwise be left in limbo as television stormed on. This is perhaps the earliest example of Corning using military work as a means of pushing technological development it would otherwise have let lie. Though the company remained leery of accepting public funds for R&D, its ability to demarcate between basic technologies associated with the material itself and the specific product the military wanted allowed it to negotiate a satisfactory position.

In its bid for this contract, Corning cited six examples of its optical glass experience, of which five were clearly of a military nature, and the sixth— fourteen-by three-inch discs for "interferometer use"—was likely military in origin as well. The proposal also mentioned Corning's nascent attempts to develop radiation-proof windows for "nuclear research work." Such antecedents proved relevant: Corning met air force demands for optical purity primarily by refining its stirrer technology under the guidance of C. F. DeVoe and R. C. Cleveland. Interestingly, the original proposal to the Air Force stated that "stirrers of the type currently in use would presumably be used in such [a] furnace [for melting the glass to be used in Massive I] and would be modified as necessary for use in the delivery system," suggesting that researchers at Corning had already put some thought into how to improve their optical glass production processes; as always, Corning was happiest working for the military when such projects advanced the company's already established research goals.[58]

The air force was apparently pleased with the results: officers from Wright-Patterson returned in the mid-1960s with a new request. The military was just beginning to investigate the possibility of satellite surveillance, a high-tech endeavor that was likely to require optical elements "even more homogeneous than those of Massive I by about one decimal point, and in a volume 8 times larger."[59] Though air force requirements were more demanding, Corning was also more experienced. "For a decade," the proposal boasted, "Corning Glass Works has produced optical glass at Harrodsburg, Kentucky, of a quality adequate for ophthalmic glass, radiation shielding windows, lens blanks, and massive optics requiring 2×10^{-5} refractive index homogeneity." This new program, though challenging, was believed to be of a piece with that work.[60] A team was assembled and air force specifications met in the R&D stage, but no production contract was forthcoming: "The [air force] optical designers learned how to do it with mirrors."[61] The company could not have mourned this loss for too long: the R&D had been paid for, related applications abounded, and Corning was still the preeminent source for this technology. Indeed, when in 1968 the Air Force Systems Command established "a new program aimed at production and inventory of high quality optical glass blanks of twenty-eight different compositions" Corning was still the only American company capable of undertaking such work.[62]

Yet what had kept the company's hand in this business, far more than an occasional military contract, was its interest in ophthalmics. Corning's wartime peak in optical sales had come in 1945 and amounted to almost $700,000. With the cancellation of military supply contracts, that figure dropped in the following year to just over $200,000. By 1948, however, optical glass sales had returned to and exceeded wartime levels; that year saw Corning break the $1 million mark.[63] The difference lay in its ophthalmics work.

Corning began production of bifocal eyeglass buttons (the blanks from which lenses are ground) in June 1946, but the decision to do so had been made during the war, when company planners realized how powerful their new continuous melting technology was. A 1944 company memo notes:

Some feelers have been put out in an effort to find out whether we can use the knowledge we have gained in optical glass manufacture to enter the ophthalmic field (spectacle lens blanks). From the standpoint of volume, the business is very attractive; that is, 20% of the normal peacetime market for blanks would be a million dollar business. Another enticing feature of this business is the prestige value which attaches itself to manufacture of glass for spectacle lenses and other optical equipment.[64]

What Corning's planners did not recognize at the time was the wide range of specific formulas necessary to service the market: process knowledge alone would not be enough. The task of developing some fifty formulas for the eyeglass industry fell to William Armistead, who had joined the company in 1941. Building on Gage's work, he systematically developed compositions to cover the entire range of glasses needed for ophthalmic ware. That task took about six years, at the end of which production was moved to the Harrodsburg, Kentucky plant. Opened in 1952, Harrodsburg was the inheritor of Main Plant's wartime projects and became a steady source of commercial revenue.[65]

From Radomes to Roasting Pans

The discovery, in the mid-1950s, of a new class of materials by Corning researchers provided another opportunity to solve a problem for the military and another example of the company's habit of seeking commercial applications as well as military ones. These materials, called glass-ceramics (and trademarked by Corning as Pyroceram), were markedly rugged, had very low coefficients of thermal expansion, and were very good at transmitting certain sorts of radiation. All three of these characteristics recommended glass ceramics to the military, which had something of a standing order for materials of that sort. A series of lucrative contracts resulted, but instead of resting on these financial laurels, the company initiated an entirely separate development project specifically aimed at finding a commercial use for the new material. That effort, which produced Corning Ware, was spectacularly successful, and once again the company found the commercial route to sales far more lucrative than the military one. The military work, however, moved more quickly.

The Johns Hopkins Applied Physics Laboratory (APL) was the first to suggest that Pyroceram might be useful for radomes—electromagnetic "windows" that allow missiles in flight to receive and transmit control and telemetry signals. Under contract to the U.S. Navy for development of Terrier and Tartar missiles, the APL was seeking materials capable of handling supersonic rain erosion and extreme thermal shock while maintaining radar-transmitting capabilities. In fact, the navy had already approached Corning seeking a glass that could be made into a nosecone while retaining the characteristics of a radome (i.e., transparency to the desired signals). The samples Corning was able to supply, however, were insufficiently rain resistant, and this fact was known to the laboratory staff. The hardness of glass ceramic, many times that of most glass formulations, must have suggested its suitability for the navy's needs.[66]

As usual, simply having the right material did not translate into being on the verge of a successful product. Nosecones were a difficult shape to cast,

This advertisement for Pyroceram, "A new wide-range basic material," appeared in both the popular and business press. In addition to celebrating a feat of research, it asked the public to provide suggestions for its application. Response to this request was so encouraging that the company was misled into thinking it could rely more heavily on an arms-length approach to customers instead of its traditional practice of co-invention with a lead customer.

and they had to be made out of a material with homogeneity levels approaching that of optical glass. By this point, however, Corning had answers to both of these challenges. The technique of centrifugal casting, well understood in terms of CRT production, was adapted to the cone shapes necessary for a missile nosecone, and the continuous melting first developed for optical glass made it possible to achieve high levels of homogeneity even for the smaller quantities needed to produce the critical test samples.

Supersonic missile radomes were (and are) a classic defense technology, marked by ultra-high performance requirements in terms of strength, resistance to heat shock, and especially transparency to microwave and other forms of radiation. Radomes made of code 9606 (a glass ceramic) and code 7941 (a multiformed fused silica) were used in a variety of missiles and rockets, including ones designed for reentry into the earth's atmosphere (i.e., ballistic missiles).[67] In 1958 alone contracts included APL and Convair (both Tartar), Hughes Aircraft (Falcon), China Lake (Sidewinder), Raytheon (Hawk and Sparrow), Douglas, Northrup, Bell Aircraft, and the Swedish Air Force (Svenska). Corning also worked closely with aviation electronics suppliers like Hughes and GE on these and other programs. By the end of 1963, Corning had sold at least 3,400 radomes, for a total of something over $8.5 million in sales.[68]

A chart from that year showing "historical performance data" for Corning's radome project demonstrates that Corning was able to supply these items at ever declining prices over time. The graph shows sales of 2 units at $10,000 a piece in 1957, 21 units at an average price of $6,500 in 1958, 39 units at $4,000 in 1959, and 428 at $2,000 in 1960. This form of pricing, often known as learning curve or experience curve pricing, was commonly associated with aircraft production and required the company to approach cost reduction in a systematic way, relying on learning from accumulated production in a multitude of ways. Corning mastered this approach for radome production but did not apply it to its commercial lines, an opportunity that, with hindsight, was unwisely overlooked, especially in regard to color TV (see chapter 7).

Having established the material's usefulness to the military, Corning researchers attempted to broaden Pyroceram's appeal. The announcement of the existence of glass ceramics had prompted "10,000" or so requests for information, each associated with a commercial possibility; of these, *"none were found to be of any significant or lasting commercial interest."*[69] At various points the company experimented with glass-ceramic versions of "brake shoes, architectural curtain walls, high-temperature ball bearings, household cooking ware of all types of stove and serving service, godet wheels, pump parts, thread guides, and even piston heads for internal combustion engines."[70] Major efforts were undertaken to develop a glass-ceramic stovetop (the so-called counter that cooks) and miniature capacitors, but the one failed in the marketplace and the other ultimately led to Signetics, which was no success. All of these failures were more than matched by the one enormous success, the consumer product Corning Ware, which by 1965 was the best-selling single line of housewares in America.

Sales of Pyrex, Corning's long-standing consumer staple, had sagged after the war. Waterman, who had recently been hired as the head of the consumer products division, was known to be actively searching for Pyrex's replacement; in this sense, Corning Ware was created, like Pyroceram radomes, in response to a standing order from upper management. Pyroceram recommended itself for the job because it combined a minimal coefficient of expansion (i.e., the ability to withstand temperature extremes) and great strength with relatively low production costs. Unlike radomes, however, the target market for Corning Ware required a good deal of education. Waterman's image of the problem his salesmen faced was a housewife

> who believes she owns all the pots and pans and serving dishes she needs, who doesn't know a radome from a radiator, who thinks of missiles only in terms of doom and destruction, who has become wary of product claims—and figure out how you are going to get her to plunk down twelve dollars and ninety-five cents for a cooking-serving dish she doesn't even know exists![71]

Oddly, it was precisely this connection with missiles that proved among the most popular advertising claims associated with Corning's newest consumer line. The centerpiece of the product launch was a thirteen-minute film titled *American Women—Partners in Research* featuring shots of rockets

Playing on Space Age themes and the use of Pyroceram in missile nosecones, Corning Ware was often pictured with a rocket in the background. Ironically, though the brand was developed as a high technology ovenware able to go from refrigerator to oven to table, the kitchen proved a harsher environment than space for the epoxies that held the popular Corning Ware percolators together. Corning recalled the percolators in 1975.

streaming away from their gantries. "Corning Ware," the print ads declared, was "made of an astounding new missile material, Pyroceram—for all its beauty, it can't crack for heat or cold."[72] The assumption the consumer was expected to make was that if the material could handle the rigors of atmospheric flight, it would have no difficulty with the average kitchen. More generally, it was hoped that the prestige of military high technology would rub off on its more down-to-earth counterpart.

In light of this, it is notable that the technical achievements associated with the production of Corning Ware were greater than those generated in the process of learning how to produce an acceptable missile radome. "Ceramming," or partially crystallizing the glass, usually involves some shrinkage in the product, a change in volume that was felt more keenly in smaller pieces (roasting pans) than in larger ones (radomes). Early attempts to crystallize cookware produced surrealist vignettes, with semimelted pots and pans sagging in response to the heat of the ceramming process. And, as always, mass production brought its own challenges: demand for Corning Ware quickly outstripped supply, a felicitous but difficult problem that was solved by Jim Giffen's invention of the so-called Hub Machine. It is hard to say precisely what is high tech and what low, but on balance, *more* tech was required for the successful production of commercial products than for military ones.

Massive Optics: Failure in the Postwar Period

It would be misleading to give the impression that Corning's work for the military involved only a continuous stream of success stories and highly profitable commercial spin-offs. The company did have a number of flops, products that could not find a market because they were either unable to meet a technical challenge or able to do so but at too great a cost; even the military must sometimes work within a budget. While Corning's R&D capabilities had been greatly augmented both during and after the war, there remained tasks beyond its abilities; in the postwar period the company's reach sometimes exceeded its grasp. Corning's seven-year long frustration with "massive glass" provides an excellent example of a major R&D effort that ended in failure, one that we will detail below. This failure cost Corning little more than some unreimbursed research funds. Its foray into products for the nuclear power industry, by comparison, took a much greater toll, including the failed joint venture Sylcor (discussed in chapter 5).

The term "massive glass" refers to very large glass castings intended for use as part of a deep-sea or "hydrospace" system. The company's interest in massive glass appears to have been sparked by a materials engineer from the Naval Ordnance Laboratory, who visited Corning in 1961.[73] Glass was thought to be ideal for this application as it is tremendously strong, particularly under compressive pressures of the sort to be found in the ocean depths. Furthermore, many glass compositions are extremely resistant to salt water corrosion and are far less prone to attack by marine organisms than most types of metal.

Corning continued to work with the ordnance research laboratory for some time, and by 1968 had developed a range of hydrospace products. As with massive optics, the most immediate problem was not size. Rather, the essential challenge in manufacturing massive glass for hydrospace exploration would be one of surface quality: to cast pieces that were as nearly flawless (and thus as strong) as possible and, where necessary, to seal those pieces as perfectly as could be managed. By 1968, Corning could boast of having "demonstrated the capability for forming and finishing glass hemispheres up to 56" in diameter," and Corning researchers felt it was possible "to produce 6' to 10' hemispheres" via sagging or pressing of ultralarge glass sheets.[74] Combined with electric sealing of the glass, the possibility of forming very large shapes was apparent. And, as with all glass, these pieces could also be chemically or thermally strengthened.

But the sheer size of these castings did pose at least two unique problems. First, statistically speaking, the probability of defects showing up in a casting six feet in diameter was so high that 100-percent shrinkage was a real possibility unless each piece were individually inspected and repaired. And second, though the compressive strength of glass is enormous, any significant surface flaw reduces that strength considerably; as a result, "handling of these massive pieces will require special care to avoid damage to the surfaces,"[75] and such handling would, obviously, be complicated by the size and weight of these castings.

The navy may well have been willing to work around these difficulties, but in addition, Corning noted, constructing hulls six feet in diameter would require specialized facilities, which would both raise the cost and time necessary for production. The half million dollar cost was probably less off-putting than the estimated four-year construction time, but in any case the navy chose not to take Corning up on this particular offer. A letter from Amory Houghton Jr. to Secretary of the Navy John Chafee in 1968 suggested that Corning had been encouraged to pin its expectations in massive glass on promised initiatives in naval research that never materialized. The reply, sent by Undersecretary Robert Frosch, stated once again a belief in the potential of massive glass but offered a reevaluation of program priorities only by and by. Even that potential was undermined by a series of tests performed by outside researchers that revealed serious difficulties with glass/metal interfaces, a necessity for almost any imaginable vehicle. With neither a perfect technical feat nor an aggressively priced product to offer, the company had to write off the project.

THE PRICE OF BEING ALOOF

By the mid-1960s Corning had ensconced itself on, and helped to define, the active periphery of the military-industrial complex: it continued to take government contracts as it felt best and carefully avoided further ventures of the sort represented by the Sylcor disaster. Nevertheless, Corning's relationship with the military was not, on the whole, cordial, nor did its executives easily recognize just how important a niche it filled. Chuck Lucy recalls being told that the company was a proverbial source of trouble for the army development labs in World War II: "We always said," one veteran of that organization informed him, "we had to fight three enemies: the Germans, the Japanese, and Corning Glass Works."[76] This antagonistic relationship was undoubtedly at least in part a product of Eugene Sullivan's resentment of what he perceived as a military takeover of his labs, but neither the end of the war nor Sullivan's retirement resolved it.

In 1958 Amory Houghton Jr. initiated a study of Corning's relationship with the federal government. Updated in 1963 at the behest of Mal Hunt and others, the report painted a troubling picture, one worth analyzing in detail. Defense spending was continuing to climb and government investment in R&D was now three times that of industry. Furthermore, the top 100 defense contractors were all huge companies taking between them almost three-quarters of federal defense contracts, with most of what was left going to small businesses which, as a group, were politically protected; "This," the report noted, "forecasts trouble for the middle-sized corporations."

As bad as the environment itself was, Corning's position in it was even worse. The report claimed that "serious attempts were made in the previous study, in this study, and frequently in the five intervening years to find other companies whose problems and products involving the Federal Government were "reasonably similar" to Corning's.... Lack of results leads us to honestly believe that Corning is unique."[77] The report also noted that "30 of our major customers [totaling some $90 million in sales] are among the top 100 suppliers to DOD and NASA" but that relations with these customers and with the government were far from cordial. Specifically, it recommended that the company "better define the types of government business we would readily accept or reject... [and] improve our techniques of rejecting undesirable patent or data clauses without embarrassing or irritating customers and the government." Yet even if Corning communicated perfectly with the defense establishment, the fact remained that it was a sole source supplier in an industry with an abhorrence of the dependency that created; this, the report noted, "will continue to be a thorn in our side" when dealing with the military and its contractors.

In fact, it was not until the 1980s that Corning managed to iron out its communications with the military. It did so by hiring Frank Kapper, a former adviser to the Joint Chiefs of Staff and a Pentagon intimate, to oversee all of the company's contacts with the military. The decision to bring in someone with these credentials was prompted by the Reagan-era arms buildup, a surge in defense spending that was marked by a greater permissiveness in terms of government title to intellectual property rights. To quote one Corning manager, previously the government's attitude had been "paid for by public funds and therefore, guys, it belongs to the public." With Reagan, the perception was that "things have since changed associated with government funding. You can end up negotiating with the government and get rights to the technology."[78] In light of this, Corning hesitantly began to explore the possibility of increasing its percentage of government contracts.

Initially a part-time consultant, Kapper took a full-time position in response to a particularly bad flare-up between Corning and the Pentagon. General Abramson, a major figure in the Star Wars initiative, had publicly criticized Corning for, in Kapper's words, "not doing the quality job it should have."[79] This, for obvious reasons, stung, but only Kapper realized just how serious such an allegation could be: "This is a matter for the CEO and president to talk to General Abramson about because what you've just witnessed is somebody venting their spleen, either valid or otherwise, and you have to go challenge them face to face." Kapper was able to arrange a meeting at which it was discovered that Abramson's impression had been unduly influenced by a report written by a Corning competitor. This was followed by a visit to the Canton plant, and the discovery that, of the mirrors supplied to the Star Wars program, only Corning's met the military's requirements.

The Reagan era was, however, of limited duration, and while Kapper could smooth Corning's relationship with the military, he was not able to speed the company's planning. Ultimately, there was little change in the percentage of products being sold to the government but an apparent improvement in the handling of what sales there were. While having a professional dedicated to that issue undoubtedly helped, changes in the military's understanding of its own priority vis-à-vis the commercial economy likely also worked to bring it into sync with Corning's natural inclinations.

On the Edge of the Complex

Like any other contractor working with the postwar defense establishment, Corning was confronted with onerous secrecy, accounting, and other requirements, as well as the problem of the divergence between military priorities and commercial needs. It avoided the most dangerous pitfalls, especially those that involved raising internal barriers to the easy flow of information by carefully limiting its exposure to the military-industrial complex.[80]

A 1963 letter from Amory Houghton Jr., written in response to an inquiry by NASA head James Webb, shows how its policy toward government work had consolidated:

> Corning's sales for Government end use are currently running about 6% of total company sales. Of this amount 5% is to higher-tier contractors and 1% as a prime contractor. The greatest portion of our business is in standard commercial product lines and is obtained competitively on a firm-price basis. Last year only two-tenths of one per cent (0.2%) of our business was under cost-type contracts.
>
> It has long been the established policy of Corning Glass Works to limit the use of cost-type contracts and to quote wherever possible on a firm-price basis. We have adhered to this policy for long-term contracts, even though the inherent risk was recognized. It is our belief, based upon experience, that better results in product, price, and delivery are achieved when there is a self-imposed goal to be met.[81]

Houghton's explanation shows Corning's deliberate efforts to leverage its government connections at their most skillful. In a "permanent war economy" that had transformed many companies into permanent government dependencies, Corning was attentive and alert but not mobilized or controlled. Identified with no one particular government agency, it kept lines open to all of them. It did the important work on its own money. It chased no ambulances but accepted government projects that advanced its own aims. The few exceptions to these policies, such as the program-distorting massive glass, proved the merit of the general policy.

Corning paid a price for its independent stance toward the government, its unwillingness to dangle juicy new ideas in front of military program officers, its refusal to become dependent on public funds. This price was to be labeled aloof, even uncooperative. In communication with sources of funding, but not in any inner circle, it forfeited some of the critical access it needed to information and decision making, a gap that even the most assiduous government affairs office could not close. One casualty of its policy may well have been its electronics business, which never shook the laggard's position after the 1960s. But by guarding the integrity of its program and the character of its innovative culture, Corning was among the few hightech companies of the era that came through the formative years of the Cold War with its horizons expanded and its fundamental approach to innovation largely intact.

REINSTITUTIONALIZING R&D

TV, CORNING WARE, AND

THE SEARCH FOR BREAKTHROUGHS

> *Even with the most effective management guidance, the technical*
> *effort will not be productive without creative people. . . . These*
> *proven creators normally can be counted on to create over-and-over*
> *again, and are the key people of our organization.*
>
> —W. H. ARMISTEAD
> "THE FUTURE OF RESEARCH"[1]

THE EXPERIENCE of World War II changed Corning in many ways—its place on the national stage, the range of businesses it would engage in, and the kinds of problems it was capable of solving. It also paved the way for its major new business, television. Corning's president, Bill Decker, realized that television required an unprecedented concentration of technical resources and an immediate emphasis on achieving advanced production techniques. But he and other managers soon understood that longer-term technical efforts needed to be directed at more ambitious projects to provide other big business opportunities for Corning, repeatedly and on demand. This implied a new model of innovation appropriate to a larger, more visible, and more diversified company, and consistent with the most up-to-date thinking of the time. Recent wartime experiences offered such a model based on the atomic bomb and radar, which demonstrated what could be accomplished if massive resources were concentrated and mobilized.

After the war, new leaders took charge of Corning's technical organization with the goal of bringing it in line with the best of what was known outside the company. This meant constructing new self-contained R&D facilities, putting together and restructuring a more comprehensive technical organization, and hiring a new research staff. Underlying these steps was the by now nationally accepted notion of technological innovation as a "linear" progression beginning with a fundamental scientific breakthrough and more or less inevitably resulting in large-scale new businesses on the order of DuPont's nylon. These radical innovations were known in some venues as "blockbusters," or in Corning's term "home runs." The research component of this process patterned itself on the way radio was perceived to have emerged in a straight line from scientific work in the first half of the century.[2] Corning's leaders called this "pioneering research," and it was predicated on the objective of hiring exceptionally creative people and giving them the kind of environment and resources that would support their best efforts. E. U. Condon, one of the chief wizards in the wizards' war and Corning's research director for a brief period, put together the blueprint for this postwar research renaissance. But it was a group of younger people— men like Bill Armistead and his office mate, Don Stookey, and Jim Giffen, Corning's resident mechanical genius, who epitomized the new approach for Corning; their personalities shaped the evolving R&D organization.

This recast version of R&D grew up in the shadow of Corning's most demanding business to date. The television bulb business, for which Corning was a leading glass supplier, inevitably formed the context for all of Corning's other technology-related efforts. Black-and-white bulbs were already in production, and they required huge amounts of ongoing product development. Color, by contrast, was a planned research effort, though not a pioneering project, as Corning did not hold fundamental patents for it. Begun in 1951, the color program was charged with anticipating what OEM customers would want and supplying whatever that might be. This costly effort gave Corning a dominant position in color bulbs, but at the expense of a strategic vulnerability to its lead customer, RCA. The push to keep up with television also left the company with a depleted research arsenal at just the time when industrial research of a fundamental sort was coming to be regarded as the obligation of all patriotic enterprises in support of the Cold War.

This chapter covers Corning's attempt to support, and then replicate in business terms, its television bulb business. This attempt took the form of a series of pioneering projects, made possible by the rebuilding of its research staff and the consolidation of all its corporate technical efforts under one big organizational umbrella called the technical staffs. Compared to other companies that mounted similar corporate efforts, Corning's would have to be judged a qualified success: few of its projects proved to be dry holes, though several failed in their initial objectives. Nevertheless, the linear model of innovation beginning with a research breakthrough and ending in a new market eventually fell into disrepute at Corning, as it did nationally. Over time it isolated the technical organization from the rest of the company and from its customers, both historically fruitful sources of innovation at Corning. Another cause of this isolation was a growing estrangement between theoretically trained researchers and practical floor-level people, which even devices like pilot plants, or later the Process Research Center, could not overcome.

At its peak, pioneering innovation created a different climate of expectation for Corning's research staff. Franklin Hyde, the lone exploratory researcher, had been an anomaly in his time and had not been considered especially productive in a commercial sense for over five years; but the eventual success of his endeavors with silicone had led to great expectations for his successors. The norm of Corning's prewar organization had been Harrison Hood's "glass technologists together," but in the postwar era the ideal would be a creative individual like Donald Stookey.

CRACKING FAMILY SECRETS:
THE EARLY DAYS OF DONALD STOOKEY, 1940–1947

Stookey was the first Corning researcher to invent an entirely new family of glasses, a breakthrough on a par with the invention of borosilicate glasses. If others, like H. P. Gage had been networkers, establishing Corning's most reliable pattern for "hitting singles," Stookey was at the other end of the research spectrum, a lone explorer intrigued by the unknown. His work yielded Corning patents on photosensitive glasses, chemically machinable glasses, and glass ceramics, the last of Corning's greatest research home runs.

While others were inspired by ideas they gleaned from frequent contacts with customers and colleagues, Stookey worked partly on hunch and intuition about the behavior of atoms and ions.[3] Arthur Day's ideal for the Corning laboratory, the Kodak model combining researcher freedom with discipline, was designed to accommodate both types. Stookey's undeniable success as a glass inventor, or as he termed himself, a "pioneering researcher," showed just how well Corning had managed to achieve Day's intended middle way over the decades. By the time Stookey came along, in 1940, the middle way had become a Corning tradition and training a researcher in it, a Corning habit.

\

The Formation of a Glass Researcher, 1940–1947

Glass was unknown territory to Donald Stookey when he launched himself on the precarious 1940s job market, his newly defended Ph.D. dissertation in physical chemistry from MIT in hand. He was not among the top scholars in his year; he had barely scraped by in his graduate mathematics and physics courses, which were far more advanced than the work he had done at Coe College, Iowa. By his own account, most of the top scholars graduating from MIT that year had been snapped up by DuPont and Eastman Kodak while he was still hoping to find a job. Still, thinking these large places were likely to be regimented, he was far from disappointed. Stookey knew what he wanted; what really excited him was the chance to explore. The problem was that scientific frontiers seemed to be few and far between: few real secrets seemed to be left in what he called the "conventional sciences of Chemistry and Physics." When research director Jesse Littleton and William Taylor showed up at MIT looking to fill three Corning positions, Stookey considered glass for the first time. But what, he asked, would a chemist do with a substance that would neither crystallize nor dissolve in nor react with anything?

Stookey was invited to interview at Corning as a candidate for a position as a glass technologist, overseeing melting research in the production department under Corning's chief engineer, Walter Oakley.[4] His lackluster record at MIT had not prompted Littleton the physicist or Taylor the chemist to consider him as a candidate for the fundamental research slot: investigating opal glasses. But somehow by the end of his visit Stookey had convinced Littleton to hire him for that research position, with an annual salary of $2,500.

He joined the Corning laboratory just as it was about to occupy new quarters—the first laboratory built especially for research. It had a distinguished and productive technical staff, and the quieter times of the Depression had allowed it to pursue a thorough program of fundamental research that had yielded a great deal of knowledge and some surprising results, including the breakthroughs of Franklin Hyde and commercial silicone. Not long after Stookey arrived in 1940, Harrison Hood, veteran researcher of two decades, gave him an orientation in what had become "the Corning tradition." He tutored Stookey in the science of glass, showed him the factory operations, and then started him on a small project that would teach him how crystals formed. Few people that Corning hired were trained in glass chemistry, and it was generally expected that it would take them a few years to do something really useful. Stookey's first six months—hot and dirty months—were spent in an office and laboratory in the big dusty attic above the batch mixing room for B Factory, before he became one of the first tenants in Building 50, the new laboratory. It had an experimental glass-melting facility with a not especially satisfactory "muffle oven." This replaced the previous arrangement for experimental batches in B Factory, which had consisted of a clay melting pot for hand-shop glassblowing, run by veteran glassblower E. A. Wood. In the new building the researchers were on their own, but its advantage was its excellent modern equipment for physical measurements and chemical analysis.

Over the course of a few months, Stookey's supervisors, Harrison Hood and Robert Dalton, introduced him to further aspects of opal and ruby glasses. These provided intriguing material answers to the questions he had raised at the start as a mystified neophyte. Opal glasses are opaque and white in nature because microscopic crystals of fluorides or phosphates of sodium and calcium have precipitated in them as the glass has cooled. Similarly, gold and copper ruby glasses are given their color by metallic crystals that precipitate in them, but only when reheated. Both of these glasses, the opals and the rubies, had been known in antiquity and their origins were the stuff of legend. This aspect of the science appealed to a deep romantic streak in Don Stookey.

Eugene Sullivan was known to attribute a large part of Corning's success through the 1930s to Corning's early practices of secrecy about glass composition. Glass compositions were still not published and were disclosed even to Corning researchers on a need-to-know basis. The only people who had access to all the formulas were Sullivan and the Houghtons. Stookey set out to crack these family secrets: no one, he noted, ever objected when he succeeded. Yet for Stookey the mystery of glass and its traditions would remain one of the enduring fascinations and motivations of his work, even as he tried to build scientific understanding about it. He thought of himself as rediscovering knowledge about colors and properties last known to medieval alchemists.

One of Stookey's mentors, Robert Dalton, had discovered in 1937 that the copper-ruby color could be intensified by irradiation. Dalton had been trying to find new ways to decorate glass. Stookey tried to replicate this work, discovering at first only what Dalton knew but had not yet revealed to him: that what was usually a simple process of solution, supersaturation, nucleation, and precipitation of metallic copper, was much more complex in the case of copper-rubies. Stookey wrote that "the mechanism of reaction was very sensitive to oxidation-reduction reactions involving copper in its various valence states. The roles of temperature, viscosity, and of [various] multivalent reagents . . . were unraveled. This resulted in my first invention, photosensitive copper glass."[5]

It turned out that the ability of the copper to develop a pattern when reheated was due to a latent image at room temperature that consisted of photoelectrons trapped at one stage of the copper when unheated and reacting into visibility when reheated. As would be true of much of Stookey's work, this phenomenon had been known in practice for years but had not been understood scientifically. The first patented commercial application of this work was to develop opacity in thermometers.

Stookey next turned to the general problem of copper glass chemistry and from there to the question of gold-ruby glass, where existing literature suggested that there was no oxidation reduction mechanism. Stookey went on to show that the literature was misleading, and that a different sensitizer was needed to cause the gold ions to react; he identified cerium oxide as one possible sensitizer. Meanwhile, another young chemist recently hired by Corning, Stookey's office mate for years, William Armistead, had also become interested in Dalton's work and went on to develop photosensitive silver-yellow colors.

Armed with a theory and the prior work of Dalton and Armistead, Stookey went on to find the mechanism for making photosensitive glasses with many different kinds of crystals, learning to adapt the cooling and heating cycles for the particular crystals involved. It was the most recalcitrant of all—the sodium fluoride crystals made into photosensitive sodium fluoride opal glasses—that would eventually find commercial use for Corning, but not until thirty years later. Then they would be used for architectural lighting and control purposes in spectacular venues like the walls of the United Nations Assembly building in New York City, which were made to look like marble. At the time these developments were unforeseeable: Stookey had invented a curiosity. It was, nevertheless, out of these efforts to understand the photosensitive glasses that a commercially important discovery was made. Luckily for Stookey, who had been around for longer than Hyde before turning up anything that looked commercially useful, this work offered the timely prospect of solving a very difficult problem for a new Corning product program, aperture masks for color television. Television glass was becoming an all-consuming drain on Corning's technical resources, and anything that could not demonstrate potential relevance to its television problems risked being shut off.

.

TANGLING WITH TELEVISION, 1947–1951

Corning entered the 1950s grasping a tiger firmly by the tail: television glass was far more unruly than any of its previous businesses had been. It faced one significant competitor, Owens-Illinois, and powerful customers, some of whom were bitter rivals and several of whom had both the financial resources and the technical capabilities to consider integrating backward into glass. Although Corning was recognized as the leading innovator in the demanding area of glass enclosures and was the preeminent source of critical technical expertise for the industry, it had no contact with the end user and only tenuous control over the course of its own technology.

Bill Decker would describe the years 1948–1952 as the "really hectic" ones for television. "The first thing we did, we licked metal. The second thing, we never did permit our competitor to get a very big share of the business. They did not catch up—because our quality is ahead of theirs, our service is better, and our research."[6]

Corning endured four such hectic periods in television during its first fifteen years: the initial development of black-and-white bulbs, a similar but far more complicated period for color bulbs, the creation of the so-called laminated tube (tube plus faceplate), and the conversion to rectangular bulbs.

Glass Versus Metal

A contest between metal and glass had been waged on and off since the 1930s, when radio bulb customers first tried to substitute metal for glass in smaller vacuum tubes. In the case of television more was at stake. RCA was accustomed to controlling all of its technology through an elaborate "radio related" patent collection inherited from its founding companies, and it objected to Corning's prospective control of television bulb production technology and the profits that control would bring the company. It also shared the concerns with glass bulb design and performance that tube and radio set makers had been voicing: their weight, fragility, high defect rates, and expense.[7]

In 1948, just as Corning's push to improve its production methods had begun to bear fruit under Forrest Behm's leadership as Pressware's plant manager, RCA came up with a glass-metal hybrid, a metal funnel designed to be used with a glass faceplate. By offering the metal funnel approach as a package, complete with well-specified methods and technical support, RCA had persuaded many of its licensees to adopt this new approach as well. RCA canceled its largest order for bulbs right before Christmas, forcing Corning to lay off workers at the Pressware plant, just as they were expecting to earn big rewards for improving production. Forry Behm never forgave RCA for this, the single worst moment in his career:

My integrity was questioned, because I promised them something and I
couldn't deliver. That hurts me even today to think about that. It was just
unnecessary. RCA lied to us. They had told us nothing. They had kept it
absolutely secret. We had sales people and engineers down there and everything else. They had done World War II secrecy on us. Why? They never
explained why.[8]

In reality the possibility of taking bulb production away from Corning
had long been a topic of debate at RCA headquarters. Ironically it was a
comment by a Corning employee that was rumored to have precipitated the
decision. Ernie Ling, Corning's closest link to the electronics industry, had
declared in a meeting with customers in 1942 that the largest commercially
produced glass television bulbs ever likely to be produced would be twelve
inches in diameter. Corning had never been able to press Pyrex platters
larger than twelve inches and did not as a rule make one-piece (blown) bulbs
larger than eight inches. RCA seized on Ling's pronouncement as a firm
technical limit on the all-glass bulb and began research into a glass/metal
bulb in earnest.

RCA eventually produced several metal bulbs for black-and-white television and, later, a prototype for color. Corning engineers continued to work
with RCA and relations remained cordial. Though Corning had been
burned in business terms over the black-and-white bulb, it still had a lot of
RCA's business and did not want it integrating into other types of bulb production as well. There was no denying that the thin metal funnels were
lighter and cheaper than the glass funnels. However, tube producers who
switched to metal discovered that RCA's design did not entirely overcome
significant electrical interference problems inherent in the material; there
were tradeoffs with both types. The contest was decided by Corning's
invention of centrifugal casting for funnels, a novel production technique
that allowed the company to produce bulbs that were much thinner and
therefore both lighter and easier to seal reliably. It also proved significantly
cheaper, tipping the economics of tube production in favor of glass.

The contest with RCA was a foretaste of the kind of business television
was always going to be for Corning, so unlike the more orderly prewar businesses that had been protected by long-term contracts and cross-licensing.

Jealous of its own position as technology leader in its industry, RCA would always be a customer that might at any point become a competitor. Demand for television bulbs would periodically even out to some extent, but it would never be predictable; while the technology might stabilize a bit, such plateaus would always be short. On the other hand, the television business had two redeeming features for Corning: it was very big and, as long as Corning could remain ahead technically, it was very profitable.

Three technologies, in addition to the expertise in overall bulb design exhibited in the fight with RCA, were crucial to Corning's continued leadership of the business and its ability to survive those trying times: special television glass compositions, electric sealing, and the centrifugal casting of funnels. Though a great deal more went into Corning's successful pursuit of this market, these three areas of innovation represented the company's most important and fruitful fields of endeavor.

Television Glass

In the immediate aftermath of the war (as discussed in chapter 4), William Armistead, working with American Optical as lead customer, had meticulously produced an extensive series of ophthalmic glasses. He now used this acquired knowledge to develop a more suitable television glass. The result of this work was formula 9010, Corning's first no-lead television glass. Much harder to melt than any of the lead-oxide formulas previously used, 9010 necessitated major changes in refractories, melting methods, and molds. Such problems were too complicated and too interrelated to work out either in the laboratory or on the production floor, so Corning assigned them to a pilot plant (later known as Pilot Plant 1). Meanwhile Jesse Littleton asked John Sheldon, manager of the television department, to tackle the problem in a different way.

The key insight Sheldon pursued was that a bulb need not be made out of a single formula. Only the neck, the smallest and most easily formed part of the entire bulb, required the high electrical resistivity that demanded lead or some other metal as part of the glass composition. The rest of it could be made out of any number of compositions, chosen for their workability or for other reasons, but not solely for their electrical characteristics. After surveying the main customers, Sheldon determined that the funnel and panel required only a tenth as much electrical resistivity as the neck for black-and-white applications. The resulting composite bulb could be made of as many as four different types of glass, which, while a manufacturing problem of no small complexity, allowed much greater flexibility in designing the final product.

With this new approach in mind, Sheldon and Armistead began an intensive research project aimed at finding optimal formulas for each part of the bulb: the neck, the funnel, and the panel. Armistead melted and Sheldon formed. Together the two tried many compositions before settling on a 12 percent barium oxide glass to be used for everything but the neck, which was made out of the 30 percent lead-oxide formula. In 1949 these new formulas entered full-scale production and, with minor adjustments, remained the industry norm until the mid-1970s.

Sealing

Sealing of multi-piece bulbs was a vexing problem even at the relatively sedate production rates of radar; with the advent of television and its greatly increased demand, it became an absolute bugbear. In 1943 a special sealing department was set up under the direction of Ed Leibig, and in 1948, when larger bulbs compounded the challenge, sealing operations were transferred to the Pressware plant. The devices used at this time for sealing larger bulbs were awkward and dangerous, real Rube Goldberg contraptions. Forrest Behm found this process the most inefficient operation in his entire plant:

> The burner was mounted in the center, and you swung this burner in so that flames went up to the panel and flames went down to the funnel. The burner had a ring of fire twelve inches in diameter with burner tips about as big as my finger placed very close together all the way around this thing.

The amount of heat that came out of one of those was like a hundred blowtorches. You swung that under there, and then by eye, you determined whether it had melted the funnel edge and the panel edge enough and you swung the burner out, and then you squashed them together and worked them a little. We shipped bulbs that all came back because they had a very fine hairline and when they went to test them, the water came out.[9]

This method was based on those used to seal glass blocks, but with CRTs they could not guarantee that the glass to be bonded was melted through (the bulb pieces were thicker than the ones out of which blocks were made). Furthermore, the excessive heat of the flames produced a condition called "reboil" in which tiny bubbles or seeds appeared in the remelted glass, which increased the bulbs' susceptibility to thermal shock.

In 1949 a group working in Corning's physics division under veteran researcher E. M. Guyer invented its own technique for electric sealing of larger CRTs, a hybrid system that used both flame and electricity. Their system worked well but could not be automated: the eternally varying demand for different bulb sizes made the economics of such an investment untenable. Manual electric sealing of bulbs became the norm, with each larger bulb size (15-, 16-, and 19-inch) first tried with flame sealers and then adapted for electric sealing.[10]

Corning's ultimate success with electrical sealing was the work of many engineers and scientists, and the lessons learned there spread through this network to many other products outside the television business, including fluorescent lightbulbs and sealed beam headlights, both major product lines in their own right. A constant presence throughout this work was Robert Dalton, who was Corning's point man when it came to sealing technologies. His career as sealing expert involved him in close working relationships with RCA, Westinghouse, and Sylvania. These relationships, in some periods involving daily letter exchanges, were one way Corning acquired essential understanding of its customers' technologies and their needs. In turn, Dalton's confidantes at RCA and Philco frequently entrusted him with technical findings and even confidential reports intended only for their own in-house use.[11]

Centrifugal Casting

Corning's work with glass formulas and new sealing techniques matched much of its other research: based on deep reserves of technical knowledge and practical experience and developed via a measured and painstaking program of experimentation. In contrast, the adaptation of centrifugal casting (a not particularly common method of glass forming that relied on the centrifugal forces generated by a spinning mold to force a molten gob of glass to assume a given shape) was a classic flash of genius reduced to practice. Though no one innovation accounted for Corning's leadership in black-and-white television bulbs, centrifugal casting, perhaps more than any other, proved crucial.

Jim Giffen, at that time the sole member of Corning's new machine research department, had been asked to look at new ways of casting Pyrex casseroles, but he soon determined that the casseroles were poor candidates for this technique. It was typical of Giffen that, if momentarily stymied by one problem, he would apply himself to another. It was also typical of Corning to support crossover technologies. In the words of

James Giffen's development of centrifugal casting for television bulbs gave Corning its crucial advantage over metal bulbs. Here Giffen hovers above the spinner machine, which is designed to spin a gob of molten glass into a funnel shape by application of centrifugal force, assisted by Arthur Pierpont, a member of his machine research group.

Otto Hilbert, "Jim Giffen set up a mould spinning device, and with J. Over-meyer as gatherer, found out that moulds used for pressing could be used to make spun funnels satisfactory for sealing. This was the start of cen-trifugal casting."[12]

The phrase "satisfactory for sealing" was the heart of the matter, for Giffen's spun funnels had much thinner walls than the usual pressed or blown funnels. The immediate benefit of this was that sealing, whether flame or electric, was much more effective because the thinner glass soft-ened more quickly and evenly. Giffen did not fully develop his process until 1949, when RCA's metal challenge to glass funnels made it necessary to find a cheaper approach, and did not patent it until 1953, by which time he had extended the technique to spinning rectangular funnels.

Centrifugal casting of round bulbs was relatively simple: a hot charge of molten glass was deposited in a cone-shaped mold, which was then spun, forcing the glass to climb the sides of the mold. The resultant cone could be automatically trimmed to the desired size. A rectangular shape, demanded by the industry's move to rectangular screens, was another mat-ter. Howard Lillie, a Ph.D. specializing in flow mechanics in the research division's physics department, wrote a detailed report showing that it was theoretically impossible to adapt centrifugal casting to rectangular shapes. The essence of the problem was that a liquid will climb the corners of a spinning shape more quickly than the sides because the corners are mov-ing faster owing to their greater distance from the center. Lillie's report declaring the problem insoluble prompted Giffen, who held all academic degrees (and especially the Ph.D.) in contempt, to produce his solution the very next day. He used a mold rigged with dams in the corners to give the liquid on the sides a head start over that in the corners. In his model the molten glass in the corners flowed around the dams before it could head up the sides, thus arriving at the same time as the slower glass nearer the center. Giffen's patents for centrifugal casting formed two of the key tech-nologies that Corning later licensed to parties overseas to produce televi-sion bulbs.

Researchers like Dalton, Armistead, Nordberg, Guyer, and Sheldon, and inventors like Jim Giffen and Stewart Claypoole (who invented the critical sealing compound called the frit) contributed countless particulars to the linked technologies that together helped Corning gain and maintain its leadership in television bulbs from 1947 on. In addition to the significant inventions singled out above, Corning's mastery of this market was based on many small, painstaking developments and years of integrative work carried out by these men and their groups working in conjunction with customers. It was the cumulative effect of their work, not only in television but also in prior specialty areas, that enabled Corning to establish the all-glass television bulb as the dominant design in the black-and-white industry, definitively closing out RCA's attempt to substitute the metal bulb.

TV: PREEMPTIVE INVENTION, 1951–1957

A principal accomplishment of the laboratory... is that it was an important factor in helping Corning to keep in the forefront of this vital new industry (television). In retrospect it can be seen that much work could have been left undone had we not been determined to be ready to "go" whenever color went commercial. This is the price of leadership.

—JOHN SHELDON, 1954 ANNUAL LABORATORY REPORT

When black-and-white television had been at the point of takeoff in the late 1940s, Corning had barely been in position to take advantage of it. By the time color entered the picture, Corning was in the thick of things. The company's advantages were obvious: it had a wealth of experience to draw on and was widely recognized as the technological leader in the industry. But Corning's position in black-and-white meant that color had to be developed in the context of an active and growing black-and-white business without disrupting ongoing production; Corning simply could not afford to experiment on the factory floor. Nor did it. Early on the company organized its technical approach to color in a very different way, pursuing an integrated program of scientific and engineering research begun in 1951. When the surge in color came a decade later, Corning was ready.

The Korean War in 1951 and 1952 halted all production of television receivers, since their production required scarce weapons-grade materials. The prohibition halted all but two color television research programs, RCA's and Philco's. When the Korean action was over and television production resumed, a lingering uncertainty around what color standard would be used also came to an end. The FCC and the industry, which had long been feuding over whether to adapt RCA's NTSC standard or another field sequential system pushed by CBS, grudgingly accepted RCA's standard as a fait accompli. By that time so many black-and-white sets, which all used the NTSC standard, had been sold that choosing the incompatible CBS color system would have infuriated consumers.

Until this time, a handful of other approaches to color television had been in limited production, and neither Corning nor anyone else could predict with surety which would come out on top. As a result (and, because it wished to avoid accusations of anticompetitive behavior following the antitrust judgments), the company had had to work with all comers. To quote John Sheldon, manager of the television department:

> The tube industry, against a backdrop of bitter commercial rivalry, has been groping for the color television tube that can be produced at a suitable price. A variety of independent approaches by our principal customers made the picture quite confusing at times. Each temporary advantage of any one quickly obsoleted the others, leading to a leap-frogging situation. The rapid rate of obsolescence was particularly trying to Corning, for we have tried to serve the needs of the industry in its effort to evolve "the" commercial tube.[13]

From its inception color television, superficially so closely related to black-and-white, followed a different trajectory. This was partly because the color television bulb under the NTSC system was a nightmare of technical complexity. Because of the precision required in aligning its millions of phosphorescent dots to a pattern of holes, no amount of floor-level ingenuity could make up for the problems it posed in design and production. These required deep understanding of fundamental phenomena. Besides, Corning had learned several organizational lessons from black-and-white. It was crucial to anticipate both the volume of demand and the shape of the competition. The climate had changed drastically since black-and-white television had been developed. Black-and-white's development was a prewar invention controlled in the final stages by a relatively few companies. Color, on the other hand, bore the stamp of its postwar development: the majority of Corning customers were running active research programs staffed with credentialed scientists. To achieve not just the knowledge and foresight but also the customer relations necessary to anticipate developments in the industry, Corning treated color television as an integrated research project in its own right, not as an ad hoc incremental development from some other product.

The research program Corning put in place in the early 1950s had several major parts. The generic problems, such as achieving an all-glass bulb or finding a suitable method for sealing the bulbs (a much more difficult process for color than for black-and-white), were extensions of the previous developments discussed above, now treated in a more systematic way. Dalton's work in sealing, for example, was the basis for the critical breakthrough that made it possible for Corning to grab and hold the lead in bulbs for color television. Because of the complexity and expense of color television bulbs, shipping them whole risked a prohibitive amount of breakage. Corning developed a frit, or special low-melting-point sealing glass, that allowed customers to assemble and seal the bulbs in their own plants. That breakthrough belonged to Stewart Claypoole, whose patent for the frit was issued in 1963; this became one of the chief patents that Corning supplied to its color TV licensees.

But Corning's research program was also driven by the diverse technical concerns of its various customers. Philco, one of RCA's chief technical rivals, for instance, inspired a systematic search for a one-piece color bulb. Another challenging example of customer-driven work was the aperture mask Corning made for use in producing RCA's shadow mask bulb. Though this component itself was never adopted for commercial use by color television manufacturers, both its spin-offs and the failure to capture the market taught Corning important lessons about the value and danger of pursuing stretch goals, (i.e., goals that would cause the company to attempt far more than it knew how to do).

Glass Aperture Masks: Dead End with Unexpected Results

As already noted, the technical problem with RCA's color tube was that the phosphor dots coating the inside of a color CRT faceplate had to be laid down with extreme precision, not once but three times (blue, red, and green being required to achieve full color). This was done with the aid of an aperture mask through which the phosphor could be applied. In essence a very precise stencil, such a mask had to be extremely rigid and yet pierced by millions of tiny holes in a perfectly regular pattern. Jesse Littleton, research director at the time, believed that glass might offer a solution to this problem; certainly the material's inherent stiffness was promising. The approach Corning took became characteristic of its manner of attacking many such research problems: Littleton invited his leading researchers to brainstorm as many different solutions as possible and then selected from these the few best prospects for further research. Donald Stookey was one of those researchers, and his method was chosen.

Even Corning's best brains were hard-pressed to find answers to the problem at first. One idea was to seal together a million small glass tubes, stretch the bundle, and then saw slices from it. Recognizing in this proposal a potential production nightmare, Stookey thought he had a better idea. Because he had been working with various photosensitive opal glasses without commercial result, Bill Decker had been pressuring him to find commercial applications for at least one of his brainchildren. Up to this point Stookey had focused on the visual characteristics of these glasses, but he had earlier recognized that solubility was another distinguishing property of this glass. Experiments with various solvents led him to the finding that lithium silicate glasses in particular could be etched slightly more than the opals around them by means of a hydrofluoric solvent. In effect, the material was chemically machinable. "'A miracle,' I thought to myself," wrote Stookey later in his characteristically dramatic style. "Another secret door had opened."[14]

This "miracle" was not enough to win the day for glass aperture masks. Hammond Munier—another key figure in product development for television—undertook an extensive project in Corning's pilot plant lasting several years and succeeded in producing from Stookey's material a prototype aperture mask with the required number and configuration of holes. But for financial reasons the industry settled on a metal aperture mask. It soon became clear that the product wouldn't last long enough to justify Corning's investment in its commercial development.[15] Nevertheless, Stookey's attempts to adapt his photosensitive glasses to this previously unimaginable use had other fruitful outcomes. One was a family of chemically machinable glasses trademarked as Corning's Fotoform. Another was a stream of research pursued by new fundamental researchers. Robert Maurer, for instance, a physicist who joined Corning from MIT in 1950 and later did essential work on optical fiber, took Stookey's results as a jumping-off point for studies of the nucleation kinetics of the self-nucleated gold and silver glasses. Most important of all, while heating working samples of the Fotoform product in 1952, Stookey himself made the discovery that led to the whole new family of glass ceramics that Corning called Pyroceram. This in turn led eventually to a new consumer product line—Corning Ware, a story we will detail later in this chapter.

A New Blend of Craft and Science

As a rule, the more radical the demands of television technology, the more necessary it was to experiment with its production and the more difficult and costly it was to try it out on the regular production floor. With black-and-white this problem was compounded by the new research staff's lack of practical experience. Before the war, when novices arrived fresh from university, a friendly but firm plant manager generally warned them never to tell an operator what to do or how to do it. By the early 1950s, when a majority of new hires (not just researchers but also production engineers) had advanced university degrees, and with the status of theoretical research in the scientific culture at large making it hard to attract and keep good people, the technical balance of power had shifted. Even Corning's skilled plant personnel were no longer presumed to know best. In such circumstances ways had to be found to reconcile the different working styles of several different cultures. Both the pilot plant, where Munier made the Fotoform aperture mask, and a second similar installation served this and several other important purposes. They not only kept experimental activity from disrupting the production floor, but they also provided a physical and organizational space where new patterns of developmental working could be introduced and green personnel trained to achieve productive professional-professional and worker-management relations. Not least, they also provided a neutral place to work with customers without allowing them access to actual production facilities.[16]

In pilot plants various forms of expertise from different parts of the company could mingle on common ground: research, machine research, engineering, and production. Corning's television department was divided by function into design and testing, glass-metal sealing, glass-glass sealing, and equipment and metal fabricating, and they worked closely with a fifth group, the laboratory machine research group under Giffen. As John Sheldon reported at the end of 1954:

> These five groups have worked as a team on the complex problem of designing a bulb, designing experimental equipment and developing production methods, producing samples for evaluation tests and customer samples and in carrying out extensive evaluation tests. . . . As in the past, an important aspect of our work was virtually continual contact with the technical and management people of our principal customers.[17]

Pilot Plant 2 was set up on Tioga Avenue in Corning in 1951 when it became clear that customer demand for sample bulbs could not be met by piecemeal production in the lab or elsewhere. The pilot plant had a full-scale furnace and hydraulic glass press that were both capable of producing significant volumes of glass. Its broad mission was to lend technical support to new product and process innovations, as well as improving processes in the existing business. Among the many types of equipment it helped to develop was Giffen's centrifugal spinner (which in 1951 was refined into three distinct types for different types of bulb housings), an improved stirrer, and automatic panel-sealing lathes intended to eliminate the labor expense of hundreds of hand polishers.

From 1951 to 1957, the period of most intense color television development, Pilot Plant 2 was home to a high-powered set of Ph.D. chemists and engineers working to develop experimental glass compositions and the new forming methods. They were well suited to work with the technical staff in the television department, but they could achieve almost nothing without men who had solid plant experience to translate their ideas into workable methods.

An episode recounted by Jack Carpenter, later of Corning's Process Research Center, was typical of the kinds of cultural encounters that this mix produced. In 1954 a problem arose during an attempt to use hydrofluoric acid to strengthen television faceplates. Carpenter was summoned from Wellsboro because of his experience using hydrofluoric acid to frost light-bulbs. Because color television bulb faceplates could not be pressed precisely enough to conform to customer specifications, diamond drilling had been used to finish them off. This method weakened the faceplates, which then required hydrofluoric acid treatment to strengthen the glass by removing the thin, scratch-filled layer of glass. Unfortunately, this approach produced smooth but uneven glass surfaces that caused serious optical distortion in the color bulbs.

Carpenter arrived from Wellsboro to find a group of top technical people, all Ph.D.s, deep in discussion. Each man advanced a different theory as to which elements of the glass were reacting to the acid and how the composition might have to be changed, but no one had observed the actual process of acid strengthening. A look at the operation in progress on the pilot plant floor showed Carpenter that the hydrofluoric acid was forming a residue that collected unevenly on the inside of the faceplate. He borrowed a rubber glove from the operator and instead of letting the acid sit in the faceplate, swished it around for the prescribed period. The result was a faceplate unmarred by the usual distortion. "When I told them I could make good faceplates right away," he said, "they couldn't believe it. From then on we spun the faceplates on fixtures mounted on bearings during the acid treatment operation, and they came out just fine."[18] Later the scientists would in fact come up with a systematic understanding of which glass compositions tolerated the acid treatment, but these efforts would take many more months.

This episode was emblematic of a change that was taking place in Corning's technical culture and in that of many companies like it. A growing estrangement between the theoretical knowledge of the Ph.D.s and the practical know-how of those working on the floor led many companies to stabilize their production processes and then force new products to accommodate themselves to the existing process constraints. This was a serious limitation that Corning managed to avoid with devices like its pilot plants. Corning was continuing to develop new processes along with, and often independently of, new products, and this was in no small part due to the company's ability to keep scientists and engineers talking to each other.[19]

Pilot Plant 2 was both expensive to run (by 1956 it was costing the company $1 million per year) and challenging to manage. In June 1954, when problems arose with its management, Bill Armistead was asked to take over its direction. Armistead later described this brief experience as one of the most stressful of his entire career. "I was an individual researcher, not used to working with other people or depending on them for my success. Every noon I had to go home and lie down. But I performed."[20]

In 1957, as an economy measure, Pilot Plant 2 became an adjunct to Pressware, a sort of smaller production facility. This move was vital to free up funds for other research. Though Corning's commitment to research as a long-term necessity had not wavered, the company had allowed television to drive out or significantly reduce its other research efforts. It was generally recognized that Corning now had to play catch-up, for in the glass industry at large, research was getting more attention than ever before. At least two other glass companies — Owens-Illinois and Pittsburgh Plate Glass — had been steadily increasing their R&D investments in the 1950s. For Corning, reallocating money and attention were not enough, however; several familiar obstacles to rebuilding an effective research program also had to be overcome: the state of Corning's research facilities and, as always, its location.

REBUILDING RESEARCH, 1950–1967

Corning under Decker was more focused and purposeful than it had ever been, but these factors held few attractions for aspiring research personnel. Unlike Corning of the 1930s, when its differences from other research-performing companies had given it hiring advantages, it was in no position to attract the graduates of leading research universities. When Edward Condon arrived in 1951, he described the scene in sobering terms: "we had only the very crowded facilities of the old lab next to A Factory with essentially no modern scientific equipment. There were 98 technical people, 8 clerical staff and 91 technical support people."[21]

Condon's contribution in the brief period he served at Corning was to put the company on the path to doing fundamental research once again, in fact, pioneering research, explicitly aimed not just at mastering existing technologies through better scientific understanding but at achieving a leader's advantage in new areas of technology for new markets. Condon was a true believer in the linear model of innovation that had emerged from the successes of World War II. Some companies were using fundamental (or in government funding terms, "basic") research as a way of attracting leading researchers into industry. Nor were immediate practical results considered the sole legitimate objective for industrial research. At a time of national peril, with the Cold War becoming more frigid by the month, many thought it was the patriotic duty of technology-based companies to add to the general knowledge base. Edwin H. Land, founder of Polaroid, wrote in 1945:

> Industry can provide a much larger field of inquiry for pure science and much greater human stimulus to many of the young scientists than are now provided by the university. In short a continuum between pure science in the university and pure science in industry should stimulate and enrich our social system.[22]

It is hard to know whether Condon would have gone as far as this at Corning had his personal difficulties with security clearances (see chapter 6) not brought his time there to an abrupt end. As it was, his first task in laying the groundwork for an improved research program was to acquaint Corning's management with the need for a new laboratory facility and to persuade them to create an environment that would be conducive to hiring a first-class research staff in the competitive labor market of the 1950s. To this end he set up and fostered a fellowship program patterned on one he had created at Westinghouse before the war. He also acquired for Corning

Research Director E. U. Condon (center) examines a glass aperture mask with Donald Stookey (right), then a young researcher. This key part of color television production was one that Corning did not in the end master, but the attempt to do so led Stookey to his invention of Pyroceram.

state-of-the-art research equipment and improved its methods for documenting its discoveries, both necessary infrastructural elements to restarting fundamental research. Finally, and perhaps most important, he picked Bill Armistead to be his successor as research director, after putting Armistead through his trial by fire running Pilot Plant 2.

The location of the new laboratory could have been a matter of debate. Many companies were treating as gospel the notion that a research laboratory should be remote from any manufacturing facility. But, as Condon noted, research on glass was hard to do away from production facilities. Had pilot plants been possible to locate in nearby Ithaca, it might have been possible to take better advantage of Cornell University as the closest academic research center, but Corning's pilot plants were already in place, and forty-five miles was too great a distance. Instead, Condon acquired new property near Corning's recently built Glass Center across the river from the main part of town and close to the heart of the company. Condon convinced management to allocate as much space there as possible until a new, $3 million laboratory could be built on a larger campus. Condon's most compelling argument for this improvement was its contribution to researcher productivity. With each researcher now averaging roughly $10,000 per year in operating costs, he reckoned that an annual capital cost of $1,300 per researcher was a wise investment. A new facility could be expected to greatly increase researchers' productivity if outfitted with the right equipment and adequate space to operate it.[23]

A lack of good facilities was not the only obstacle to pursuing a vigorous program of research. Although Condon himself adapted well to Corning and was able to maintain his unparalleled set of connections within the scientific community, he knew that neither his reputation nor his charisma was enough to attract to the Chemung Valley other scientists of the caliber Corning hoped to hire. In the 1950s industrial research in general had lost status compared to a now more generously funded university research establishment. For highly trained scientists academic jobs were abundant, and a combination of increased government secrecy and competition among industrial research performers meant that industrial posts offered limited publishing opportunities. Few leading researchers could be enticed away from the university or the government laboratory, both of which needed many people and offered the chance to publish.

Even current Corning employees felt acutely the difference in the new climate, though they might be seasoned enough to understand the reasons for it. As early as 1947 Frank Hyde wrote ruefully to a fellow chemist at the University of Buffalo denying the fellow chemist's request for help in reviewing his academic work:

> I am hesitant for the following reasons. We are definitely in serious competition with other organizations, who are turning out research work at a rapid rate. There are scarcely any publications coming out which do not come close to work that we have done or are doing. It is unfortunate that the results of industrial research cannot be made immediately available to all as in the case of research at academic institutions because of economic considerations. . . . On this basis we cannot afford to give our competitors a single clue. This may seem a very selfish and unscientific attitude from the

academic side of the fence, but it is the same competition that rapidly and efficiently brings new things to a practical stage of development to the benefit of all, including the academic institutions which must supply the additional trained personnel needed.[24]

Program planning for research also required Condon's immediate attention. The parlous state of fundamental research in glass compositions and surfaces, as well as the difficulty and expense involved in hiring researchers to do this sort of work, prompted some research managers to propose procuring fundamental work from outside Corning altogether—from universities and independent research firms like Arthur D. Little. It was noted that Owens-Illinois had set up a fundamental research program several years before and was spending upward of $200,000 on programs at MIT, Michigan, Kentucky, and Stanford. Owens-Illinois's arrangement was to spend $5,000 per award recipient on what amounted to short-term contract research, with a particular project assigned to a given professor.

Corning did sponsor a few specific research projects at several universities, like the small-angle X-ray scattering project at the University of Wisconsin, which involved collateral activities at the leading Bay Area electronics firm, Varian Associates, as well as at Alfred University. But such work was viewed as transitional and was intended to be transferred in-house as soon as Corning had appropriate staff and facilities to absorb it. Perhaps the memory of the complications of working through Mellon Institute in the 1930s checked the impulse to outsource too much work of this nature. Corning also initiated Condon's proposed university fellowship program awarding annual fellowships of $7,000 at seven different universities. Later, at Condon's urging, this program was regularized and the stipends gradually increased to a very generous $10,000 per year. Few of the actual fellows ever became Corning employees, but the relationships that were established with faculty members were viewed as significant and the program continued well into the 1970s.

By late 1954 one report indicated that Corning was spending roughly 4.5 percent of its $1 million R&D budget on fundamental work. Two departments accounted for most of this money: physics and chemistry. In chemistry the projects so designated included work on glass structure, glass composition, photosensitive glasses, and glass surfaces. In physics they included physical properties[25] and dielectric studies. Condon's committee concluded that there was considerable overlap among these programs and that communication needed to be improved.

Condon later regretted that the need to achieve immediate success with color television and to revamp the work in Corning's core glass technology had kept him from launching Corning on a more adventurous research program, particularly in solid-state physics. As he wrote to Armistead in 1962, "If the management had known you well at the time, it would have been much better to put you in charge of the general glass research program, and to have brought me in to organize a new laboratory staff for solid-state physics."[26] But in the early 1950s Corning was still marked by a small-company mind-set, not yet fully aware of either the opportunities or the necessities for growth that television was generating. The limitations of this mind-set would become very apparent later when the company tried to diversify its businesses into related technologies, including the solid-state electronics Condon regretted not having led the company to explore earlier.

Armistead in Charge

When Armistead succeeded Condon in December of 1954, his new boss, Bill Decker, gave him a succinct double-pronged mission: to get color television done and to keep Jim Giffen, Corning's maverick machine researcher, happy. Although the second task was not so easily accomplished, the first was already well in hand.

Several more years of intense effort on color television were needed, coming to a conclusion when the goal of achieving a one-piece, all-glass bulb sealed with Corning's new devitrifying solder was reached. Armistead applied here the "all-hands" approach he had learned from his mentors, Decker and Littleton. He concentrated resources and he tried ideas from many different disciplines. In a report summarizing color television engineering activities from 1951 to 1957, the author J. F. Frazier described this last part of the program as the culmination of the combined efforts of chemistry, engineering, and heavy machine research. After years of work in so

Taken in 1966, this photograph of Corning's color television production process at Bluffton, Indiana shows bulbs for color picture tubes coming off the line.

many areas the bulb program could draw on a multitude of prior developments in process research equipment and techniques. Frazier wrote:

> When the decision was made in Sept. 1956 for an all out effort on the all-
> glass solder glass bulb sealed with a devitrifying solder glass, it was done
> with a knowledge of the extensive effort that had gone into the devitrifying
> solder glass up to that time.... A massive effort, involving a large number of
> additional laboratory personnel, was directed to this phase of the program.
> The total effort was successful for in March it was possible to melt large
> quantities of 186 type solder glasses that were superior to those previously
> melted. In April it was possible to supply RCA with 1,000 pound lots pre-
> pared by blending from 150 pound ball-mill charges.[27]

As for keeping Giffen happy, Armistead found that his only recourse was to
the top of the company. Giffen alternated between complaining that he had
too little help and wanting to fire all who worked for him because they got

in his way and required him to spend too much time on administration. After one particularly trying episode with a disgruntled Giffen, Armistead called on Bill Decker for help. Armistead and Giffen were invited to Decker's office, where Decker inquired of Giffen what he needed to be happy in his work. Giffen replied that he wanted to spend more time hunting and fishing at the new home he had acquired in Florida. At the end of the session Decker had given Giffen leave to visit Florida six times a year, along with the additional salary needed to cover tickets for himself and his wife. It was also agreed that if Giffen were needed while he was in Florida, his men would be sent down to join him.[28]

With his first two objectives met, Armistead recognized that his chief priority had to be to continue redressing the balance between television and the rest of Corning's technical program, in order to do the kind of research that would lead to major new products and processes. While short on suggestions for specific new products to pursue, management proved to be long on support for research. Decker understood completely the need to retain Corning's research staff at a time when other companies were on the

William Decker and William Armistead around the time of the opening of the Process Research Center at Sullivan Park.

lookout for experienced researchers to hire, and the Houghton family continued to view research as one of Corning's defining characteristics.[29]

Hiring significant numbers of Ph.D. researchers was essential to Armistead's plans for pursuing pioneering research. When Donald Stookey recognized that he had a breakthrough in 1954 with his controllable glass ceramics, he lacked colleagues of comparable training to help him exploit it. A year later several other chemists had joined his effort, but more sustained work had to await better staffing. Despite a worrisome economic downturn in 1957, the buildup of Corning's technical staffs under Armistead's leadership stayed the course prepared by Condon. Both Lee Waterman, who succeeded Decker as president in 1957, and the new senior vice president of corporate staffs, Amory Houghton Jr., (known by all as "Amo") were strong supporters of Armistead in this matter. As senior executive in charge of the technical staffs, Houghton realized not only that the television effort had depleted Corning's technical capability but that its accustomed investment of 3 percent of revenues on R&D needed review. While respectable for a glass company, the sum was modest when judged by the standards of large technology-based companies like GE and IBM, which were investing between 5 and 6 percent of revenues annually. The percentage was increased by 50 percent.[30]

In 1957 the new Sullivan research center located adjacent to the Glass Center opened for business as part of a new headquarters complex called Houghton Park. One of its first inhabitants was Tom MacAvoy, a Ph.D. in physical chemistry from the University of Cincinnati, in the vanguard of a cadre of the research and development personnel Corning's new facility was attracting. The plan was to grow the technical staffs by 10 percent annually, doubling it in ten years. The research staff built up gradually but steadily from then on, a handful of professionals arriving each year, many with Ph.D.s in physics and chemistry. It was a cosmopolitan and heterogeneous group, reflecting the brain drain from Britain and the Commonwealth and drawing from many institutions outside the small group personally known to Corning research leaders.[31] Only the members of machine research department under Giffen had no advanced degrees, and in fact almost no college degrees at all.

Numbers swelled in Corning's R&D organization to over 900 professionals evenly divided between research and engineering; the organization also added a managerial layer, including twelve new research directors appointed in 1964. Some of these directors represented new responsibilities for Armistead, for with the formation of the Technical Staffs Division he controlled centrally not only research and development but also engineering and the Process Research Center. Management was becoming a highly rewarded activity, and growth created a demand for research managers. Some of the most active researchers were quickly promoted to head groups. Another perhaps inescapable change to the culture was that researchers in the various scientific disciplines became more inward turning, specialists more inclined to stick together and less inclined to mingle with those in other disciplines. Small projects proliferated as researchers had a good deal of freedom to pursue the questions that most interested them.

In 1962 Condon, who was an active consultant still on the Corning payroll, wrote to Armistead marveling at the change from the Corning he had known ten years previously: "(a) we have splendid facilities, as good as the best and improving right along, (b) we have a strong staff of fundamental

As Corning's technical staffs doubled in size in the early 1960s the central technical organization added a new layer of managers. Here the Sullivan Park research directors gathered on the stairs (in descending order) include John MacDowell, James Giffen, Ray Voss, Charles Wakeman, and Donald Stookey.

research people . . . (c) the growth goal has been set for the next decade and I am confident that the management will achieve it."[32] Armistead did not stop at increasing the research staff. He also recognized the need to balance Corning's research capability with greater capacity in the patent department. In 1961 (as described in detail in chapter 8) he made the case for a significant change in patenting policy. His concern with the issue resulted in the patent department's being placed under his direction. This was far more than a simple change in reporting status, for putting patenting under the control of the central technical organization ensured that patent priorities would serve Armistead's broad pioneering strategy and that the patents filed would be relevant to the breakthrough priorities of the company as a whole.

At no point during the decade, when Corning's research budgets were increasing and staffs expanding, did cost cease to be an issue. Inflation was the norm in the economy at large and the cost of research was going up fastest of all. From 1957 to 1967, the period of most rapid growth in the size of the technical staff, annual expenses for research rose from $5.6 million to $19.2 million. While the number of people employed by the central technology group rose from 700 to 1,300, the expense per person nearly doubled from $8,000 to $14,800 per year. Of these people perhaps 400 were technical professionals required to file annual reports. During the same period Corning's annual sales went from $159 million to $444 million.[33]

In point of fact, Corning did not increase its research investment much past 4.5 percent of sales until 1968. Compared with many other companies, it was getting a lot for the money. Corning employed roughly 10 percent of the technical people working in the glass industry worldwide at that time. Only Owens-Illinois, Pittsburgh Plate Glass, Pilkington, and St. Gobain had larger research programs, and all were much, much larger companies. In 1957 Corning received twelve patents and filed for thirty. By 1967 the number of patents received was 148 with an additional 111 filed for.

Maintaining a Research Culture

In his various comments to Armistead on staffing, Condon had worried not only about the problem of attracting high-caliber people but also about the character and nature of research culture. In a time when young Ph.D.s were in high demand, they were, he warned, a "spoiled" bunch who often turned up their noses at industrial research. He recommended bringing young scientists to work at Corning during the summers on a generous internship program, where they could get to know the culture and the excitement of the work. He suggested further that William Shaver, one of the second generation of researchers at Corning soon to retire, be retained as a consultant to mentor the interns. A somewhat different plan was actually adopted, but Condon's concerns about the culture were addressed much as he had proposed. The grand old men of research—Harrison Hood, Robert Dalton, Martin Nordberg—remained at Corning into the mid-1960s, and some stayed as consultants past their retirement, serving as mentors and guides to Corning's unique culture. Partly through their efforts, and partly owing to self-selection by those who chose Corning's offers over others, the central research culture in the Chemung Valley managed to retain a strong element of continuity even as it doubled in size.

Though the technical staffs division inevitably took on a certain amount of bureaucracy as its size increased, it was still governed by patterns established in earlier decades. MacAvoy, whose mentors included Nordberg and Sheldon, was surprised, and at first put off, at how quickly he was taken by the latter to visit customers. This was not the norm at other corporate laboratories. Old-timers at other labs in the 1950s, often inventors and engineers, either were dispersed to divisional laboratories or were expected to adjust their style and way of thinking to the new generation of theoreticians.[34] At Corning the ultimate respect was still reserved for all-time "heavy hitters," researchers who had produced technology that had been commercialized. Whether or how much they had published was of relatively little concern. Thus the stars of the day continued to be Hood, with thirty-nine patents to his name; Martin Nordberg, who with Hood invented 96 percent Silica (Vycor); Robert Dalton and Donald Stookey, honored for their work on photosensitive glasses; and William Shaver, head of atomic research and later in charge of international research, traveling the world on Corning's behalf.

Nevertheless Corning's technical culture was changing in important ways. Symbolic of this was the appearance of the new R&D campus,

which, according to plan, was constructed only a few years after the opening of the research laboratories at Houghton Park. Named after Eugene
Sullivan, this complex in fact conveyed a completely different relationship
between R&D and the rest of the company than had existed under Sullivan.
Sullivan Park was located at the top of a hill in Erwin, three miles outside
Corning, and its design, short on windows on the upper floors except in a
few management offices, had the appearance of a landlocked space station
or a modern fortress, impenetrable and unwelcoming to outsiders. According to an exchange of memos between Armistead and Amory Houghton,
the design of the building caused a considerable outcry among the younger
members of the research staff, who were particularly unhappy about the
lack of windows in laboratories. But Armistead defended the design on the
grounds that it represented the most modern thinking about supplying all
needed facilities to laboratory space. The first group to inhabit this new
structure was the Process Research Center.

The Process Research Center

An important feature of the technical staffs, as Armistead constructed them
in the 1960s, was their even balance between process and product research.

Sullivan Park complex, c. 1970. The Process Research Center on the right.

The Process Research Center under the direction of Tom Howitt was a modern outgrowth of Corning's pilot plants, intended eventually to be conveniently located adjacent to the researchers instead of spread in temporary locations all over town. Armistead was insistent that product work not be constrained by known processes. He required that a representative of the PRC regularly sit in when researchers were reviewing their projects, not to emphasize the limits of Corning's processes but so that process researchers might get early warnings about new processes that might be needed. Not surprisingly, the 1967 advisory group convened to review Corning's technical effort recognized the Process Research Center as one of Corning's unique strengths. In the collective experience of these scientists, drawn from outside Corning, few other companies could boast of organizations as sensible, or as necessary, as this kind of an experimental halfway house between research and production. The Process Research Center was crucial in developing new methods, in transferring technologies into the plants, and in integrating new technologies into existing processes. It would become even more important in the 1970s, when Corning would take the unusual step of hiring union members to work in the Process Research Center.[35]

The PRC, however, was not the recognized source for the most important inventions for brand-new products: that honor remained with Jim Giffen's machine research department, which was made up of Giffen and as many as fifty assisting technicians. This continued commitment on Corning's part to a maverick was wholly out of step with the trends of the time and its purpose was not easily grasped by outsiders. The 1967 advisory committee on R&D expressed surprise at the seeming low caliber of some of Corning's employees among its engineering staffs. The committee members found it hard to believe that a company that put such emphasis on quality personnel could retain a pocket of people whose only credentials were their craft expertise. But difficult as he was, Giffen continued to justify the company's investment in him. His invention of key equipment such as the Hub Machine, first developed to press black-and-white television faceplates and later applied to ovenware, was crucial in making Corning Ware a profitable product.

Armistead's focus on pioneering research, especially after 1957, became the working philosophy of Corning's entire technical staff and translated into a continuing search for new products and in particular the elusive home run. In earlier times the company had nurtured a multitude of small projects and watched an unpredictable number of them grow into big businesses, worrying that this growth would overstrain management capabilities and threaten the Houghtons' control. But there was the alternative example of Franklin Hyde, whose exploratory work in the 1930s, defensive though it set out to be, was still providing a seemingly inexhaustible supply of commercial opportunities, not just for Corning's venture partners but for Corning itself. Now on the lookout for other technologies that showed promise of becoming big businesses from the outset, the company moved in the direction of trying to plan its innovations from the top down and concentrating more of its efforts on its most promising projects.[36]

In 1957, in addition to the first commercial color television bulbs, Corning introduced a line of electrical resistors and the first commercial fused silica (used for military delay lines). Both of these products exceeded $1 million in sales that first year. In the course of the next decade, there were only three years in which Corning did not announce some new product that achieved that level of market acceptance; in some years two or three did. From 1957 on, Armistead and Ray Voss, who was head of new product development, made this concept of the million dollar business into an important indicator of success for the technical program. Once again one of Donald Stookey's discoveries played a key role.

Serendipity Strikes Again: Pyroceram and the Road to Corning Ware

Stookey's machinable glass idea had not led to success in the aperture mask project, but chemical machining was likely to have other applications. It was while working with some of the trademarked material Fotoform that Stookey made his next important discovery:

My next discovery came as the result of a laboratory accident. I was heating
a plate of pre-exposed Fotoform© glass at 600°C in a study of its crystallizing behavior; but the automatic temperature controller misbehaved, and
when I came back the temperature had shot up to 900°C ... I expected to
see a pool of melted glass, but to my surprise my plate still had sharp corners. I took it out of the hot furnace with tongs, but it fell on the floor with
a clang like a plate of steel, and didn't break.[37]

Although the new material was the result of a succession of accidents,
subsequent experimentation with it was carefully directed. As it later came
to be understood, the process relied, paradoxically enough, on partially
crystallizing the glass, or "ceramming" it. Almost any glass formulation
could be so treated, and to varying degrees. The range of properties that
could be induced in a glass ceramic was thought to be practically infinite,
but in most cases at least one benefit was found: the glass was strengthened
considerably.

In response to this perceived potential, "the research project," as
Stookey recalled, "changed from a low-key, one-man exploration to a recognized breakthrough, and every available glass composition researcher was
enlisted to contribute his effort."[38] The purpose of this research was
twofold: to build a sufficient case for patenting it as broadly as possible and
then to find applications. Lee Waterman, who arguably understood the discovery's potential better than Stookey himself, commented at one point
that "if the Patent Department can give us a three-year lead in the marketplace, no one will ever catch us!"[39] That it was possible to turn glass into a
crystalline form was not news to glassmakers of any stripe. For them vitrifi-
cation (degeneration of glass into a crystalline structure) was a familiar
worry. But the mechanisms for the control of nucleation had not been
patented, and Stookey's claims were filed and patented in a very broad way.

The properties of this new material were potentially ideal for many
products, but the two that emerged most quickly were glass ceramic
radomes (discussed in chapter 7) and ovenware. It was not hard for almost
any Corning researcher to make the connection between the promise of
Stookey's crystalline material and the pressing needs that Corning had iden-

tified in its ovenware line years before. The limitations of Pyrex ovenware, in use by consumers, were only too familiar. Although Pyrex was supposed to be attractive enough to put on the table, baked-on food particles eventually spoiled its appearance. Hardened Pyrex had been sold for certain types of stovetop cooking, but extreme caution was required to use it in this way.

Corning wanted to overcome these drawbacks and extend its line of cookware. Within months of Stookey's discovery of a zero-expansion form of Pyroceram, Corning's technical staffs had launched its effort to make ovenware from the new material, encouraged by Lee Waterman's enthusiastic reception. Recruited from W. T. Grant to revamp Corning's consumer product line, Waterman was known as a consummate merchandiser who also had strong marketing skills. He readily spotted the appeal of Pyroceram as a space-age material for consumers, and he was politically astute enough to form an alliance with the company's technical staffs. As long as Waterman was directly responsible for consumer products, and even after he became president, the technical staffs enjoyed infusions of financial support and the pull of executive interest from the consumer products part of the business.

Corning Ware was Corning's second really successful new product of the decade after television bulbs. Although it succeeded in reaching the market in a rapid two years after discovery, it involved years of further testing and continuous process improvement. New process innovations came in the form of ceramming and forming. Starting out as a product that was so difficult to make that Corning complained of wrapping up $500 with each piece, Corning Ware costs eventually dropped dramatically. One big improvement was Giffen's Hub Machine, which not only increased the volumes and reduced the cost of forming the new material but made it possible to make products, such as large platters, that could not previously be made at all. In 1961 the new hub-formed Corning Ware was listed as a second million-dollar business developed out of Pyroceram.

The Martinsburg Plant

After several years of making Corning Ware at Corning's Pressware plant, the company opened a new plant for the ovenware at Martinsburg, West

Virginia. This required adapting heat treating techniques for ceramming that had previously been used mainly in the production of roofing tiles. While not new in principle, it had never been attempted in such volumes at Corning or many other places. Corning Ware pieces traveled on belts through long kilns where the temperature gradients were precisely controlled from start to finish. The effort to produce Corning Ware in the high volumes required involved close and intensive collaboration between Corning's heat treating and other process specialists, as well as with Stookey and his research group and the new plant staff at Martinsburg. Stookey became so involved with the Martinsburg plant over time that he tended to treat it rather like his own pilot plant. Even though they were a few hours' drive from the Chemung Valley, the Martinsburg technical staff were responsive to this treatment. In fact, their distance gave them some independence. Under the leadership of a proactive plant manager and a keen process engineering staff, they even came up with products of their own. Norval Johnston, a process engineering head, remembered the atmosphere at Martinsburg in the early days of Corning Ware as electric with creativity: "The excitement in Martinsburg in those days was equivalent to my friends who have gone into Photonics [the latest new business at Corning]. Well, it was that exciting for Corning Ware at that time. We developed new products. There was never anybody holding us back as far as money was concerned to develop new products."[40]

Corning Ware appeared to validate resoundingly Armistead's philosophy of pioneering research. The only problem was that glass ceramics had been an accidental by-product of television R&D rather than the deliberate outcome of directed research and a linear development process. In other respects, though, it definitely supported Armistead's approach: a crash research program resulting in a blockbuster commercial product. Announcements of the new material generated a flood of inquiries from potential customers in all kinds of industries, proposing novel uses of the new material.[41] For Corning's consumer business Pyroceram not only produced two generations and many variations of new products but also led to the further discovery of a chemically strengthened version of the material adaptable for fine tableware—Centura—a material developed by another Corning chemist, John MacDowell. The natural lesson for Corning to draw

from the Pyroceram experience was that a new product with radically superior properties could be expected to create its own markets.

The one aspect of pioneering research according to the linear model that
appeared not to be under control was achieving breakthroughs like Pyroceram on demand and on schedule. According to orthodox management theory, what was needed was greater top management attention to
high-priority projects, ample resources, and strict accountability to goals
and timetables. By the early 1960s, with its first cadre of new hires in place,
Corning was prepared to conduct its innovation efforts in a more systematic
and concentrated way. A succession of very expensive projects, some of
them ultimately successful, and some costly failures, came out of this
approach. In most instances, Corning's traditional persistence kept these
investments from ending as complete write-offs; but none were episodes
that anyone wanted to repeat, and together they spelled the end of a self-
sufficient, generously funded, and aloof technical organization.[42]

Chemcor and Project Muscle, 1962–1971

Armed with its new research force, Corning was in a position to address the
problem that both Decker and Amory Houghton (now known as the
Ambassador) had been pushing for years. "Glass breaks," Decker had once
commented to Armistead. "Why don't you fix that?"[43] Armistead set out to
do just that, launching a systematic effort to pursue and refine a set of techniques for strengthening glass. This time the linear model of R&D applied
from the outset with a problem identified as a priority at the highest levels
of the corporation and assured of getting all the support it needed.

    Armistead dubbed the undertaking Project Muscle and invited his tech-
nical directors to list and investigate all known forms of glass strengthening.
The only one in common use was thermal strengthening (i.e., tempering),
which had been practiced for centuries. The layering of glasses with different

coefficients of thermal expansion, such that compressive forces are induced on cooling, had also been known for some time (it had first been tried by the German company Schott before the turn of the century) but was not used for any commercial product. A third approach, one that had been tried only in laboratories, was a postforming chemical treatment known as ion exchange. Corning, in a research program carried on with great intensity in the early 1960s, refined the latter two and won four basic patents in the field. It termed the strengthened products thus produced "Chemcor."

By early 1962 Chemcor was deemed ready for unveiling to the public. What was lacking was a list of equally promising product ideas to make use of the strengthened glass. In September of that year, Corning, following the earlier Pyroceram model that had produced such an overwhelming response, broadcast its new process to the world at large. "Corning Develops Method to Make Glass So Strong It Bends and Twists" proclaimed the *Gaffer*. The company's public relations department sent a seventy-two-second film clip to over 200 television stations and gathered eighty-five members of the national press together for a conference in New York City. The coverage would be outstanding: the effort resulted in articles in major papers and magazines across the country ranging from *Aerospace Engineering* to *U.S. News and World Report*.[44]

The day before the press conference the technical products division sent to eighty-eight Corning executives a packet of instructions concerning the sensitive matter of handling outsider ideas, especially how to identify good potential products while protecting the company from future claims against its intellectual property. The press conference featured a cast of Corning's top management, including both Bill Armistead and Amory Houghton Jr. The press was treated to a display of glass sheets being bent and twisted, saw some sample pieces tossed on the floor, and were told of an experiment wherein glass tumblers, treated by a Chemcor process, were dropped from the top of the research center at Corning onto steel plate without breaking. But they saw no actual product and were told almost nothing about planned applications. As Armistead noted, "These new strong glasses have been made only in the laboratory. We expect it will be some time before they are in commercial production."[45]

Houghton offered the following invitation:

[We] hope that not only design engineers but everyone throughout the country will be intrigued with glass so strong it can be bent and flexed repeatedly. Historically, Corning has solved many problems brought to us from the outside. We feel other manufacturers may very well see uses for these new materials in other products—applications which we might not consider.[46]

One reporter interpreted the invitation in a somewhat negative light: "Scientists have been dropping cups and saucers from the top of a nine-story building in Corning, N.Y., but don't ask them why. They're not sure."[47]

Corning did have a few ideas of its own for Chemcor applications. The architectural and building applications, a business that Corning had been trying to penetrate further for decades, seemed obvious, and they were, in fact, the first such applications to be noted. One Corning salesman suggested that the company start working with record (LP) manufacturing companies, which required a smooth substrate for the casting of master discs. The potential thinness of the glass prompted another employee to suggest that it be used as a lining for tote boxes and other containers. Corning marketers estimated that a million dollars or more annually might come from using Chemcor plate in casting plexiglas and other plastics.

A list from early 1963 contained over seventy potential applications generated by the publicity effort, many of which ("detention windows for Penal and Psychiatric institutions," for example) were quite specific. The Air Force asked if it could help sponsor work on Chemcor fibers in particular. Despite supportive press coverage, however, the process did not capture the public imagination as Pyroceram had. Perhaps this was because the breakthrough had occurred along the process dimension rather than the product one and involved a level of process know-how on the part of those who adopted it that few companies might possess.[48]

Consistent with the top-down approach to strategy setting, Corning devised detailed plans for Chemcor to generate millions of dollars in sales. Half a year before the public announcement of 1962, Project Muscle was already projecting revenues reaching over $42 million by 1969 from new products in architectural, lighting, and automotive markets. Almost none of these would materialize. The numbers, it turned out, were goals rather than projections; prior to the September announcement, the only chemically strengthened product Corning had to show was its Centura line of tableware, a relatively weak glass laminate invented by researcher John Mac-Dowell, which the company had brought out in 1961.

In the end, only a fraction of the predicted volume of Chemcor-generated revenues materialized in markets Corning was not already in during the 1960s. Of the many ideas circulated within and without the company, a few became prototypes; fewer still were actually produced. Bell Telephone, urged on by designer Henry Dreyfuss, considered Chemcor-strengthened glass for its vandalism-prone telephone booths but decided to stick with tempered glass. The New York City public school system also tried Chemcor in the hopes that it would lower its annual replacement glazing bill but eventually settled on wire mesh screens instead for cost reasons, despite the fact that the screens reduced the amount of light in the classrooms, presented a fire hazard, and gave the schools an unpleasant high-security atmosphere.[49]

The two new applications for Chemcor that Corning pursued most directly, both to an unsuccessful conclusion, together help to explain Chemcor's lack of success as a generator of new business for their research breakthroughs. The first was the company's attempt to develop a market in chemically strengthened lenses for safety eyewear. Until the early 1960s, all such lenses were tempered. Corning's Chemcor techniques offered greater strength and less weight, both obvious benefits to eyeglass wearers. The lens manufacturers showed interest, and at least one of them brought chemically strengthened safety glasses to market. But worries "about strength variability, the effects of scratching and pitting on the compression layer, and the extra cost" soon sank the project. More specifically, as reported in a 1965 issue of *National Safety News*,

> One Eastern manufacturer . . . called back chemically-strengthened lenses
> he had sold after "discovering that when these lenses are scratched they can
> be more hazardous than ordinary heat-tempered lenses. The surface com-
> pressions in the chemically-tempered lenses are so great that when
> scratched even a light impact will cause the lens to 'explode'—instead of
> losing an eye, the wearer could suffer brain damage."[50]

Corning responded that the tests leading to these hazards did not reflect normal use and that nobody would use such an obviously damaged lens. But the lens manufacturers preferred to take no chances and, lacking its own direct access to eyewear customers, Corning had to depend entirely on them, though its experience with this product helped when it later introduced photochromic lenses.

The Market That Wasn't There: The Safety Windshield

The second example—in many respects the epitome of the Chemcor experience and its gravest disappointment—was Corning's safety windshield project. Laminated windshields had been introduced to American automobile production in the mid-1930s and had been required by law since 1938. A glass/plastic/glass sandwich became the enduring industry standard at that time: in essence, the plastic functioned as a net to catch the vehicle's occupants in the event of a head-on collision, and the glass served to protect the plastic. At a time when highly publicized episodes like the Chevrolet Corvair accidents had increased public concern about car safety, Corning saw Chemcor as a way to get windshield glass to do a great deal more.

Much work had been done over the years on the plastic interlayer, but both it and the glass on either side had remained more or less constant in formulation and assembly until the mid-1960s. Tempering had never been adopted for windshields because it required too thick a glass to achieve the desired strength, and optical distortion became a serious problem with thick glass. Chemcor, however, could be used to strengthen any thickness of glass, and if a windshield could be made with a strengthened glass, the laceration threat could be reduced considerably, for the glass would break into small, harmless cubes rather than the shards typical of nonstrengthened glass.

Early tests confirmed what the theory had predicted about Chemcor's advantages, but further testing also indicated serious liabilities. A Chemcor outer layer did not hold up against even moderate gravel impacts. The compressive skin on a Chemcor-treated glass could not be made thick enough to make it immune to piercing by such stones, and if it were pierced, the entire window behaved much as the eyeglass lenses had: it crazed as the internal tensions let loose. Various attempts to protect the outer layer with such coatings as silicon and mylar all proved fruitless; Chemcor could be used as the inner pane, but it would require an outer pane of some other glass, most likely the annealed glass commonly used in safety windshields.[51]

Corning researchers then tried an all-glass approach, dispensing with the plastic layer, which tended to bond poorly with glass anyway. In 1964, Corning researchers Stuart Dockerty and Clint Shay in the glass forming area had come up with an exciting new method called fusion for making thin flat glass that required no grinding or polishing.[52] The windshield project settled on this very thin sheet glass made with the fusion process and strengthened using the Chemcor technique. This piece was then sagged and bonded directly to a typical soda-lime, annealed outer pane. There was one big disadvantage to this approach: its entirely novel manufacturing process was certain to be costly. But Corning moved as quickly as possible to address these problems, especially the differences between the two layers of glass in softening points, annealing points, and processing time. By early 1969 resolving these issues was an urgent matter: the windshield was a big piece of what the company planned as an important new market—its overall automotive glass market. Management assigned additional manpower to various parts of the project and spread the development burden among no fewer than seven groups in a variety of locations. Subjected to this combined attack, the technical difficulties began to succumb.

The resulting windshield was a technical masterpiece. It used the fusion process to produce very thin, flat glass and then chemically strengthened the piece to the point where it not only flexed under strain (something no other windshield design has done to this day) but, if flexed to the point of breaking, did so in relatively safe pieces rather than in a mess of pointed shards. Furthermore, the degree of strengthening could be tuned so that the dicing pattern did not even obscure vision: the car could be safely brought to a halt even with a shattered windshield. The product looked so good that Corning invested several million dollars in revamping a furnace in the old Corning A Factory to melt the glass for the fusion process.

Still the company had made a crucial mistake: it spent large sums of development money before locating a definite market for its improved windshield. Small, little more than sample-sized quantities of Chemcor glass were purchased by several car manufacturers beginning in 1964, but this was mostly for use in the smaller windows on convertibles. The only Chemcor windshield used by one of the Big Three was in Ford's winning 1967 Le Mans entrant, which was, of course, not a production model. The designers' interest was in the flexible design possibilities for specialty windows, not in the large market represented by windshields. American Motors used the Chemcor glass on one production model, the Javelin, but that company was barely limping along itself. Project manager Joe Littleton (Jesse's son) later recalled that Corning had paid the "whole shot" without ever receiving any commitment on paper from the company it considered its target customer.

When Corning's management finally asked the large automotive manufacturers directly whether they would consider adopting the new safety windshield design the answer that came back was a flat no. Littleton again:

> We told them it was safer. Safer doesn't sell an automobile. It only discourages the sale. If people go in to buy a new automobile, they don't visualize themselves wrecking it down on the superhighway and crawling out of it barely alive when they would have been dead otherwise! They visualize themselves screaming down the highway enjoying this brand new car, having fun! ... But why should the automobile industry take any risk at all to put us into business? They were in good shape with the suppliers they had. They would have been happy for us to go over to Pittsburgh Plate or Libby-Owens-Ford and license them to whatever we had and let them work it up. This won't sell an extra one. You are dealing with a market that had no response to an innovation.[53]

In fact both Pittsburgh Plate Glass and Libbey-Owens-Ford did respond indirectly to Corning's innovation—by adopting another company's process innovation that appealed to them for reasons of cost. This was Corning's second mistake: underestimating the technical competition, specifically Pilkington's revolutionary float glass. This British glassmaker's new technology, which became available in the late 1960s, was universally and quickly adopted by the existing windshield glass companies. The float glass windshield was more appealing to the auto companies and their suppliers because it was a direct and, crucially, cheaper substitute for their existing windshield glass. It did not require changes to windshield design; it simply provided a much improved and less expensive process for making the basic sheet glass used for the outer layers of the safety windshield.

Corning finally gave up on the windshield project in September 1971. Before that, Tom MacAvoy, head of Technical Products and soon to be Corning's president, called upon contacts of his own at Pilkington to see what Pilkington was doing with float glass at its plant in Canada. What he saw there convinced him that Corning had grossly underestimated the economic potential of the float glass process to undercut their windshield approach: contrary to initial predictions by company scientists, the float process could make quite thin glass and, whether thick or thin, could do it at low cost. Tests at the Blacksburg plant, where Corning's new glass had been transferred for production in June 1971, saw some improvement in the production process pointing to lower costs, but with a negative response from Detroit there was little reason to continue.[54]

The Limits of Technology Push

The picture of a company led on by its own technology was only a mild exaggeration on Littleton's part: throughout a long and very expensive development cycle Corning had been so obsessed with its own definition of consumer safety in windshields that it had ignored some key market factors. While the auto companies had been "intrigued with styling possibilities of a side window that could be curved," that was not what they were willing to pay for.[55] The market information that had so encouraged Corning in the formative phases of its project had not come from the auto companies, but from third parties with an axe to grind. These were chiefly the auto safety organizations and auto associations who believed that conditions were ripe by the end of the 1960s for government to impose much more stringent requirements for safety measures on carmakers. Conditions were indeed ripe, but there turned out to be multiple remedies.

Happily for Corning, it was never inclined to throw out or denigrate the entire chemical strengthening enterprise because of the failure of one portion of it, no matter how publicly embarrassing it might be. The failure of the highly visible windshield project did not mean the failure of Chemcor. Inside Corning's consumer business, with Stookey cheering them on, the Martinsburg plant adopted chemical strengthening in the form of ion exchange to enable the design of several new products. In the late 1960s other applications of Chemcor—combining strong compositions with lamination processes—appeared in consumer projects code-named Hercules, later known commercially as Corelle. By 1967 twenty-three different chemical strengthening processes were considered part of Corning's repertoire.[56] Still, Chemcor did not create a genuine new business worth more than a few million dollars, and that prompted a reassessment of a linear approach to R&D.

Diversification Beyond Glass, 1962–1972

In earlier years Corning's senior management group had reaffirmed its commitment to glass as a Corning identity issue: "Corning is not primarily a glass company making unique products, but a unique products company making glass," was its slogan as late as 1964. But by 1966 the wind had shifted. When Amo Houghton addressed the invited guests at the dedication of the new Sullivan Park laboratory, he noted that there was "a constant and characteristic dissatisfaction with staying where we are. As there are Venture Capital companies," he continued, "we are a 'venture research' company continuing to explore the still untouched world of glass, yet moving in other directions where there is a need and where we can establish pre-eminence."[57]

In fact, this strategy was already under way even before the move to the new quarters in Sullivan Park, first in the hiring of researchers from new disciplines like biochemistry to do exploratory work as early as 1963, and later in Armistead's thorough recasting of his 1967 budget and all resource allocation procedures related to it. As a practical matter, Corning's effective long-term strategy was being formulated in the deliberations between senior management and the head of the technical staffs. For budget year 1967 the shift out of a concentration on glass compositions and processes was significant. Just over a third of the budget was allocated to glass projects, and an additional 12 percent to refractories and related ceramics, including auto emission products. The remaining 50 percent was divided between electronics research of various kinds (40 percent, including laboratory and medical instrumentation), diagnostic materials and devices, sensors, and other devices that would eventually lead to computer-based diagnostic systems. In a sign that Armistead and Houghton were ready to concentrate resources once again after a period of relative far-reaching exploration, the number of small funded development projects was cut back drastically, from a high of 185 to 67.[58]

Another way Corning intended to enter new businesses was by acquiring other businesses: controlling them completely instead of combining with them, as it had with MacBeth Evans, or partnering with them, as with the three earlier associations. The appeal of acquisition was that Corning could book the revenues directly and thereby achieve the growth it needed; and, of course, it did not have to share the expected profits with any other party. Perhaps most compelling, if it acquired a new company in a different business, it did not run the risk of the kind of antitrust action it had faced with Owens-Corning, still very fresh in the collective memory. Out of its foothold in laboratory glass and diagnostic equipment, for instance, Corning began in the 1960s to seek acquisitions in the medical diagnostics business. But the fast-growing business area that held the most attraction for Corning was electronics, where the company already had business to protect—a significant sideline in passive components (capacitors, resistors, and other simple electronic components).

A Blind Alley in Electronics

Corning had played an important role in the development of many electronic products, from the lightbulb to radar to metallized glass components. In almost all instances, the company had explored a new product line in response to specific direct customer demand (Edison's request for bulb blanks, for example, or the navy's wartime call for CRTs), not in anticipation of it. In the early 1960s, however, Mal Hunt, manager of Corning's electronics division, tried to change the way Corning did business in this industry.

Corning had become solidly ensconced in a comfortable niche—manufacturing—by the time solid-state electronics began to make a major impact commercially. It was profitable work; the company could count on selling high-margin bulbs for power tubes to both military and commercial customers. Corning was also producing ultrasonic delay lines for Philco's distant early warning radar systems throughout the 1950s, its fused silica production facilities located first on Denison Parkway in Corning. Solid state, the company feared, might disturb those sales lines. The semiconductor was a particular threat.

Mal Hunt complained that Corning's central laboratories were not giving his electronic components business the support it needed to ward off the solid-state threat. Nor, he argued, were those labs properly equipped or manned for intensive research in this field. Real growth was not likely to come from his existing product lines. Corning's mastery of materials was unparalleled, but the production of electronic components required more than materials knowledge. Not long after gaining top management permission to move his electronics business to Raleigh, North Carolina, Hunt also arranged to set up a satellite laboratory there. This represented a challenge to the centralized, corporate model of research, and Armistead was opposed to the idea. While allowing it to happen, he left the formation of the new lab almost entirely to Hunt and his people.

Though it was located near the Raleigh factory, the Raleigh laboratory was not intended to be a works laboratory in any sense; it was meant to produce next-generation ideas for the electronics business. The intent was to explore niche areas of electronics that would allow the business to draw on the expertise in Corning's central laboratory and adapt them for Corning's electronics business. Hunt hired Charles Wakeman, an outsider to Corning and a Ph.D. in electrical engineering, to set up and run the new lab.

The small new facility that Wakeman put together by the mid-1960s consisted of fifty professionals in five departments: electro-optics, microwave, systems development, microcircuits, and fluidics. Condon's oft-voiced concerns about the difficulty of getting good research people were evident from the start in Raleigh. At the time, Wakeman found it next to impossible to hire scientists of the stature Corning typically worked with in a place so far removed from the major academic centers of electronics research—Cambridge, Princeton, and the San Francisco Bay Area—and for a company unknown in electronics circles. Corning may also have been reaping the consequences of its standoffishness toward government work in an as yet unforeseen way. Companies that performed significant government contract work were part of a privileged network. They not only received considerable government funding but also were in touch with what was going on scientifically among other government contractors. It was almost impossible for a group of researchers to be cut off from this network and successfully participate in leading-edge electronics.[59]

Hunt had certainly achieved the organizational distance from the Chemung Valley that he hoped for but had so little familiarity with the Corning research community that there was little chance for the researchers in Raleigh to draw on its expertise. Even Gerhard Megla, Raleigh's most eminent scientist, a defector from East Germany, found it hard to establish contact. By 1967 the technical advisory committee charged with appraising Corning's technical effort raised concerns both as to the caliber of Raleigh's personnel and the ability to integrate Raleigh's efforts with the central laboratory.

Before the Raleigh laboratory was even up and running in 1964, Hunt hedged his bets in a different direction: he persuaded Corning to purchase Signetics, a small west coast semiconductor manufacturer, that had its own lab, its own fabrication facilities, and, as it turned out, its own agenda. Corning's idea was not just to buy into the semiconductor business but to apply its traditional leverage principle to what it viewed as complementary knowledge and skills between Corning and Signetics.

Armistead was even less enthusiastic about the acquisition than he had been about the Raleigh lab, arguing from the start that the Signetics people were mere technological followers unworthy of Corning's attention. For Armistead, who believed passionately in the strategic importance of pioneering in technology, the "me-too" philosophy that Signetics displayed was little short of contemptible. This acquisition was one of the few areas where he and Amo Houghton openly disagreed. Houghton was also listening to the advice of fellow executives in television and other Corning electronics businesses, and he would support Signetics for the better part of a decade.

A Downward Spiral: Signetics

Signetics was a classic Silicon Valley start-up: located in Sunnyvale, California, it was founded in September 1961 by four engineers from Fairchild Semiconductors, a dominant player in the semiconductor business. By July of the following year the newcomer was shipping highly specialized transistors to its customers in the military/aerospace industry. Four months later, Corning purchased a majority interest in the company.[60]

The sensitivity that Corning normally displayed in forming its joint ventures was absent with Signetics. Though the new company badly needed the infusion of capital that Corning's offer represented, its founders resented what they considered Corning's hard-nosed bargaining tactics; the purchase was made for five cents a share.[61] Furthermore, Corning's customary assumption of leverage, that its own expertise might be applicable to Signetics's business, was ill founded. Instead, as Amo Houghton noted a few years later, "We found we had nothing to give them."[62] This is something of an overstatement; there was much that Corning might have taught the fledgling company about efficient manufacturing practices, statistical process control, and successful technology management, but Signetics employees expressed no interest in learning these things from its patron.

To some extent, the attitude of Signetics's management was simply an expression of the cultural values of the semiconductor industry and its home, Silicon Valley. Corning's central process research organization shared information within and among divisions; Silicon Valley was secretive. According to Jack Carpenter, a former head of the Process Research Center who was sent by Corning to work with Signetics,

> One of the problems that the semiconductor people had was it was very closely held technology at the time and nobody wanted to let anybody know anything. I have seen some of the operators ask some junior engineer, "Well, why do you want to do this?" and the junior engineer would say, "None of your business. You will do it this way, and that's how you will do it."[63]

Most of the success Signetics attained came with little input from its corporate owners. Any success was slow in coming. Despite projected profits in 1964, that year the company lost $1 million in sales, a direct result of Fairchild's sudden announcement, in September, that it was cutting its component prices in half. This was indeed a business in which it was crucial to be a leader. Signetics entrepreneurs, for all of their Silicon Valley breeding, lacked the proper mentality for success. Tom MacAvoy, who later inherited the organizational responsibility for Signetics when its financial demands had become too overwhelming for Corning, shared Armistead's verdict: "they were followers and not leaders." Signetics never did rise higher than fourth in the field.[64]

Despite the loss, 1964 was something of a turnaround: Corning appointed James Riley, a marketing manager from Raleigh, to run Signetics. Riley did a better job than others of negotiating the tricky cultural and communication gaps between the two companies, partly by insisting that Signetics be run like a California company. In 1965 Signetics had the first in a string of mildly profitable years. Riley gave stock options to a third of his staff (at a time when fewer than 5 percent of Corning employees held Corning options) and created a program of profit sharing to motivate and retain employees. In the eyes of middle management back in Corning such a program was unthinkable. Although Riley's methods were successful in the short run, they further widened the cultural chasm between the two organizations.

Signetics grew steadily for several years after this, opening a plant in Utah in 1966, another in Seoul, Korea, later that same year, a second in Utah in 1969, and one in Scotland shortly thereafter. The company also diversified away from fickle and demanding high-performance military sales to commercial ones, and established itself in a number of product lines other than the bipolar, ultrareliable circuits demanded by the government. In mid-1970, however, Riley resigned, and Charles Harwood, a long-time general manager of the Science Products Division assumed control. At this point Corning's hopes for making something out of its acquisition started unraveling. Signetics began demanding larger and larger amounts of capital to be competitive in what was getting to be a crowded business, even while Corning—which was running into expensive troubles in its core business, television—had less and less capital to supply. In the late 1960s Corning's television bulb business was coming unglued in just the way management had long feared it might.

TV CHICKENS COME HOME TO ROOST, 1966–1971

Sylvania, Corning's closest and most reliable television customer, was threatening to start up its own glass production in the late 1960s. Corning gave this matter its undivided attention. Working to persuade the company that it was very much outside its own interests to make such a move, it invested heavily in locating plants close to Sylvania's plants, and it organized itself to behave like Sylvania's own development department. Still not convinced that Sylvania's threats were mere negotiating tactics, Corning even commissioned an in-depth study from Arthur D. Little, analyzing the economics of such a move from Sylvania's point of view. The study concluded that the economics were marginal for Sylvania. Ironically, the consulting company based its conclusion not on actual data from Sylvania, which was not available, but on data from RCA.[65]

RCA, it turned out, used the same information to make the opposite decision. Its leaders believed that it was a superior company technologically and that it could with its superior science easily master glass technology, which they scornfully regarded as a black art. Moreover, it knew it did not have to produce all of its own bulbs, just the ones that required the least expertise. In 1968 RCA announced plans to build its own glass plant in Circleville, Indiana, to supply television bulb enclosures to its Lancaster tube plant as well as its television plant in Indianapolis.

Having absorbed this bad news from its most unpredictable customer, Corning worked hard to retain the remainder of its business. Corning turned its attention to finding new methods of cost reduction in its television manufacturing processes. But this was to be the first engagement of a losing battle, for beginning in the late 1960s Corning's domestic television customers were running into fierce competition from Japanese imports and Corning's demand was wholly dependent on theirs.

It was at this rather low point that Corning's pioneering research effort proved its ultimate worth. Although the company would not be counted among the most profitable American corporations for decades, it did have several healthy new products to fall back on, cumulatively more than sufficient replacement for the dwindling television business. For more than two decades Corning would rely on a diversified portfolio of smaller technology-based businesses rather than on any one blockbuster.

The "Technological Till"

Throughout the 1960s there were always smaller businesses, clustered in several divisions, that remained outside the spotlight of intense top management interest (Advanced Products, Electronic Products, Science Products), and each fostered a number of research and infant development projects relative to their product lines; the number of individual development projects alone reached 185 in 1966. Even during television's heyday, roughly 33 percent of Corning's business, and perhaps the same percentage of the research budget, was still organized more along the lines of the specialty glass business, operating beyond the confines of either television or the consumer business and fragmented into a number of small products and processes.

Researchers became involved in these areas either because they offered a problem to pursue or because a problem they wanted to pursue on its intrinsic merits could be construed as relating to one of these areas. In the early 1960s there was little in the broad area of specialty glass that a Corning researcher would not have the freedom to pursue if that was what caught his fancy and his participation wasn't immediately crucial to one of the large projects.

The problem with wandering off the map was that while a project could continue for years as a research or small development project, it was hard to get follow-on funding from the corporation and it was hard to compete with the big programs for attention from Corning's patent department. Though the smaller businesses frequently complained of being short-changed and the development projects linked to them sometimes went nowhere, collectively they played a critical role of a sort that was found only rarely in other companies. They contributed crucially to what Chuck Lucy, one of Corning's internal entrepreneurs who joined Corning because of his background in government electronics, called the company's "technological till." These various small enterprises stored a collection of working, ever developing materials and processes, and the human expertise needed to deploy them. This reservoir periodically produced a process or product crucial to a much larger new enterprise. Processes like vapor deposition, as well as literally thousands of glass and ceramic compositions, were thus more or less ready for rapid, if not instant, deployment. As we describe in chapter 9, it was these processes that would come to the rescue during the difficult adjustment period of the 1970s, when the big projects failed and television took a premature nosedive.

THE SELF-CONTAINMENT TRAP AT MIDCENTURY

Consider the occupational hazards of pioneering even for a proven creator like Donald Stookey. From Pyroceram on, he enjoyed the highest status a Corning researcher could attain: his work had resulted in conspicuous commercial returns for the company. Yet Stookey was the first to admit that research was often a hard and anxious life. Exploration on scientific frontiers could be exhilarating, but frequently it was lonely work marked by long dry periods. Furthermore, even Stookey could not ignore Armistead's calls for help on high priority work not his own. At Corning when the call came, all hands were expected to show up, whatever their current preoccupation. Stookey came to enjoy an unusual degree of support among his colleagues and from younger researchers who chose to follow in his footsteps, but he hit some low points on his way to that enviable position.

The loneliness of Stookey's exploration also had something to do with the small number of glass researchers outside the company, especially in the nascent field of glass ceramics. One form of psychic reward for exploration, after all, is to share new findings with scientific colleagues. At one point Stookey presented his findings at an international symposium of the American Chemical Society. Of 10,000 papers delivered at that symposium, his was the only one on glass. Presenting his work in the middle of a session on elastomers and plastomers, he felt, as he often did, more like a curiosity than a colleague.

Yet Stookey shared with many of his colleagues on Corning's technical staff a strong personal identification with the company and its leadership. In his personal account of his career, *Journey to the Center of the Crystal Ball*. Stookey compared his position at Corning to that of a medieval alchemist under powerful patronage. At one low point when he felt he had no more inventions left in him Stookey announced his intention to leave Corning. When his old friend Bill Armistead mentioned this to the Houghtons, "the Ambassador" offered Stookey a paid sabbatical. The break proved rejuvenating and Stookey returned to do more creative work.

The story underscores not only Corning's loyalty to a valued employee but the company's commitment in the 1960s to maintaining the right climate for individual creative work. Pioneering research was believed to depend crucially on the value of the gifted individual—the source of all breakthroughs. Corning's technical community had been optimized for this conception of what it took to hit a home run. In the process its technical staffs division had become an institution that neither depended on nor shared much with outsiders; it was, by location and orientation, absorbed in its own self-generated technologies.

Stories about Bill Armistead's position in the company, his ability to maintain high levels of corporate funding, the heads of Corning's businesses approaching him hat in hand to beg for technical help, were all indications of this view of the self-contained role of R&D. While true for their time they assumed mythical proportions not just in Corning but in many major research-performing companies. Effective while old relationships endured to bridge the boundaries, this model became less effective as technical communities lost contact with the rest of their organizations and with customers and they no longer enjoyed the cumulative value of everyday interaction. Furthermore, organizations that staked their worth on a few high-visibility projects tended to be judged by those projects and were hurt badly when even one of them failed. In Corning's case, pioneering research produced a number of technologies that were ahead of their time and had staying power. But the popular nickname for Sullivan Park, Ponderosa (named after the isolated homestead in the popular TV western *Bonanza*), was telling. It indicated the difficulties the organization would have in reengaging the rest of the company, especially once top managers recognized that complete innovations were neither individual nor linear and depended on the collective ingenuity of the company at large.

Meanwhile, the disastrous experience with RCA and the disappointing premature falloff of the television bulb business held some important lessons for Corning. One of these was the danger of investing heavily in businesses over which it had little or no proprietary control. This lesson, carried forward, helped make Corning's pioneering research eventually pay off in other ways. As we discuss in chapter 8, after years of reacting defensively to prewar antitrust problems, the company developed a much more proactive strategy based on its intellectual property.

INVISIBLE ASSETS

INTELLECTUAL PROPERTY AND THE

SEARCH FOR COMPETITIVE ADVANTAGE

> On Tuesday an opinion was handed down by the U.S. District
> Court in Toledo in the case of United States of America vs. Hart-
> ford-Empire et al, in which the Court declared that in conjunction
> with many other companies and individuals the Corning Glass
> Works and myself have been guilty of violation of the anti-trust
> laws of the United States. My directors are insistent that I return
> home to take my part in the many necessary decisions affecting the
> operations of the business including those involved in an appeal.
>
> AMORY HOUGHTON, LETTER RESIGNING FROM THE WAR
> PRODUCTION BOARD, 28 AUGUST 1942[1]

THE TENSIONS between creativity and control, so evident within the Technical Staffs after World War II, as they pursued innovation on demand, were playing out on the national stage as well. Nationally, Corning's position as a technology leader in the glass industry forced it to contend with the shifting sands of domestic antitrust policy. To avoid having to share its most closely guarded secrets with competitors, Corning had become more self-sufficient technically, guarding many of its discoveries in the form of trade secret.

This largely reactive approach to managing intellectual property after World War II was shaped by the set of antitrust cases that convicted both Corning and its management of monopolistic behavior in the period before the war. For similar reasons the company largely abandoned its strategy of association. But when RCA, Corning's largest customer for television bulbs, set up its own glass factory to produce bulbs for cathode ray tubes (CRTs) it called Corning's ways of protecting its intellectual property in the post-war era into question. Corning's commanding position in television glass had relied as much on its know-how in such areas as funnel spinning as it had on gaining an ironclad patent position in glass compositions. But the RCA experience suggested that Corning's future strategy for its intellectual property needed to be crafted more deliberately, to form a more secure foundation for any new business that Corning would launch.

This more proactive approach to the exploitation of intellectual property was slow to emerge. For most of the post-war period Corning was careful and reactive: careful to ensure that its brands were precise guides to the real value of its products, reactive only to the most egregious attempts to violate or infringe its rights. The risk of attracting further unwelcome government attention was too great and the cost of litigation much too high.

A new era dawned with fiber optics. A form of relationship reminiscent of the old associations was the only way Corning research entrepreneurs could find to keep this technology alive in its early years. In the end this proved to be one of several lucky breaks. The sustained support of some large future customers in exchange for regular glimpses at Corning's developing knowledge base were crucial to keeping the program afloat. But it was Corning's skill in managing and using its intellectual property for strategic positioning that gave the company the lead it needed to establish itself in an industry where the barriers to entry seemed unassailable. At the same time, the renewal of association with much larger enterprises, this time on an international scale, while essential to the development of the company's waveguide business, illustrated in painful detail the tensions and hazards that could attend that strategy as well.

TROUBLES WITH ANTITRUST, 1938–1945

As the epigraph reveals, in 1942 Amory Houghton left his position as director general of operations with the War Production Board to marshal his own troops in Corning's struggle against the Department of Justice. The company had pleaded nolo contendere to an antitrust charge in 1941 and

had been named as a defendant in four other antitrust cases over the course
of the previous two years. During the fall of 1942 the Corning forces were in
the midst of a rout.

The company's run-in with the Department of Justice had been a long
time coming. It was, in essence, the closing parenthesis of a period of
remarkably weak antitrust enforcement that had begun in the 1920s, when a
strong economy and a business-oriented national leadership had turned
political attention to other matters. In 1926, GE won a landmark case
brought by an already much-attenuated antitrust division, which served to
establish the ability of a patent holder to dictate price and marketing characteristics to its licensees. On the back of this decision, and in the relative
absence of antitrust oversight, the Glass Trust, established in outline as
early as 1912, solidified its hold on the container industry.[2]

Both the trust and the political-economic environment that supported it
persisted until well into the Great Depression. Presidents Harding,
Coolidge, and in particular Hoover had all worked to promote government-
business relations. Hoover, first as secretary of commerce and later as president, was a particularly avid supporter of business self-regulation, for which
industry associations were considered an excellent mechanism. But just as
the recessions of the 1870s and 1880s had generated public outcry against
the evils of monopolists and their favored vehicles, the trusts, so too did the
Great Depression of the 1930s.

Stimulated by the uproar, Congress created the Temporary National
Economic Committee to look into the question of excessive concentration
in the American economy. The committee held hearings between December 1938 and May 1940, issuing its final report in March 1941. Corning
appeared as a subject of investigation twice, once in a series of presentations offered by the Department of Justice between 5 and 16 December 1938
concerning the Glass Trust, and again in relation to testimony on Owens-
Corning concerning the cross-licensing of patents used to establish international cartels.[3] The essence of the department's assertions in the former
instance is epitomized by the figure on the next page.

The government's lawyers would argue in a series of cases that Corning
and the Houghtons were at the center of a widespread conspiracy to control the entire domestic glass industry—specialty, flat, and container alike.

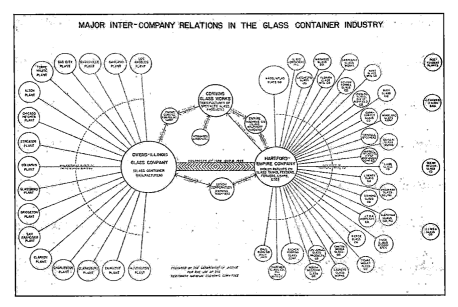

This diagram prepared by The National Economic Committee (TNEC) during Roosevelt's New Deal administration was used against Corning and its associates in congressional hearings and the court cases that followed. Corning's position in the middle of the diagram was meant to show that a small and relatively unknown company had gained an improper degree of control over the whole glass industry, and those who would try to enter it, by placing itself at the knowledge center of the industry.

Suddenly, Corning's technical and intercorporate connections, its wide-ranging contributions to glassmaking technologies, its extensive library of glass formulas, and even its joint ventures—undertakings the company was proud of, not least because they allowed the business development of entirely new classes of product—all appeared as the ties and girders of an industry-wide oligopoly.

Even as sympathetic a source as *Fortune* magazine had to admit there was something to the government's charges. "[The Houghtons'] relations with other companies," the magazine conceded, "probably made them and their glassworks considerably more powerful in the glass industry than research alone would have made them." But, the article continued, Corning and the Houghtons were hardly villains: "the philosophy of law changed with the philosophy of government and the inevitable happened: Corning, the Houghtons, and the glass industry ran head on into the Department of

Justice."[4] Under another political regime, and certainly under previous ones, what was now seen as an illegal trust would have been nothing more than a rational and innocent way of doing business in oftentimes difficult and chaotic markets.

Whatever *Fortune's* beliefs on the subject, the fact was that Corning and its close associates had been vilified in public hearings before Congress. Hartford Empire was described as a "concern, whose office is the maintenance of a strict discipline over technology," and "overlord to the glass-container industry." Far from being progressive or a technological innovator, Hartford Empire, in collusion with Corning and others, was depicted as trying "to advance the art just fast enough to keep alive a few basic patents." Its goal, critics claimed, was to "stagger invention, prolong the life of old processes, withhold novelty until it is needed. The company [is] a creature of the dominant concerns. . . . A private corporation has in short established an industrial government; it maintains law and order within a province of the national economy."[5] This same writer described the creation of the Glass Trust as beginning with a "rapprochement [that] led to an anschluss," followed by "a blitzkrieg . . . directed against the independents," fighting words for the day.[6]

Under the leadership of Thurman Arnold, assistant attorney general for antitrust, the Department of Justice pursued separate antitrust actions against GE (one each directed at incandescent and fluorescent lightbulb production), the Hartford Empire Company (containers), Libbey-Owens-Ford (flat glass), and Owens-Corning (fiberglass); in each case Corning and the Houghtons were named (often along with other companies and individuals) as codefendants. And the department won: where the matter was not settled by a consent decree, the defendants were invariably found guilty. Though each case had its own set of serious ramifications, the heart and soul of the matter was *United States v. Hartford-Empire Company, et al.*

United States v. Hartford-Empire Company, et al.

On 11 December 1939, Arnold filed suit against the Hartford Empire Company, Corning, the Empire Machine Company, Owens-Illinois Glass Company, and a host of other glass concerns. Amory Houghton, Arthur

Houghton, and Alexander Falck were named as defendants in association with Hartford Empire; the three, plus Arthur Day, in association with Empire; and all four plus Eugene Sullivan, William Curtiss, and J. L. Peden in association with Corning itself.[7] Attempts to negotiate a consent decree proved fruitless, and the case came before the U.S. District Court for the Northern District of Ohio in Toledo in March 1941.

The Justice Department contended that Hartford Empire, Owens-Illinois, and Corning were monopolizing the $1.6 million domestic glass container market and were further using their control of patents for glass-making machinery to draw and preserve boundaries between the various branches of glass manufacture (flat glass, containers, and specialty glass). At the heart of this alleged conspiracy lay a series of detailed patent licenses apportioning various classes of containers, divvying up domestic markets and setting prices for the licensees, which included all but three struggling independents, two of whom were being sued by Hartford Empire for patent infringement. This situation had been carefully constructed by the leading executives of the various companies involved—many of whom held positions at more than one of the corporations named in the suit—and was grossly anticompetitive and therefore in violation of the Sherman and Clayton Acts. So said the government.

As evidence for the above, the government's attorneys pointed to a series of agreements among the defendants: the 1916 cross-licensing agreement between the Empire Machine Company and the Hartford-Fairmont Company, their subsequent merger, and a second cross-license between the newly formed Hartford Empire Company and Corning, both of the latter having been executed in 1922. Similar contracts made in the 1920s and 1930s between Owens-Illinois and Hartford Empire and between the two and a third company dedicated to glass forming machines (the Lynch Corporation) formed a second leg of the conspiracy, according to the Department of Justice. Closing the triangle, they noted the existence of the recently formed Owens-Corning Fiberglas Corporation which was, of course, a fifty-fifty venture between Owens-Illinois and Corning.

In August 1942 the court handed down a sweeping judgment against Corning and the other defendants. It declared that in addition to bringing about an uncompetitive market for glass containers, the agreements excluding Corning from the manufacture of glass containers and forbidding the rest from engaging in specialty glass production had allowed Corning to similarly monopolize the market for "laboratory, electrical, paste mold, signal, optical, oven ware, chemical-resistant and heat-resistant ware, and bulbs, tubing and cane"—in short, essentially every form of glass at the time produced except flat glass, containers, and fiberglass and silicones.[8] The court levied a draconian punishment. Hartford Empire was forced into receivership. Corning and the others were ordered to eschew price discrimination of any sort. All of the defendants' patents for glassmaking machinery were to be made available to all comers on a royalty-free basis, and future patents for glassmaking machinery won by the defendants (both corporate and individual) were to be licensed, again, to any who made the request, for a reasonable royalty. Finally, licenses on both present and future patents were to be accompanied by the relevant "drawings and patterns relating to licensed machinery or methods used in the manufacture of glassware."[9] Such a ruling would include even Corning's Ribbon Machine.

Amory Houghton's subsequent resignation from the War Production Board prompted a small flood of letters of commiseration from various industrialists, in particular those engaged in manufacturing optical instruments, some of whom had had their own run-ins with Arnold and his trustbuster. George Wells of the American Optical Company wrote to say that "Judge Kloeb...went 'down the line.' Sorry for you," he continued, "imagine our turn comes next!"[10] M. H. Eisenhart of Bausch & Lomb offered his support as well, noting that "I was simply astounded to see the extent to which the Court laid down decisions in connection with the Glass Container Suit, and yet I suppose in view of the temper of the times and the accusation of the Anti-trust Division, this is the kind of conclusion which is quite inevitable."[11] A couple of years earlier Bausch & Lomb had negotiated a consent decree with that division for cartelization of the world military optical instruments market but had been placed under burdens that now appeared relatively insubstantial in light of Corning's adjudicated penalties.

As promised, Houghton led his company in its appeal to the Supreme Court. Corning's attorneys, led by Thurlow M. Gordon, attempted to distinguish Corning from the container manufacturers; their argument took a number of curious turns in the process. They pointed out that the latter industry had abandoned hand shops in the face of the successful Owens machine, whereas "Corning continued hand operation in many branches of its activities to the date of the suit" and could not therefore be said to be competing solely, or even mainly, on the basis of superior and restricted equipment. Indeed, Corning's greatest technical triumph, the Palomar mirror blank, was, it was emphasized, "made *by hand.*" Likewise, Steuben glassware was also manufactured by hand, "or by simple presses which have nothing whatever to do with the machinery developed by Hartford-Empire."[12] The high-volume container industry was, by contrast, heavily automated.

The appeal gained Corning some important concessions, but the essential point of the government's victory—that a trust had existed and had resulted in an uncompetitive and illegal structuring of the glass container market—struck the Supreme Court as self-evident. Furthermore, the court held Corning guilty of extending its borosilicate patents via illegal trust agreements. However, the lower court, in seeking to draw the teeth of an illegal combination, was seen to have taken along a good bit of the jaw. In particular, the Supreme Court found the open-ended nature of Judge Kloeb's rulings to be unwarranted: the purpose of the case was to break up the trust, not to strip all involved of their fundamental rights associated with patent ownership nor to be (and here the Supreme Court quoted the brief prepared by Corning's lawyers) "so vague as to put the whole conduct of the defendants' business at the peril of a summons for contempt."[13] Hartford Empire was removed from receivership and enjoined, along with the other defendants, to license its patents without bias toward any applicant according to a regular scale of royalties. Significantly, the Court also struck down the lower court's order that the patents were to be licensed royalty-free. The higher court in general placed much closer bounds in terms of time and the precise nature of the patents that should be subject to control of the sort outlined by the lower court and, much to Corning's relief, exempted all but that company's ovenware patents from the decree.

Further Trials

Though the Supreme Court's judgment alleviated the burden of guilt somewhat, Corning and the Houghtons had been dubbed major players in a conspiracy by the highest court in the land and had been held to have used patents as blocking and fencing instruments in support of that conspiracy. A series of related suits, also prosecuted by Arnold's Antitrust Division, revealed that similar arrangements had resulted in uncompetitive and illegal situations in other glass-related markets. While *Hartford-Empire* alone made it impossible for Corning to continue business as usual, these latter cases added further twists of their own.

The first, *United States v. G. E., et al.*, was directed at the lightbulb industry. Corning and GE (along with Libbey Glass) had been enjoined from dominating the lightbulb market via market-sharing agreements as early as 1911 (this thanks to a consent decree brought under the Sherman Act). Nevertheless, GE's powerful patent position made it the chief concern in the market for finished lightbulbs, and Corning's invention of the Ribbon Machine returned the two to a position of dominance almost immediately thereafter. By 1928, the two companies formally established a second set of similar agreements. It was these latter contracts that the government's lawyers attacked in two suits, one against incandescent bulbs and the other against fluorescent ones (the first filed in 1941, the second a year later). These suits were postponed at the behest of the military, but there could be little doubt but that the relationship would have to end with the war. This effectively brought to a close Corning's longest-standing technical partnership, one that might otherwise have served the company as a direct model for its soon-to-be-burgeoning television bulb business.

The second case, the so-called flat glass case (*United States v. Libbey-Owens-Ford Glass Co., et al.*), was in many respects a duplicate of *Hartford-Empire*: Corning and the other defendants (primarily the major domestic manufacturers of flat glass) were enjoined from agreements contributing to control of the market for flat glass, and, as in *Hartford-Empire*, patents were specifically cited as a mechanism that had been but must never again be used as an instrument of such control. Corning was forced to grant nonexclusive and unrestricted licenses for the patents listed in the decree to any comer willing to pay a reasonable royalty. The key difference was that this case was settled by consent decree in 1946; Corning and the glass industry as a whole had lost their taste for court battles in the wake of *Hartford-Empire*.

A third important case, *United States v. Owens-Corning Fiberglas*

Corporation, et al., was also settled via consent decree; Owens-Corning, Owens-Illinois, and Corning denied any violation of law but accepted the cancellation of a number of overseas contracts. Once again, the court ordered that a defendant (in this case Owens-Corning) issue nonexclusive, royalty-free licenses to all comers (though a specific list of such patents that were to be so treated was provided by the court) and, as in the containers case, the court did not overlook the fact that the patents alone were of only limited value; Owens-Corning was ordered to "furnish for a period of five years . . . to each licensee . . . a written manual describing all methods, processes, etc., employed by Owens-Corning at the date of the decree in its commercial production of fiber glass products involving the use of a licensed invention."[14]

As often happens when the government brings an antitrust case, private suits followed. A number of independent lamp manufacturers sued Corning for damages associated with its refusal to sell bulb blanks to the independents for the same price charged GE. Owens-Corning also paid fines related to similar suits. These actions added to the cost of litigation and the eventual penalties paid, both in terms of dollar amounts and the attention required by management and legal counsel.

Though a convicted monopolist, Corning never saw itself as a corporate criminal; the company—and the Houghtons—were mystified by the vitriol of its attackers. As *Fortune* commented, "Corning is something of a contradiction among corporations. Monopoly charges were proved against it in the glass container case and it faces others, yet it has consistently broadened its field by research, by producing new products, and by reducing prices— functions that monopolists, according to classical theory, customarily avoid."[15] Classical theory is hardly the best guide to actual business practice, but this quote does capture the sense of things: though Corning had helped create a technological oligopoly within the glass industry, it had never rested on its laurels or abandoned its search for new glass technologies.

Eugene Sullivan, in a monograph written for the joint patent inquiry of the National Association of Manufacturers, the National Industrial Conference Board, and the National Engineering Council (all three notably conservative organizations) noted that "today a manufacturer will take a responsible competitor through his plant, feeling that so long as his own developments are secured to him by patent protection cooperation will work to the general good of seller and consumer alike. Such cooperation and such contacts are a vital factor in the leadership which American industry enjoys today."[16] Corning and the other major players in the industry had established a gentlemanly—if rather patronizing—control of things, but this was hardly a covert matter or something of which Corning and the Houghtons were ashamed, as Sullivan's frank comments indicated:

> The real need for patent protection is against irresponsible competition. A responsible competitor unless he takes with him some new feature will not enter a field in which there is insufficient business for himself as well as for those already in it and in which, therefore, at best a superficial success can be attained and that only by cutthroat methods. An irresponsible competitor, ignorantly or deliberately selling below cost, will skimp quality and eventually harm the consumer as well as himself.[17]

As Sullivan noted, "Prices [in the container industry] dropped 22 percent between 1925 and 1937,"[18] and consumers were, he argued with complete sincerity, in other ways—most notably in the reliability of the purchased products—far better served than they had been under the more chaotic regime that had prevailed previous to the Glass Trust's coming to power. Be that as it may, the law of the land was the chaos of competition.

In Terrorem

For over a decade then, Corning was under more or less concentrated attack by the Department of Justice. This, and particularly the harshness of the 1942 ruling in the glass container case, produced a siege mentality at Corning that affected its approach to licensing, patenting, and the government in general for at least the next forty years. The company, its lawyers claimed, had been "placed in terrorem" by parts of the 1942 ruling;[19] a frightened organization, it would be shocked further as the various antitrust actions wound to a close.

Nor was Corning alone in this: the entire industry was thrown into

chaos in the wake of *Hartford-Empire*. The lay of the land had been deci-
sively altered by the antitrust convictions. Although the main attack on anticompetitive behavior in the glass industry was clearly over, the threat of
further action remained omnipresent. Even careful consideration by legal
counsel could offer nothing better than best guesses as to who could purchase whom or what company could contract with what other within the
industry. The implications for patent policies were particularly acute. In
more than one case, Corning and others had been specifically enjoined to
supply licenses to both present and future patents on demand. Upon appeal
these demands were modified somewhat, but none of the main players in
the now defunct Glass Trust could have any doubt but that the slightest sign
of favoritism or cronyism in the pattern of license awards was likely to have
dire consequences. The field of play was therefore limited. As with other
process industries (e.g., aluminum) that were forced to license all comers,
the problem of having to provide not only the patents but also accompanying documentation raised questions as to whether licensees might even sue
if they could not achieve the desired results by using the technology in
question.

In the midst of all this (April 1945) Corning became a publicly traded
company. *Fortune* hazarded that the decision was made in an effort to garner
"good public relations," which seems likely given the considerable drubbing
the company was receiving in connection with its various court cases.[20]
Certainly matters of estate taxes among the Houghtons had been a factor as
well. The decision to "go public" was undoubtedly made easier by the fact
that so much of the company's formerly confidential financial dealings had
been dragged into the open in the course of those same cases.

The root of Corning's troubles lay in shifting social attitudes. Performing R&D was no longer seen as an industry service that justified certain
kinds of monopoly; such behavior, especially when linked to a company's
wider circle of industrial colleagues, had come to be interpreted as controlling technology for the purposes of controlling the competition, and
intellectual property had been demonstrated to have been at the very heart
of such arrangements. Some companies that were caught in this bind simply rejected further patenting as a regular option, but Corning would ultimately come to rely even more heavily on intellectual property in future

decades. A long period of retrenchment and reanalysis would come first, however.

A NEW WAY TO COMPETE, 1945–1967

Corning's antitrust difficulties had repercussions far beyond the glass industry. *"Hartford-Empire,"* one authority has noted, "ushered in an era in which patents were looked upon with jaundiced eyes, the scope of the grant narrowly construed and many restrictions imposed by patentees upon their licensees invalidated."[21] A number of the landmark cases in antitrust following the war focused on alleged abuses of the patent monopoly. Among the first of these was a major government offensive launched against IBM in 1952. Settled by consent decree in 1956, the case bore many similarities with that of *Hartford-Empire*, as was noted at the time.[22] The government also settled via consent decree another major suit in 1956, this one against AT&T. The Department of Justice had originally hoped to force AT&T to divest itself of its equipment-making subsidiary, Western Electric, but settled for, once again, compulsory licensing of patents at reasonable terms, though in this case AT&T's entire patent pool, numbering some 8,600 patents, was included in the decree. Furthermore, AT&T was required to provide the necessary background to make the patents useful. "Simple access to a patent," remarked one "Bell man" to a reporter, "isn't always enough to get some good out of it. You've got to know how to apply it, and that's what we've got to tell them now."[23]

While *Hartford-Empire* marked the high-water point in the energetic attack on the patent monopoly led by Thurman Arnold, these subsequent cases showed the legal environment in which high-tech companies formulated their intellectual property strategy to be permanently altered.[24] Corning, for obvious reasons, was especially marked by the pressures of this new environment. Where it had once actively developed and exploited its patent holdings and, via the Glass Trust, engaged in litigation on a regular basis to police its intellectual boundaries, it now became leery of licensing and loath to sue.

Corning could not, however, ignore intellectual property for long.

However Arnold's crusade may have undercut the patent's monopoly value, the patent monopoly's patents remained a powerful tool in shaping markets and, with R&D funding levels climbing rapidly in many industries (including glass), patent production filings were on a similar upswing. If nothing else, Corning had to patent defensively or face the possibility of being excluded from markets new and old. Furthermore, while the Glass Trust in containers and similar arrangements in the flat glass industry had meant many things to Corning—not least a constant flow into the corporate coffers and the Houghtons' pockets—perhaps the most important function it had served from a business perspective was to outline the borders between flat, container, and technical glass, and to further define the last of these as Corning's exclusive demesne. In the wake of *Hartford-Empire* and *Libbey-Owens-Ford*, these walls were down. The struggles with GE over Hyde's priority in the silicone arena (already mentioned in chapter 5) demonstrated what that could mean.

Nevertheless, in the immediate postwar period Corning turned inward, coming to rely as never before on trade secrets and tacit knowledge even in an industry as competitive and chaotic as television. While the company did not altogether neglect its patent portfolio, it largely focused its energies elsewhere. As expressed in a *Fortune* article from that period, "Chairman Houghton and President Cole ... are confident that they can meet any new competitive threats from within the industry by virtue of their guarded, almost personal techniques—what they like to call their 'unpatentable know-how.'"[25]

Trademarks: Pyrex and Its Heir

Patents are not, of course, the only form of intellectual property that can be used to shape markets and achieve a competitive advantage. Corning had long used another powerful tool, trademarks, as a means of distinguishing itself from other manufacturers in the field. Some of Corning's earliest product lines were trademarked very successfully, in particular Pyrex, a trademark that covered the bulk of the company's prewar sales (in fact, some thought was given to renaming the company accordingly in the

1930s). None of the antitrust judgments touched directly on trademarks, but even here Corning felt hesitant to assert its rights. It was not until the 1960s, under the leadership of Lee Waterman, that the company began once again to utilize and expand its trademark holdings. Drawing on a long history of success with Pyrex, Corning constructed—and gave its name to—its most successful foray into consumerware ever: Corning Ware.

Though accused in the Hartford Empire trials of using its patents to avoid having to innovate further, Corning had in fact devoted considerable effort in the early 1930s to finding a patentable replacement for Pyrex or, failing that, a significant technical lead over competitors who might enter the market in 1936, when the Pyrex patents were due to expire. This push to find new formulas and products that could be used under the Pyrex trademark (which Corning used to cover most of its low-expansion glass products) produced, among other things, the line of stovetop ware that was developed in the early 1930s.

In the wake of the dissolution of the Glass Trust, Corning's fears were quickly realized: by 1945 Anchor Hocking had secured a license from the

A sampling of Corning's most widely recognized trademarks.

receiver of Hartford Empire for the machinery necessary to make Corning-style borosilicate kitchenware and had succeeded in producing a line of products that competed with Corning's Pyrex line. Superficially, they could hardly be told apart, Anchor Hocking having dubbed its new cookware "Fire-King," an obvious reference to Pyrex's apparent etymological roots, "pyro" and "rex."

Anchor Hocking did innovate in one important respect: it cut prices. Corning had long charged a premium for its borosilicate products, and its competitor took direct aim at those profit margins, advertising in *Good Housekeeping* and similar magazines that "New *Fire-King* costs you less— *saves you up to a third on price* ... gives you the greatest value in ovenware today!"[26] That Anchor Hocking's ability to make borosilicate glass was dependent on Corning-developed refractory materials could only have added to the irritation caused by this copycat product. Despite such provocation, in the wake of *Hartford-Empire* Corning chose not to react.

With Pyrex sales undercut and no replacement on the horizon, the consumer business languished in the immediate postwar period. But in the mid-1950s a literal white knight was found in Pyroceram. Corning quickly seized upon Don Stookey's invention, glass ceramics, as Pyrex's successor in consumerware. The ceramming process that transformed glass into glass ceramic produced an extremely strong material, allowing development of a cookware that could withstand even the most drastic heat differentials of freezer and range top.

As noted in chapter 6, glass ceramic's first application had been a military one: radomes, used to protect sensitive electronics in missiles and rockets. Corning turned this fact to good advantage in its new line of consumerware, trumpeting it across the land as part of the company's most aggressive advertising campaign to date. The basic appeal of Corning Ware was its ability to go directly from cold storage to hot cooking surface, a fact Corning communicated in its promotional image of half a casserole embedded in a block of ice and its other half being heated by a blowtorch. But Corning Ware's most distinctive advertising theme was a timely appeal to the space age. In one classic product shot, a Corning Ware percolator appeared resting atop an electric stove coil while a rocket launched in the background, the legend "From Rocket Research" modestly applied in the lower right-hand corner. Distributors picked up on the theme, advertising it as "the cookware that came from the moon" and helping promote it as Corning's technical partnership with the American housewife.[27]

Corning had, of course, also patented Pyroceram (its trademarked name for glass ceramics). Stookey filed for a patent to cover his basic process for ceramming glass in June of 1956. A fairly lengthy series of exchanges between Corning's attorneys and the patent office was required before patent 2,920,971 was issued, this in January 1960. Three years later Anchor Hocking, having secured a copy of a patent Corning had filed in Belgium, introduced its own models of glass ceramic-type cookware. Corning was loath to see the maker of Fire-King profit from its marketing efforts. Even worse, Anchor Hocking's product was not as durable as Corning Ware, and it was feared that confusion between the two might undermine the value of Corning's expensively developed and marketed product. Corning found itself once again facing litigation, this time as the plaintiff.

Once again, Corning's competitor had replicated not only the material but also the shape and even something of the decoration of Corning's own product (Anchor Hocking's line featured a blue stylized wheat sheaf placed precisely where Corning's sported the blue cornflower). Again, their advertisements stressed price, promising the consumer that this product would always be "at least $1 less per dish than other ceramic cookware."[28] If Corning allowed this to pass as it had the Fire-King line, Anchor Hocking's market share seemed assured; if, on the other hand, Corning sued for patent or trademark infringement, then the defendant would have the opportunity to challenge what it saw as an invalid patent. Corning's patents rested on a phenomenon widely recognized among glass technologists: the tendency for glass to crystallize if not handled properly.[29] Anchor Hocking's desire for a confrontation seemed to be written in the product name itself: Corning Ware's challenger was marketed as "Anchor Hocking Cookware."

Corning sued in November 1963. Fish, Richardson & Neave (the New York firm that was to become Fish & Neave), prosecuted the case, aided by Corning lawyers Clarence Patty and Clint Janes. It brought to the stand not only the intuitive Don Stookey but also his young protégé George Beall, whose incisive testimony about ceramic structures helped convince the judge of Corning's position on several key points at issue. The defense argued that the patent was invalid because of the "obviousness" of Stookey's work and the existence of certain prior art. Anchor Hocking's lawyers even claimed that Corning had engaged in fraud in the course of pursuing the patent application by willfully misrepresenting the state of prior art to the patent examiner. In addition, Anchor Hocking charged Corning with attempting to monopolize the glass ceramic cookware market and counterclaimed for damages.

In March 1966 the district court in Wilmington, Delaware, ruled against Corning. Most of Anchor Hocking's claims were declared unfounded, and the court went so far as to characterize Corning's patent as "a basic and pioneering advance in glass and ceramic technology."[30] Nevertheless, the court found the patent to be invalid and unenforceable for the simple reason that, in 1956, when the patent had been applied for, there had been no standard or common technique for determining the degree of crystalinity of the glass ceramic. Corning's patent rested on the key claim that it could control the crystalinity.

Corning's glass ceramics by this time had become a major—and growing—revenue stream for the company. Radomes had brought in over $10 million in contracts from the government, and Corning Ware itself had sold over ten times that much by the time the adverse ruling was received. Various research efforts had succeeded in developing a space heater, a laboratory hotplate, a deep-sea submersible hull, and the Cercor heat exchanger as part of an ongoing program to exploit Stookey's discovery. The invalidation of the patent underlying all of this work was a major threat. Corning appealed immediately.

A year later the Federal appeals court in Philadelphia handed down its verdict. The lower court's assessment was declared too narrow a grounds for invalidating the patent, which the higher court characterized as "a great basic invention which has brought substantial benefit to the public at large."[31] The case was returned to Delaware, where Anchor Hocking was accordingly found guilty of infringement and ordered to abstain from further such activity. Corning, however, chose not to collect damages or court costs; Anchor Hocking's antitrust charges were still pending and Corning bought relief from those actions by forswearing further punishment of its competitor.

Anchor Hocking was not the only concern interested in producing Corning's new material. In 1967 Corning learned that Owens-Illinois and Pittsburgh Plate Glass were both taking orders for products made of glass ceramics that Corning believed violated the claims in the Stookey patent.[32] The former was using it for large mirror blanks similar to ones that Corning was producing for NASA and for military surveillance operations. In a visit to Corning in early January for the purpose of obtaining Corning's technical assistance with a television funnel Owens-Illinois was producing, patent counsel for that company offered to discuss "any other areas in which Corning felt that O-I was 'stepping on its toes.'" When Clarence Patty, Corning's patent counsel, demurred, refusing to discuss anything other than the funnel, his counterpart became more direct, raising the matter of the Stookey patent, then still under reconsideration by the courts. In what was taken as a clear warning, he informed Patty that his company had been advised that Anchor Hocking had contested Corning's patent in the wrong way by failing to introduce into evidence what Owens-Illinois believed was the most compelling (though unspecified) example of invalidating prior art. "I listened," wrote Patty in a report to Amo Houghton.[33]

In fact, Corning had already decided not to send notices of infringement to either of these larger corporations because it did not want to give either company a basis for filing its own suits requesting declaratory judgments while the Anchor Hocking case remained on appeal. The company's lawyers reasoned that there would be time to claim damages from Owens-Illinois at any point before the mirrors or other products were actually delivered. Meanwhile, the outcome of the appeal in the Anchor Hocking case would determine how they chose to treat the matter of licensing potential competitors in the future. Unlike Anchor Hocking, which had openly followed and copied Corning, doing no research and only copycat development and threatening the reputation and performance of a class of products that Corning considered central to its business, Owens-Illinois and Pittsburgh Plate Glass were not just competitors. As joint venture partners with Corning, of much larger size, and with substantial investments in their own research (though hardly in fundamental research), Corning considered them peers in the industry. As such they were not only worthy opponents but allies of a kind whose contribution to the industry's collective knowledge and know-how Corning needed and valued. In any case Corning remained gun-shy.

The Power and Vulnerability of Brands

The ultimately successful prosecution of the Anchor Hocking case did much to reinvigorate Corning's faith in the purposeful management of its intellectual property. Corning Ware's enormous sales and its high-profile market position similarly demonstrated the benefits of another form of intangible asset: the association of Corning's high-tech status with its brand, thus leveraging the name into a powerful sales tool. Patents per se might not sell product, but they protected the brand and lent a space-age halo to efforts to market the product. This was the ultimate connection Waterman had made when he persuaded Corning's management to name its Pyroceram product for the consumer market "Corning Ware."

Corning had already devoted decades of effort to developing a trustworthy identity with consumers in its Pyrex business by establishing its home economics laboratory under Lucy Maltby in 1929. It had also invested in firsthand market research, engaging with ovenware users throughout the country via demonstrations in department stores.[34] In terms reminiscent of Arthur Houghton's industrial design initiative of the late 1940s, the company's policy statements for the consumer products division read, "Everything we do must make sense to consumers or end users. This includes not only products we make but how they are advertised, displayed, merchandised and sold."[35] Time, money, market research, and constant vigilance were required to keep the brand fresh. Once invested, however, the returns could be considerable.

Unfortunately, the returns were not guaranteed. The Anchor Hocking case served as a warning that a strategy of developing brands as a means for establishing market share brought with it large areas of vulnerability. As the antitrust trials had demonstrated, litigation was terribly costly, even beyond the dollars spent directly, in that it absorbed a great deal of management time and attention at the highest echelons of the company. In the Anchor Hocking trial this involvement penetrated through the ranks to Don

Stookey, George Beall, and other Corning researchers, and to patent lawyers who had to spend days testifying and as much time or more complying with requests for documentation and clarification of their work. Like so many other aspects of managing intellectual property, the cost in researcher time lost for research, not only in documenting the discoveries but in establishing the initial market position, was enormous. Furthermore, the Anchor Hocking case had been a close call. The damage that could have been done to Corning's expensively won brand and market position, had it lost the appeal, was incalculable. In short, Waterman's approach to the consumer market on Corning's behalf was a powerful and effective, but by no means risk-free, method of exploiting Corning's intellectual property holdings. Nevertheless, it had one great advantage: although it could offer less apparent protection from the anarchy of competition than earlier trust arrangements had afforded, this solution to the problem of competitive advantage was uncontestably legal by modern standards and fell well within the mainstream of the political economy of American competition.

There was a further danger associated with the Corning Ware strategy, however: the company's good name, carefully linked with the quality and satisfactory performance of millions of pieces of consumerware, could be destroyed by flaws or performance failures in even a few of them. This fact would become terribly clear through a series of consumer accidents with Corning Ware percolators in the mid-1970s. Each percolator was equipped with a handle affixed to its body by a stainless steel band. In earlier models this band was designed such that the geometry of the two pieces kept them together. In later versions, however, Corning relied on a novel sort of glue: epoxy. Another miracle product of the space age, epoxy was trusted by Corning engineers as Norval Johnston, a consumer process engineer, recalled, it was "regarded as a wonder material. It was used in high speed aircraft." Unfortunately, the Corning engineers who redesigned the product seeking cost reductions overlooked an important fact: for epoxies, the home environment was harsher than that encountered by military jets. "The thing that people failed to recognize was the thermal cycling along with detergent that occurred with its use in the household. There was a leeching process that went on as the product was used and run through the dishwasher and thermal cycle, and the material . . . became brittle, started to shrink."[36]

Decayed epoxy could result in the sudden separation of the handle from the percolator container. In a few cases where this occurred the result was scalding coffee in a hapless consumer's lap.[37]

It is likely that Corning would have responded to such a situation with a recall, even had its name not been attached to over 300,000 of these items, but it took the company time to arrive at the unprecedented step of retrieving such a large number of items on the chance of a small number of mishaps occurring. What clinched the matter was not consumer complaint (Corning Ware users, and especially percolator users, were a loyal lot, in some cases reluctant to surrender their pots even when asked to do so) but employee morale, which had recently been battered by the widespread layoff known as the Guns of August (see chapter 9). Tom MacAvoy, who was president at the time, had come to realize that further delay would cause employees to lose faith in the integrity of the company; such a threat to morale was intolerable.[38]

The percolator recall eventually cost the company well over $10 million and was, at that time, the largest such undertaking ever attempted in the United States. As it happened, Corning's public relations department had written up general guidelines for consumer recall in 1975 and was thus as well prepared as it could be. "The overall objective," a review document later noted, "was to make the recall a classic—the best recall ever."[39] To this end public relations sent out over 1,200 mailings to newspapers, slides and a script to some 300 television stations, and a tape explaining the recall to 400 radio stations, and this in the first wave of announcements alone, a combined effort that dwarfed even such previous Corning media blitzes as the Pyroceram or Chemcor sales campaigns. It was followed by more such communiqués, as well as over $1 million worth of in-store display material sent to almost 90,000 retailers.

Although the recall had the desired effect, removing the percolator from many hundreds of thousands of homes, the Consumer Product Safety Commission declared that Corning had not recognized the hazard quickly enough and fined the company a record $325,000. Reminded once again of the hazards of the consumer market, Corning subsequently hired Susan King, who had chaired the commission during the recall. Placed in consumer affairs, she brought a much deeper understanding of the government's role in the commercial market to Corning's consumer wing. As a consequence of the way it conducted the recall, Corning's name sustained little if any harm and in some circles its brand was enhanced: *Business Week* and a variety of trade publications praised Corning for its efforts.

REAPPRAISING PATENT POLICY, 1961–1968

While branding made Pyroceram a success, it was the underlying patent that made it Corning's success alone. The vindication of that patent in court might have been taken as evidence that the company's approach to such things was correct. In fact, it was seen as proof of the exact opposite and came at a time when Corning was reconsidering its patent policy from the ground up.

As noted above, the subject of intellectual property at Corning had received very little notice from either research or central management throughout the late 1940s and 1950s. Though Frederick Knight, Corning's corporate counsel, had served a brief tenure as a U.S. patent examiner in the 1930s, he appears to have raised few, if any, issues about patent policy during his time at Corning. Higher up the corporate ladder, attention to intellectual property was diverted by the overwhelming pressure of the television business, which relied mainly on know-how. And the memories of the antitrust trials, which transformed the entire area of intellectual property into a strategic minefield that few dared cross, remained painful.

Nevertheless, a flare-up in 1960 of a long-standing dispute between research and engineering and the patent department over "what is, or should be, Company patent policy"[40] forced management to focus directly on intellectual property practices. Recognizing the issue as both complicated and politically charged, Corning executives asked McKinsey & Co. (a management consulting company with strong ties to Corning executives through the Harvard Business School) to study the situation. The consultants produced two reports, one in 1960 and a follow-up in 1961, entitled *Protecting Research and Development Expenditures in the Years Ahead*, which served as reference points throughout the subsequent debates on the subject.

The reports dramatized both the relatively haphazard state of Corning's patent policy and the nature of the threat involved. The consultants remarked on Corning's sparing use of patents only to protect major innovations and its reliance on " 'know-how' and trade secrets" to cover those of lesser perceived importance, "even when patent protection might be available."[41] Furthermore, they noted that while the researchers instigated most (though not all) patent applications, the patent department itself had final say as to whether or not, and how vigorously, a given patent would be pursued. While such a minimalist approach to patenting was not uncommon among companies that had been targets of antitrust attacks in the 1940s, McKinsey pointed to these characteristics as weaknesses, thus siding with research and engineering in its call for increased overall patent activity.

Three points suggested that Corning would need to invest more in patents:(1) the "dramatic increase in industrial research expenditures," not least in the glass industry;(2) the growth in employee mobility, which lessened the value of trade secrets; and (3) the fact that Corning was beginning to look to entirely new product areas, in particular electronics, where defensive patenting was the rule.[42] McKinsey's follow-up report in 1961 was more favorable to the patent department itself, focusing on the fact that it was underfunded and overworked as a result of Corning's greatly increasing the number of researchers and research projects without similarly raising the department's budget. The result, according to the consultants, was that "discoveries of both major scientific importance and commercial significance have been found, which are not adequately protected." Such oversights constituted a major failure to learn from previous experience; recall that Hyde's difficulty in solidifying Corning's patent position on his pioneering work in silicones had stemmed in part from the company's failure to get timely advice from its patent lawyers. More recent experience showed similar lapses: McKinsey pointed out instances where "competitors have obtained patents on unprotected discoveries made by Corning Glass Works."[43]

The consultants did not underestimate the difficulties involved in creating a larger patent department. More people would have to be hired and all patent attorneys would have to be better paid, or turnover would cause the costs of patenting to spiral out of control. While Corning's top executives might have balked at the added costs or worried about revealing company secrets in the patent applications, ignoring McKinsey's advice would have meant alienating their director of research, Bill Armistead.

Though others at Corning contributed to the debate, it was Armistead's usually quiet voice that rang above the fray. Under his guidance, trusted as only Sullivan's had been before him, the laboratories were growing steadily and making notable achievements, but his philosophy of pioneering research had little chance of ultimate success without a corporate commitment to the more aggressive pursuit of patents for that research. For this reason Armistead strongly supported McKinsey's conclusions, noting that if anything they were too uncritical of the present situation.

All parties, then, agreed that the patent department needed to be enlarged, but the problem was not simply a matter of sheer numbers. As Armistead noted in 1963, two years before the Anchor Hocking case was filed, "Corning has tended to rely on coverage obtained with *one* broad patent for each major development. A much stronger patent position results if significant features are patented in addition to the broad concept." Or, as he expressed it elsewhere in the same memo:

ARE WE ADEQUATELY PROTECTING OUR MAJOR DEVELOPMENTS?
I DON'T THINK SO.[44]

The fact that in the Anchor Hocking case a single judgment could jeopardize Corning's proprietary position in glass ceramics vindicated this assertion.

To eliminate further disputes, the patent department became part of the newly formed technical staffs division under Armistead. As noted in chapter 5, as much as any other measure this gave Armistead substantial influence over Corning's strategic positioning until well into the 1970s. After clearing these hurdles, the department began to grow and, with it, the number of patents filed for each year. The total had already been increasing since 1959, the first year that could be expected to produce new results after attention had shifted away from television and toward a more balanced technical program. Over the course of 1962 it had nearly doubled, from 70 to 138.

According to both the researchers and the patent attorneys the effect that reporting through the technical staffs had on the work of the patent attorneys was salutary for the core technologies, glass and glass ceramics, in this respect as well. Better communications between patent lawyers and inventors produced better patents—broader, more capable of withstanding

scrutiny and challenge, more truly representative of the invention as practiced. Over the course of the 1960s and throughout the 1970s communication between the two groups was intimate. As George Beall, a scientist who
worked at Corning during this period, noted, "The patent attorneys at
Corning [have] a very unusual understanding of materials." Beall worked
closely with Clint Janes, who had a degree in chemistry. Janes, he recalled,

> would actually write a creative patent if he felt that an [internal report] or
> something that I wrote lacked a certain explanation, he'd put in his own
> explanation, actually. Sometimes they were hare-brained and sometimes
> they were surprisingly insightful. But no matter what they were, they led
> you to think about things. It wasn't just a job where you write something
> down and then somebody takes care of it. It was an iterative process.[45]

Where this close working relationship broke down was in the newer diversification areas of electronics and, later, biological and medical technologies. Here the geographical distance separating the researchers in Raleigh
from patent attorneys in Corning worked against the researchers, and complaints from the operating management in the electronics division about
the lack of legal resources devoted to their area of research mounted
steadily through the 1970s and into the 1980s. Part of the problem was, of
course, that the majority of the patent staff were trained in glass technology, and people with the appropriate expertise could not simply be hired off
the street: the entire area was still relatively new even to the U.S. Patent
Office. Discontent about this matter was one of the factors that would lead
in the 1980s to the decentralization of funding for the patent department
and its organizational relocation under the operating divisions. Until that
time, though, the patent structure established in the 1960s remained in
place, serving Corning for a full generation.

Patents for Licensing

The patent policy finally set to paper in 1964 also contained a key provision
that changed the company's stance toward licensing its technology. Previ-

ously, Corning had eschewed licensing for fear of creating competition. The revised policy now required that licensing potential be considered a key factor when establishing patent priorities. Inventions falling in what was labeled category 1 (having appreciable commercial potential and likely to be disclosed through commercial activity) were now to be filed as a matter of course if a review of the prior art indicated the possibility of "useful" patent protection, that is, if it would force a potential competitor either to use a less desirable alternative or to pay royalties for a license under a patent. This was such a change that Amo Houghton still felt qualms about the draft. Following the long-standing preference of his family, he jotted in the margins the one-word note: "Secrecy?"[46]

Category 2 inventions were those that would be patented only if there was a chance of receiving reasonably broad patent protection. Otherwise, or if known only to a few key employees, they would be kept as trade secrets. To offset what he viewed as the perils of letting out too much information, in the next several years Amo Houghton pushed for much greater secrecy in the way Corning managed its technology in other respects, including halting even the publication of laboratory annual reports.

Corning was changing its practice with respect to outsiders and technology, in part out of necessity. In 1968 Armistead announced that since 1957 Corning had negotiated (i.e., obtained for use) thirty-two patent licenses and was given eleven.[47] Among the technologies obtained was a royalty-free license from Philco to use their basic patent on the "counter that cooks," which Corning then made out of Pyroceram. Another was the new electric melting furnace technology that they had from Vermel for use in their own internal processes. In glass-related areas Corning usually had technology to offer in return, of sufficient value that the terms for the licenses it negotiated were either minimal or royalty-free. In new diversification technologies, however, the picture was very different. Company executives discovered this to their chagrin after acquiring Signetics. Initial assumptions about the synergies with Signetics notwithstanding, Corning found that obtaining access to solid-state electronics technologies essential to the new business was quite difficult. Despite its significant and growing investments in electronics research, Corning had to use some of its own core technologies as bargaining chips to get the technology Signetics needed.

A Lesson from Western Electric

Nowhere was this more evident than in a painful negotiation Corning conducted with Western Electric in the fall of 1968 on behalf of Signetics. As indicated by the roster of high-level Corning attendees, this was a crucial meeting: Bill Armistead, vice president and director of technical staffs; Thomas MacAvoy (then the new general manager of electronic products); James Riley, president of Signetics; Frederick Knight, corporate counsel; Clarence Patty, head of the patent department; and Chuck Wakeman, director of physical research succeeding MacAvoy. On the other side of the table sat four members of Western Electric's specialized patent licensing department. As the manufacturing arm of AT&T, which had been forced by consent decree in the 1950s to license its technologies to all comers, Western Electric employed a full-time staff of specialized license negotiators. While Corning had engaged in fewer than fifty such negotiations in the past ten years, Western Electric had been through hundreds, if not thousands.

Signetics had a Western Electric license for its semiconductor technology before it was acquired by Corning. With little to offer in return, it had obtained the standard unilateral license that Western Electric was required to grant under the consent decree, on the order of 4-percent royalties. Upon acquiring Signetics, Corning had obtained a bilateral license from Western Electric on a modestly reduced royalty basis; Corning's negotiators had assured Western Electric that they were researching materials technology that would be of interest to AT&T. In 1968 Corning was back to renew its agreement with Western Electric, hoping for even more favorable terms for Signetics.

Corning's Frederick Knight opened the meeting with a review of the company's previous relations with Western Electric. He acknowledged that Corning had formerly refused to grant licenses to Western Electric in Corning's own areas of expertise, owing to its traditional nonlicensing policy. Now, in what he clearly viewed as a valuable concession, he offered to grant Western Electric licenses in formerly off-limits technologies in glass, glass ceramic, and ceramic research on a royalty-free basis in return for similar treatment for Signetics.

Instead of jumping at this offer, Western Electric's representatives asked for a more detailed accounting of the technologies that Corning felt were worth a reduction in the royalty rate. This turned out to be a sticking point because a huge imbalance existed among the dozen or so "semiconductor" patents that had been issued to Corning and Signetics in the past five years and the hundreds that Western Electric had obtained in the same period. According to Western Electric's negotiators, Corning had failed to earn even the half percent reduction in royalties it had been granted five years before.

Having neatly turned the tables, Western Electric's representatives proposed a new agreement: Signetics could have a reduced royalty in the desired semiconductor area in return for blanket royalty-free cross-licenses to Western Electric in all its areas of interest. In one area of particular interest to Western Electric, the new area it called "optical communication systems," where Corning had done research but had patented almost nothing, Western Electric required the license to run only in its direction, and on a royalty-free basis.[48]

In 1969 representatives of Western Electric visited Corning to hear a review of the work they were doing in all areas of mutual interest. Based on that assessment, Corning struck a somewhat better deal: the two companies granted royalty-free use of each other's technology in the glass-related areas, and Western Electric reduced the semiconductor royalty for Signetics to a more tolerable 2 percent. By that time, however, Signetics was suffering from the sharp recession in electronics, and even a tolerable royalty couldn't improve the picture much. Even so, Corning's electronics venture still looked like one of its most promising new businesses. In allowing Western Electric (and through it, AT&T) access to its work in "optical communications systems," Corning was giving away little more than access to a few good ideas and a handful of experiments; it was a matter of exchanging an unknowable future advantage in a field of technology that was believed to be decades from commercial application for an important cost factor in a currently hot business. Only later would it become clear that Corning had given its sole potential domestic customer and future key competitor free access to all of its patented technologies in what would come to be called fiber-optic communications. Criticized by some after the fact as an unpardonable lack of foresight, in fact there were some significant compensating factors. The arrangement created an early community of interest between

Corning and AT&T's Bell Labs in the crucial formative stages of what was eventually to become a huge new business for both companies, and it gave Corning access to ancillary technologies it would have lacked without the contact with AT&T.

POSITIONING WITH PATENTS: OPTICAL WAVEGUIDES, 1966–1987

Although Corning was shifting the balance of its research investment into a more diversified portfolio during the 1960s, Armistead continued to emphasize the importance of patenting in Corning's central field of activity—specialty glass. He had, however, abandoned his original all-or-nothing view of the need to possess the fundamental patent in a field. It might be equally important and just as effective, he now believed, to control other key patents and to barter them for the intellectual property Corning did not possess. His research philosophy had also adapted: "Corning Glass Works supposedly is in the specialty glass business... We should then enter all specialty glass business which appears significant, regardless of who invented what."[49] If Corning had a toehold and some licenses to trade, it could compete effectively on a combination of broad expertise and speedy response. Armistead's chief example: the nascent field of fiber optics. Although it was American Optical that had pioneered this field commercially, Corning had recently matched American Optical's sales, and this despite the fact that Armistead himself had at first ignored the opportunity: "Some years ago I was asked to undertake this project in the laboratory; I turned it down because American Optical had the patents and it looked like we had no place. Obviously that decision was wrong, because... we've made a place for ourselves."[50] It had been one of the operating divisions (specifically, new business development in the Television Division) that had seized this particular opportunity. Initially, Corning had followed American Optical's lead in fiber optics, but it soon chose a different route that led the company to pioneer in a new and extremely lucrative area within the larger field: low-loss fiber optics for optical waveguides. The successful establishment of a strong patent position in this field brought together all of the elements of Corning's postwar intellectual property strategy.

Introduction to Fiber Optics

The fiber-optics technology that Armistead had first misjudged was a far cry from the low-loss fiber that, used as optical waveguides, later became a core business for Corning. Both functioned on the same basic principle—that light can be channeled inside glass. The fiber optics of the 1960s, however, were high-loss: they served to direct the light but absorbed so much of it in the process that after several meters little if any signal was left. This characteristic severely limited their utility. Corning and others manufactured image intensifiers, endoscopes, and similar products that did not require the light to travel very far within the fiber in order to achieve their effects. Together these made a sizable market—totaling several billions of dollars, much of it demand from the military. But at that time neither Corning nor its commercial competitors saw optical fiber as an imminent contributor to telecommunications applications. Only a few large communications laboratories were doing theoretical work in the area, much of which focused on light pipes, not fiber.[51]

And so it might well have remained had not Corning responded to an inquiry from the telecommunications industry in the spring of 1966. In 1965, parties from the British ministry of defense and the British post office joined forces to define a new communications infrastructure for Britain. Both the military and the post office (which handled the British national telephone network) could envision a time when more than just voice transmission would be crowding the wires. The military, for instance, had a device called a Vidiphone, which provided point-to-point video transmission (conceptually similar to the more elaborate commercial Picturephone that Bell Labs was developing in the United States) but needed a great deal of bandwidth to do so. Optical fiber, it was thought, could provide the desired capacity.

More specifically, the two organizations were looking for contractors to develop an optical fiber that could be drawn in kilometer lengths and would transmit light with less than twenty decibels per kilometer (db/km) loss (called "attenuation"). That this was at least theoretically possible had been suggested by a paper published by Charles Kao, a researcher at the Standard Telecommunications Laboratory, who had hypothesized that pure silica had the potential to transmit light with virtually no loss whatsoever. After trying in vain to encourage the drawing of high-purity glass fiber in several domestic firms, the British organizers had accidentally learned of Corning's extraordinary expertise in glass when they were approached by the company's Electrosil subsidiary in Sunderland, which hoped to sell them electronic components.

Veteran Corning researcher William Shaver, at that time serving as International technical liaison for R&D, attended a meeting with a delegation from the British signals division (including representatives of the British aviation and radar ministries) arranged by Electrosil. This turned out to be the first of several such meetings with the British post office, which eventually took over national coordination of both military and commercial requirements. Shaver found the meetings intriguing enough to bring along his chosen successor, Gail Smith, who in turn invited Corning physicist Bob Maurer.[52]

Initially, the British wished to see how low an attenuation could be measured in the best currently available glasses. Corning supplied three different samples of optical-quality glass rods, which when tested measured a bare 200 db/km attenuation. While this was far better than standard fibers (which had losses of around 1,000 db/km), it was still a long way from the 20 db/km goal. This figure was a matter of finance rather than science: it represented the point at which such a line would require amplification of the signal no more than once a kilometer, the same interval at which the electrical signal in standard copper cable required boosting.

Kao's paper had offered no better suggestion than to make a fiber out of pure silica and embed it in ice, that being one of the few known substances that had a lower index of refraction than silica itself.[53] No one had ever made such a fiber, and the major research competitors already in the field (Nippon Sheet Glass was rumored to have work going on, as was Bell Labs) had not taken that approach. Shaver and Smith sent back reports including these details and soon stirred interest in several quarters at Corning. The television division in particular was looking for new business, and one of its chief new business developers, Chuck Lucy, expressed an interest in the project. He convinced Robert Maurer—an old colleague from the delay line project and the same physicist who had joined Shaver for meetings with the BPO—to look into the matter. Maurer was in many ways the ideal person to take the project on. For one thing, he was familiar with ultra-high silica: he had been a leading scientist on the Corning team that had successfully developed the fused silica delay line for the Philco Corporation over a decade earlier. More recently he had done intensive research on light scattering, and he had spent some time looking into glass lasers—all aspects of the project as the British had defined it.

Armistead had his doubts about the wisdom of initiating a research effort in this area. Although he believed in allowing researchers to pursue what they chose when possible, fiber optics seemed very long-term at a time when he was being pressured to come to closure on a few large and imminent opportunities. On the other hand, if fiber optics could be used for telecommunications the resultant market was likely to be very important. Since such an application would almost certainly necessitate a totally novel approach to fiber optics, a practical technology would presumably be patentable. The balance was favorable: Maurer began research in the fall of 1966.

A team formed. Maurer hired Donald Keck, fresh out of Michigan State, in January of the following year. Also an experimental physicist, Keck was given the job of focusing on measurement problems. He soon joined forces with Peter Schultz, a glass chemist who himself was new to Corning, having been hired from Rutgers six months earlier. Schultz was a protégé of Bill Dumbaugh, another Corning chemist, who was determined to resurrect the fundamental work that had been done by Hyde and Nordberg on vapor-deposited silica. This technique was in use at the Canton plant, which made mirror blanks using the vapor deposition process; Schultz became involved with their work. Though it was used for production, no one had closely studied the materials produced by vapor deposition, and Dumbaugh believed this work needed to be done.

Given this background, Maurer elected from the start of the project to inhabit terrain no other group had explored: pure silica. As Keck later described it:

Bob's view was to play to win, to be a little contrary, that if you did the same thing everybody else did, the best you can do is tie. While the rest of the world in fact was heading toward these more conventional optical glasses and trying to make fibers out of better raw materials, Bob said, "No.

Let us go this other approach. The glass's high temperature is harder to work, but it's simpler and we'll keep it simple."[54]

Although Corning was alone in investigating this route, few had the expertise to follow even if they had chosen to do so. Pure silica required extremely high temperatures for melting and working, and that high temperature ability would have to be acquired by copycat organizations.

Maurer was right about something else as well: Corning would need to be different if it wanted to compete in an arena dominated by the international communications giants. Nothing short of an ironclad patent position would allow Corning to enjoy the fruits (if any) of its labors. With this constantly in mind, each time a project member wanted to try something new, such as Keck's early efforts to use a sputtering technique to deposit silica inside a glass tube, Maurer would hand him an invention disclosure form to ensure that the earliest possible date of discovery was documented and witnessed.

The practical challenge was to come up with suitable compositions and to find a way to draw them into fibers made up of a "core" and, surrounding it, a "cladding." High-loss optic fibers had a thick core and a thin cladding; the reverse proved true for waveguides, as the low-loss fibers came to be called. The first goal Maurer set for his team was to draw a kilometer of testable fiber using a block of titanium-doped silica that was left over from a mirror prototype produced at Canton. He had a summer student cast it into a rod and draw it out. Frank Zimar, a scientist in the development labs who had an ultra-high temperature furnace used for earlier semiconductor materials work, joined them in this effort, making the tubing into a fiber.

The project proceeded in the proud tradition of experimental physics, scrounging stray materials and using bits of "string and sealing wax" to build equipment. Early attempts to use vapor deposition involved drawing the vaporized titanium silica through a hollow tube using a vacuum cleaner for suction. Pete Schultz's technician Fran Vorhees, who much later became involved in transferring the process used in development to a full-fledged plant, described the process of making the early preforms from which the fiber would be drawn:

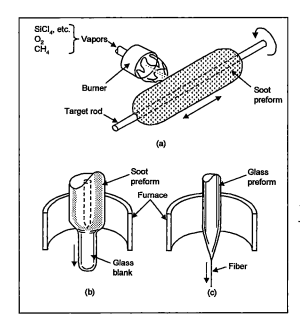

This diagram illustrates the process used to produce optical fiber, starting with a boule (or soot preform) of high-purity silica which is then drawn into a fiber.

We had a burner, which is close to what we are using now. It was actually what they used in Canton for the ULE (Ultra Low Expansion) processes. It was a two inch round burner as a deposition. We aimed that out into the room, and then Pete Schultz would stand there with a piece of transcyte and hold it in front of the burner, and I would wheel this lathe table up and line it up with the burner. Don Keck had the stopwatch. Don would say, "Okay." Pete would pull the transcyte away, the flame would be shooting into that hole with a vacuum cleaner sucking on it, and then twelve seconds later, Don would say, "Okay." Pete would put the transcyte back in, and I would wheel the table out of the way so it wouldn't get anymore.[55]

Progress was halting at first. Summer students and other temporary participants came and went, but two years into the project the core team of Maurer, Keck, Schultz, and their technicians, Fran Vorhees and Jerry Burke, found they were able to produce a clad fiber that measured only 100 db/km attenuation.

The original pace of the project was deliberate because this was fundamental work from which no one expected instant results. Two serious hurdles changed this. The first was the apparently unfavorable licensing agreement that was negotiated with AT&T/Western Electric. Because no progress at Corning could possibly threaten AT&T under the terms of this license agreement, Maurer found that he was able to strike up a good working relationship with Stu Miller, the Bell Labs researcher coordinating AT&T's work on "optical communications systems." This was a crucial connection, allowing Maurer and his team access to other parts of the optical system—especially the sources (lasers) and the detectors—that might otherwise have been much harder to get. This obstacle, then, actually sped things up considerably.

A second apparent setback was also turned to the team's advantage. In 1969 Armistead warned that the project would not receive money much longer out of the general research budget. Though Maurer and his team were making measurable progress, the funds under Armistead's control had too many demands on them already. If the project were to proceed, he wanted it to find a patron in one of the businesses at Corning.

International Partners, Domestic Competitors

Chuck Lucy, who had taken an interest in the project almost from the beginning, had his own business development budget and was an obvious source for further funds. The resources he controlled were not, however, enough for a sustained, long-term effort of the sort that was likely necessary. He persuaded Armistead to continue some funding until he could find other partner companies to help with the financial load. AT&T had indicated that they would never buy fiber from an outside supplier, and someone had remarked that the only other likely customers would be the foreign telecommunications companies.

Raising outside funds, however, would be difficult or impossible without encouraging results from the laboratory. Maurer's team redoubled their efforts, testing sample after sample until in 1970 they hit upon one combination of composition and fiber design that achieved the goal they had been seeking: a measurement of under 20 db/km. In fact, they had overshot, registering 16 db/km, a sensational result. The news would have to be published in some way: Lucy needed to share the information with those he was courting as research partners, and Corning needed to alert telecom companies and other potential customers to keep them from investing in and becoming committed to an alternative technology.

The team wrote a brief paper, little more than a note, for a conference in England. Buried near the end of the paper, as if an afterthought, was the statement that they had crossed the desired attenuation threshold. In order to keep other researchers from guessing that they were working with something other than the kind of optical glass that they had supplied to the British for testing, they left Schultz's name off the paper; his presence on the team would have instantly pointed to work with high temperature silica vapor deposition. This stratagem gave them time to file the necessary patents without bringing others into the same line of research.

Their announcement in 1970, modest as it was, attracted attention and sparked efforts to imitate the feat in R&D facilities the world over. Jack

Robert Maurer, Peter Schultz, and Donald Keck were the three men credited with contributing the most to the original Corning inventions that gave the company its strong proprietary position in optical fiber.

Hutchins, a senior research manager who would later succeed Armistead as head of R&D, described the episode vividly:

> Bob went to England for some scientific meeting.... And there were guys from the British Post Office and the guys from AT&T, and there was Bob.... The British Post Office guys [gave] the pitch that Gail had heard: "Here's what we need to make optical waveguides work, but we can't make it work...." And the AT&T guys are going down the path to try to make window glass pure enough to work and they say it can't work. Bob gets up and effectively says, "I didn't know it couldn't work, so I did it." And he announces this 20 decibels per kilometer.... I used to call that statement of Bob's "the optical shot heard around the world."[56]

While Lucy searched for international patrons, the team continued its work. The important step, more important than the 20 db proof of concept, was to demonstrate commercial feasibility. That required finding superior material compositions and producing fiber strong and flexible enough to be used in real installations.

Meanwhile, Lucy's money-raising labors bore fruit. By the end of 1972 he had signed on a small host of companies from Britain, Germany, France, Italy, and Japan.[57] By the terms of what were dubbed joint development agreements each group agreed to supply $100,000 per year for a minimum of five years. In exchange, the partners were promised an exclusive license on any patent filed in their home country as well as license under the U.S. patents that Corning generated in the course of its fiber-optics research. The agreements further provided for confidential technical exchanges between Corning and its partners. This was intended to make it possible for the partners, which in each country included at least one company with the capability to make copper cable, to develop techniques for cabling glass fibers. It had the added benefit of giving Corning's researchers a knowledgeable and committed audience for their work. Perhaps most importantly, it also meant that the company had made a serious commitment to pursue this research to businesses it respected and did not wish to disappoint. As much as the funds themselves, this guaranteed the immediate future of waveguides at Corning.

The joint development agreements effectively conferred prospective rights to licenses for patents Corning did not yet have, offering a piece of a market that did not yet exist. When and if that market did form, the arrangement would exclude all but the five JDA partners from having a place in it. When the time came to develop a Corning business strategy for optical fibers, this arrangement caused a good deal of heartburn to those who had to work with (and around) it. Corning's legal department, though by now a full generation beyond *Hartford-Empire*, was still guided by its antitrust history. Lee Wilson, who took responsibility for plotting the first business strategy for fiber optics when he was made head of the electronics division, was dumbfounded to find that the technical agreements had effectively selected Corning's international business partners without evaluating their capabilities as commercial competitors, and in some instances had also given them access to the same markets Corning would naturally want to supply:

> When I read these [joint development agreements], I went down to Bill Dana, who was then the international lawyer. I said, "Bill, why are these agreements written like that? We didn't need to give them a license under our U.S. patents to have a joint development agreement." And Bill said, "Well, it was because of the antitrust implications. If we did that, then there was no way that we could ever be accused of antitrust, because here we were opening up our market unit, we were being completely unselfish."[58]

In an effort to ensure against antitrust charges, the legal department had apparently given away much of Corning's prospective international business.

Yet the greatest commercial frustration was the absence of a domestic market. AT&T was still the sole long-distance carrier in the early 1970s, and its trunk lines were the preeminent candidates for upgrading from electrons to photons. The AT&T cross-license was not without its advantages; for one thing, it served as another guarantee against antitrust recriminations. As Wilson noted, "Nobody could really accuse us of any kind of an antitrust violation when we had licensed free ... the biggest user."[59] But as one internal history put it, without the market AT&T represented, "[a]ny IRR calculation for a large commitment for ten years or longer duration would be most discouraging."[60] As luck would have it, however, a more varied domestic market did form in the wake of the AT&T breakup: MCI, the first of the serious long-distance challengers, decided to stake its future on Corning waveguides.

In Defense of Waveguide

> There are 12 basic patents in the field and we have all 12 versus none in integrated circuits [referring to the Signetics disaster]. It's our turf with our patents.[61]
>
> —AMORY HOUGHTON JR. (FORBES, AUGUST 1977)

The waveguide team's labors were captured in a series of patents that established Corning, its JDA partners, and AT&T as essentially the sole source of feasible waveguide technology. As Maurer had suspected, the competing research projects based on conventional glass-melting processes proved unsuccessful.[62] The battle for intellectual property, however, had only begun. Though Corning had defended its patents in court before and still employed a number of legal staff who had worked on the Anchor Hocking case, the magnitude of the trials that followed could not have been anticipated by the most seasoned or even the most cynical. The Anchor Hocking case, Corning's largest to date, had been a matter of one relatively small glass concern fighting another. In what was to come, Corning would play David to some of the biggest Goliaths in the corporate world.

Corning's success sparked frenetic research activity around the globe. The basic techniques were, of course, revealed in the patents the company filed in the United States and many other countries. On the basis of the knowledge revealed therein, several concerns managed to establish manufacturing facilities for waveguides, and, in a clear test of Corning's resolve, some even went so far as to begin producing and selling what Corning held to be its product. Among the first and the largest of these was International Telephone and Telegraph, better known simply by its initials: ITT.

ITT was one of the largest U.S.-based conglomerates. It had grown throughout the 1960s and 1970s via acquisitions in hotels, food manufacture, and a variety of other businesses, most of which had nothing whatever to do with telephones or telegraphs. Nevertheless, telecommunications remained a core business, and ITT had both the research and manufacturing talent necessary to follow Corning's trail. It also had very deep pockets. The size of the challenge, and of the challenger, did not dissuade Corning's management; indeed, to Wilson in particular, it seemed an advantage: "I wanted to sue ITT because they were the biggest. . . . it was saying to the whole industry, including the telecommunications industry, that Corning was going to defend their patents."[63] What Wilson's statement does not indicate is that Corning's suit against ITT was in defense of the patents and little else: there was as yet no market to contest. Unlike the Anchor Hocking case, Corning had not sold any significant amount of product, much less the millions of dollars of Pyroceram that had justified that action over a decade before; indeed, waveguides would not pass the $10 million mark until 1982. Even ITT was not selling fiber on the open market, but by contract with an obvious customer: the U.S. government. Corning's legal action was a very expensive leap of faith and was only taken after attempts to negotiate another solution failed.

Corning filed separately against ITT and the government in July 1976. Both parties responded that Corning's patents were invalid and, just as in the Anchor Hocking case, ITT counterclaimed with antitrust charges. ITT itself knew a good deal about such matters; it had had an extended run-in with Richard McLaren, assistant attorney general for antitrust under the Nixon administration, its own version of Corning's multiyear battle with Thurman Arnold's Department of Justice. The case against the government was stayed until the ITT case was adjudicated, which left the former matter pending for several years.

As with the Anchor Hocking case, Corning chose the firm of Fish & Neave to pursue the case. Yet even with an outside firm handling the prosecution itself, the case would need to be managed within the company and a suitable point man found. As Wilson put it,

> We decided that we really had to have a lawyer who was an expert in this
> whole field and who had an entirely different approach and background
> from all the patent attorneys we had in the company who . . . knew how to

draft patents. How to use those patents, how to use that intellectual property as a major asset and strength of the company to develop and maintain
markets and market positions was something they just couldn't think
about.[64]

Corning turned again to Fish & Neave, hiring Al Michaelsen, one of their
attorneys. If nothing else, this guaranteed smooth communication between
the firm and its client. The case produced more than enough work to keep
Michaelsen fully employed. What came as something more of a surprise
was just how long the matter dragged on. ITT, more used to purchasing
"small" companies than to respecting them, simply assumed that Corning
would eventually give up. In Lee Wilson's words, "ITT's attitude was, `You
may have the invention, but we've got the money,' and it cost us $1 million a
year to pursue that suit."[65] Money was only part of it. Corning executives
spent literally thousands of hours preparing for and submitting to cross-
examination by ITT attorneys (Lucy alone was required to give depositions
for twenty-two days), and ITT's lawyers demanded hundreds of thousands
of documents in the course of discovery.

    Corning, however, did not give up. Sticking it out in this way was a
costly enterprise and a decision that had to be made at the highest levels of
the company by Amo Houghton and Tom MacAvoy. They were criticized
for not giving up and allowing ITT a license, which is what ITT clearly
expected to happen. Instead they held fast to the strategy that Wilson, with
their blessing, had established. When the judge finally called the case in July
1981, ITT realized that Corning would not give up and settled. The defendant admitted infringement, paid a multimillion dollar penalty, and signed a
license agreement, dropping its antitrust charges as part of the out-of-court
settlement. The government case was settled out of court in 1983, with the
defendant agreeing to pay $650,000 to the company and agreeing to pay
more if it purchased infringing fiber in the future.

    The delay had been costly to Corning by putting off the victories to the
point of diminishing returns. The decisions came too late to have the
impact Corning had hoped for: others were already entering the field and
challenging the company's patents. Even before the ITT case closed, Corning learned that Philips, the Dutch electronics giant, was selling fiber in the

United States via a subsidiary called Valtec; this prompted another suit, which was not settled until 1984. Again, the outcome was successful (Philips dropped the business, selling its subsidiary to ITT, which could, under the terms of its postsuit license agreement with Corning, use its production capability), but this time it had been a two-front war: Corning had sued Canada Cable and Wire, which had purchased and resold waveguides in violation of Corning's patents, even before finishing its suit against Valtec. This suit moved much more quickly: Corning won in 1983, a year before the Valtec suit came to a close.

Still the trials were not over. Canada Cable and Wire's infringing waveguides had been manufactured by Sumitomo, a major Japanese company, which had indemnified its customer against the possibility of action by Corning (and covered the Canadian firm's litigation costs). Not deterred by the indirect costs it had already had to bear, Sumitomo decided to raise the stakes by beginning export directly to the United States. Corning filed suit with the International Trade Commission, claiming that this action would grievously harm the domestic waveguide industry. Corning's patents were upheld in that forum as well, but in a January 1985 ruling the ITC failed to find the harm serious enough to warrant action on its part.[66]

Yet even before this case was settled, Sumitomo took a further step: it began construction of a plant in North Carolina. Though the structure was originally (in 1984, when it was announced) tagged as an R&D facility, Sumitomo was obviously intent on producing waveguides in the United States and signaled this in the clearest possible terms: it sued to have two of Corning's basic waveguide patents declared invalid. It was all but inevitable at this point that Corning would sue directly for infringement, and Sumitomo may have hoped to seize some sort of high ground in going to court first.

Needless to say, Corning countersued, seeking damages for infringement on the same two patents as well as a third. Corning won its case against Sumitomo in October 1987 (upheld on appeal in 1989). Sumitomo's arguments—the same ones it had used in defense of its customer, Canada Cable and Wire, and before the ITC—were again rejected, the judge even going so far as to commend Corning for its technical contributions. The company, the court noted, had "literally created a new industry of substantial size" and deserved the full fruits of those labors.[67] The victory was not, however, complete: only two patents had been found infringed; the third, which covered an important step in the fiber-producing process, was not. Sumitomo, which had been providing roughly 10 percent of the U.S. market, announced plans to simply buy drawn fiber from licensed suppliers and to use its facility in North Carolina to finish and sell them; in the end, however, it gave up, paying Corning $25 million, comparable to if not greater than the total of its waveguide sales to date.

The New Antitrust Environment

As important as these cases were in establishing Corning's intellectual property position, the most important suit was the one that never happened: the government never came to view Corning's power in the waveguide market as undue or unlawfully achieved, for a number of reasons. First, AT&T's power in the market and its access to Corning technology made any early claims that Corning aimed to dominate seem laughable. Other reasons were peculiar to Corning's handling of waveguide development and production, while still others related to changes in the larger environment for antitrust. Corning's most heated battles in defense of its waveguide patents came while President Reagan was in office, and his administration, in keeping with its general probusiness bent, oversaw an across-the-board lessening of antitrust activity. The most important factor of this sort, however, was the establishment in the 1970s of judicial support for single-company monopoly (as opposed to trusts or cartels) when based on a strong patent holding. Corning was following the example set by much larger companies in the 1970s, specifically the *Xerox v. IBM* and *Kodak v. SCM* cases, both of which helped reestablish an era of sympathetic court judgments for the holders of fundamental patents in lucrative commercial fields. These cases had found that a company had the right to refuse to license.

While such cases likely encouraged Corning to adopt an aggressive stance toward infringers of its waveguide patents, there could be no guarantees against antitrust action on the part of the Department of Justice. Corning continued to live with reminders of its wartime antitrust trials: it was not until 1984 that the restrictions on the company's ownership of fiberglass manufacturers, handed down as part of the original 1940s settlement of the fiberglass suit, were raised.

Corning continued to structure its approach to the market so as not to draw the ire of government trustbusters. But, as the business matured, patent protection would become less important than the other forms of knowledge that Corning was fast accumulating. Even the harshest of antitrust decisions were never able to touch know-how. As Wilson later recalled,

> One of the reasons I was so fussy about protecting our patents and being really stuffy about it was that I knew that by the time this got to be a big business, our patents were going to be pretty long in the tooth.... I wanted to have such a lead in know-how and keep pouring on the coals technically so that our know-how would be so far advanced ahead of anybody else, that even though they could read our patents and theoretically make it, they just would never be able to compete.[68]

INNOVATION AND INTELLECTUAL PROPERTY

Technology is intellectual property.

—ALFRED L. MICHAELSEN (PROPOSED
PATENT DEPARTMENT MISSION STATEMENT, 5 JUNE 1985)[69]

Corning's experiences developing and defending waveguides had as signifi-cant an effect on the company's approach to intellectual property as those of any other era in its history, not excepting the antitrust trials of the 1930s and '40s. As one internal memo stated it,

> Prior to approximately the mid-1970's, Corning had relatively little direct competition.... There was, in fact, little patent strategy because, if one has no real competitors, there is little need for a strategy.... The situation changed as Corning entered the waveguide and medical business. In wave-guides, the strategy was (and still is) to use patents aggressively to define a place in the market. That strategy had been used before. This time, how-

ever, the setting was different because (1) our potential customers (cablers) didn't want us, and (2) our potential competitors (most of whom were also our potential customers) had the technical resources to make the product and were not adverse to a patent fight.[70]

William Ughetta, writing in the same year, noted pointedly that "we have had more litigation in the past nine years than we had during the previous twenty-six" (i.e., since the last of the antitrust actions wound to a close).[71]

Though recognizing an increase in litigation as a necessary part of its new intellectual property strategy, Corning, in each of the cases discussed above, used the courts as a last resort, albeit one to which the company was forced to turn repeatedly. Unlike the antitrust actions, in the bulk of these cases Corning was the plaintiff and, of course, in all of them Corning won. Yet, as noted above, even victory before the bench was not without cost, nor could Corning choose its battles as it liked. Once it entered upon a strategy of aggressive defense of its waveguides patents, cases such as that against Sumitomo (even had Sumitomo not initiated the action) were all but inevitable. This was recognized by management, and a heightened awareness of and preparedness for legal conflict came to be seen as a cost of doing business in the adversarial (as opposed to the prewar trust) model.

Furthermore, the cost of waging a protracted legal war on behalf of a business that for many years had no revenues had to come out of the other Corning businesses. One of the more contentious issues in what was already a very difficult period for the company was how the waveguide litigation soaked up the lion's share of Corning's legal and patenting resources, leaving other developing businesses feeling neglected and unprotected.

Though the switch to a more aggressive, litigatory stance appears to have been a product of the waveguide experience for Corning, its roots, like so much else, extend back to the war. World War II changed the landscape of American business in many ways, but the most noteworthy was the rising tide of competition—both domestic and, as Europe and the Far East recovered, international—that was most marked in high tech industries. Franklin Hyde's comment in 1946 that Corning was "in serious competition with other organizations, who are turning out research work at a rapid rate" indicates just how quickly the scientists' war became the scientists' peace. In such a peace, one that amounted to industrial war for high tech companies, "patents and the capacity to rapidly attain industrial production [were] the only protection...for the millions of dollars...invested."[72]

Those were also the words of Frank Hyde, who regretted the tremendous changes in the climate for scientific discovery after the war, the increased hazards of sharing even with colleagues in universities, and the impossibility of sharing with scientists in other industrial laboratories. Yet the phrase "intellectual property" conveys a more definitive sense of ownership than could ever be the case when the primary form chosen for protection of commercially valuable knowledge was to patent and license it. Patents almost never served as Corning's first line of defense, not even in the heart of the waveguide battles. For Corning, as Wilson and others knew, the real first line of defense was two key elements of intellectual property which, taken together, represented assets more valuable, and in their way, more formidable, than the company's patent holdings: trade secrets and tacit knowledge, the latter more commonly called "know-how."

One of Corning's greatest fields of invention for most of its history was glass formulation, later extended to embrace other synthetic materials as well. For many years the sheer number of formulas held in Corning's vaults were pointed to as a proxy for the success of the company's research efforts and as a reminder of all the many corners of the sandbox Corning researchers had explored. The number was, however, unverifiable, because the formulas did sit in a vault, with all that implied. The situation was a constant in the industry: "Glass formulations are tremendous in number, and exact contents generally remain a closely guarded proprietary secret."[73]

Corning patented only a tiny fraction of its proprietary formulas, relying instead on the power of trade secrets and the preeminence of its research infrastructure in the industry to protect its ownership of these assets. As noted in one internal memo, "Most of [Corning's] products were proprietary because of know-how, rather than patents, although patents supplemented the know-how position."[74] Not only had Corning researchers undertaken experimental melts on a more or less on-going basis since well before World War II, but in pilot plants and later the PRC, they had continued to develop better forming methods, and they had kept in touch with process improvements made in plants throughout the Corning system.

The new formulas and the countless other internal processes and practices known only to Corning insiders, were Corning's real stock-in-trade, part of the "till" from which its researchers and product developers, and process engineers all drew when called upon to solve problems for customers. Trade secrets, therefore, lay at the heart of Corning's research efforts, as important a part of the company's intellectual property as patents or trademarks, but, by their nature, a good deal easier to overlook.

Corning was able to rely on knowhow and maintain it as community property, rather than the province of individual experts to a greater extent than many companies. It had created and continued to maintain for this purpose ideal conditions that few companies enjoyed after World War II. It had a loyal stable workforce in somewhat remote small town settings, a high degree of continuity and communication among its employees, and a respect for craft that coexisted with the more readily documented knowledge of the scientists and engineers.[75]

Though Corning could not have been aware of it at the time, even RCA's move to integrate backward into glassmaking, though a major breaching of Corning's defenses, would actually show what a powerful advantage Corning's knowhow afforded. For although RCA did eventually produce acceptable glass for its highest volume CRT's, it came very close to failure because of discord between engineers who disdained craft as "black magic" and conflicts between glassworkers from different glassmaking traditions whose local knowledge was not easily meshed.[76]

The conditions needed to keep regenerating and reinventing Corning's know-how while protecting its room to maneuver with patents could never be taken for granted. These advantages had endured for a long time, but they could be disrupted or even lost entirely, and they very nearly were during the 1970s and 1980s when Corning, like most other U.S. companies, faced the full force of competition. As we show in chapter 9, the struggle to grow in bad economic times, and the attempts to impose greater measures of control in the name of productivity, would erect barriers between Corning's technical community and its businesses that would undermine, though not destroy, Corning's innovative vitality for an entire generation.

THE END OF THE

"AMERICAN CENTURY"

WRESTLING WITH DIVERSIFICATION

AND CONTROL

Our goal is to be the best. This happens now to be glass. We hope to evolve to a point that we could include glass-ceramics, ceramics, refractories, and products related to a more embracing system which springs from our technology or other assets—possibly different in form from anything we've ever done. In other words, we must now more than ever utilize all the resources of Corning Glass Works, not just the technical, to create something better and different than anyone else. What is the change—the difference? It does not always have to relate to glass.

—AMORY HOUGHTON JR.
ADDRESS TO THE 1968 MANAGEMENT CONFERENCE

"I N THE NEXT decade we must find a better way to use what we have, our total resources. At the moment we appear to be using only part of that system." This comment could have struck an audience filled with hard-charging young executives at Corning's 1968 management conference as a mere course correction, one in a sequence of gradual strategic realignments that had issued from Amory Houghton Jr.'s office during the 1960s. But it was far more than that. The comment augured a significant reappraisal of the company's strategy, a response to the intensifying challenge of meeting a 10 percent annual growth target while adhering to a research-driven strategy during a period of economic transition.

Developing a strategy for intellectual property (discussed in chapter 8) was an essential but insufficient step for Corning to take to prepare to harvest the fruits of its investment in R&D in the 1980s and beyond. As Amo Houghton recognized at the outset, there were systemic issues, operational and cultural, that had to be worked out if American companies were to become truly productive in a more competitive world. For many companies this was an exercise in learning by doing. Corning's efforts in the 1970s and 1980s to identify and master these issues were wide-ranging, and they ultimately produced a whole new set of abilities for the company. But these gains were overshadowed in the short run by the struggle between two different philosophies—one of achieving productivity through control and the other of innovation through support of creative individuals. Finding the balance between these different poles was the hard and frustrating work of an entire generation of Corning managers.[1] It affected projects as diverse as substrates for catalytic convertors, laminated dishware, and fiber optics; it also played out in areas of diversification like biomedical research, as well as in the developing relationship between Corning's domestic and international laboratories.

A New Era

The sudden and premature end of what Henry Luce had dubbed the "American Century" came as a shock to American industry as a whole. The euphoric days of the postwar boom had led Corning's management and many others to think that their successes had been entirely of their own making. Corning had become accustomed to hiring managers straight out of leading business schools and then giving them a fast track course of on-the-job training. Marty Gibson, fresh out of Wharton, occupied four completely different line jobs in the Science Products Division in five years, ranging from sales and production to controller. Van Campbell, later Corning's chief financial officer and executive vice chairman, had begun his Corning career out of Harvard Business School by bouncing between positions in production and finance.[2] Now it seemed that such management practices during which youthful managers had little time to accumulate any particular expertise (and no time to live with their mistakes) were a luxury of the high-margin business, and such margins were shrinking fast.

Market forecasts also suggested that in some of Corning's highest-growth markets, their products were maturing and losing market share. High-purity (greater than 95 percent) silica, for example, had been growing at 15 percent per year. Although Corning had almost half of that market at the end of 1967, its Vycor products were falling short of the needs of the fastest growing part of the market—semiconductor tubing and ware—and other competitors were producing the superior quality of fused quartz considered necessary to match rising demand.[3]

When Corning had faced such serious difficulties as international competition and recession after World War I or the calamitous drop in demand of the Great Depression, it had stuck tenaciously to its own path, rejecting the rigid control measures of more "scientifically managed" mass production enterprises. It had protected hourly workers in Corning with short hours, and it had never laid off salaried workers without cause. This time circumstances were different. Corning was no longer a privately owned enterprise immune from stock market pressures, and there was less conviction about the efficacy of its unique solutions.[4]

As a result of the prolonged period of postwar prosperity, the Corning of the early 1970s had become a much larger enterprise. Revenues increased from over $500 million in 1968 to nearly $1 billion five years later, around 190th on the list of industrial companies. As the world's largest specialty glassmaker, it had greater visibility than its size alone would warrant. It also had critics: stockholders to please, unions to contend with. And it had new classes of employees, each with its own sense of entitlement: youthful professional managers who took pride in working for a high-tech company and cohorts of first-class researchers, some of whom had been hired to do exploratory research. For these people Amo Houghton's vaguely dire prediction of April 1968 would turn into very bad news indeed. In a futile search for profitability, Corning's executive corps would be compelled to carry out a complete overhaul of its operations, and the company's leaders would become embroiled in two decades of frantic experimentation before settling on a new way forward.

The implications for change in the management conference presentations were greatest for the operating divisions being asked to shoulder more initiative. In the decade just past, the strategic emphasis had been on "home runs" hit by the technical staffs and supported by senior management; in the one to come, all of the heads of Corning's operating divisions would be expected to grow their businesses by 5 percent annually and to embrace large research-based opportunities when they were offered, but they were also charged to add substantial chunks to their revenue streams through acquisition. The cumulative result of all these efforts was expected to be 10 percent.

Houghton acknowledged that however attractive the approach might be as a way of acquiring chunks of new revenue while Corning's stock price was high, an acquisition program could have grave implications. During the previous decade companies well-known to Corning, like the old Radio Corporation of America, which had recently become RCA, or the former International Telephone and Telegraph, now ITT, had sought to manage their cyclical risk by conglomerating. The mixed outcomes of such ventures had plainly showed that to acquire others successfully a company had to know itself well.[5] As it happened, Houghton's concerns were more justified than he knew. The identity issue, like some untimely genie released from a bottle, would haunt Corning for more than two decades. If Corning were no longer to mean "research in glass," what else might it mean?

A TIME OF TRIALS, 1968–1975

The first stage of what turned out to be a major reversal of fortune for Corning came shortly after the 1968 management conference broke up, when RCA announced its intention to integrate backward into television bulb production. In retrospect it seemed that Corning had been leading a charmed existence for more than a decade. RCA, with one swift stroke, broke that charm, leaving Corning's senior leadership in the 1970s, Tom MacAvoy and Amo Houghton, in the words of another top Corning manager, "desperate to find breakout opportunities from [the] death spiral of the traditional OEM glass business."[6] Although Corning moved with dispatch to head off any further defections among its television manufacturer customers, the damage was serious. The loss of RCA's bread-and-butter nineteen-inch bulb sliced away the most profitable core of the television business, the high-volume, high-margin piece that made the whole extremely profitable. With this one development Corning's television bulb business went from a strategic star, in portfolio matrix terms, to a business with shrinking margins that had to be defended. Its managers went from the privileged to the beleaguered almost overnight, with serious problems for management morale.[7] In general Corning's chief strategic problem had seesawed from growth to cost control.

Within a year of this first setback, conditions in the general business environment took a dramatic turn for the worse. Domestic television makers faced an onslaught from increasingly powerful Japanese competitors, culminating in the consumer electronics recession of 1970. No one had recovered from this shock before the economy as a whole took a nosedive. The Nixon administration's effort to cope with the macroeconomic problems caused by its predecessor's decision to fight a war in Southeast Asia without moving to a wartime economy was further undermined in 1973–1974, when the Middle East oil crisis pushed energy prices through the roof. The cumulative effect of these powerful reversals produced a novel economic malaise dubbed "stagflation": a period of low growth coupled with accelerating inflation. Capital became difficult to get and very costly. Houghton's dire predictions of early 1968 had turned out to be all too accurate: "Unless our government...faces up to the present financial crisis, we could be living in an atmosphere totally foreign to anything we have ever seen—and I include the depression!"[8]

For materials companies like Corning these developments were especially onerous. Sitting near the end of their various supply chains, they suffered the cumulative reverses of all their customers. Big energy users as a rule, their production costs shot up but they were prevented from raising prices. Concurrently the government was putting pressure on such companies to clean up their manufacturing processes, which in Corning's case entailed serious efforts to reduce air pollution. It is difficult to recapture the sense of things before the late-1960s awakening of an environmental consciousness, or rather to recapture the *lack* of a sense of things. Remembering the surprises of this period, engineering manager Dave Leibson commented, "Along about this period of time comes pollution." Corning acted quickly in response to its "discovery" of pollution, developing and importing a variety of techniques for limiting its impact on the environment. This initiative began in 1971 and cost the company around $60 million over the course of the next decade.[9]

With the OPEC embargo, concern about energy conservation became another element to be considered in striving for corporate good citizenship. Though utterly dependent on a steady supply of energy for its daily operations, Corning was better prepared than many to deal with the effects of the embargo. The company had long been sensitive to fluctuations in the price and availability of the fuels it used in its furnaces (oil, as it happens, was not one of them). Natural gas shortages in the 1930s,[10] energy rationing in both world wars, and constant attention to the best mix of energy sources for the furnaces served to make the 'energy crisis' of the early 1970s one in a long line of similar challenges. Compared to the logistical difficulties involved in switching from coal-fired to gas-fired furnaces and, later, from gas to electric (both of which had improved the energy efficiency of production and, secondarily, cleaned it up considerably), the OPEC challenge struck less fear into management's heart than one might have expected in such an energy-intensive business.

Nevertheless, the whole period was grim. The oil crisis and the ensuing economic nightmare negatively affected Corning's previously impervious revenue stream. Profitability started a steady downhill slide in 1969, sinking from the 10 percent plateau of the 1960s to a low of 3 percent in 1975. Even revenues contracted, moving lower in 1971 for the first time since World War II and repeating the slump in 1975. And as if this were not enough, this same period saw Corning's worst natural disaster in forty years.

The Flood

In June 1972, the tail end of Hurricane Agnes caused the Chemung River to flood. Trusting the Army Corps of Engineers that had supposedly tamed the river with flood control projects, the entire area was caught by surprise. The deluge wrecked the headquarters data processing center, tore through the Main Plant area, devastated the Pressware and Fallbrook plants, shut down Steuben's furnaces, and came very close to scuttling a vital crash program on one of Corning's most important and time-sensitive new product programs, the ceramic substrates for automobile exhaust systems called Celcor.

Happily, Corning already had in place its government affairs office set up in the 1960s, a relatively new institution for most companies. While this office had proved itself of some value to the company, this disaster provided the occasion for its first major triumph. Alan Cors, the director of that office from 1968 until 1999, recalled the urgent summons that told him of conditions at headquarters:

> The gas lines have been ruptured and we don't have gas for the city. We've got these glass tanks that are going to freeze up. We've got to have gas to keep these things going. And the [Army] Corps of Engineers is saying they're so busy with every other community. What can you do to help?[11]

As it turned out, Cors was able to do a good deal via contacts in the Pentagon who were willing to reorder corps priorities. For the next year or more Cors and his office did nothing but deal with the aftermath of the flood, helping bring federal aid to the area (not just the company) in the form of disaster relief and Small Business Administration loans, which it later also helped get forgiven. Cors was eventually elevated to the position of vice president and the GAO taken out from under public relations, where it had previously reported, and placed in direct communication with the CEO and other top management. Communications between the GAO and headquarters became much more regular and formalized; the company had recognized the worth of this asset and managed it accordingly.

EXECUTIVE SOUL-SEARCHING

Good times cover many defects. Where the general mood at Corning during the television era of the 1960s had been self-congratulatory, in the midst of a succession of setbacks, the focus naturally turned inward. Sober reflection was the order of the day, though conclusions varied widely as to the causes of Corning's predicament.

The first conclusion with major implications was that the past decade's effort to spawn whole new businesses chiefly from big research ideas coupled with strenuous engineering pushes, all under the direction of a powerful, self-contained technical staffs organization, had been too big a stretch. Corning's strategic directions had typically arisen from Amo Houghton's ongoing dialogue with the chief of Corning's technical staffs, Bill Armistead; often they mirrored initiatives already under way at Sullivan Park. More recently they had also been influenced by consultations with Walker Lewis of the pace-setting Boston Consulting Group. As of the management conference two quite new initiatives formed part of the proposed plan, which gave research-based innovation a considerably more modest assignment than responsibility for the entire future direction of the company. Amory Houghton's five strategies were:

- Defending the OEM business, the specialty glass that was still the locus of Corning's identity

- Growing existing businesses, already quite diversified (43 businesses, up from 30+)

- Extending more aggressively into overseas markets where such legal constraints on glass-related activities as antitrust were not as confining as they were in the United States

- Innovating in new markets based on nonglass research

- Outright acquisition of domestic companies in nonglass but related industries.[12]

The last two were the novel ones, though they were not wholly unrelated to Corning's previous research-based strategy. Corning's already substantial stake in electronics was partly an outgrowth of its glass research. Biotech, another nonglass research area being pursued as part of the laboratory program, was similarly still regarded as a way to open up new markets for porous glass, not an end in itself.

The technical community responded to Amo Houghton's five-point plan with caution. Reluctant to contradict a chairman who had long been his staunchest ally, Bill Armistead still argued that it was premature to look for further research areas outside glass until they were in a better position to exploit the research opportunities already at hand. While not denying that conducting research in another emerging technology was a matter worth considering, Armistead urged that the difficulty of attaining research productivity in such a field not be underestimated. "We have not," he concluded, "reached the 'sunset' of glass research":

> All of American industry faces the problem of maintaining corporate growth and profitability in the face of steadily rising salaries, wages, purchase costs and taxes. We face this same problem in research and development. [To] increase our output without a corresponding increase in numbers of people... we must: 1) manage better 2) find and make the best use of creative people 3) identify and concentrate on the big opportunities, and avoid frittering away our effort on small projects 4) transfer people from where they can be spared to "where the action is."[13]

To that end he had already instituted Corning's "technical request system," which was working well as a way of seeking operating managers' guidance. The key problem in Armistead's eyes, however, was ensuring that there were enough high-caliber people to do the research. No amount of management guidance could produce a productive technical effort without creative people or without the years invested in building an effective research organization to enable the success of their work. According to Armistead's numbers, Corning had achieved this desired state only in glass technology. In the other research areas, electronics and composites, "my main conclusion is that we must tackle new fields of research with proven creators from other laboratories, (5 or more patents, as young as possible)." This was especially crucial in electronics.

Ray Voss, head of new product development, and Bill Decker, former Corning chairman of the board and CEO and still an influential force in the company, both argued strongly against further diluting the efforts of technical staffs by adding more kinds of research. They maintained that the R&D program needed to concentrate on one or two major opportunities.

Decker expressed the further concern that the R&D program in electronics was not even strong enough to keep up with the leaders, let alone excel them in Corning's usual fashion.[14]

The themes of productivity and creativity and their relationship to growth infused Corning's internal debate for the next decade. Amo Houghton's technical staffs file drawer bulged with straight-talking memos from senior Corning managers, reviewing the weaknesses they perceived in the way Corning was managing its innovation process. Several charges appeared in most of these critiques: a lack of initiative among Corning's general managers, too little clarity about vision, and a tendency to stretch too thin Corning's fund of managerial experience. Each only underscored the general point that the problem was not a shortage of novel ideas but an inability of the system (i.e., all the parts of the company working together) to exploit them. Where these various memos disagreed was in their choice of two very different and possibly mutually exclusive solutions: cost reduction based on improved productivity, versus innovation aiming at enhanced performance. As Corning had seen in earlier periods, the two emphases might not inherently conflict, but the former certainly had a tendency to crowd out the latter.

The bitter RCA experience supported the cost-reduction solution. Among the many unambiguous lessons Corning could take from that experience, the most obvious was that Corning could no longer depend on being able to charge a higher margin for better performance, either for new product capabilities or for superior service. At first it might seem that this was a life cycle matter—that television was simply a maturing product and that new products would still be able to recover higher margins as before. But gradually the shape of a new and different reality set in: cost cutting had to be assumed, and planned for, from the design stage, and certainly by the moment a new product hit the market.

As they were for many American companies at the time, improving production targets and output were central to cost-cutting efforts. Corning's first step in meeting enhanced overseas competition, particularly from the Japanese, was organizational: restructuring its engineering forces, most of which had been reporting as part of the ttechnical staffs division to Bill Armistead. A major portion of engineering was transferred to a strong, centralized manufacturing and engineering (M&E) division under fresh, aggressive leadership. This organization received the mandate to get technology into the plants more quickly, to smooth out new product introductions, and, significantly, to improve the gross margins of the existing plants. The leader named to head this effort was Dave Leibson, who had already made a name for himself by solving a number of seemingly intractable production problems, including some key snarls in television bulb production.

Leibson soon had a force of eighty people working for him, of which more than half were credentialed engineers. He used them to create detailed standard operating procedures (SOPs) for every Corning manufacturing process, which in many cases superceded the discretionary practices and rules of thumb of the operators. He also had the power to allocate the pot of resources for plant modernization and new product introduction. After negotiating with the general managers, Leibson would henceforth decide which of the many projects in need of support the M&E group would take on in any given year. Finally, during the 1970s Leibson managed career tracks within manufacturing, deciding the career pattern by which promising young managers would be developed.[15]

Leibson's objective, set directly by Amo Houghton, was to increase the gross margin of every plant to 50 percent. An "impossible" goal, noted Leibson, but he accepted that measure of performance as one "to strive for." The chief difficulty he found lay in "breaking down the barriers between

David Leibson, head of the central manufacturing and engineering organization which in the 1970s controlled how manufacturing resources were deployed all over Corning. M&E was responsible for starting up many crucial product programs including Corelle and Celcor.

research, engineering, and the plants and then getting productivity as a goal." Leibson later noted that "the plant managers hated [the gross margin measurement], 'it was no good, it wasn't accurate', but it was a good measure of productivity and year after year we would make 6-percent gains in productivity—which was very, very good."[16] Senior operations managers like Forry Behm had been complaining for some time that Corning did too little to prepare the plants for new product introduction, especially when it came to process development and training. They also complained that during the 1960s too many resources had been lavished on business development projects at the expense of the general level of preparedness in the plants. Leibson was the first to acknowledge that Bill Armistead had not undervalued manufacturing himself, but his people had placed their emphasis on new products to please him. In any case, many production research projects had only been emerging in the 1960s. Corning had been early to experiment with computer-controlled processes under its senior engineer at the time Art Weber, for instance, but they were only in their infancy and not up to the rigors of a regular fast-paced production environment until the 1970s.

Under Leibson's direction Corning also initiated a new integrated project management team approach ensuring that research, development, melting, process, and manufacturing engineering would work together early in the product cycle. This replaced the more sequential methods that had prevailed previously, paving the way for demanding new products to reach their production targets more quickly. One of the first projects to benefit from the new approach was Corelle, Corning's laminated glass consumerware. In fact, without this new approach Corelle, which would become Corning's largest-selling consumer product, might never have reached the market. According to Armistead himself, "Corelle was far and away the most difficult project I ever did in the lab to take it to production."[17]

CORELLE: JIM GIFFEN'S TECHNOLOGY, 1955–1977

Of all the major products Corning brought to market, only a few took longer to develop technically than they did to develop commercially. Corelle, the result of a long and tortuous technical development, was one of these. It incorporated forming technologies that Corning had worked with as early as 1955. The glass formulations and product specifications followed in the 1960s, but it was not until 1970, when the new project management approach (discussed above) was introduced, that the most serious bugs in the process could be worked out. By contrast, only three years after first appearing on store shelves, Corelle became the best-selling tableware in the United States.

At the center of Corelle's technical development was the iconoclastic inventor Jim Giffen. The Corelle project manifested the self-confidence and bulldog tenacity that Giffen relied on to bring his ideas to fruition. It also displayed the full extent of Corning's commitment to following Giffen almost anywhere he wanted to go. In the case of Corelle this combination led to a high-speed process for manufacturing extremely thin dishes out of a highly strengthened glass laminate. There were, however, serious drawbacks to Giffen's idiosyncratic character and unique approach: his way of doing things created production and morale problems of their own. The very challenging new processes that he developed called into question Armistead's dictum that existing processes should never be treated as constraints.

The first of the basic technologies that contributed to the creation of Corelle was vacuum forming, a method Giffen had worked on in the early 1950s. At that time his priority was television production, but he had tried a variety of molds while tinkering with the process, including such consumerware items as pie plates. The consumer division, and Corning's president Lee Waterman especially, noted these experiments and, with the development of Pyroceram, requested that Giffen combine his process and the new product to make lightweight dinnerware. Giffen did so, creating the so-called Hub Machine for the purpose. Described by one author as "a flaming Ferris wheel,"[18] it was in essence a more spectacular version of a Ribbon Machine, and it could well have been the Ribbon Machine that inspired Giffen in designing it.

An experimental version of the device was installed in A Factory in 1958, and it went into commercial use at Martinsburg in 1961; Pyroceram plates manufactured on the machine made their market debut that same year. Giffen used the opportunity to broaden the range of shapes he could vacuum form and the Martinsburg hub machine continued to produce the

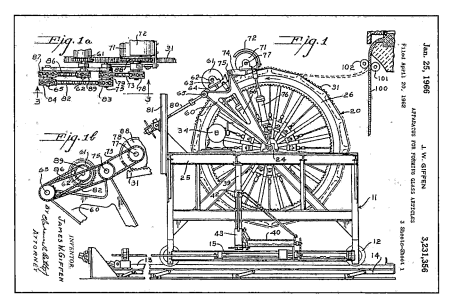

The Hub Machine, shown here in a patent drawing, was one of James Giffen's major inventions and was vital to the production of Corelle dinnerware. The centerpiece of the Hub Machine was an oversized wheel, the outer surface of which held a series of molds. When rotated, the wheel, or hub, would present a constantly new face to the ribbon of glass to be shaped, sucking it into each mold as it came in contact. An automatic trimmer cut off excess glass, allowing the machine to churn out an endless stream of formed pieces.

largest pieces in the Corning Ware line, but the effort required to find a more suitable glass composition for dinnerware was not undertaken. Rather, the lab and Giffen alike turned their attention to strengthened glasses as part of what would come to be called Project Muscle.

One of the strengthening concepts revived in the course of that labora-tory-wide investigation was glass lamination: using two or more layers of glasses with different coefficients of expansion to achieve the desired com-pressive stresses in a finished and therefore strengthened piece. The technol-ogy had ancient roots, but Corning's researchers improved it considerably. Giffen, meanwhile, set out to do something entirely novel: to form pieces from this laminated glass on a continuous, reliable, and high-speed basis. The project, officially begun in 1965, was dubbed "Hercules" in tribute to the expected strength of the product and, perhaps, in subconscious anticipation of the labors that lay ahead. Giffen had hoped to use his new laminated glass for architectural materials like roofing tiles, but he was persuaded first to

apply his new discoveries in the market where Corning already had its bearings: consumerware.

It is difficult to overestimate the complexity of the task Giffen had set for
himself and Corning. The obvious problems—finding a pair of suitable
glass formulas, merging them into layered but not intermingled streams,
and maintaining them within an inevitably narrow working range—were
only a few of the more difficult ones encountered along the way. Initial trial
runs in the Sullivan Park Process Research Center took place between January and May 1966 and led to reworking Pilot Plant 2 for the next stage.

This step was taken before a suitable opal core glass had been found, but
such a glass was necessary if the final piece was to be opaque.[19] Opals,
though soft, were suitable for a laminated glass because they would be sealed
within layers of a much tougher, transparent formula, opaque and hard at
the same time. Unfortunately, Corning's opals required long times in a lehr,
and even then they did not achieve opalization uniformly. This produced dinnerware in unacceptably varying shades of white. Hercules was saved by
"spontaneous opals." These glasses invented by Bill Dumbaugh and James
Flannery would achieve opalization almost immediately upon cooling below
their softening point and were much more uniform in their behavior.

The search for a suitable formula took over a year, and the pilot plant
tanks were not filled with this formula until July 1968. Where further
process problems remained to be overcome, Giffen again proved both his
genius and his no-holds barred approach to getting his way: Armistead
recalled his astonishing request for an electron beam welder, a rare and
expensive piece of equipment for the time:

> I say, "What are you going to do with it?" He says, "Well, I'm going to put
> this feeder together with it." I said, "Have you tried it?" He says, "Oh
> sure . . . " I said, "Are you sure it will work?" He says, "Yes." I said, "You need
> an appropriation request because this is worth $300,000." And he got it in
> and it had to be in an air conditioned room because the temperature . . . was
> very important. Well, he made the feeder.[20]

The feeder in question was the orifice that shaped the two flows of glass
into a multilayer laminate and became another patentable technology in

Corelle's development. The device, as Giffen envisioned it, required platinum forming of extreme precision, beyond the capabilities of any of the platinum experts employed by Corning for more typical uses of the metal. Using the electron beam welder, Giffen hand-built an orifice that was capable of producing a three-layer laminate; later he adapted it to produce a seven-layer laminate for roofing tiles.

Giffen built the platinum orifice in 1969 and, having proven its utility, had most of the pieces for the new dishware in place: the glass would flow from two tanks through his platinum orifice, which would shape it into a laminated sheet and pass it to rollers that would introduce it to the Hub Machine. The Hub Machine would stamp out the pieces, which would be trimmed and sent along for fire polishing. Further work was required to produce a formulation that would be malleable enough for this process, but by January 1970 Bill Dumbaugh had produced both a core and skin glass that met with everyone's approval.[21]

Ironically, even though Giffen personally provided many of the solutions for Corelle, including a number of smaller metallurgical advances, he was also one of its most serious obstacles to commercialization. The scale up to volume production did not initially result in significant cost savings per piece, a disaster from a profitability standpoint. Armistead, Waterman, and Houghton called in Leibson and asked him why, with Corelle "bleeding money" his manufacturing engineering people weren't doing something about it. After investigation, Leibson returned with the unwelcome news that Giffen was at the heart of the difficulty:

> I'm letting them talk and letting them talk, and then I finally said, Amo, we can do nothing as long as Jim Giffen is in there because he won't let go. He won't accept any suggestions from our people; they are trying hard; they are getting nowhere. We will get nowhere as long as he is there. . . . Amo says, Oh gee whiz, and Armistead said nothing. . . . Waterman said, 'Okay, Dave, well I guess that takes care of it. Thank you.' And I am gone. I have no idea of whether I am going to be fired the next day or what, because I know they value Jim Giffen more than they value me.[22]

The next day Waterman called Leibson back. "Okay, Jim has gone back to the lab, now fix it!" The problem was, observed Leibson, that Giffen's machine was still a laboratory prototype. As a consultant, Leibson brought in a retired naval maintenance expert whose specialty was developing standard operating procedures for a whole production process. With his help, Corning's process engineering group reengineered the Corelle production process for high-volume production, and Corning had a product at last.

Marketing Livingware

Having made the product, Corning still had to sell it. To match the technical achievements of Giffen, Dumbaugh, and the rest, the consumer business put together Corning's most detailed and careful publicity campaign ever, using a Madison Avenue publicity firm. The new dishware was to be "primarily a middle to low-end product" and was expected to "ultimately level out in a market mix comprised of hardware, variety and mass merchandisers" in addition to department stores. The consulting firm insisted on picking a name that contained the prefix "Cor" for Corning. Madison Avenue proposed "Corever" and Corning countered with "Corelle."[23]

The remaining technical challenges delayed full market introduction until 1970, but Corning used the intervening months to test and retest consumer response to the new product. Corning market researchers followed women into their homes to see how they actually used the dishes. Focus groups were assembled, and patterns, prices, packaging, and names were tried out. Home economists and marketers in the company's employ spent a total of five years preparing for the big day.

Actual introduction of the new dishes, dubbed "Livingware," was accompanied by a number of firsts. Corning offered a two-year warranty and promised to keep any discontinued patterns available for two years. In point of fact, only four patterns were originally introduced, of which three continued in production for over a decade. The new product was an astounding success. Corning sold over 400,000 pieces in the last quarter of 1970. The following year that number leapt to almost 40 million, and by 1977 it had doubled again. "The consumer loved us," wrote one marketer. Corelle's success was a windfall for Corning. Projected sales for Corelle in the early 1970s were on the order of $20 million, rising to $35 million by 1976. In fact, sales reached into the hundreds of millions annually, and by 1977, what journalists referred to as the dishes made from "this glass equivalent of plywood" held an astounding 20 percent market share.[24]

But success also brought with it a new air pollution problem. Corelle relied on a glass containing fluoride, a potential air pollutant that was typically removed using smokestack filters called "baghouses." Since these filters were expensive and high maintenance, Waterman hoped to do away with them. Under pressure from him, Leibson and Armistead decided to take the step to vertical, "cold crown" melting. This technology had been introduced to Corning (as well as to many other American glass manufacturers) by Preston Laboratories, a small consulting lab run by a British scientist who argued that glass should be melted in giant cylinders, with the heat being applied electrically within the batch, and new batch materials added at the top in such a manner and amount as to blanket the molten glass with a solid layer of unmelted material. By eliminating the volatile surface of a molten bath, this system, called a Vermel (for "vertical melter"), did away with almost all particulate and gaseous emissions from the melt. The experiment was a success, and the Corelle line was retrofitted with Vermel furnaces, making that technology yet another in a string of important innovations that contributed to Corning's dinnerware line.[25]

Home Run Exhaustion

Corelle was manufactured at Pressware, the hometown plant built in 1938 for Pyrex bakeware production, shifted to making television bulbs in the 1960s, and shut down in 1969 when TV declined. Converted to Corelle production in 1970, with its new all-electric melting tanks, the plant operated essentially nonstop for nearly three decades.

Corelle was a success by any standard. On 29 February 1984, Corning's steamwhistle blew to mark production of the one-billionth piece of Corelle. The extreme technical challenges this high-tech consumerware presented also had important benefits for the company. Corning secured patents on the key parts of the process and on the concept for the product itself. That Corelle production remained entirely within the Pressware plant spoke to the amount of local and tacit knowledge required for its production.

Although Corning tried to produce Corelle elsewhere—especially in its Sunderland plant for the European market—it did not succeed. As one author commented, "The process is so complex and the investment is so great, that Corning has never built another factory to make Corelle. It would take a Jim Giffen to make it happen." Corelle was, in this sense, a case of creativity allowed too free a rein. Corning needed to get beyond Giffen and its idealization of his unbridled genius if it was to be competitive as a manufacturing company in increasingly demanding markets.[26]

The possibilities of laminated glass did not stop with plates and bowls. In one of the relevant patents the authors—Dumbaugh, Flannery, John Megles, and John Smith—noted vehicle windshields as one possible application of their "Method for Making Multi-layer Laminated Bodies." Giffen was anxious to find ways to produce his preferred tile and roofing products, and Corning was still expecting to break into this architectural market in a far more substantial way. From the early 1970s on, however, neither the consumer business nor most of the glass-related businesses were aligned with the strategic guidelines that Corning had developed for concentrating its innovation activities. Corelle had been such a near thing that it left few people with the stomach to try anything like it again soon. Indeed, there was a generalized desire not to concentrate too much of the company's effort in any one area, especially if it was glass.[27]

Coming at the same time as the unambiguous strikeout of the Chemcor windshield project (chapter 7), the difficult aspects of the Corelle project served to emphasize the object lesson learned from Chemcor about the costs and risks of top-down home run projects in general. Not only did these projects absorb resources that otherwise might have improved the cost structures of Corning's television plants, but they undermined the company's confidence in the old alliance between research and top management. They especially called into question the wisdom of allowing that alliance to champion products for entirely new businesses. Millions of dollars had been invested on the basis of untested assumptions—that the auto companies would be compelled by public opinion or government regulators to embrace a safer windshield, that a proprietary production process would be better than one that was easier to install and control—what was to prevent senior management from making such false calls in the future?

THE CONSULTANTS CONSULTED, 1970–1975

With both its revenues and profits falling, Corning could hardly claim that its customary iconoclastic approach was giving it any advantage over other companies struggling to respond to a crisis of international competition. Even its elder statesmen could hardly remember a period of such peculiar and difficult challenges. Unsure of the times and of themselves, Corning executives sought more and more professional management advice from outside the company. A hardly unprecedented decision—Corning was as well connected to professional management circles as any company of its size in the country—the call summoned a succession of consultants, business school professors, and top management consulting firms. All framed and described Corning's problem in much the same way, though their proffered solutions varied.

One perennial message, long brushed off by Corning's senior management, was that glass was a maturing technology to which Corning had remained tethered for too long; this was commonly accompanied by a prescription to drive the business more from a marketing perspective. The second message was that at a time when professional business was increasingly dominated by analytics, or a "management by the numbers" ethos, Corning's numbers were out of line. The obvious message was that "the numbers" had to be reined in to improve profitability for the shareholders, a group that was becoming a more important focus of attention as growth slowed.[28]

Consultants had been offering similar advice for years, but Corning's new president, Tom MacAvoy, was sensitized to the impact of economics on the company by the recession of 1970–1971, and he gave both of these criticisms a fresh hearing. MacAvoy had joined management's ranks from the laboratory and had learned much of what he knew about professional management on the job. He keenly felt the handicap of managing in the 1970s without benefit of professional management techniques, and he pursued the subject of productivity, in particular, with a convert's zeal. In his view, one of Corning's major strategic weaknesses was that its technical community had been insulated from economic reality while it was effectively shaping the company's strategy.[29]

Though sure of himself and empowered by his position to dictate the changes he felt necessary, MacAvoy recognized that he and his accomplices faced an uphill struggle:

> I was constantly talking with the plant managers about the importance of productivity, which they understood ... but over time it became quite apparent that productivity has zero sex appeal for the organization. In the theoretical sense, managers understand it and they're "committed to it," but the people don't go for it. It's threatening to them.[30]

In fact the productivity drives had a number of downsides for Corning, which many people whipsawed by them recognized. While they delivered short-term economic gains, they increased manufacturing managers' resistance to changing processes and especially to bringing in new products. They also reduced the amount of collateral work that plants were willing to perform in favor of optimizing the one central productivity measure. Moreover, the centralization of decision making in Leibson's engineering organization gave operating managers a diminished sense of control over their own destiny. Someone else was deciding whether their projects were the most important on the basis of market growth rather than local performance. This "productivity dilemma," as several widely followed renegade professors at the Harvard Business School termed it, was a problem that had stifled innovation in earlier periods in U.S. industrial life, and it had raised its ugly head again in many American companies. Middle-level managers had reason to feel threatened, and the events of the mid-1970s undermined their morale still further.[31]

Downsizing: The "Guns of August"

Faced with problems none of the Corning management team had encountered before, the company asked McKinsey & Co., which was already involved in organizational development at senior levels of the organization, to lead an assessment of its productivity. In essence this meant applying at the middle management level the kind of generic tools that had previously been reserved largely for manufacturing and operations—a white-collar Taylorism for the 1970s. At Corning, of course, such tools had been used sparingly in earlier periods, even at the operating level.

The original intention of conducting an overhead analysis at Corning was to produce an orderly plan for personnel reductions. But the recession of 1974–1975 got ahead of them. In a layoff popularly memorialized as "the Guns of August" 1,500 people of management rank were let go, many of them at headquarters. Corning had been good at weeding out nonperformers, but laying off satisfactory performers in a small town like Corning was a bruising experience, especially when done en masse. Even the R&D organization, which had traditionally been spared, was required to take a 10 percent cut, most of which came from the "R" side. The new head of R&D, Jack Hutchins, was warned that his participation in layoffs was mandatory if he wanted to have any voice in management circles going forward. For research in the 1970s, lacking such a voice would be dangerous indeed.

Strategic Planning

For Sullivan Park the 1975 layoffs marked the beginning of decades of constant cutback: not only was it necessary for research to adapt its effort to shrinking budgets, but new strategic planning approaches and financial controls pointed to fashioning a research program that aimed at target market areas instead of capitalizing on perceived technical opportunities. The source for new business development strategy had moved to a corporate development committee, which itself was heavily influenced by a new management orthodoxy.

The new strategic planning method, using a growth matrix system currently in vogue, divided the company's businesses into four categories based on sectoral growth rates and Corning's share of each of these markets. The committee had first issued its recommendations in 1971. These placed highest strategic priority on making suitable, non-OEM acquisitions, on the grounds that Corning's high stock price made them the cheapest avenues to growth. The committee also noted that since research and development expenditures had manifestly not generated enough profitable products to offset the life cycle of Corning's high percentage of OEM businesses now classified as "mature" (TV, lighting, electronics, and optical),[32] R&D should be oriented away from the mature, lower-growth businesses, where its expertise was concentrated, toward newer ones and should be enrolled in contributing a portion of its expertise to aiding cost-reduction programs. According to consultants from the Boston Consulting Group, (not known for their technology expertise), this could be done without injuring Corning's position in glass research. Product modification and development in the consumer and science products businesses should continue (though only where strong proprietary positions were the anticipated result), and, prefiguring the eventual sale of the foundering Signetics, Corning's electronics research should be redirected into biomedical research. The committee implemented all three suggestions.

The committee's guidelines spelling out Corning's market-driven philosophy was a clear reversal of Corning's traditional approach to strategy formulation. The senior Amory Houghton's oft-expressed conviction—that a desirable enough material, or even a powerful enough product or process, could be depended on to transform a market—was no longer to be the guiding spirit. Gone too was Armistead's simple $10 million rule of thumb. Instead, the new strategy welcomed research-based breakthroughs only in businesses where the payoffs were assured, not where they were uncertain or risky.

Even though this market-driven perspective was in its preliminary form in 1971, it was developed enough to influence Tom MacAvoy when he became Corning's president. He moved quickly to evaluate Corning's portfolio of new products, examining fifteen "developing businesses" that had been sponsored from the top of the organization. While some were relatively small, several were consuming resources at the vigorous clip of $1 million-a-year and already had substantial capital invested. Urged by Amo Houghton not to act precipitously, MacAvoy checked them out with customers at the highest levels. His conversation with Ed Cole of General Motors put an end to two in one sitting: the automobile windshield and Cercor, the ceramic heat exchanger for gas turbine engines. Customarily Corning ended projects by moving the people working on them to higher priority projects. This time some projects ended more abruptly. By the third quarter of 1971, MacAvoy had "dropped" the windshield and the ceramic heat exchanger altogether and had marked "probation" alongside more than half of the remaining items.[33]

Although no existing project had been planned to absorb the manpower freed up by these discarded efforts, one was about to take on a new urgency: automotive emissions control. Judged by the criteria applied to the others, it seemed an odd choice. Another OEM product for the auto industry, it was extremely hard to produce and was a product the industry vehemently opposed in spirit. Given the politics of air pollution at the time and the opposition of the auto industry to emissions control, many observers believed that it had a very slim chance of enduring for more than five years. By almost any standard calculation its net present value worked out to less than 7 percent. In short, the product violated most of Corning's new guidelines. But it had this to recommend it: the auto companies might dislike it, but they needed it badly and they needed it quickly.

CELCOR, 1970–1979

The February 1970 meeting with GM at which Corning executives realized that the auto industry would never adopt their Chemcor windshield was a low point in Corning's long-standing relationship with Detroit. Corning had been an important supplier of sealed beam headlights to the industry for decades. The company's attempts to anticipate other car company needs beyond that relatively small piece of the automobile, however, had been unsuccessful: the Chemcor windshield was a failure and Cercor, the ceramic heat exchanger designed for gasoline turbine engines, was losing money, with little prospect of profit in the foreseeable future.

Corning had been working on this latter project primarily at GM's behest, but GM's president Cole, when quizzed by MacAvoy, had to admit that the gas turbine had dim prospects: "We've got a dozen manufacturing lines to make internal combustion engines that cost 300 million dollars a piece. You don't displace that kind of stuff overnight,"[34] MacAvoy recalled Cole as saying. Cole proposed a different use for the Cercor ceramic: perhaps Corning could help on a project to develop catalytic converters to limit the air pollution generated by internal combustion engines. MacAvoy pointed out that lead in gasoline destroyed the metals used in catalysts and could even eat away the underlying ceramic. Then Cole revealed that GM had just convinced Exxon to start manufacturing unleaded gasoline by committing to design its future cars to run on this modified fuel.

Armed with these new facts, MacAvoy seized the opportunity to pursue catalytic converters. A week later he and a small team visited GM again, this time to talk with a group directly involved with catalytic converter development. Visits to Ford and Chrysler yielded similar findings: the catalytic converter, in whatever form, was likely to become a standard part on new cars, and—this the key lure for Corning—nobody knew how best to make one.[35]

The Right Place at the Right Time

The basic characteristics of the Cercor product did match those needed by a catalytic converter. Cercor was initially meant to serve as a heat exchanger in a gas turbine engine, using the hot exhaust to preheat the engine's air intake. This required a high thermal shock resistance and as much surface area as possible in order to maximize the transfer of heat from the exhaust gases to the incoming air. The device also needed to be as light as possible. Corning technical reports had already noted its possible use "as catalyst supports."[36]

But Cercor was not in large-scale commercial production, and its current forming technique did not lend itself to scaling up sufficiently to meet projected demand: paper impregnated with a ceramic slurry was wound on a spool to form a large cylinder; this in turn was fired, which burned off the paper and left behind the ceramic exoskeleton. Cercor's formulation was also insufficiently heat resistant. A considerable R&D challenge lay ahead: to compete in this nascent market Corning would have to find both a better material and a faster means of producing it to shape.

Several factors, beyond Cole's word alone, prompted Corning to accept this challenge. Cole's hand was being forced by a growing political movement in favor of sweeping governmental regulation of air quality and other environmental standards. In 1970, Congress passed the Clean Air Act, mandating drastic reductions in automobile emissions beginning with the 1975 model year. As one of the companies trying to find a technology to meet that mandate, Corning knew both the deadline and the general specifications it had to meet. Through its government affairs office, it also had good access to relevant government information and increasingly sophisticated ability to interpret it.

Gun-shy after the windshield project, Corning wanted to be certain of each point in the chain of logic. Dave Duke, a member of the original team that had met with GM's technical staff concerning specifications for the desired catalytic converter, performed due diligence. He and several others visited not only the technical staffs of the Big Three but also their purchasing departments. They also talked with the companies offering the catalysts (i.e., the coatings that prompted the necessary chemical reactions). And they went to Washington:

> We visited with Senator Muskie...the leading environmentalist at the time. We talked to the staff people in Washington who were writing the bill. It was clear after just two or three months of interviewing all these people that the Clean Air Act would be signed by President Nixon at the end of 1970, that catalytic converters of some type would have to be put on cars for the 1975 model car, which meant they had to be available by early in 1974, so they could be made so that the car models could be ready to go by the summer of '74, and that no one had the ideal solution yet. But it would happen.[37]

Preliminary R&D had already begun, but with the information that Duke had collected in hand, plus assurances from Exxon's Cliff Garvin that unleaded gasoline was indeed on its way, upper management, and in particular Armistead, decided to put everything behind the project, now dubbed "Emcon" for EMissions CONtrol.

This decision was prompted by one other factor: the competition. Three other corporations were contenders—the American Lava Corporation with a process very similar to the Cercor approach, chemical company W. R. Grace, a 3M subsidiary. A much larger corporation, and one renowned for its inventive abilities, 3M's chances looked best, but size worked against them. As MacAvoy recalled,

[3M] had organizational walls that didn't allow them to throw people in from the side. Whereas we had a style of operation that went back to our TV days of throwing everybody into the act. Armistead did this on a massive scale. He could get away with it. I mean people would get bent out of shape, but you were in war. It was the whole attitude of the thing.[38]

Corning's approach to amassing as many researchers as possible on the emissions control problem would later be known as "flexible critical mass." At the peak of its research stage, well over half of Sullivan Park would be at work on Emcon. Sheer weight of numbers was no guarantee of success, however. Corning had to develop both a superior product and an efficient process for manufacturing it, under unprecedented time pressures.

The initial Emcon research program followed a familiar pattern: brainstorming resulted in half a dozen or so approaches, each of which was pursued until Armistead and others felt certain they could pick the most likely candidate. Work on process and formulation went forward hand in hand. The company also hired catalyst experts to try different approaches with the various metals that were considered potential coatings for the final product. By early 1971 researchers had hit upon both a promising process—

Rod Bagley and Irving Lachman displaying samples of the extruded ceramic material that became Corning's successful Celcor subtrate for catalytic convertors. Lachman worked out the composition and Bagley discovered the extrusion process, two critical interdependent aspects of the Celcor innovation.

extrusion—and a ceramic with the necessary thermal characteristics—a cordierite.[39]

The material came first: Irv Lachman and Ron Lewis, both in the ceramics research department, developed the cordierite, a ceramic made out of magnesia, alumina, and silica, and secured a patent on it in 1975. For help in forming it, they turned to ceramics researcher Rod Bagley. Extrusion—Bagley's idea—was a common forming technique in the plastics and metals industries, but it had never been used to make a Cercor-like structure, that is, one with very thin walls (on the order of a couple of sheets of paper) separating hundreds of spaces per inch. To do so required the development of a die capable of withstanding tremendous pressures. Bagley won a patent for this extrusion process in 1974.

Further work, at least as involved and challenging as the initial discoveries, served to marry the two. Dave Duke recalls:

> When it was clear that we could extrude these—in fact, as soon as we saw the first little samples, that they could be extruded—we all looked at it and said, "Wow. This is the way to go." Instead of debating it and talking about it for a month or two like most people would do, we sat down and Bill Armistead said, "This is clearly the way to go. Let's take all the people off all the other ones."[40]

Further development was required (the extrusion process turned out to change the operating characteristics of the cordierite), but the main challenge at this point was clearly production. The key to moving speedily from research into production was good communication. Fortunately Duke, who had started out in the laboratory as a geologist, was a good communicator and a superb motivator. His own formative experiences had made him especially good at crossing the boundaries between laboratory, engineering and production.

The Bet-the-Company Deadline

The crash R&D program that led to the decision to produce ceramic substrates via an extruded cordierite, for all of its speed and intensity, was

leisurely in comparison to the production and marketing frenzy that followed. Though representatives of the car companies continued to try to
stop or delay the Clean Air Act and the newly formed Environmental Protection Agency, behind the scenes they were putting considerable pressure
on Corning and others involved with catalytic converter production to integrate with their assembly lines on schedule. Corning itself, prototypes of its
ceramic substrates having been tested by the catalyst companies, was confident by 1973 that it could make the deadline and testified to that effect in the
congressional hearings prompted by the car companies' complaints.

This rapid progress took place despite the damaging delays caused by
the June 1972 flood, which all but destroyed an important testing facility and
completely disrupted the lives of many of the employees engaged in the
Celcor project. The intensity of the project, however, brooked no delay;
more than one manager associated with it recalled extended periods of 100-
hour weeks. At the same time, the new organizational approach to getting
different departments to work in parallel caused large amounts of friction
that not only held up or frustrated key decisions but added to the pressure
for those who were working on it. The factory, located in nearby Erwin,
New York, was begun in 1973, even before the process was well worked out,
and was producing by April of the following year. Skip Deneka, who took
the project from the lab to the factory, understated it thus:

> We had a large auto company, actually several, that could not sell product
> without our component after a certain point in time. . . . And trying to
> develop a product, develop a process, and make samples for a customer to
> do their testing, and then start the manufacturing plant essentially simulta-
> neously required a lot of effort.[41]

Yet the pressure the car companies put on Corning also showed how badly
they needed the glassmaker this time. Corning took advantage of that fact
to negotiate guarantees into its contracts: if the automobile industry succeeded in getting the Clean Air Act provisions delayed, the contracts called
for reimbursing Corning for its capital expenditures as well as its samples.
The money at stake was considerable: hundreds of Corning employees
were involved in scaling the project up to produce the millions of pieces

required by deadline, and capital expenditures alone were in the tens of millions of dollars. Sales, even in the first year, were greater: on the order of $100 million.[42]

Corning's negotiations were spearheaded and coordinated by the manager of the technical products division, Dick Dulude. Dulude had been running the opththalmic products operation at Harrodsburg, where they had introduced several difficult new glasses, including photochromic glass, into a plant that had previously been doing the craft-centered job of making old-style opththalmic glass for many years. With a highly effective combination of product engineering and customer experience, Dulude managed to take advantage of the difficult spot the auto companies were in, landing Ford and Chrysler, as well as Volkswagen, Mercedes, and Volvo among European manufacturers. Even in bad times the auto companies were hard customers to pin down. Once again Corning's original contact for catalytic converters, GM, had decided to go with its own competing technology, a metal cannister using alumina beads, as the filter. Dulude described the start-up this way:

> We didn't get General Motors for a customer until a long, long time afterwards.... I'll never forget: we built the factory [at Erwin] and it's in production.... And we had the board of directors out there for a visit. And [MacAvoy] was showing the board of directors—it's a show and tell sort of a thing; "Here's our product, goes in this little can, and who are the customers?" It's Chrysler (And Chrysler was almost on their back then) and Ford was another customer. And so they had these little cans. And then here's the General Motors' bedpan. You know, it's this tall, this round, and it looked like a bedpan filled with beads. And I can remember the board members saying, "Now let me make sure I understand this: You're selling to Chrysler and Ford, and General Motors isn't buying it. They're not even using the same technology." ... I could see them saying, "I hope he knows what the hell they're doing."[43]

In the late 1970s Congress lowered the allowable percentage of emissions even further. The GM technology, which in any case suffered from a relatively short lifespan due to the constant jostling of beads against each other, proved unable to meet the tougher standard, and Corning added the last of the Big Three to its customer list. By 1994, the product had generated $1 billion in sales for the company.[44] Perhaps just as important for Corning in the longer term, Celcor, with its extremely aggressive schedule, forced the company to adopt a project management approach to getting the product up and running that was tighter than any it had used before, and the focus, from the beginning, was on moving down the learning curve. Celcor was the first product for which the fear of competition motivated the company to obsolete its own product generations. It would not be the last.

A New Manufacturing Model

The contrast between Celcor and the early stages of the color television tube business was not lost on Corning management. After a short period of high margins, Corning knew that there would inevitably be serious price pressure from Detroit. As MacAvoy recalled, "We started working like crazy to reduce the cost. . . . Our reaction is, we're not going to get stuck by that dumb thing again, that television thing. Anybody who was associated with television would tell you we made a big mistake there."[45] Part of the secret to reducing cost meant keeping alive a supporting research effort in the laboratories. This was not easy to do when financial measures were rigorously applied: given the uncertainties of future demand, Celcor never looked attractive on a net present value basis. Nevertheless, Corning committed itself to adopting a pricing approach based on the learning curve technique first adopted by defense contractors during World War II (but largely forgotten by American industry following the war): selections increased steadily on a planned schedule thanks to the experience gained from increasing volumes, a focus on continuous process improvement, and stricter and stricter goals. This also meant that the large Celcor workforce required in the initial rush to meet deadlines had to be drastically reduced as the process stabilized and then improved.

Employment instability proved to be endemic to Celcor anyway due to Corning's place at the end of the supply chain. As MacAvoy later realized, legislated changes in acceptable emissions levels would have a huge impact on Corning's production lines: "tightening it up a tenth of a percent would have us building another factory. Loosening it would have us close a factory."[46] This dependence on factors beyond Corning's control would remain characteristic of the catalytic substrate market, and it was one of the many things that Celcor would have in common with a later product, namely, waveguides. Such was Corning's concern with the matter that it initiated an ongoing relationship with Mike Walsh, a former chief of the EPA's mobil source emission group, and assembled a group of interested industrial parties (for the most part, companies producing one part or another of the entire catalytic converter assembly) into a Corning-led association dubbed MECA: Manufacturers of Emission Control Apparatus. The need to closely monitor the impact of government legislation on the company's markets, as well as the fact that Corning would need to improve the production process aggressively in order to be able to continually lower its prices, made Celcor an excellent learning experience for what was yet to come.

LONG BALLS AND SINGLES

Apart from Corelle and Celcor, the nearly wholesale discontinuation of projects that had been sponsored at the highest levels of the corporation in the early 1970s might easily have spelled the end of all such long-term investments for Corning. In many companies that was precisely what was happening during the 1970s. The use of financial benchmarks and net present value calculations rigidly and ruinously applied was widespread. Laboratory after laboratory abandoned their long-term investments in technology. Corning's technical community came under this same kind of financial scrutiny, and many projects fell short of the mark.[47] But Corning's top management played a crucial protective role. Switching from their old offensive game to a carefully defensive one, the team of Amo Houghton and Bill Armistead saw to it that certain high-priority projects were protected no matter what. Chief among these was the optical fiber project, which during the late 1970s required high levels of investment while generating very little revenue for an extended period.

Fiber Optics Development

The aggressive intellectual property strategy Corning was pursuing (described in chapter 8), was only one of three major activities it needed to build a foundation for a strong competitive position in the global telecommunications market. It bought time for Corning to build its business. But as Corning's optical waveguide patents began to be issued in 1974, two other major tasks remained to be accomplished. The second task was to create an interrelated product and process technology that was superior to any other in the world. The third, and most difficult, was to prove Corning's commercial credibility as an upstart supplier of a novel technology to one of the most conservative industries in the world: state-owned, or at least state-regulated, telephone companies. As Chuck Lucy told Corning's board of directors, waveguides were only the channel via which information was transmitted: a lot more technology needed to be developed by others if that channel were to be of use to anybody. As Lucy put it, "A lot of the keys to success are on other people's keychains."[48] These other parties were by no means ready to think of Corning as a credible supplier.

Since most industry experts predicted scant demand for waveguides in long-distance communications until after the turn of the century, the fiber optics project flunked every internal financial measure that was applied to it. Houghton and Armistead, however, had their belief in the opportunity reinforced by unambiguous advice from an unlikely source. Corning director Jim Fiske of Bell Labs said simply, "Keep at it: it will be important."[49]

Emboldened by this and similar observations from his colleagues on the boards of IBM and AT&T, Amo Houghton went along with Lee Wilson, when as head of the electronics division, he committed Corning to the audacious and costly step of pursuing ITT and other infringers through the courts. But as this move tied up most of Corning's legal resources, waveguide became unpopular in many quarters of the Corning organization.[50] Veterans of previous ventures like Dave Leibson and Al Dawson made no secret of their belief that trying to break into the telecommunications market was the ultimate fool's errand. AT&T, the domestic customer that controlled 80-90 percent of the potential market, had made clear its intention to supply its own needs. Al Dawson, whose recent contacts with the phone company over Signetics had been cautionary, was quoted as saying, "If AT&T wanted to stop us they could step on us like an ant."[51] Given such a forbidding competitive prospect, only Amo Houghton and Bill Armistead—with MacAvoy's strong concurrence—could have found the money the project needed to carry it even through the pilot stage.

Achieving Feasibility for Fiber

Waveguide continued in the relatively inexpensive research stage well into the 1970s, largely supported by the annual research contributions from the first five international development partners. Even though the research team under Bob Maurer had achieved its first objective of less than 20 db/km attenuation in signal in 1970, the question of commercial feasibility had not been resolved. Early projects producing experimental optical cable for military uses uncovered no compelling military need for video or voice data transfer to support the initial development cost. Commercial development was the only route, and that meant that both fiber costs and signal attenuation had to be low enough to justify its use in the commercial telephone network. Huge challenges remained in producing glass fiber that would not break, that would be malleable enough for cabling, and that could be produced cheaply in volume.[52]

Ironically, the very processes that had made the original titania-doped fiber a success also made it too brittle to be practical. Other dopants were needed. It took two more years of work from Maurer, Schultz, Keck, and those working with them to achieve technical feasibility of the kind that showed the fiber could be produced. The breakthrough came in June 1972, when the Corning team achieved an attenuation of 4 db/km using a germania-doped material. As though to herald a major breakthrough, Hurricane Agnes struck at just this time, suspending all work while everyone lent a hand to help clean up the devastated Corning community.

Corning kept its new dopant secret for many months, Schultz playing coy with fellow researchers at conferences by calling the material "fairy dust." Finally another researcher let the cat out of the bag, prompting Keck, Maurer, and Schultz to write a paper summarizing the prospects for low-loss fiber in December 1972: "total attenuation of about 2 decibels per kilometer in the region beyond 800 nanometers thus appears possible." If this claim held up, fibers of doped silica could perform at least ten times better, that is, carry light ten times further than even Charles Kao's theory had originally predicted. From this time on, Corning stopped sharing information with AT&T, though it still had to cross-license its patents. AT&T in turn pressured Bell Labs to come up with higher performance technologies of its own. The two companies were now in competition for a market that AT&T had not intended to develop for decades. They would soon be joined by other companies around the world.

With other companies getting involved, Corning had to explore more than one process for producing its fiber. It added people to both the composition and design teams—composition and process led by Pete Schultz, design and measurement led by Don Keck. Meanwhile a small fiber marketing effort began under Fred Quan selling experimental fiber in small quantities to customers and learning everything possible from customer needs. In the early days, when it was hard to keep the fiber production process under control, different fiber batches had quite different characteristics, so the fiber marketing group took orders for specialty compositions and characteristics and then sorted through the bins of cast-off fiber for batches with the properties that matched each specialty need.

By the late 1970s Corning had completed four critical inventions, as well as a myriad of lesser ones, placing it well along the steep path to commercialization. In addition to the first material inventions consisting of fused silica doped with titanium and later germanium (which, as Bob Maurer had recognized early on, had enormous intrinsic purity advantages over the purest regular glass) the other two inventions involved two different processes—the inside process (IV) and the outside process (OV)—for making fiber. "IV," or "inside vapor deposition," began with a tube of silica as the outer cladding and then deposited the doped fused silica core material on the inside in the form of a soot, heating the whole afterwards in order to consolidate it. OV involved laying down the soot on a cylindrical mandril, which was removed before the resulting form was consolidated. Corning researchers recognized that the OV process would ultimately be better from a cost standpoint, but it was more technically challenging.

Corning's relative obscurity in the communications research world was an advantage in the early years. Mainstream research competitors, already focused on different interim conceptions like millimeter waveguides and lightpipes, were slow to recognize the revolutionary significance of Corning's initial breakthrough. They were also deterred from simply adopting Corning's approach, not only by Corning's solid patent position but also by the sheer difficulty of working with materials at the high temperature melting points that fused silica required. But in the mid-1970s two companies performed actual field trials of real optical fiber installations—Standard Telephones and Cables in Dorset, England, and AT&T in Atlanta. At that point competing research efforts expanded enormously, and small start-up enterprises began to form.

AT&T and others adopted multimode (or graded index) fiber as its standard. The larger core of a multimode fiber was required to couple with an LED (light emitting diode) light source. (Reliable semiconductor lasers were not then available.) Corning, still hopeful that it might be permitted to supply some of AT&T's requirements, or at least those of its smaller competitors, followed the direction of the industry. At the same time it kept particle physicist Bob Olshansky at work on single mode fiber. With no stake in conservative approaches such as AT&T's, it recognized that single-mode fiber's advantages in bandwidth would quickly prevail if certain breakthroughs were achieved in other critical system components like lasers. Internationally, many giant competitors stepped up their activity on fiber optic research. These included the British Post Office, soon to become British Telecom, and the Japanese NEC.

Development Partners

When AT&T, implacable about opening the domestic market to anyone else, offhandedly advised Corning to seek out international customers. Corning responded by cultivating further its existing relationships with its largest potential international customers, a group of companies representing the lion's share of the cable supply to the world's phones outside the United States.[53]

Chuck Lucy handled the delicate responsibility of sharing the technical information with the joint development partners, as per their various agreements. The trick here was not to divulge information received from one JDP to any of the others. Not since the early days of color television development had Corning been involved in such a diplomatic tangle, though in this instance there was the obvious advantage that the JDPs did not see themselves as competing with one another.

Corning's relationship with each of the five international enterprises was different. First among these equals was Siemens, the only JDP with which Chuck Lucy had discussed forming a joint venture for fiber production, should the happy day of full commercialization ever arrive. Their agreement, only verbal, was the product of a close relationship between Lucy and Bernd Zeitler of Siemens Research Center. When Lee Wilson took over as Lucy's boss some time after these early negotiations, he refused to honor this nonbinding commitment until he had reviewed the range of possible Corning partners. His attitude temporarily damaged Corning's close relationship with Siemens, but the marriage was saved when a months-long study by a team from the Boston Consulting Group declared Siemens an excellent partner for such a venture.[54] Siemens and Corning accordingly created two joint ventures (Siecor Corporation for cable production in the United States and Siecor GMBH in Germany which produced fiber for the Siemens cabling operation), the first and closest of several international joint ventures to spring from the joint development agreements.

While these negotiations were proceeding, Maurer and others in charge of production were frantically trying to supply sufficient quantities of testable fiber to the JDPs. By 1975 it became necessary to open a pilot plant for this purpose. From this point on development was carried out in parallel, with the laboratory in charge of research and the pilot plant responsible for process development. Always an expensive proposition, the appropriation request for the pilot plant crossed Amo Houghton's desk at almost the same time as the order to commence the mass layoff of the Guns of August. He signed.

Finding a Leader for Fiber

The reorganization that accompanied Corning's 1975 layoff, though devastating and confusing, led to a determination to make a concentrated push on the waveguide business. Celcor had provided the focus for pulling out of the slump in 1970–1971; Corelle was also going strong. Waveguides were the next apparent candidate to lead a recovery. Ironically, some casualties of the August layoffs were employees of the nascent fiber business. Rich Cerny and Eric Randall decided to go off on their own, eventually hiring away other Corning people to join them. Still convinced of the ultimate value of fiber as a product, they looked for and found venture capital backing to set up a fiber company called Valtec, one of several start-up operations that hoped to give both Corning and AT&T a run for their money.[55] As of late 1975, with Corning's sample sales of optical fiber still well under $1 million, it was agreed that the key to rapid commercialization would be strong entrepreneurial leadership, the best Corning could produce.

The leader chosen to build Corning's fiber business was Dave Duke, who had distinguished himself on Celcor, who was known to be a tenacious team developer, and whose ego might be able to withstand what could seem to many successful managers like a demotion. When he received a call from Tom MacAvoy, Duke was general manager of Corning's materials business, which totaled around $100 million in sales. He recalled, "I was just learning about that, visiting the customers and getting that turned around, and starting to make really good money, and really liked what I was doing, a big office, a secretary and all this, and I get a call." Duke was familiar with the waveguide technology from his early days in the laboratory and he knew of the substantial technical effort under way, but the commercial side was almost nonexistent—less than a million dollars in sales and six people to report to him. "Tom," he asked, "what did I do wrong?"

One positive thing Duke could see was that, compared to the Celcor project, there was time to do things right with fiber. Absent the fear of shutting down production in some of the largest companies in the country, waveguides were not the pressure cooker that Celcor had been during its first few years; Corning was running against no clock but its own. For Duke, taking over the little fiber business was the beginning of a ten-year engagement. By the time he left waveguide to run Sullivan Park, fiber optics would be well on its way to becoming Corning's largest business.

From Pilot to Production

Duke's first major decision was settling the IV/OV debate. The pilot plant, which had begun operations at the Erwin plant complex in 1977, was supposed to be where the lowest-cost approach to producing optical fiber was demonstrated. A team of thirty-five engineers, led by Gitimoy Kar, had the task of transferring the knowledge out of R&D and setting up the first commercial optical fiber preform fabrication facility. The greatest challenge was not mastering the preform production process but working out the disciplined approach necessary to bring all different types of expertise from research and development, manufacturing and engineering, and the Erwin infrastructure into a smooth working relationship. When Kar arrived, the facility had just missed a delivery deadline for its first significant commercial OV order for twenty kilometers of fiber for General Cable company. The process was not even up and running. According to Kar,

> unfortunately, this single order for 20 kilometers of fiber had pushed the plant into round the clock production involving engineers and production people for nearly six months. Three or four weeks after I arrived we actually produced the order because we were able to use the knowledge we already had effectively.[56]

Corning ran both the OV and IV processes in tandem all the way through the pilot phase into the 1979 start-up at the Wilmington plant, which already produced electronic components. When the time came to scale up, Duke insisted on phasing out IV and concentrating all efforts on OV. The reasoning behind this decision echoed Corning's technical decision making throughout the fiber program: "if we use the IV process the best we can do is tie" and "if we tie, we're going to lose."[57] In this case the tie would have been with AT&T, which, lacking both Corning's peculiar technical skills and its nearly desperate motivation to remain in the technological lead, had placed its bets on the inside process.

Continuity of management was one of the few advantages the Corning project enjoyed. Skip Deneka, who had worked closely with Duke five years earlier on the Celcor start-up, volunteered to set up the first commercial fiber factory. He worked in the waveguide pilot plant while it was struggling to master the technology and production organization, and the two together planned the design and start-up of a new fiber plant in Wilmington, North Carolina. Deneka had also done much of the early plant design and initial startup for Celcor and had stayed on through the early phases of delivery. But because he lacked the necessary production background to be the plant engineer, Dave Leibson had insisted that he retread his career to acquire the necessary on-the-job training before he could be eligible to become one. This time, having acquired the necessary experience in plant systems, he became plant engineer for the waveguide operation in Wilmington, North Carolina after it was up and running. "It was interesting designing the Wilmington plant and knowing I would have to live with my mistakes," he said later.[58]

With the Celcor experience still fresh in his memory, Deneka formed an integrated design and production team for the new plant, organized from the start to avoid the kinds of friction the Celcor project had had to endure. He intermingled the plant and M&E groups so that everyone working on a particular part of the process was co-located with everyone else so assigned, regardless of their departmental affiliation. The result was that "in this entire startup we only had one major conflict compared to weekly conflicts on the Celcor project startup." Deneka stayed on as plant engineer to supervise the dramatic changes in the process that were taking place, at first, roughly every two years. After concentrating its efforts on OV, Corning then moved from one generation of fiber making equipment to another in an effort to achieve constantly improved product at ever lower costs. Behind these moves was the research team at Sullivan Park that kept on the leading edge both in composition and in product design. This regular reinvention cycle, coupled with an emphasis on continuous improvement in quality terms, allowed Corning to drop the selling price steadily from $3 to $5 per meter on the earliest production fiber to well below $.10 a meter twenty years later. Corning gradually learned to modify the composition and design of waveguide to produce different fiber products for different applications.[59] It was a classic engineered material.

The Wilmington plant's initial planned capacity was 30,000 kilometers per year, expandable to 100,000 kilometers. Actual production quickly ramped up to 200,000 kilometers per year, twice its maximum anticipated capacity. With twelve to eighteen months lead time required before new capacity came on line, Corning had to build well ahead of demand. Amo Houghton charged Duke "never [to] run out of capacity." He backed up this injunction with the necessary support to get Duke's appropriations past Corning's financial watchdogs, who had acquired more and more teeth as the 1970s progressed.[60] On more than one occasion Duke reported to Houghton that his appropriations had been bottled up in finance but that he had already ordered the steel and was building the building anyway. Ultimately, the Wilmington plant would produce millions of kilometers of fiber per year.

Achieving the volume sales to pay for these redevelopments was a far from orderly matter. Corning had to prove a laundry list of capabilities: that the optical fibers worked and that they were reliable, that they wouldn't break, that they could really carry information, and that they could be installed. But to convince the ultimate customers, the telephone companies, it was first necessary to overcome the skepticism of their suppliers, the cable companies. This required an odd combination of experimentation and relationship building. Chuck Lucy, as architect of the joint development relationship, devoted himself to keeping the joint development partners happy with visits and regular reports, samples and test measurements, and helped sponsor the pilot plant as well. Later he would build several of these looser relationships into joint ventures, also forming a network of other international connections for Corning. Meanwhile, Corning integrated forward into the cabling business.

Fiber Optic Cabling

Corning's contacts with its JDPs had taught it a great deal, but in order to secure the confidence of the national phone companies that it hoped would place orders, the company had to gain hands-on knowledge of optical fiber in its final form: cable. This required more than just exchanging technical information through the JDAs. Armistead, to whom Dave Duke turned regularly for help and advice, believed that, although Corning generally avoided competing with its customers, in this instance it would have to do so. It needed to learn how to make its own cable.

Under the auspices of the first fiber joint venture, Siecor, the beginnings of a tiny cabling operation were established in 1978 in a former Robert Hall clothing store in the Corning vicinity. Progress was slow, and after two years it was still unclear how Siecor would gain market access in the United States.[61] To build the operation more quickly and to gain access to the cable market, Lee Wilson decided, and Amo Houghton approved, the purchase of a small copper cable outfit, Superior Cable, in Hickory, North Carolina, at the relatively high price of $50 million. The acquisition raised hackles. When the appropriation request reached Al Dawson—a member of the executive committee of the Corning board at the time and Wilson's predecessor as head of the electronics division—he walked down the hall to Houghton's office to register his dismay. For Dawson, the forced sale of Signetics was still a fresh memory:

> Why in the world are we doing this? It's crazy. They have 4 percent of the
> copper cable business and they're located in a place that nobody ever heard
> of. We're going to try to run it by osmosis from Corning and it's going to
> fail. And Amo said, "No, the guys who are running the business want it."
> Sure enough they did it, and sure enough it did get in trouble.[62]

And sure enough this time Dawson was called to the rescue. As he had predicted, managing Superior Cable from afar did not work, and it was decided to move the Siecor operation (still only twelve people) to Hickory, North Carolina, where it would be much closer to the new optical-fiber plant site under construction in Wilmington, North Carolina. As usual with successful Corning joint ventures, each partner assigned some of its best people. Siemens was sending some of its leading experts in cabling technology, and Corning proposed to assign one of its most experienced managers in Al Dawson. But when asked to go to Hickory to put the fledgling Siecor operation on its feet, Dawson suspected a backhanded attempt to get him to retire. "Why should I give up running the biggest, most profitable part of the company and go run a business that we never should have been in the first place?" he queried. "If you want to fire me, I'll leave quietly."[63]

Reassured that the need was real (and that the position came with a company plane and twenty-four tickets to the Masters Golf Tournament), Dawson turned his attention to building Siecor. He began by getting rid of the copper cable business, which he judged to be too low-tech to make the jump to fiber. Drawing on his deep experience in establishing commercial relationships, he established connections with all the important potential customers in telecommunications. Then Dawson set about building from scratch an enterprise capable of delivering what was then expected to be modest amounts of cable made from multimode fiber. Both expectations were quickly proved mistaken: as detailed in chapter 10, single-mode fiber, and lots of it, would soon be what was required. Superior Cable was the vehicle necessary to get Corning into position to supply the need.

The Problem of Laboratory Morale

As the only research project at Corning that did not suffer deprivation during the mid 1970s, fiber optics incurred resentment from other projects and researchers who were operating in a radically changed research environment. Fortunately for R&D, Armistead had worked with the operations managers on a few management disciplines that served well in this new climate. Hutchins kept these and refined them. One was the aforementioned technical request system, which established research priorities on input obtained from general managers. A second was the $10 million list that no longer had strategic significance but helped account for R&D. The lab kept track of the growth of businesses that, having grown out of R&D projects, had achieved $10 million in revenues in five years.[64]

The laboratories also adopted a "management by objectives" system requiring explicit goals and timetables for research projects and tying them to particular products sponsored by operating divisions. This new practice frustrated researchers, especially the cadre of individual performers who had joined Corning in the 1960s. Hired into an organization that encouraged them to pursue whatever they liked on the assumption that their work would produce commercial results over time, they felt betrayed by the new rules. In an article prepared for publication by *Biotechnology Patent Digest*, Ralph Messing, the biologist whose small group of "oddballs" had lived an unfettered and generally quite productive existence in the laboratories, voiced his concerns. The new productivity measures were having a catch-22 effect on Corning's traditional climate for research. Reviewing the work that he had done during the 1960s and early 1970s, Messing pointed out that it was the freedom to pursue anomalies and to follow up on unexpected developments that could never have appeared as objectives that had led to his most important work for Corning.

> This [management by objectives] was the harbinger of tighter research control and a more restrictive atmosphere for industrial research efforts with less opportunity to investigate basic problems. Ultimately this type of atmosphere tends to stifle creativity, since it does not allow for failures and discretionary investigations. As productivity falls in terms of research the control becomes tighter and innovation is reduced even further. The ultimate is the transfer of authority to initiate research from the R&D division to the Operating Division. Once this occurs, the research scientist tends to become a fire-fighter. Research programs must be defined in terms of operating division's products and processes rather than the pursuit of knowledge with the opportunity for creativeness.[65]

Messing's complaint was heard in research organizations across the country in the 1970s and early 1980s. Researchers who had been wooed for their originality, as valuable high-status individual performers, now found themselves stigmatized as self-indulgent individualists who were not team players. Though Corning had never allowed its research culture to get quite so far out of line with the rest of the company, Messing's sentiments accurately reflected the state of morale in Corning's R&D community during most of this period. Starting in the early 1970s, a number of researchers at Sullivan Park were asked to retool or to drop what they had been doing to work in areas for which they had not been trained. Inorganic chemists like Harmon

Garfinkel and Augustus Filbert even redirected their work toward the biotech projects. Almost two-thirds of the remaining research staff was drafted onto the Celcor project. MacAvoy described this latter process:

> Armistead and I, with Amo's blessing, had control of these people, we could say to a guy over in here, a very good mathematician who was doing modeling of hydraulic systems in melting tanks, we'd say, "We need that effort here on this ceramic thing. It has to do with extrusion of ceramic mush through a complicated mask, but theoretically it's similar. Help us on this thing. Then you can get back to this modeling thing where you are."[66]

With R&D in disfavor across the country and professional management ascendant, researchers inevitably sought to transfer to that latter, now more prestigious and better rewarded, career track. Corning gained some excellent managers in this way, but such promotions could result in creative researchers becoming mediocre administrators. The process was largely halted at Corning when Jack Hutchins strengthened the dual ladder for promotion, making it possible for scientists to be promoted to higher levels of compensation without becoming managers. The new arrangement evened up the ratio between senior research associates and managers, and resulted eventually in the creation of the research fellow, a position organizationally considered to be on a par with division manager and responsible in each case for a given research program.

Having stood at 25 percent in the late 1960s, the research portion of the technical budget was steadily reduced in favor of development and engineering and the pressure was there to reduce it still more. Hutchins, who believed fervently in what he called the "Dr. Sullivan Principle," that studying Mother Nature directly was the surest way to ensure commercial opportunities in the future, was worried about the dramatic reallocation of his resources.

In 1979 Joe Littleton prepared a brief analysis in response to Amo Houghton's request for perspectives on Corning's growth problem. Littleton observed that expectations might be at fault, that the company still tended to think about research and development solely in terms of producing big hits with its technology. While "longballs" (as he termed them) such as Pyrex or Corning Ware had been crucial to the company's history, so too had the cumulative effect of smaller innovations, the "singles" such as sealed beam headlights or ophthalmics, which did not necessarily originate with research ideas. This analysis took root among Corning's senior managers, and the now demoralized laboratory community took the argument as yet another attack on long-term research, especially as Littleton traced many of the base hits to sources outside the Corning technical community altogether.[67]

Meanwhile in the traditional research areas of glass technology promising ideas for new technologies were going begging for lack of takers in the operating divisions. One in particular was transparent glass ceramics, which had been shut off because the consumer business thought it might cannibalize the sales of Corning Ware. Of course a major part of the problem was that businesses that would traditionally have carried new products to the market now faced fierce interest rates, as well as more restrictive conditions generally. In the consumer business, in particular, the old Fair Trade laws, which had for so long supported smaller-scale retailers and higher margins, had disappeared, making way for the discount stores with their much lower margins. Researchers often didn't see the forest for the trees and tended to assign the blame for the lack of receptivity to research-based products to the leadership factor. Armistead had been legendary as a figure to whom operating managers had come hat in hand. When Hutchins succeeded him, they believed they had lost their champion. Most researchers were unaware of the larger changes in the way Corning had come to view its strategy in the 1970s, with an emphasis on high-growth markets and already existing or recycled technology.

Operating managers complained just as loudly that they had too little control over how R&D spent their money, and even less over engineering, which they criticized as unnecessarily expensive. They agitated to break up these centralized organizations and take them under their own control. MacAvoy, backed up by Houghton and Armistead, turned a deaf ear to these requests, believing that glass-related technology, especially the process aspects, was centralized by nature. But with so many complaints coming from the divisions, even the suggestion from such an influential figure as Corning board member Arthur Houghton—that it might be prudent to allocate more money to research—was rejected. Money was tight. When television plants could not get the money they desperately needed to retool, investing extra money in research would be perceived as a matter of organizational inequity.[68]

In the latter years of the 1970s, though the company's fortunes improved, the fortunes of the technical community located at Sullivan Park did not. There were, however, two exceptions to this general state of disaffection besides the waveguide project. One was the French Laboratory in Avon, later called the Fontainebleau Laboratory. The second was the biomedical area, where research into laboratory uses of porous glass was evolving into one of the most advanced biotech efforts in American industry.

INNOVATION ABROAD: THE FRENCH LABORATORY, 1968

Corning's decision to make its French laboratory a full member of its technical community put it well ahead of most American companies in terms of operating an internationally distributed R&D structure. The laboratory,

The leadership team that had the dubious duty of taking Corning through its most difficult transition period in the 1970s included Amory Houghton Jr. as Chairman and CEO, Thomas MacAvoy as President, William Armistead as Vice Chairman Technology, and James R. Houghton, Executive Vice President, International.

located at Avon on the edge of Fontainebleau, repaid the trust placed in it by functioning as a fertile source of continuing innovation for Corning at a time when the headquarters R&D organization was going through some painful transitions. Surprisingly, Sullivan Park did not reject Avon's efforts but treated it as a small yet potent source for renewal. Avon was the first of several international laboratories Corning ultimately included in its R&D network. It would be followed by a lab in Japan, one in Russia, and still later, the former British Telecom Lab in Ipswich, England; but Avon laid the foundations for the whole.[69]

The Avon laboratory originated in 1968 when Sovirel, a joint venture between Corning and the venerable French glassmaker St. Gobain, consolidated its various factory laboratories into one small research center. The first five years saw the construction of a facility and assembly of a small research staff, but the purpose of the laboratory was ill defined and the group was too small and too varied to achieve critical mass around any project area or subject. Sixty people covered a very broad portfolio, including consumer products, optical process, optical glass development, and technical support for Sovirel's manufacturing processes. When the profitability of its European ventures began to deteriorate in the early 1970s, Corning moved to combine its holdings, first buying out St. Gobain's share of Sovirel in France in 1972 and then the remaining shares of Jobling in England in 1973. For two years following this, Avon was in limbo. Its collective experience covered such diverse areas as industrial glass piping systems for chemical companies, production processes for sunglasses and other optical and opththalmic glass, and delay lines for European television. Avon survived on government grants and contract work while trying to find new technology-based products for Corning's French businesses to pursue.

Armistead, recently elevated to the position of Corning vice chairman with responsibility for technology, took on the task of defining the purpose for an international laboratory in early 1973. His initial idea, to select a neutral site and staff it with the best researchers from the several countries that Corning served in its international operations, boded ill for Avon, not least because he specified that it be English speaking.[70] He also suggested that the initial program be "applied" in nature, related to filling European needs, as well as "on the basis of ability to handle" official technical requests that could not be handled in the United States. If these guidelines were observed he predicted that Corning would have a "fully competent" lab in five to ten years: "able to invent, able to develop, able to put into production."[71]

What Corning had in Avon, however, was a French laboratory, and although the company might prefer to locate elsewhere, such a move would entail significant delays. Moreover, the cultural differences in the practice of science were sizable, suggesting that a productive cross-cultural laboratory might well prove elusive. Avon had the advantage of already being in existence, and it was close enough to Paris to have a chance of hiring good people. In line with Armistead's other guidelines, two important decisions were made at that point: first, to give Avon a clear mission as a development laboratory with some real and desirable assignments and, second, to send a respected member of the Corning community to help turn Avon into a productive laboratory for Corning.

The choice of the new director—Chuck Wakeman—might have seemed, on the face of it, somewhat odd. Wakeman had been the founder of the Raleigh laboratory (for electronic components), which had not been an especially successful part of the Corning R&D community. In practice he turned out to be an inspired choice. Wakeman had been a Corning outsider when he started the Raleigh laboratory in the early 1960s; by the time he went to France in 1974 he knew not only Corning headquarters and Bill Armistead intimately, but he also worked well with director of research Jack Hutchins and head of development Ray Voss. Most important, Wakeman had learned from his experience at Raleigh the importance of integrating a remote laboratory into the Corning R&D structure as closely and thoroughly as possible.

Though Wakeman spoke no French to begin with, Avon's researchers recognized in him an ally, appreciated his tenacious efforts to learn the language, and welcomed the chance to be truly linked to Corning. They had suffered from the lack of definition in their organization since its inception and especially from being left to their own devices for nearly two years while Corning worked out what their role should be. Now they had a role— to get Corning's European operations to make better use of R&D and to become a fully developed member of Corning's technical community. They also had a mission: to "provide Technology that will lead Corning to its growth and profitability goals and have fun doing it," as Avon's second director, Jacques Lemoine, defined it.[72]

Wakeman accepted the assignment to make Avon an active development lab and with the help of Ray Voss chose several projects that were going nowhere back in Corning. These included fusion glass, photochromic glass, and cookware made of a transparent glass ceramic, later called Visions. Fusion had been dropped from the Sullivan Park repertoire after the disastrous outcome of the windshield project. In France it was thought it might be used for large photochromic architectural panels that would have natural shading properties; Avon briefly pursued the idea of producing such specialized building materials. Ultimately Avon's marriage of the fusion process and photochromics, transferred to Corning's Harrodsburg plant, gave the company a small but very profitable business in light-sensitive sunglasses.[73]

The third product, the transparent glass ceramic cookware, was an idea proposed first by Sullivan Park. With the domestic consumer business still focused on the high-prestige, high-margin ovenware, Corning Ware, a transparent version held little appeal. The French, however, did less cooking in the oven and much more on the top of the stove. This distinction had already led Corning in France to offer a Pyrex line capable of stovetop use, but that line was threatened by the advent of hotter stoves in the 1960s and 1970s. The French consumer business needed something that was both more durable than Pyrex and, ideally, cheaper than Corning Ware.[74]

Partly as a result of Wakeman's leadership and partly because of the sense of frustration Corning's glass technologists had experienced as they tried to gain a hearing for their own product ideas, relations between Sullivan Park researchers and researchers at Avon were good. Key Corning people, like George Beall and Ted Koslowski, worked in France for extended periods, and Wakeman in turn persuaded Jacques Lemoine to spend more than a year at Corning. Other French researchers also worked with several Corning plants, most notably Harrodsburg on photochromic glass and Martinsburg on the Visions cookware, to capture the production technology they needed. After nearly four years as head of Avon Wakeman returned to the United States, leaving Lemoine, a French national, to take over. By that time Avon was an accepted part of the Corning R&D community, though its period of integration continued until 1983.

Avon had advantages that older Sullivan Park researchers were able to recognize. It was small and its researchers were versatile, were willing to engage in multiple projects, and were able to take on multiple parts of a project if necessary. It was also possible for personnel at the French laboratory to have direct contact with its customers and occasionally even with end users like chemical plants or government contractors, a practice that had been common at Corning's central laboratory at one time but had gone by the board as Sullivan Park expanded and its researchers specialized.

Once proven by Avon, processes and product ideas that had attracted no support from the domestic organization became more certain and therefore more attractive in the United States as well; several of the technologies developed by Avon for the French market were picked up back in Corning. Avon took on a wide range of Sullivan Park's diverse offerings as well as electronics research for the French and English governments and, later, optical waveguide and early telecommunications devices like planar couplers. It even became involved in early biotech, a controversial and somewhat peripheral line of research at Sullivan Park but one that was pushed aggressively by Corning's international organization headquartered near the Avon laboratory.

By the end of its integration phase the Avon laboratory could claim several clear successes, including photochromic sunglass products (dubbed Aton [1976] and Superaton [1979]) and Visions (brought to market in 1980). It contributed usefully to waveguide development and maintained and improved fusion draw capabilities, among other things. In short, at a time when Corning's main laboratory bore the stigma of being the proponent of what Corning's strategic planners were viewing as mature or even "spent" technology, Avon was playing a vital role in reinvigorating that technology and Corning's system for exploring and exploiting it.

BEYOND GLASS, 1963–1982

Another area around which Corning's senior management opted to throw a protective shield in the troubled period of the 1970s was work in the emerging field of biotechnology. This was, after all, one of the few areas of technology in which Corning met the twin criteria of the decade: low on energy consumption and not in direct competition with the Japanese. Corning's foray into biology, specifically biotech and medical applications, had its roots in both the lab's core technologies (glass and glass ceramics) and management's strategies for growth and profitability in the 1970s and 1980s. Though at crucial points highly profitable, it was, like Signetics, an uncomfortable technological fit for the company. Unlike integrated circuits, however, the company's various investments in biotech were repaid with respectable if not spectacular interest, and Corning's contributions to the field itself were significant.

In the early 1960s two factors led Corning to engage in biological research. The first was that labware, which had long been a Corning staple, needed to keep up with changes in laboratory technology and practice. In physics Corning followed its market by developing specialized products for high-energy physics, nuclear physics, and so forth. Biologists still required a simple beaker, but they too were beginning to demand more complicated research equipment. Second, Corning executives were searching for opportunities to diversify: Hutchins joked that Corning had hired a biologist to find ways to grow lightbulbs. In fact the rationale was closer to that of hiring Hyde out of organic chemistry: opportunity might exist in the boundary regions between glass and biology.

The laboratory hired its first biologist, Ralph Messing, in 1963, eventually placing him under the direction of Jack Hutchins, who was the manager of surface chemistry research. Messing, given no clearer mandate than to study the interface between glass and biology, decided to investigate how certain plants metabolize silicon.[75] This project proved a dead end, but Messing made a valuable contribution when he explained a puzzling problem concerning Corning's porous glass. This glass was an intermediate form made while producing 96 percent silica glass, and it contained billions of minute holes, allowing it to be used as a filter, or, more technically, as an extremely efficient chromatographic separator. But early experiments with this filter found something surprising: an aqueous solution containing proteins, if poured into a piece of porous glass, would come out the other side as an aqueous solution with no proteins—plain water. Messing was able to explain this to Hutchins's satisfaction: "Ralph now understands the surface chemistry, the surface charges on proteins. He understands by his association with people in glass that there are also charges on the surface of glass. And it turns out that the combination of those two are such that the charges are opposite so they attract and they get adsorbed."[76] Messing was also able to see an important commercial application in this phenomenon. Trained as an enzymologist, he recognized that what was a problem when separating proteins might be an advantage when working with enzymes, since enzymes held in place could serve to catalyze a variety of successive biological reactions.

Messing began experimenting with enzymes stuck to the surface of glass beads. Because the beads were essentially nonreactive, the enzymes themselves remained chemically active. Furthermore, they remained so for many months; the glass preserved them in a usable form. This was in contrast to other methods of enzyme capture, and it suggested that Corning might have a product of considerable interest to the various industries that rely on enzymes as an ingredient in their production processes.

In order to push his researches into what came to be called immobilized biologicals, Messing hired a second biologist, Howard Weetall, in 1967. Weetall was an immunologist and was more interested in antigens—proteins that stimulate an immune system response—than enzymes. His work quickly diverged from Messing's, and the rivalry that sprang up between the two of them was later reflected in the two branches of biological products that Corning eventually entered: industrial biotechnology and medical applications. By 1970 the two scientists were on quite different tracks, but by that time the company's biological program as a whole was also bifurcated.[77]

At the research level both types of biologist were cultural misfits among the glass technologists. Not surprisingly, given the menagerie of goats, rabbits, and lobsters they installed on the roof of Sullivan Park for use in antibody research, they were viewed with a kind of suspicion that even the electronics researchers had not suffered.[78] The early difficulty in communicating the nature and purpose of biological research to others in the research organization would long plague the new undertaking. But the commercial value of their work was soon evident.

Biotech

Compared to its efforts in medical products, Corning's development of products for industrial biotech applications was straightforward. The company's glass-based immobilization technology was similar to its fiberglass or silicone inventions of an earlier era. Corning had a proprietary position in a novel capability that was of obvious interest to companies unfamiliar to Corning. As it had with fiberglass and silicone, Corning ultimately addressed this difficulty by forming joint ventures. Alliances, as they were now coming to be called, were getting to be standard in the emerging biotech industry. Often they involved small entrepreneurial biotech firms providing their patents and expertise to large pharmaceutical firms. Corning, of course, had a tradition of forming joint ventures, but the ones it formed in the biotech arena departed in key respects from its own successful formula.

After some time spent working with a number of domestic and foreign companies on various projects related to this technology, Corning struck a deal with the Kroger Company, a Cincinnati-based manufacturer of foodstuffs. The plan was to use Corning's immobilization technology to convert cheese whey into higher-value food products, a process that Kroger had some knowledge of. Created in 1981, the joint venture, called "Nutrisearch," ran into insurmountable difficulties from the start. The Corning managers in charge, in too great a hurry to find growth opportunities, had not looked carefully enough at the technology Kroger was proposing to match with Corning's offering. The factory they built did not function; the venture failed, and by 1982 Corning had sold its interest altogether.

Difficulties with Nutrisearch made Corning more wary but did not derail its move into industrial biotech. This time Corning found a partner that was both competent and on the leading edge: Genentech, the leading recombinant DNA firm of its day. Genentech's work with recombinant DNA allowed it to tailor enzymes and other proteins for Corning's immobilization process. This was a much more advanced approach than the standard methods used by Nutrisearch.

Dick Dulude, general manager of the science products division, negotiated this deal, as he had the previous Nutrisearch venture. Genentech rejected his initial proposal that it engage in contract research on Corning's behalf but was willing to form a joint venture in what by this time could only be called classic Corning style: a new company to be equally owned and managed by each partner, the Corning name to come last. Unfortunately, Genentech did not have sufficient funds available for a project of the scope Dulude envisioned. Dulude by this point, however, was convinced that Genentech was the right partner for a major commercialization of Corning's immobilization technology, and he offered a solution: Corning would invest $40 million in Genentech, and Genentech would in turn invest that money in the joint venture. Corning would thus have equity in both companies.

Genentech agreed, and the two together founded Genencor in 1982, Dulude serving as its board's first chairman. Genentech brought to the table considerable experience in recombinant DNA technology, the technical key to tailored enzyme production. The combination of the two capabilities meant that Genencor could offer a wide range of standard enzymes (as well as specially created ones tailored to individual customer demands) packaged so as to make them usable in continuous processes of the sort common in industrial practice.

Genentech's willingness to work with Corning was, unlike the earlier West Coast start-up experience with Signetics and integrated circuits, based on more than just money. Corning's technical contribution was considerable, and while it had only a handful of biologists on its research staff, the work they had done had led them into areas no other company had colonized. Jack Hutchins, head of R&D at Corning in the 1970s, recalled that Corning had after all come close to starting its own program in recombinant DNA but was deterred from this plan by the layoffs of the Guns of August. Hutchins noted:

> Now stop and think about how far we've come in terms of diversification. I mean we're at the technological forefront in an age associated with modern biotechnology. I'm talking about recombinant DNA in the spring of 1975 ... So in '75 we decided not to do recombinant DNA. Genentech does because they've got venture capital money. Genentech becomes the leader. But later on, based in terms of what we're doing with the immobilized

enzymes, we do get into recombinant DNA, and the combination of those technologies has a glass company able to talk to the leader in biotech, which is Genentech.[79]

With $80 million of Corning's money invested, Genencor dwarfed the company's other biotech ventures. It did eventually manage to turn a profit, though it was not a major success. By 1990 both Genentech and Corning had sold their holdings in it, the latter as part of its move to exit the field of biotech. The company's investment in Genentech itself, however, was repaid many times over when Corning sold its shares in the 1990s This money not only paid for the Nutrisearch losses but also covered the investment in medical applications that made up the other half of Corning's investment in biological products. Although that business saw a number of ventures that earned Corning money, it had more than its share that did not.

Medical Products

Corning's made its first foray into medical instruments in 1964, when the company began selling a line of pH meters based on chemically sensitive glasses it had developed some thirty years previously.[80] The meters proved a success, and Corning grew to become a major supplier of these devices. The company centralized this and related work in its Medfield, Massachusetts plant, which opened in 1964 with seventy-five employees. Guided by Marty Gibson, who believed the growth potential in science products lay in focusing on medical testing devices, that product line underwent a transformation. Gibson believed that clinical labs were about to become a huge market:

> Of all the laboratories ... that was the fastest growing by an awful lot. ... Everybody was building new hospital facilities. People were getting older. Medicare at age 65. There was a tremendous demand and technology was exploding on the applications side. Here was a great chance. There were no powerfully entrenched competitors ... I was given a green light on almost everything we wanted to do.[81]

The relatively simple pH meters had already, in the mid-1960s, been adapted to detect other basic ions, and on the basis of these abilities Corning began to produce blood-gas analyzers and other more sophisticated equipment for the clinical lab market while continuing to manufacture hot plates, stirrers, and other basic laboratory tools, which Corning sold via its Science Products Division. By 1976 Medfield was employing 500 people and was only one of several Corning sites contributing to its medical device production.[82]

Progress was not, however, entirely smooth: two major speed bumps appeared during this period. As Dick Dulude recalled, while beta testing of the blood-gas analyzers went smoothly, actual market rollout was a disaster. Corning had done its beta testing with top-notch lab technicians, but, as Dulude later realized, this was a mistake: a "good lab technician initially can make anything work," but the average technician proved unable to do so. The entire medical products business at that time was less than $4 million in sales, and a full recall of the blood-gas analyzers was projected to cost as much as $400,000. Nevertheless, Dulude decided to recall and refurbish the machines. While expensive, "that established our credibility in the business."[83]

The second stumble was both more serious and more costly. In the early 1970s the company began work on a machine designed to tackle one of the few routine diagnostic tasks remaining to be automated, the white blood cell (or leukocyte) differential test. Corning's was only one of five such serious development efforts; major medical products companies and electronics manufacturers were both involved in the market.[84] Corning succeeded in developing a functional device, a machine it dubbed the leukocyte automatic recognition computer (LARC).

LARC represented an enormous leap in complexity beyond any device Corning had ever brought to market. Whatever the production challenges of annealing enormous telescope blanks or forming Corelle tableware, Corning had never attempted to sell a product that was itself so inherently intricate. LARC was not one product, but three: a "spinner" (a small centrifuge designed to produce a monolayer of blood for transfer to a slide), a "stainer" (an automated system that fixed, stained, and buffered the spun blood sample in a temperature and humidity controlled chamber before drying it), and the "classifier" itself.

Corning sold the complete LARC system for around $100,000. *Business Week* and Corning had estimated that at that price around 1,000 of the devices would be sold, for a total market of $100 million. They had not reckoned with other competing devices. In fact, potential customers were not prepared to make the investment, only in part because of cost. As Harmon Garfinkel, by then Corning's director of Research, pointed out, "if you had to choose between a CAT scan, which is much more expensive than a LARC, and a LARC . . . you said, '[The CAT scan] gives me new information. The LARC is just a quality control device for the person who's counting the red and white blood cells. Therefore . . . I'll take the CAT scan.' "[85] Wakeman summarized the effort as "a naive attempt by someone who had not built electronic equipment to achieve a useful objective."[86] Ultimately, the failed product cost Corning around $25 million, with little to show for the trouble. It was the final blow for the Raleigh lab.

Even before the LARC came on the market, sales of a variety of devices for clinical lab use had grown to such an extent that in 1973 Corning formed a new division dubbed medical products, with Gibson as its vice president. Senior management looked to this product line and its associated services business to help grow the company in difficult times; medical equipment looked like one of the few areas likely to grow faster than the gross national product, the benchmark used at the time. With a clear mandate from the top, Gibson moved to take medical products farther.

The creation of a separate division had implications for research. Before 1993, Gibson's group had relied partially on the central lab's research capabilities, especially on Howard Weetall and his group, while work on blood meters of various sorts had demanded electronics expertise that only existed at Raleigh. That connection with Raleigh led Gibson's group to become increasingly estranged from the central research organization— practically, if not personally. Gibson recalled that "Jack [Hutchins, director of R&D] and I formed kind of a bond and really began to assign more resources to our area. Unfortunately, there wasn't much that Sullivan Park could contribute to this because the technology was so different from anything they had done historically before."[87] Nor did Gibson believe the company should develop such expertise under the existing research structure.

Hutchins agreed and subsequently moved Weetall and his work to Medfield.[88] This represented a final estrangement between industrial biotech and medical technologies: the one stayed in Corning, the other went to Massachusetts. By 1975 the Raleigh lab closed, many of its scientists moving to Sullivan Park while a few joined the Medfield operation. Medfield eventually grew to house over 100 researchers.

Even with a dedicated lab, development of new products for this line came slowly. The process was hastened considerably by Corning's purchase in 1980 of Gilford, an Ohio-based manufacturer that sold a broad variety of instruments to clinical labs and hospitals. As part of Corning it continued to produce those devices and expanded its line to include over 100 different lab and hospital instruments. Corning also sought to accelerate its growth in this field via joint ventures. The first such undertaking involved Swiss pharmaceutical giant Ciba-Geigy. Corning created Cormedics in 1969 to develop and market disposable syringes prefilled with a variety of drugs. The company had been selling glass tubing for use in the production of syringes since the 1950s. A sleepy product line, medical products in general focused attention on this as it grew. Even as Corning was developing expertise in syringe production, it began to look elsewhere for help in filling the syringes.

Like the other joint ventures in biotechnology, Cormedics departed from the classic Corning pattern: Ciba-Geigy was asked to join with a 20 percent share only. Corning hoped its partner would provide the technical expertise and market knowledge necessary for Cormedics to succeed, but Ciba-Geigy manufactured encapsulated drugs (pills, capsules, etc.), not bulk drugs sold by liquid measure of the sort that would be injected, and it did not know that latter market. With a mere 20 percent stake in the matter it never made a serious attempt to develop and communicate the necessary understanding of prefilled syringes. As a result, Cormedics itself never developed an accurate picture of the market and failed to seize a superior technological position. With well-entrenched competitors already in the field, it was not surprising that the venture had folded in 1971.

When asked what he thought Corning had learned from the venture, Joe Littleton's answer showed how far Corning had departed from its successful prewar model of productive venture formation:

> In our management of the business, there was a great lesson to be learned
> and that was we put enthusiastic, highly-motivated people down there. In
> their frustration to show good results under very difficult conditions, I think
> that they tended to push too hard. Some of the staff reacted badly. I proba-
> bly pushed too hard for profit.[89]

The focus had been on profit rather than on forming a truly viable venture
based on typical Corning values. Ciba-Geigy had sent people who were
largely peripheral to its business. Moreover, Corning's top management had
had very little to do with either its formation or its subsequent conduct.[90]
Interestingly, Corning did not take away from the Cormedics flop a sense
that Ciba-Geigy was a poor match; indeed, some fifteen years later the two
formed a much larger joint venture (this time arranged along more traditional—for Corning—lines) called Ciba Corning Diagnostics.

MetPath

Corning's foray into the broader medical market did not end here; if anything, this was where it began. Corning's work in medical products served
to familiarize it with the clinical lab business and provided the company a
bird's-eye view of the spectacular growth in that industry in the 1970s. In
1973, at the urging of Marty Gibson, who was running Corning's medical
products business, Corning purchased 9 percent of MetPath, one of the
larger such labs, "just to see how it looked." The drive for growth and high
margins, which had motivated so much else in Corning's exploration of
biotech and medical products, drove the company here as well, with the
result that it found itself, for the first time, in a service business. But as Gibson reiterated to Amo Houghton and Tom MacAvoy, the clinical lab business "doesn't use energy and it doesn't use raw materials and Japan doesn't
compete with it!"[91] Furthermore, it was extremely lucrative at first.

  After a five-year hiatus as Corning's head of personnel, Gibson returned
to the health and sciences group (an umbrella organization formed to contain both the old science products and the various new ventures in biology).
Noting that none of Corning's ventures were doing particularly well, he

suggested to Houghton and MacAvoy that the time had come for Corning to buy MetPath outright. It had in the meanwhile become one of the largest suppliers of testing services in the country. Corning had begun offering test-ing services in the 1970s. Although those efforts had seen some growth, it was clear that the company by itself would never become a major player in that field. MetPath was a major player already, and Gibson believed it had the potential to become even bigger. In 1981 Corning bought Metpath outright.

Gibson would ultimately be proved right about MetPath's potential to grow. But before the new acquisition could start making its contribution, a great deal of work needed to be done. In its eagerness to close the deal, Corning had made this largest of all its acquisitions with the least attention to due diligence. The result was a $20 million write-off in receivables. Hav-ing paid, Corning still did not find itself in possession of a profitable outfit. Two years of constant restructuring and streamlining under Roger Acker-man ensued before a properly pruned business could emerge out of the tan-gle to become Corning's most profitable business in the 1980s.

PROFESSIONAL MANAGEMENT AND DIVERSIFICATION: MIXED RESULTS

Having slogged through a a ghastly and wearing decade, coping with new crises every few years, with margins declining more or less steadily through-out, the management team headed by Amo Houghton and Tom MacAvoy ran out of steam in the early 1980s. The optical waveguide business seemed always on the verge of breaking even; the medical business proved not to be as recession proof as Gibson had claimed it would be. By 1982, one of the worst years on record, profitability had sunk to a dismal 1.8 percent.

In 1981 Jamie Houghton did a strategic review of all the company's busi-nesses, in preparation for succeeding his brother as chairman and CEO. His analysis divided the company's businesses into three categories—those that were doing fine, those that could be fixed, and those that no longer had the growth potential and therefore the dynamism to warrant fixing.[92] In the lat-ter category were businesses like lamps, steel refractories, and portions of Europe's glass-based businesses. The lamp business was especially hard to consider shutting down for sentimental reasons. At a time when so much had been lost and identity was an issue, the Wellsboro and Central Falls plants took on particular significance. They were the oldest plants outside Corning proper, with strong associations with the Ribbon Machine. To Amo Houghton it seemed like selling "members of the family." If Corning was not synonymous with "research in glass," it still aspired to be synonymous with loyalty to people. Wanting nevertheless not to leave Jamie with all the negative tasks to perform when he took over, Tom MacAvoy and Amo Houghton took that step themselves and then stepped down in 1983.[93]

In future years those who had led Corning through the painful transition of the 1970s would rightly be remembered for their courage in staying the course. One reason the course had become so very difficult was the self-inflicted dilemmas associated with the 1970s brand of professional management.[94] The first dilemma revolved around the internal conflict set up in this organization (and in many others) between systems intended to promote efficient management and the previously untouchable technical organization, which had been structured and charged to innovate almost single-handedly and now was completely out of sync with the rest of the company. A second dilemma of similar provenance arose out of the effort to find greater security in diversification and international adventuring, which could only be regarded as a way to avoid risk if all expertise, local knowledge, and experience had no value. No longer convinced of its own ability to navigate the "uncluttered path" and driven by increasingly impatient money managers, Corning pursued many of the same dead ends that most other U.S. companies did, but with one critical difference: it hung on to some of the old practices even as it adopted the new ones.

Ironically, though Amo Houghton had exhorted his management colleagues to exploit all parts of the Corning system, incentives had been created to make all parts of the system work at cross-purposes. In many companies this same problem would spell the end of further efforts to produce blockbusters, or home runs, as Corning termed them. It did not spell the end at Corning, but for a time top management's reluctance to cancel all truly long-range projects would seem dangerously out of step to almost everyone inside and outside the firm. Companies long admired for their inventive genius would produce such fiascoes as AT&T's Picturephone,

The Decker Building contrasted sharply in design and function with the almost windowless Sullivan Park. Championed by David Leibson, it was designed to promote group interaction. The building was completed at about the time Leibson's powerful centralized engineering organization was disbursed to divisional control.

Kodak's Disk Camera, DuPont's Mylar, and the one that helped bring about the premature demise of Corning's old rival, RCA's VideoDisc.

Most of the companies survived these major failures, but few of their technical establishments emerged unscathed. In some cases the failures were fatal and had lasting consequences for more than just one firm. RCA's reabsorption in 1985 by the General Electric Company led in turn to the virtual demise of the consumer electronics industry in the United States. In all of these cases a major factor in the failure of products that ought to have been successes was internal conflict among independent or nearly autonomous divisions, and the tremendous complications introduced by widespread diversification.

Corning's internal conflicts would become more severe in the early 1980s, when the company decentralized most of its technical establishment except the R&D laboratories and gave control of most R&D funding to the divisions. No wonder that at Corning it became received wisdom that any innovation, to be successful, needed a "champion." An innovation champion was indeed needed at Corning, as at many other formerly successful innovating companies, to take on the increasingly hostile environment for new products that the professionally managed company of the 1980s had become.

10

RECOVERING CORNING

A RETURN TO THE SPIRIT OF SPECIALTY

MATERIALS

Over the course of our history, we've managed to [market technology profitably], and we've discovered two things: First we must accept a climate of constant change. It's driven by innovation and we not only accept it, we encourage it. Second, we've been able to participate broadly in the technological revolution of the twentieth century.... You have to count down 222 places on the Fortune 500 to locate us. And yet, we've supported nearly a century of technical growth and even inspired some of it.... Naturally, there's an interaction between what you do and what you are. Participating in such explosive technological growth has made restructuring a way of life.

—JAMIE HOUGHTON
ADDRESS TO THE INDUSTRIAL RESEARCH INSTITUTE, JUNE 1993

C REATING the "more embracing system" that former Corning chairman Amory Houghton Jr. had called for in the late 1960s proved to be no small matter; in fact, it was the work of more than one generation of managers. To generate a structure that could renew itself for creative purposes, even as Corning became a multibillion dollar company, involved institutionalizing innovation in its broadest sense: taking it out of the realm of technology alone and making it an activity that pervaded every part of the company.

Before this could be achieved, however, it was critical to resolve the outstanding identity issues that had arisen over the course of the 1970s transition: whether the company was to be defined primarily by its technologies or by a particular market focus, whether it would maintain a special emphasis on building relationship as a key strength, and how to resolve the seeming conflict between what was needed to be a productive company and what was needed to be a creative one. Some of its executives wanted to make Corning the largest venture capital company in the country; others believed it could still be one of the most innovative companies technologically, while still others believed that it had to become the lowest-cost producer of optical fiber and ceramics. At the time these strategic options were viewed as mutually exclusive, but Corning would eventually prove otherwise. By reinventing its approach to innovation and succeeding beyond all expectations with its fiber-optic business it would prove to itself that it could have a future as a high-tech company in the twenty-first century.

First, a balance had to found between the pursuit of productivity and the need for continuous innovation: the one could no longer be allowed to jeopardize the other. This involved adopting a total quality management (TQM) program, but counteracting its static effects by formalizing the process of innovation and making explicit commitments to diversity. Second, Corning's leaders rediscovered the importance of relationships—the individual as a productive member of a team, partnership between the company and its unions, and joint ventures between the company and other companies—which had fallen out of favor during the professional management era of the 1970s.

Along the way, market focus, regardless of technology, received a strategic emphasis it had not enjoyed since the days of television. In the 1980s and early 1990s, much of Corning's management attention was diverted to the fast-growing market for diagnostic laboratory services, even though Corning had little technology advantage there. This diversion forced the company's leadership to take a hard look at its profusion of product lines, some of which it had been producing since before the turn of the century.[1] Ultimately, Corning would divest almost all of its slower-growing businesses, even the consumer business that bore its brand name.

To resolve its several strategic issues, Corning employed many of the same tools that other companies were using at the time. Words like "quality," "diversity," "networking," and "restructuring" became standard parts of the company vocabulary. However mind-numbing and sometimes meaningless these buzzwords could be in the wider industrial culture of the 1980s and 1990s, Corning put them to use in its own unique ways, pushing them to their limits, working them longer, and insisting that they serve rather than subvert company values and purposes. Whatever the label, Corning's intention, and often its achievement, was not to use these concepts as mere rhetorical devices but to pursue the ideas behind them until they became effective disciplines inside the company.

Behind these efforts, and providing some of the driving force, was the sense that the Houghton family's influence, important as it had been for a century and a half, was diminishing and might even disappear. Despite major efforts to achieve continuity in leadership philosophy, the precarious-ness of relying on leadership alone became poignantly evident when Jamie Houghton barely survived an accident in 1993.[2] Therefore, Corning's efforts to institutionalize innovation from the mid-1980s to the mid-1990s were in part directed at embedding in the company's culture the kinds of policies and disciplines that would sustain cultural continuity even if the Houghton family was no longer there to support it.[3]

Alongside these efforts, and forming the context for all of them, was the contest between Corning's two new developing businesses—fiber optics for telecommunications on the one hand, and medical electronics and testing on the other—both representing powerful growth sectors of the economy, but with the potential to lead Corning in radically different directions. The latter sections of this chapter present the development of each business as a case in point, flip sides of Corning's new approach to innovation.

The struggle between the two businesses, and the different Corning identities, would only begin to be resolved in the early 1990s, when a leader with a strong technology background, Roger Ackerman, was chosen as chief operating officer and likely successor to Jamie Houghton. Ackerman, the fast tracker out of ceramics engineering who had headed Corhart while still in his twenties, who had pushed Celcor into a new generation of technology in the 1980s, and who was equally successful at bringing order out of chaos at Metpath, became Corning's chief operating officer. Ackerman's selection would prepare the way for Corning to exit its medical services businesses in favor of technology-based products rooted in specialty materials for rapidly growing global markets.[4] Later, as chairman, he would support the rebuild-ing of Corning's central technical organization, which had not been revital-ized since the 1960s. In the meantime the contest between two very different possible futures would hold much of the company in suspense.

RESTRUCTURING AND FOCUSING, 1983–1991

In 1983 Jamie Houghton inherited a situation that was in many respects the mirror image of the one his brother Amo had faced in 1968. In the late 1960s the company had been in superb financial shape after more than a decade of prosperity, buoyed by high morale verging on euphoria. The key problem for Corning's leadership in the drastic transition that had followed was finding suitable opportunities to sustain the company's growth through the dramatically altered business environment of the 1970s. In Jamie's case, by contrast, the product portfolio contained more high-growth opportunities than there were financial resources to exploit them.

Corning's financial position in 1983, another recession period for the national economy, was abysmal. Profits had declined for three years in a row, reaching a low of 7 percent return on equity (compared to figures of 14-16 percent in larger successful technology-based companies like General Electric). Morale reflected not just the declines of the previous decade but the chasm that had opened up between the technical organization and the rest of the company. Corning's identity was no longer tethered to research in glass, but a coherent substitute identity of equal motivating power did not appear to be emerging. Scientists and engineers were seeing their best work ignored or abandoned by the company, not because of the lack of technical merit or even business value but because of strategic uncertainty. In addition, the company had suffered through another restructuring. Mindful of the wrenching consequences for morale of the layoffs in the previous decade, the chairman's letter in Corning's *Annual Report* for 1982 acknowledged two Corning "men of the year":

> First—the person whose employment with the company was cut short through restructuring, repositioning, or an exaggerated fall in volume. Second: the Corning prototype—the old pro, the young contributor—who time after time, as goals were met, set higher standards and proceeded to beat even them. To these men and women, a few who start new careers, the majority who continue with the company, we want you to know of our deep appreciation. 1982 is over.[5]

While the Corning business portfolio of the early 1980s had definite strengths, it also had two central problems: too many divergent options and the fact that 70 percent of its businesses were in low-growth markets. This was apparent in reading between the lines of a speech Jamie Houghton made to the Industrial Research Institute shortly after becoming CEO. In a presentation put together with Jack Hutchins, head of R&D, Houghton projected a future structured by three internally developed clusters of technology, each a portfolio with some fast-growing and some slow-growing products in them: consumer and industrial, based on strengthened glasses and ceramics applied to tableware and ovenware, along with other high-performance glass products like ophthalmic, medical products arising out of the merger of the traditional laboratory glass business with the new concentration in the biosciences, and electronic components and fiber optics for the emerging telecommunications market.[6]

In some ways this address to leaders of the industrial research community was an odd speech for Jamie to be making. While he had been steeped in technology and strategy issues over the previous several years, this was not an area in which he felt particularly comfortable. On the contrary, he felt bound by a set of intense and uncomfortable inherited obligations, not of his own choosing. There was, for one thing, the family commitment never to reduce investment in R&D spending. "Investment in R&D," he confessed in a 1999 interview, "was an article of faith in my family; my brother and I learned that as children."[7] There could be no question of breaking with that faith, but Jamie had the uneasy feeling that in the matter of support for technology-based innovation his brother's tenacious defense of fiber optics had raised the bar to unreasonable heights for future Corning CEOs.

Amo had clung to the nascent waveguide business through a difficult economic period. It was widely believed, though the actual inner workings of his management team were not public, that several times he had even had to scuttle moves to shut down further fiber-optic development when others had wanted to use the money to acquire more of the fast-growing and profitable MetPath. Jamie felt an obligation to do what Amo had done—"to find and champion my own 'big megilla,'" as he put it.[8] He was apprehensive about it, but given the rapidly decentralizing organizational structure of the company, he believed this was the sort of thing that could only be expected of the CEO. Heads of separate divisions were under too much pressure to generate steady growth, and the barriers to cooperation were too formidable to expect anyone else to achieve such a goal.

Even as Jamie Houghton sketched out the prospects for his company to the Industrial Research Institute in neat technology planning terms, it was becoming evident that going forward on all these fronts—that is, nurturing more than one demanding emerging technology—was beyond the human and financial capacity of the company. Though he told the institute that cutting back R&D would be suicide, in fact he believed that increasing the R&D budget would also lead to trouble, since it would expose the company's investment policy to criticism from the financial community that it was garnering inadequate returns. As the family's holdings in the company were declining, the analysts' views had to be taken more seriously. In the next six years, Corning would reduce its financial exposure to technological uncertainty by selling off several of its businesses: Corhart (which had hit a slower growth phase), the international laboratory glassware business, electronics, and biotechnology. The $500 million thus realized would go into acquisitions, mostly in laboratory services, that were not dependent on Corning's in-house technology at all.[9]

One of the most important acts of leadership that the new management team faced in 1983 was making decisive choices between such businesses so that resources were not spread too thin and people were not frustrated by a lack of priorities.[10] Houghton himself was ready to display as much discipline and tenacity of leadership toward the task of shutting down options as his brother had displayed imagination and courage in his task of creating them in the first place.[11] Fortunately, a management structure already existed that had a chance of resolving the apparent strategic conflicts.

The Six Pack

Jamie Houghton had opted for a management structure that appeared highly unconventional to some and downright messy to others. Nevertheless, it proved to have real advantages. He made himself the first among equals of a six-person group, immediately dubbed the "Six Pack." Besides Houghton, it included three company presidents and two vice chairmen: one president for the core businesses based on glass and ceramics technology (Bill Hudson), one for the medical businesses (Marty Gibson), and one to focus on the optical waveguide or telecommunications business (Dick Dulude). The intent of this arrangement was, of course, to give special attention to both of Corning's fast-developing businesses. The two vice chairmen, each heading staffs, were Tom MacAvoy, who covered technology and government relations, and Van Campbell, in charge of all other staff functions, his own special expertise financial.

Management by team, in the extreme form that the Six Pack represented, was new for Corning, but not radically so. It built on the executive office structure that Amo Houghton had adopted in the latter years of his chairmanship. Moreover, the team structure had become such a key part of Corning's most successful projects during the previous decade that it seemed right for top management to practice it as well. In any case, the team was a way of ensuring that corporate interests continued to be taken

The executive team nicknamed the "Six Pack" included (back row) Dick Dulude, Marty Gibson, Bill Hudson, Tom MacAvoy, (front) Van Campbell and Jamie Houghton.

into account under what was otherwise a new, more decentralized organization. For the first time business heads were to get control over most of their own resources, both financial and technical, and could allocate their own funding. Although specialty materials technology would continue to be concentrated at Sullivan Park, biomedical and medical electronics research would be separated off entirely, as electronics research had been earlier.

In the first year or so after the reorganization, the management team spent at least a quarter of all their working hours together, an incredibly intensive group effort by almost any standard.[12] They were aided in this by a succession of skilled consultants serving as facilitators and by Peter Booth, lawyer and secretary to the committee, who was intimately acquainted with Corning's international activities. During this period the management team placed a high priority on articulating and formalizing seven shared values as a way of framing the hard strategic choices that had to follow.[13] These core beliefs—quality, integrity, performance, leadership, technology (later changed to innovation), independence, and the individual—might shift in emphasis over the next decade and a half, but they would remain touchstones. The need to be explicit about these values was a sign of the times as well as the size and geographical dispersion the company had attained.

Pruning the corporation—shutting down or selling the remaining non-growth businesses—presented the leadership team with some of its hardest choices because most of these men had spent their formative years in one or another of these businesses. The second difficult, and equally important, strategic choice was deciding between the prospective growth businesses. Both the medical equipment business and the waveguide business had underlying technologies that could easily consume most of Corning's discretionary investment for years to come. What started out as a contest for resources became a struggle waged for the soul of the company. As the medical business abandoned its technological underpinnings, leading Corning into the service sector, the company's management had to choose between a technology-based strategy and one based on investment in high-growth markets, where it had no experience and little value to add.

The Business Options

The difficulty with making a definitive choice between medical technology and fiber optics in the early 1980s was that the potentially enormous fiber-optics business had been moving at the speed of molasses. Domestically it was kept from exploding by the notoriously conservative AT&T, and abroad by national government control of telecommunications monopolies. In later years this deliberate pace could be seen to have held real advantages for Corning: it was a chance to lay firm foundations for the business, to pursue an orderly scale-up process, and to learn from experience. But the delay in realizing returns on huge investments in fiber-optics research and development subjected the company to much criticism from the financial community.

Meanwhile, the medical instrumentation market was looking increasingly attractive. It was growing rapidly at a time when Corning's other businesses were in the doldrums. The company's initial attempt to deal with the resource problem for medical technologies, when most of its development resources were going into fiber, was typical for Corning: it formed a series of resource-seeking partnerships: Genencor, Nutrisearch, and, chief among them, Ciba-Corning Diagnostics.

This latter joint venture was a product of management's realization that, however healthy the past of the medical products division had been, Corning would have to delve more deeply into the basic biology underlying the division's products in order to remain on the cutting edge. Corning's own Medfield research operation lacked sufficient resources for a serious effort of this type. Lacking both money and expertise, it looked elsewhere.

By mid-1985 a deal had been struck with the Swiss pharmaceuticals giant Ciba-Geigy. Corning essentially spun off its medical products division, including its Medfield lab and its plant in Walpole, while Ciba-Geigy contributed money and expertise. The result was a fifty-fifty ownership structure of a successful company that, in a departure for Corning, did not rely wholly on Corning technology.[14] Although Ciba's percentage and its expectations for the future of the market were sufficient to maintain its interest, the joint venture lasted a mere four years. Corning was uncharacteristically impatient for quicker financial returns,[15] and its researchers' dreams of having access to Ciba technology in Basel were never fulfilled.[16] After Corning sold its share in the venture to Ciba-Geigy in 1989, what remained of the medical branch was the burgeoning laboratory services business consisting of MetPath and other related acquisitions.

Even though the largest portion of Corning's technical effort was concentrated in fiber optics, work was still carried on with other nonfiber technologies—specialty glasses, other related materials, and some organic research on plastics for laboratory ware. Products drawing on this broader research included photochromic glass for nonprescription sunglasses, ultra-low expansion glass for astronomical mirrors, plastic for disposable labware, machinable ceramic substrates for computer memory disks, and environmental products like novel applications of the Celcor substrate technologies and improved versions of refractories. Many of these technologies fell under the broad umbrella of technology products, a division that served a wide array of markets and provided the incubation function for developing new products and processes that we have previously labeled Corning's "technology till." A number of new high-potential materials seemed to be opening up in the late 1980s. It was, for instance, out of new product development in technical products, later known as specialty materials, that Corning extended its fusion glass technique to make both LCD substrates for computer displays and high-purity masks for semiconductor fabrication.[17]

Some of the businesses in the specialty materials area were very profitable for a while but lacked staying power, since those overseeing these ventures were unwilling under the new decentralized funding structure either to invest in the research or acquire the technology that would allow them to compete in the longer run. Photochromics, for instance, though never a large business, was extremely profitable for several years. It eventually started to lose ground to competitors making much lighter-weight plastic lenses with photochromic properties, but it continued to throw off welcome cash for the use of other businesses.[18] Other products that looked as though they would turn into big businesses didn't. Memcor, for instance, involved cooperative work with IBM to replace aluminum for memory disks with strengthened glass ceramic. It failed much the way the wind-

shield had failed, both by underestimating the potential in competing material and by demanding too high a price for the market to accept.[19]

In prior years the consumer business would also have been regarded as
technology centered. Now, with the decentralization of technology funding and the freedom to pursue its own priorities, this branch shifted away
from significant technical investment in favor of heavier investments in
marketing. In the aftermath of the demise of fair trade laws, the business
that had made Pyrex from strong glass, Corning Ware from high-strength
ceramics, and Corelle from chemically strengthened and laminated glasses,
fell victim to the power of big discounters like Walmart and Kmart to shave
its margins. While the consumer business continued to promote its transparent stovetop line, Visions, and found cost-saving ways revisit the idea of
"swing glass" to produce Visions and Corning Ware from the same melt
(Tavis), it basically substituted for its old technology-based strategy a new
one: using marketing and product line extensions, along with acquisitions
like Revereware, to achieve further growth and profitability.

With Corning's profitability and morale both at record lows in the early
1980s, it was not hard for Jamie Houghton to settle on the goals his management team would emphasize: profitability and growth. But how were they
to be achieved? At an offsite meeting at a Marriott hotel near Rochester, New
York, attended by the company's entire management, Houghton issued an
ultimatum. To quote one of the several hundred people in attendance; "He
fundamentally said, 'We stink. We've got to get better. We've got to use total
quality systems, and we're going to do it.' That was his speech. That's what
kicked the whole thing off."[20] Quality had already been enthusiastically promoted by Forry Behm for several years inside Corning. To his colleagues'
surprise, Jamie Houghton chose to pursue this theme not as a temporary
expedient but as the hallmark of his own leadership. As Tom MacAvoy put it,
"To our astonishment, Jamie went from being a learner to being St. Paul
in a couple of months. The first thing you know he was insisting that

Behm develop a training program and that it be ready by the first of the year, and the Six Pack was going to be the first ones to take it.[21]

Corning was hardly alone in pursuing total quality management (TQM) as a major program in the early 1980s; in fact, the company was slow off the mark compared to others with challenging manufacturing tasks. However, it was one of only a few companies in which the chairman and CEO was the most fervent and consistent promoter of this and other related disciplines for more than a decade. Jamie's choice of quality as his personal mantra turned out to reflect his surefooted instinct for a cause that could bring the Corning community both to address its profitability problems and to reconnect with its fundamental values. As it turned out, the initiative received the support of Corning's main union, the American Flint Glass Workers Union. George Parker, its visionary national head surprised Corning's management by declaring that such an effort was long overdue and giving it his wholehearted support.[22]

In superficial ways the quality initiative bore a strong resemblance to the productivity programs of the previous decade, but it was productivity with a far more positive spin. As Tom MacAvoy observed, Forry Behm's work had already demonstrated that "quality had sizzle." Most liked it, especially the Phil Crosby approach, widely adopted at the time, which Corning used in the initial training phase. And when the program evolved into its "total quality" phase, this shifted the emphasis beyond improving manufacturing and operations to a more holistic treatment, justifying the commitment of more functions. The program set the stage for broader participation at all levels of the company: ideas could bubble up rather than simply cascade down. And just as important, it helped instill throughout the company a disciplined way of working that was crucial to sustain new products past their high-margin start-up phases into the competitive long haul that inevitably ensued.[23]

The quality program went through four major stages at Corning. The early stages in the mid-1980s were similar to those at other companies — developing measurement systems, training all employees at its own Quality Institute, rerouting worker participation away from old-style suggestion boxes to "method improvement requests" and a form of quality circles. But Corning's program was distinct in two ways. First, most senior managers were rigorous about learning and doing what they were requiring of everyone else. Second, thanks to Corning's depth of activities in Asia, it had intimate access to Japanese practitioners of quality principles. Platoons of Corning employees, including union members from the shop floor, went on learning missions to Japan, visiting venture allies and customers, to experience this firsthand, often taking other customers with them to broaden the discussion beyond Corning's immediate culture. One tour took as its theme "quality in research."

Many employees were initially mystified that management would invest $5–10 million in such a program when the company was already suffering from declining profitability. Not everyone appreciated the value of requiring employees to spend a set percentage of their time (1 percent, escalating to 5 percent) on training, an investment that by 1992 amounted to 1.4 million hours company-wide, or an average of eighty-six hours per person.[24] Only the medical testing business did not invest in this training. Its managers objected to the cost of training and pointed to the initial difficulty of applying standard quality operating practices to service operations. The exception appeared to be made because of its undeniable profitability, but in so doing this business lost its chance to avoid many future problems.

There were, of course, from many quarters, the expected complaints of those who resented the paperwork involved in measurement, documenting, and complying with the quality demands. But as time went on, forming a corrective action team (CAT) or participating in a quality improvement team (QIT) at the divisional level became the natural way to get something done, and success was defined in terms of satisfying both internal and external customers 100 percent of the time, a central tenet of the quality movement.

As in most companies, the program first bore fruit in manufacturing, where Corning's products were becoming ever more demanding to produce. Here, just the basics—bringing the production process within defined control limits through measurement, operator participation, and continuous improvement—yielded visible benefits. Houghton later recalled:

> From old-style suggestion boxes that offered money rewards, we went to the quality suggestion approach which has no reward other than recognition, but also offered the chance to make a difference. We had nine times as

many suggestions as before, then after a while we had a declining number. When we checked into it we discovered that the decline signified a desirable outcome. People no longer felt they had to make suggestions for other people to carry out. They just took on the problem and did something about it.[25]

Corning's ability to survive a shakeout in the fiber-optics business in the mid-1980s—the same sort of shakeout that had undermined both the television and electronics businesses before—provided early evidence of the strategic value of having honed this set of disciplines and improved employee involvement. Corning was also making steady progress toward its financial goals, ratcheting up its performance in manufacturing year after year. By 1991 it had achieved a cumulative record of 16 percent per annum return on equity and 20 percent return on assets.

The value of the quality program as applied beyond manufacturing became more apparent when certain staff functions that had been struggling with too little for years found that they could use the TQM process to make their case for adding scarce resources. This happened early for the patent department, for instance, which had been denied the headcount it needed during the productivity-driven 1970s and early 1980s, despite the recommendations of outside consultants.[26] Angry letters and complaints had shown for years that internal customer requirements were not being adequately served. The problem was easy to measure: in the previous ten years the demands on the patent department had increased in almost all areas while the number of qualified legal staff had decreased by four attorneys, whose accumulated insider expertise was hard to replace. Under the new TQM regime, by which heads of department were invited to present their case to the management committee, it was easy for Al Michaelsen, head of the department, to prove that he needed at least two more trained lawyers and a support person to fulfill the expanding strategic mission of his function.[27] Michaelsen's request was granted. The same kind of treatment helped to get the attention of researchers, when they were able to use the quality process to get better funding for research equipment.

Nevertheless, Jamie Houghton later observed that if he had given up any time before 1990—seven years into the program—quality at Corning would

have sunk without a trace. One of the initial holdouts was the R&D community, in which the immediate application of quality procedures was seen
as irrelevant and the benefits appeared to be few. Researchers, who had been
educated in postwar science to value originality and individual contribution
above all else, were turned off by group meetings that stressed a patterned
approach to communication. They scoffed at the notion of error-free work
in a laboratory, where errors could be the major source of discovery and
eliminating them could drive out serendipity. They fumed about having to
satisfy quality program requirements by measuring the unmeasurable and
then measuring the trivial. Some observed that it was a healthy turnaround
for research to think about customers again, while others believed that the
real objections were cultural: as a senior manager in the development function observed, operating on quality principles as a way of working required
people to offer respect to those outside the scientific community, not typical
behavior for either senior researchers or research managers.

> I tried like hell, but they wouldn't listen to me. I've had a lot of meetings
> with some of the research managers, trying to give them examples of how
> we worked [in technical products development] and what we did. The
> stumbling block was the measures. But the core, I think, is that [managers]
> have to give up some power, and you have to be comfortable with that.[28]

In time visible benefits of the program also began to accrue in research, in
areas like improved laboratory services delivered (error-free testing), and
enhanced communication across functional lines. At Sullivan Park standing
quality improvement teams became the standard means to address intransi-
gent issues like the difficulty of hiring and promoting women and minorities.
Moreover, researchers who had been isolated for the past twenty years at Sullivan Park found themselves rubbing shoulders with people from other parts
of the company when they served on quality improvement teams outside the
technical community. Eventually the research organization came up with
four of its own "key results indicators" or KRIs that had meaning inside their
own community and helped them to communicate with others outside.

The commitment to working according to the tenets of quality became
so ingrained over time in most of Corning that the bureaucratic structure

and some of the mechanics were allowed to disappear.[29] The TQM emphasis changed from a measurement regime to a way of defining the company's core values: reducing hierarchy, yielding the power of decision making to a wider range of people, and eliminating old-style supervision, giving employees at many levels the tools and the self-confidence to act on their own. In short, in places all over the company Corning's approach to quality became a source of organizational innovation that tested the company's creative problem-solving ability and demonstrated the effectiveness of harnessing its collective ingenuity.

Competing Values

At the same time, it was evident to Corning's management that some central tendencies in the behavioral aspects of quality programs could run counter to key Corning values like individualism and innovation. Taken to its logical extremes, insistence on performing a process in a controlled and consistent manner, for instance, could easily translate into a culture that stifled creativity. Norm Garrity, who would lead Corning's manufacturing revolution in the latter part of the 1980s, found the quality movement indispensable in these efforts. But he also recognized its contradictions:

> We Americans are not built to follow procedure. We hate it. Why would I put that cup in that same position every time I get my coffee? Japanese will do it. They will put it right in the same spot until there is a change process.... They follow instructions. Americans: this is change and we are moving and we have to be flexible. Where it hurts us is in discipline areas. So, that is a challenge for us because everyone wants to do their own thing.[30]

Respect for the individual, another core value, had long been regarded as key to the creativity that Corning tried to foster. As one consultant publicly observed, Corning managed to avoid a common risk of quality programs, which was to put too great an emphasis on uniformity of behavior.[31] The exception made for the medical testing business was a case in point,

although this particular exception later proved to have unfortunate consequences for the company as a whole. Yet the danger of requiring too great a
degree of conformity was clearly there; it could reinforce a tendency that
small-town cultures were prone to: rejection of people who did not look
and think alike. Whether Jamie Houghton had this particular connection in
mind is not clear, but in 1987 he decided to add a "third leg" to his stool—the
only additional goal he would adopt for the company during his entire thir-
teen-year tenure.[32]

Diversity was another slogan that many companies were adopting at the
time, but few labored under the disadvantage of having their headquarters
in out-of-the-way Corning, New York. Houghton was convinced that, given
the demographics of the United States toward the end of the twentieth century (and he might have added, the company's commitment to keeping its
headquarters where it was), Corning would face serious competition in
recruiting the level of talent it needed if it did not make extraordinary efforts
to hire people outside the traditional white male category. Knowledge workers—people with particular expertise, advanced science degrees, or special-
ties in various aspects of business—are difficult to keep in any case because
of their mobility and expectations, but the hardest categories for Corning to
retain would be women and minorities. And these would remain thorny
issues: the company was bound to have more trouble satisfying all kinds of
ethnic minorities than businesses located in more urban settings. Asian and
Jewish employees, the two minorities best represented in the educated workforce, were already complaining of their seeming inability to move into the
ranks of Corning's senior executives. Even so, there was substantial dis-
agreement among members of the management committee as to whether a
push for greater diversity was necessary or desirable.

Affirmative action hiring was a program that Tom MacAvoy had encouraged and set as a personal goal in the 1970s, largely as a matter of good corporate citizenship. But Jamie Houghton pushed diversity as a matter of
corporate self-interest. With an average price tag of $40,000 attached to the
hiring and training of each employee, turnover was also a matter of short-
term profitability. It became mandatory for all managers (as reflected
in their bonuses and measured by company climate surveys) to recruit and

foster outstanding female and minority candidates. Once again, Houghton insisted on objective measurements, complete with published goals and timetables. Achieving a climate attractive to a culturally diverse workforce was not, of course, just a matter of recruiting. The company sponsored coaching programs, new work/life policies, and mandatory awareness training concerning diversity and sexual harassment, not only in the company but in the community. By 1994, seven years after adding this third leg to the stool, Corning had doubled its number of women and black employees, bringing to 29 percent the number of women managers and to 8 percent the number of black managers. Turnover for women was reduced by 50 percent and for black employees by 30 percent. Most striking of all, in a development that startled the Corning community but also showed that diversity would be taken seriously, one very successful senior manager lost his job over an incident of harassment.[33]

Innovation versus Quality

The other Corning value that had the potential to conflict with a vigorous quality program was innovation. But it was a conflict that top managers were slower to recognize, perhaps because technology-based innovation was so deeply ingrained in Corning's traditional character that it was easy to take it for granted. In this case the problem was easier to see on neutral turf. Jamie Houghton noted of a visit to Motorola that "they were proud of their commitment to achieving Six Sigma (very high rates of perfection resulting from getting the product right every time). We cared about perfection too, if we could achieve it, but we cared more about looking ahead to what we would need to do next."[34] To be consistent with Corning's values and its goals for growth, a quality program could not be allowed to impede the effective management of change. Corning chose to balance the two values by formalizing its innovation process, which previously had been defined only within the research, engineering, and product development communities, and working to make this minimalist, yet formal, process the central integrating mechanism across the broader community.

FIXING INNOVATION, 1983–1986

As vice chairman with special responsibilities for technology from 1983 to 1986, Tom MacAvoy found that he was not getting the respect from his former subordinates in the Six-Pack that his predecessors had enjoyed from their senior management colleagues. To his surprise, he found himself the target of open resentment expressed by the operating divisions, which seemed to believe that they had been bearing the burdens of an insufficiently productive centralized technical establishment for far too long: in their eyes Sullivan Park had lost its creativity in research and was too expensive in engineering. "Stay out of our hair and fix it" was the message MacAvoy was hearing.[35] Meanwhile, the R&D community was disenchanted with MacAvoy for different reasons. They viewed him as one of their own who had disappointed them by shutting down programs; he was not the kind of advocate for R&D in higher places that they had perceived Armistead to be.

Part of the problem was, once again, universal. The times were out of joint for R&D nationally. "Innovation" at Corning, as in U.S. industry more broadly in the early 1980s, was a concept that had fallen out of public favor. In addition, as already mentioned, Jamie Houghton had his own reasons for deemphasizing innovation, closely associated as it was with the previous leadership. This did not mean he would cut the R&D budget as a percentage of sales: he reasserted his personal commitment to maintain R&D spending at 4–5 percent. Although this was twice the national average and quite competitive for the glass industry, it was hardly in the ballpark for a "high-technology" company, where 6–8 percent of sales was closer to the norm.

For most organizations in the country, innovation had become identified with the R&D function and was seen as essentially synonymous with new product development. As a consequence, when innovation became more difficult to execute on a business timetable, R&D bore a disproportionate share of the blame. A few voices, such as that of John Akers, chairman of IBM, spoke out against the tendency to assign the blame for ineffective product development in this way. Claiming that the onus ought to be on the rest of the company to pull technology out of its laboratories,

Akers said, "We need to apply a suction to our R&D laboratories." Few listened, and in general R&D became viewed as one of the obvious culprits responsible for industrial woes. Another dissenting voice was that of Lester Thurow, economist and dean of MIT's Sloan Management School, who pointed out that American companies had neglected process development for decades and had therefore made new products harder to sustain in a competitive marketplace.[36]

One universal method of "fixing" R&D in the 1980s was to decentralize either the institutions themselves or the control over their funding—or both.[37] At Corning key managers still believed it was imperative to keep specialty glass and materials research physically centralized, but financial decentralization was a major plank of the profitable growth plan. The centrally located part of the technical community accordingly shrank from a high of 1,400 in the early 1970s to a rump force of 800 people, including central manufacturing and engineering. The medical products division assembled its own small laboratory, and each business took control of part of the engineering force. In France the Avon laboratory dropped the goal of integrating its program with Sullivan Park and turned its entire focus to supporting Corning's French operations. The Japanese laboratory, more recently acquired from RCA, focused its efforts mainly on supporting the Japanese television business.[38]

The larger, more autonomous business units took responsibility for their own portfolios, presumably freed up in this way to invest the money they needed to make them current. The corporate part of the technical effort, managed on a charge-out basis, would be concentrated on from two to six major opportunities, defined as greater than $100 million in sales.[39] Some of the moves to decentralize had immediate and not wholly beneficial effects for the corporation over all. Some claimed, for instance, that patenting priorities had shifted away from seeking to protect the broadest areas possible and had come to be used more tactically, in support of short-term business goals.[40]

The buck stopped with Tom MacAvoy, having become vice chairman with responsibility for technology to "fix" Corning's approach to innovation. In 1984 he set up an interfunctional "innovation task force" that was

responsible for finding out why the rest of the company was dissatisfied
with R&D, whether or not its reputation for decline was deserved, and what
could be done to improve the new product development process for business unit customers. Extensive interviews with business unit managers
yielded a frank and devastating report on the state to which Corning's overall technology had been allowed to drift.[41]

Except for a few key projects protected by top management and a few
new products that had come in from the periphery, the study revealed that
most other aspects of the R&D and engineering program had fallen into a
state of neglect. New product development was insufficient to sustain profitability, declines in new process development had allowed core businesses
and acquisitions to become unprofitable, and the manufacturing sciences
had deteriorated. There were, to be sure, pockets of promising technology

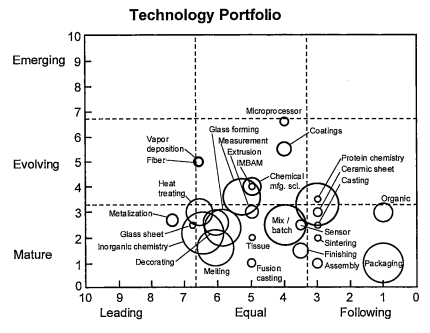

Technology Portfolio

*This diagram from the report commissioned by Tom MacAvoy when he was vice chairman
shows that during the period when Corning had been focusing on productivity improvement it had fallen behind in virtually every one of its main areas of technology.*

here and there, but they were not strategically integrated even in the desired "market-based businesses, end-use and systems-based products" like medical electronics, which had received strategic emphasis over the past decade. In the judgment of outside consultants and internal managers alike, in spite of all its efforts to change its character, Corning's greatest technical capabilities, comparatively speaking, still lay with its materials and process technologies, not with its market-based businesses.

The report concluded that Corning's defensive moves of the 1970s and early 1980s—to reduce research funding (down 20 percent in real dollar terms over the decade) in favor of development and to confine new investments primarily to low-risk product and process extensions and renewals— had set up a cycle of diminishing returns. Corning's traditional practice of sponsoring exploration and "reach" projects across the board, as well as keeping up a certain level of risk taking, had had the important side benefit of replenishing the company's "technology till." By the mid-1980s that till was in need of revitalizing.

Further, much of the rest of the company was paying no attention to innovation at all, while low morale in the R&D organization itself was undermining the effectiveness of its projects. Innovations that did occur were based on extreme measures: extraordinary leadership like Dave Duke's in fiber optics, exceptional inventions like immobilized enzymes, or special market positions. Efforts to innovate were succeeding by acts of heroism or by fighting the rest of the company.

Remembering How to Dance: Corning's Past Successes

So as not to ignore outside perspectives, the innovation task force retained consultants, but the members also invested months of their own time, most of it over early breakfast meetings. A major part of their effort consisted of a systematic appraisal of Corning's many past innovation successes and failures, from which they aimed to develop an explicit description of Corning's way of innovating—an innovation process.[42]

At the first organizational meeting, one invited observer, Marie McKee, the new head of human resources for Sullivan Park, told Tom MacAvoy that a crucial element had been missing in the discussions—people. Discussions of the innovation process at the time were typically disembodied, using the quasi-scientific representational diagrams of boxes and arrows common to engineering and systems diagramming. "I know I just got here," McKee said, "but if you need to get more ideas coming out, then linkages between the teams and between the people are going to be critical."[43] Recognizing a different and valuable perspective, MacAvoy asked McKee to serve on the task force. McKee then took on a leading role both in managing the consultants and in organizing the internal effort.

What lay behind the morale problem among the various technical staffs was a growing feeling of irrelevance to the company's strategic direction. Even the sort of recognition for innovators that had been common in the old Corning was lately in short supply. The group decided to focus on Corning's past history of successful innovation as an untapped resource, one that could be crucial to rebuilding morale. They also believed that the understanding of innovation implicit in the company's shared memory needed to be made more visible. MacAvoy proposed a slogan for this effort taken from a well-known saying of Corning veteran Eddie Leibig: "We never dance as well as we know how."

A group of recognized Corning innovators then came together as a "quality improvement team." They studied hundreds of Corning innovations, mining them for their larger meaning. Many of their generalizations matched those that were coming out in broader studies of innovation across the country: that high-caliber people who were willing to take risks and had good communication and team building skills were key. Another factor stood out at Corning, however: its ability to concentrate maximum strength on a project of major importance and to do it quickly. This method had enabled Corning to tackle outsized opportunities such as projects like Celcor and waveguides. In addition, innovation at Corning had never been the sole province of scientists or even technical people. Corning had been good at identifying and developing innovative leaders with the right qualities throughout the company in the past, but this kind of leadership had gone by the board in the face of countervailing pressures to specialize, downsize, or reduce the asset base. Finally, based on a review of current literature on innovation, the task force identified a multistage model that could be adapted for Corning's case.

Jim Reisbeck, the marketing member of the task force, cautioned against doing what many companies were doing at the time, which was to define the process of new product development in such minute detail that it reduced innovation to filling in endless checklists and inhibited creativity instead of enhancing it. The task force adopted a skeletal overview of the essence of a process, grounded in Corning's own experience, to be used as an integrative framework. This they then summarized in a simple graphic flip chart.

The group then decided on a company-wide conference as a way to focus attention on innovation and re-introduce the innovation process. To get Jamie Houghton to bless this effort, Tom MacAvoy stressed the importance of innovation in the context of TQM:

> I brought him the cost of quality analysis that said 'improving the innovation process is the most important Total Quality program in the company.' I'd worked out some very simple arithmetic. Let's say we're spending $150 million annually. We're probably wasting about a third of it, we just don't know what third it is. If quality is only about improving manufacturing we can get 5% at most improvement in gross margin. The rest has to be about improving the way we innovate. Finally I convinced him that this had to be one of the Total Quality things.[44]

Innovation Conference

The Innovation Conference was a two-and-a-half-day event involving more than 200 senior Corning leaders held at the Corning Glass Center. It included speeches by outside experts, workshops by Corning product and process champions, and the unveiling of the innovation process schematic. It reminded older generations of Corning's essential character and it acquainted newer members of the community with a history they had not necessarily understood was so central to the company's culture. It turned out to be pivotal.

MacAvoy's keynote address was in many ways his legacy to the company, for he was about to take early retirement: he reminded those in attendance that the subject matter of the conference was in fact nothing less than the company's defining activity: "In all cases technology is involved and is at the heart of what we do. We lead primarily by technical innovation. Translating technology into new products and processes, into new ways to help our customers, into new sources of profit and growth—that's what we're all about as a company."

The task force had not limited its deliberations to celebrating Corning's past achievements. It had also identified the key ways in which Corning had fallen short of innovating effectively. MacAvoy portrayed innovation as one of the top two or three quality problems the company had. Improving the innovation process by 10 percent a year could cut that cost in half. Doubling that rate would be equivalent to doubling the R&D spending level. It came down to restoring several simple elements: an environment of energy and enthusiasm, entrepreneurial behavior at all levels, the right people in the right places, sound business and technical strategies, improved processes for nurturing ideas, and organizational mechanisms that could support the organization's drive for results.

Learning how to innovate on a systematic basis over a long period of time, formerly a tacit matter, was now to be formally articulated so that it could be practiced across the company. MacAvoy summarized the objective this way: a good research laboratory staffed by good people, skilled at sensing technical trends early; building relationships with OEM customers in growing industries; excellent links between scientists and engineers and through sales and marketing groups to customers.

For those who were laboring to carry the burdens of new products and process introduction against resistance so steady that they were now called "champions," the conference was a turning point. The conceptual marriage of TQM and innovation was far more than simple rhetoric. While it would be another seven years before quality programs and innovation worked together on the same track, at least they began running on parallel tracks. A

Five Stage Innovation Process

The Innovation Process represented by this diagram, the result of a year's work by the Innovation Task Force, was introduced at the Innovation Conference in 1986. The basic stage gate process, deliberately kept very simple, left room for discretion in the way it was implemented. The motif of the three exclamation points emphasized the critical importance of people as central to the process.

full decade would pass before the change in attitude inaugurated at the innovation conference would be reflected in significantly increased R&D budgets, but a new generation of innovators with the necessary integrative skills was in the making.

Three enduring achievements emerged from the innovation conference. First, the articulated formal process provided a framework for training programs at all levels of the company, becoming part of the structure for project reviews and the basis for hiring and deploying personnel. One requirement for attending the training was to be part of an established team sent by the team's supervisor. Starting with marketing and technology and later spreading to other areas of the company, attention began to be paid to fostering innovators and creating integrated technology plans. According to Charlie Craig, later division vice president of strategic planning and innovation management for Science and Technology. "The graphic we used said it all. The exclamation points represented people, the single most important ingredient."[45]

The long-term benefit of having the five-stage innovation process and training everyone in the company in its use was that, in an era when "time to market" became the key competitive issue for industry at large, Corning had already developed the routine practice of including all major parties in any new process or product innovation as early in the project as possible. Ted Kozlowski, one of Corning's key development managers for many successful products, commented that the relations between the people was key. "In [the innovation process] we will take three people from three different functions. How they behave in the process will be influenced by the style of their own managers. It's not so much running the process [that matters] as it is taking care of the people."[46]

Another consequence of the innovation effort was a rise in internal entrepreneurial behavior, yet another business mantra of the 1980s and 1990s, but one that had real consequences at Corning.[47] At Sullivan Park in particular, technologists were allowed to supplement an essentially flat R&D budget with sales of shelf technology, sales of services in which Corning had particular expertise, and, for a short period in the Reagan era, increased government contracting for technologies they wanted to pursue anyway.[48] Those who were willing to expend the effort were given the latitude to form small enterprises. One parlayed Corning's expertise in laboratory services into a million-dollar business annually. Another sold samples of optical fiber, by-products of the effort to get that process under control, to fill custom orders for users who were experimenting with fiber themselves. A third involved licensing an oxy fuel process, invented by a Corning engineer, to the Gallo Winery along with the engineering services to make it work. Some Corning operations had been reluctant to try this unproven process; but when Gallo turned it into a proven technique, Corning adopted the oxy fuel process all over the company to cut the cost and pollution of its furnace operations.

With these projects and others like them, research entrepreneurs had a chance to learn what earlier researchers in Corning had been required to know but later generations had lost—what it means to listen to customers.[49] The ability to augment the research budget by seeding small technology-based businesses helped researchers take control of their own destiny at Sullivan Park. It kept the heart of Corning's innovation establishment intact and committed through a very trying period when Corning's management committee was preoccupied by parallel experimentation with other activities. At the same time, the years of focusing on innovation helped convince parts of the Corning leadership that had been indifferent to or skeptical of Corning's prospects in this direction to take it more seriously. One of these was Corning's executive vice chairman in charge of the financial staffs, Van Campbell. "I knew we had made an impression," said MacAvoy, "when I heard Van tell the analysts that Corning was only superior at two things, joint ventures and innovation."

A third achievement of the Corning innovation task force was possibly the most unusual for companies at the time: the continuation of a practice of collective self-examination that previous Corning generations had also employed.[50] In reviving the practice of storytelling, the task force showed that reinvigorating shared memory was a powerful way to build the company's collective ingenuity. It tied the notion of best practices not solely to the dictates of outside experts or to the examples of other companies, but to the recovery of grounded experience in the company itself. It was in this manner that the practice later called flexible critical mass—the rapid concentration of technical effort on a high-priority project—was legitimized for a new generation beyond the few managers who had been most closely involved in earlier episodes of its use. Few technical people would agree to be drafted for projects well outside their own domain without understanding this as the way Corning had traditionally taken on successful projects of the highest importance, in some cases reviving or revitalizing the technical careers of employees at the same time.[51]

Few of the other practices Corning raised to consciousness were unique or even unusual to the company. What was unusual was the company's willingness to invest time in group reflection, to examine its own shortcomings in the context of its past achievements, and to hold the community accountable for them without assigning individual blame. Echoing the message symbolized by the cracked 200-inch mirror blank that stood in the Glass Museum, those who were preparing for leadership revived the old Corning idea that there was no shame in failure, but only in failing to persevere.

INNOVATIONS IN MANUFACTURING: UNION PARTNERSHIPS, 1986

In addition to a renewal of innovation at its R&D center—the place where creativity obviously matters—manufacturing processes too benefited from a return to Corning's roots. The quality effort was already doing much to

improve manufacturing discipline in all of Corning's plants when Roger
Ackerman, who took Bill Hudson's place on the management committee in
1985, launched a company-wide assessment of its manufacturing operations
in 1986. Globalization was beginning to pose new threats to many of Corning's formerly secure businesses. The critical questions that managers had
to address were not only how much cost could be squeezed out of existing
operations if things were done right the first time, but how each of Corning's businesses stacked up against competition on a worldwide basis. Corning, which had been forming significant equity joint ventures in several
emerging economies, was well positioned to see just how threatening the
competitive scene was becoming. Ackerman, who had himself served as
head of manufacturing and engineering (M&E) in 1982–1983, chose Norm
Garrity to serve on his staff as head of M&E and to form what was known
as the "Gang of Five" to benchmark all of Corning's operations against the
best in the world. Garrity said,

> We pulled together the engineering and manufacturing and people parts of
> the company and we started to look at ourselves. We did bench markings,
> substantial bench marking in all aspects. Everything from automation to
> logistics to people treatment... we studied everything from Toyota Kaisan
> approach to the best in every area.[52]

The Gang of Five sought out companies that were doing radically different things in manufacturing in the context of a union environment. Having
looked at all kinds of innovative systems, especially those that involved pay
for performance and self-management, the team opted to do a model plant
for the environmental products business in order to increase capacity for
Celcor substrates. Despite criticism from Corning's financial community
that favored simply adding the business to the already depreciated Erwin
plant, the team decided to restart Corning's idle plant in Blacksburg, Virginia, and turn it into a model facility.

Key to the Blacksburg experiment was a partnership with the American
Flint Glass Workers Union, spearheaded by its progressive union leadership.
Union leader George Parker agreed to cooperate with an entirely new
approach to manufacturing. He was won over not only by the prospect of

new jobs for the Virginia plant but also by the chance to evaluate firsthand what the role of a union could be in a model plant organized along principles very different from Corning's usual production operation. At the outset, Corning shared information about the cost structure of the plant with the union, based on what was known from the Erwin operation. It was agreed that either party, the company or the union, could pull out of the agreement at any time with six months notice. A second key factor was an agreed-upon set of values, a statement of why both the union and the company were there and what they stood for. This statement was intended to be renewed and refreshed every time a new cohort of workers was hired. Other factors were stripped-down management, with an unusually highly skilled workforce formed into self-supervising teams and paid on a variable compensation basis akin to salary, reporting directly to the senior plant management. Such high-performance teams, also being tried by other companies at the time,[53] had the power internally to discipline or even dismiss a team member if he or she did not perform. Garrity described this experiment as follows: "We had very strong screening and qualification for the jobs. We had many college graduates. We had two Ph.D. students that got

George Parker, head of the Flint Glass Workers of America from 1961–1989, who led the union to cooperate in its quality partnership with Corning.

turned down because they didn't pass all the tests. A lot of people failed the interactive skills because in a team environment you really have to have good interactive skills."[54]

Corning initially believed that Blacksburg would serve as the model for all its plants in the future. In fact it learned from the experiment that the Blacksburg model could not be readily transferred to other plants, especially not to existing plants with different cultures and certainly with very different workforces. Such a plant required not only a well-educated workforce but one in which everyone had good communications skills. To improve its internal communications to this extent, Corning would have to raise the general level of workforce education to at least a twelfth-grade reading level, not a realistic goal for most of its existing plants.

Nevertheless, important innovations in Corning's entire manufacturing system did come out of the Blacksburg experiment. One was the adoption of goal sharing for hourly workers. Goal sharing, based on eight variables, had been used successfully as a way of determining management compensation. Blacksburg tried it with its nonmanagement workforce with successful results, and decided to extend goal sharing to the two-thirds of all Corning employees who were not management. Beginning in 1990, employee representatives from each plant got together with its management to set goals on a plant-by-plant basis. Goals could never be set lower than the ones for the previous year, but only 25 percent of the goals had to be company wide.

The very existence of Blacksburg challenged things as they were, encouraging other plants to push for their own individual ways of achieving outstanding results based on their own peculiar needs. Martinsburg, a consumer plant located in West Virginia, for instance, perfected swing glass, first discovered at Sullivan Park and revived in a project called Tavis, to make Corning Ware and Visions from one tank melt. Other improvements involved eliminating layers of management that carried significant unnecessary costs. The difference between plants like Blacksburg or a similar experimental fiber plant the company built later in Charleston, South Carolina, and older Corning plants was that people in the new plants took greater personal responsibility for their work—not only how well they did it but how well it was organized. As a result of these efforts, both Corning's ability and its reputation for quality manufacturing became so strong that it was selected as the only non-Japanese company to participate in a partnership with Japan's huge telecommunications concern, NTT, when it turned to developing the standards and the manufacturing process for its class 3 fiber.

By the early 1990s Corning had demonstrated, by means of its effective adoption of quality and innovation as complementary disciplines, that a future as a high-tech company was a strategic option. Jamie Houghton's address to the Industrial Research Institute in 1993, on the tenth anniversary of his earlier address to that body, was a sign that this was so. Speaking of the obligations of general management leadership in high-tech product development and marketing, he argued that Corning had significantly improved the effectiveness of its R&D by applying TQM principles to innovation. Innovation, he concluded, was the glue that bound all functions into a cohesive team of inventors, producers, and innovators. At Corning this philosophy was most clearly demonstrated in Corning's optical waveguide business, which was on its way to winning in 1995 the prestigious Malcolm Baldrige award for its outstanding record of serving customers out of its plant in Wilmington, North Carolina.

It is impossible to imagine that Corning could have remade itself into one of the major suppliers of optical fiber to a rapidly expanding telecommunications market without the combination of disciplines that Houghton described. The story of how the fiber business grew from a long-term wager made by top management and the R&D community in the 1970s to a multibillion dollar player on a global stage in the 1990s has to be understood against that backdrop.

CASE IN POINT: MAKING A BUSINESS OF OPTICAL WAVEGUIDES

In the early 1980s things finally started going Corning's way in the fiber-optics business. After years of investment in technology, litigation, and plant operations, all the preparation suddenly began to pay off, in ways and in volumes no one had anticipated. Emboldened by the capitulation of ITT on the eve of its court case in 1981 (see chapter 8), Corning willingly plunged into head-on international competition in the sort of venture that it would have shunned in the early 1970s. Jamie Houghton and Tom MacAvoy were ready to keep investing in this enormous gamble not only because Corning's intellectual property position gave it the sort of strategic protection that its television business had lacked but also because of its much improved project management discipline and the serious effect its total quality approach had on its ability to compete.

Establishing a commanding intellectual property position was only the first of three monumental challenges that Corning had to surmount before fiber optics could become its dominant business in the 1990s. As discussed in previous chapters, Corning had had to meet the other two—creating a superior product and process technology, and proving Corning's commercial credibility as an upstart supplier in a largely regulated industry—even as it was struggling to navigate the turmoil of the 1970s.[55] Although the company began the 1980s in a strong position strategically and with promising technical capabilities, it had a very short order book.

Although Corning had prepared itself to supply the multimode ("graded index") fiber that most telecommunications companies were specifying, following the standards set by AT&T in the United States, it was having trouble breaking into the market in any significant way. When AT&T launched its northeast corridor project in 1980,[56] Corning even filed a complaint with the FCC, charging that AT&T was deliberately limiting competition. AT&T went through the motions of considering competing fiber from other suppliers, but in the end it disqualified competing suppliers in favor of its own Western Electric, even though Western's bid was higher than Corning's by a significant margin.[57] As luck would have it, being shut out from the northeast corridor project was a lucky break for Corning, for it avoided being tied up in supplying large quantities of the second-generation (multimode) fiber when demand suddenly materialized for even larger quantities of the third-generation (single-mode) fiber. Experts estimated that the market for optical fiber cable in 1982 would exceed $1 billion by the end of the decade. Before long that estimate would prove to be wildly conservative.

In 1982 AT&T was ordered by a federal court to divest its manufacturing and research arms from its long-distance operations and in 1984 to spin off its regional operations into independent companies, the so-called Baby Bells. This was the opportunity that MCI, the upstart long-distance competitor to AT&T, had been waiting for, and it proved to be Corning's as well. MCI decided to build its own national telephone network around a fiber-optic spine, and it was not about to source its fibers from AT&T's in-house supplier, Western Electric. Moreover, contacts with the British post office had convinced it of the superiority of single-mode fiber. MCI approached Corning with a $90 million order for approximately 150,000 kilometers of single-mode fiber. Not only had Corning never produced anything like this volume of any kind of fiber, it had never produced single-mode fiber anywhere but in the laboratory. And MCI drove a hard bargain: it required a decreasing price structure beginning at the already low fee of $1 per meter and dropping from there.

Both Al Dawson from the Corning cabling venture with Siemens, Siecor, and Dave Duke of Corning's fiber operation were at the meeting with MCI when the offer—and its requirements—were presented. Both men well knew that although Corning was working on its third generation of multimode fiber, it had never actually produced single mode.[58] The two executives communicated with each other by passing scraps of paper back and forth. The first note from Dawson to Duke read, "Dave, can we make this stuff?"

The scribbled reply: "I think so. Can you make the cable?"

Back went the first scrap: "I think so."[59]

To supply MCI's cable, it was necessary for Corning to improve its draw speed from the two to three meters per second currently run to ten meters per second; this was accomplished within a year of starting the project. These improvements were achieved in the context of erecting the Marathon Tower, the first fiber draw tower Corning built. Improvements in the polymer coatings that protected the fiber from abrasion proved essential to increase draw speeds. Coatings for the fiber, which were applied as the fiber was drawn, initially had to be engineered for maximum protection and for quick curing as they were applied in the process of drawing, as well as to be easy to remove mechanically when customers wanted to cut and splice them. Eventually coatings would be custom engineered for many different applications and purposes.

Following the breakthrough with MCI, an even more unforeseen opportunity arose when the newly liberated Baby Bells realized they now had an alternative supplier to Western Electric. MCI had been following a high-tech differentiation strategy anyway and would almost certainly have come to optical fiber before long. The Baby Bells, on the other hand, had been liberated by Judge Green's key court order to make independent supplier choices for the first time, and their requirements dwarfed MCI's. Moreover, once MCI had broken the ice, other companies like MCI's competitor Sprint lost no time in following suit. Northern Telecom even switched from multimode to single mode in midstream, completing its project to wire Saskatchewan with third-generation fiber. AT&T dropped its own standard to switch to single-mode for its national backbone installations. Corning's original appropriation to purchase Superior Cable suddenly seemed inconsequential when compared to the enormous opportunity it had helped to create.[60] "Talk about long-range planning being what we're having for lunch," said Al Dawson.[61]

Siecor Finds the Cutting Edge

Siecor now had the opportunity of a lifetime, and it was up to Dawson and Wakeman, who had recently joined him to run Siecor's manufacturing operations, to see that the venture did not botch it. Siecor had some real advantages over the rest of the domestic industry because it had Siemens's patented process for assembling cable as well as the superior expertise of some of Siemens's best people, who were helping to get the process going in North Carolina. But achieving a low-cost position in fiber-optic cable would still be a challenge. Wakeman decided that what the venture needed was a quality program like Corning's. He convinced Dawson and the rest of the Siecor management to learn from Corning's effort already under way by enrolling in Corning's Quality Institute. The method caught on quickly. As a new organization, Siecor had few dysfunctional habits to overcome, and the most powerful of the new practices proved to be giving responsibility to the people on the plant floor. According to Siecor's Joe Hicks, one of the few holdovers from Superior Cable and later head of Siecor,

> When [Dawson] got down here he said, "The only people we are going to hire into this company, with rare exceptions, are going to be people coming right out of school. They've finished their degree. They're ready to go to

work." By and large, we have adhered to that over the years, and it has really paid dividends. If you look at the talent pool... around Siecor in terms of experts in their own areas and potential future general management talent, I'd put us up against anybody. One of the reasons is these people came into this business with no bad habits and got a chance to learn the business and grow up and create.[62]

Although the MCI order and the subsequent rush of Baby Bell business proved to be the turning point, there were still some anxious moments for the whole waveguide business. In 1986 several foreign cable makers entered the field and existing suppliers added capacity, causing worldwide capacity to increase to the point that existing suppliers had a sudden leveling off in sales. There was even concern that the market might be saturated, and in 1987 *Financial World* charged Corning with fumbling fiber optics in the same way it had fumbled television, ending up competing in a commodity market that had far too much worldwide capacity.[63] Siecor's market share dropped from 58 to 29 percent overnight. But this was where Corning's and Siecor's intensive efforts to adopt quality principles and stay at the leading edge of the technology both in process and product improvement could and did pay off. As Hicks recalled,

> That's the year we found out that quality was really worth something because we had been, since 1983, just like Corning, training people on the quality processes and thinking that way and working that way. But really, there is nothing that focuses your mind like hearing that you may hang at dawn, and that's exactly what happened to us there toward the end of 1986, early 1987. . . . We had to go to a different way of thinking and that is to understand that the cable industry, whether it's copper cable, fiberoptic cable or whatever, is a low margin, very volume-dependent business.[64]

The results of emphasizing quality also showed up in a steady reduction in the time it took the Siecor plant in Hickory, North Carolina, to fill an order. Almost every order was unique: in 1980 it took Siecor six months from receipt of order until the cable was delivered. Over the next decade that lag would be steadily whittled down until rush orders of forty-eight hours were not uncommon, and some orders could be filled in a day. All transfers of information back and forth between plant and office were eliminated until the point where the plant could carry the whole responsibility. Siecor's market share gradually climbed back to around 43 percent, and by the mid-1990s its sales exceeded $1.2 billion, of which about a billion came from cable.

By 1988 Corning was supplying fiber around the world, most notably to Third World countries like Brazil, India, Argentina, Mexico, Indonesia, and Thailand that were eager to use fiber-optic systems as a way of leapfrogging generations of telecommunications systems.[65] Even though they did not serve the same markets, Corning, Siemens, Siecor Corporation, and Siecor GmbH had the important advantage of working together on a steady stream of innovations in the fiber-optic cable business. In 1990 Japan's NTT inaugurated a contest to develop the next generation of fiber-optic cables—their track 3 development process—to be used in a new line of optical cables designed to take fiber to the home, each cable to contain up to 4000 fibers.[66] Corning, Siemens, and Siecor elected to participate. To quote Corning's Gitimoy Kar in new business development for telecommunications products.

> If we wanted to play in that market in any significant way, we would have to participate in this. There was no question. Frankly, I'm not so sure that the process wasn't designed maybe to keep us out. Nobody at Corning or Siemens believed we could win. I mean, it was, "Well, the Japanese are going to find some way to keep us out but if we don't try, we are surely going to be out." So we decided to bid for it. I was part of a team that consisted of folks from Siecor, Corning and Siemens and we worked hard to put together a proposal. Lo and behold, we not only got a proposal done on time, but we won and we beat out several major entrants including AT&T.[67]

The program went on for five years. By then Japan had delayed its fiber to the home initiative and wasn't buying much 4000 fiber cable. But, as a consequence of the partnership, and also as a consequence of significant pressure on Japan from the U.S. government, Japan did buy major lots of 1000 fiber cable from Siecor, more than most other customers were interested in buying.

Although Corning was able to supply such needs effectively it was clear that just supplying fiber and cable would not be enough. As its customers' uses and goals for optical systems became more sophisticated, Corning needed to have a hand in conceiving, designing and developing the systems of which they were part.

The New Modus Operandi

In the mid-1980s it became clear that if the knowledge base at Sullivan Park were not replenished, Corning and Siecor alike might falter. Corning's earliest patents were beginning to run out. At that point Dave Duke and Skip Deneka, who had been the first chief engineer at Corning's fiber facility in Wilmington, left the waveguide division and returned to Sullivan Park to begin the kind of rebalancing of R&D that had also taken place in the years after color television. Deneka first became technology director for fiber and then director of new business development. From that position he expanded the group of waveguide technologists from thirty to ninety people to get them into position to develop new technologies. He also upgraded the research equipment, which at that point was over nine years old and had been sorely neglected in favor of production equipment. Gitimoy Kar, who was then responsible for draw and coating development remembers Deneka posing an unthinkably challenging objective of 50 meters-per-second when the production drawing speed was less than 5 meters-per-second. In a few years the team demonstrated the feasibility of 30 meters-per-second in development, a draw rate that would not be equaled in commercial operations for ten years. During this period technologists developed the seventh, eighth, and ninth generations of waveguide product and process that were destined for the planned "Tower Five" expansion at Wilmington, nearly a decade down the road.

Deneka had long believed in not only preparing for, but pushing to bring about, rapid generational shifts in businesses. In 1987, he became the director of new business development in the Telecommunication Products Division where he fostered Corning work on new fiber and cable designs optical amplifier, couplers and connectors. Gitimoy Kar was closely involved in this work also: "In 1988 when Skip asked me to work for him in new business development and explained his vision of Optical Wiring System (OWS), I thought he was way ahead of our time in his thinking. So I signed up. In those days, we were working on single channel optical amplifiers for example. Now, we are making 40 channels and trying to make 80 channel amplifiers."[68]

Out of the work on couplers and connectors, much of the research for which was conducted at Corning's Avon laboratory, came a new business supplying planar couplers to telecommunications companies. This business did indeed turn out to be ahead of its time. The plant built in Melun, France, was shut down after a very short time, but the French laboratory "boxed" its development work and set it aside, its research management convinced that the time of photonics would come round again.

Meanwhile, Dave Duke had replaced Tom MacAvoy as vice chairman, in 1986, directing all of Corning's efforts in research and development and selecting a chemist, Gerry Meiling, as director, then vice president, of research. Waveguide's urgent needs for constant increments in capacity and for constant investment in supporting research had made it very evident to Corning's management committee that further hard choices had to be made. By the time Duke returned to Sullivan Park, biomedical research was gone, and much of the rest of the research effort was concentrated on extensions and renewals, first for optical fiber and then for other core businesses like ceramics for environmental products.

Another adjustment that eventually had to be made was in Corning's relationship with Siecor. Siecor had been founded according to the old non-controlling fifty-fifty formula. But this meant treating Siecor like just another customer, which according to Siecor's management came to feel like being treated worse than others in order to be kept at arm's length. Competitors, such as the powerful AT&T, had the benefits of backward integration into fiber making, and before long Corning would arrange to acquire from Siemens the controlling interest in Siecor Corporation, making it a Corning subsidiary rather than a simple equity investment. Some at Siecor disliked the loss of freedom this involved, but the closer relationship was viewed as essential to smooth the path of new product development between the two companies.

Dave Duke, Skip Deneka, and those working with them had success-fully applied the learning from their experience with Celcor to the optical fiber business in several ways. The most critical lesson was the importance of working well into the future: constant and aggressive reinvention was needed well in anticipation of anything the competition could be expected to have in mind. Under their leadership the optical fiber business and the R&D that supported it were becoming a self-renewing resource, a model for sustainable innovation that, once grasped, could be applied to all of Corning's technology-based businesses. The logic was inescapable that rein-vention and renewal could not be occasional or unusual events. They had to be standard practice, a way of life, for Corning.

Beyond Fiber

Once the management committee conceived of optical fibers as a renewable platform, it was a natural jump to thinking about other existing core materi-als and processes in much the same way. Another important piece of the puzzle was continuing to discover new materials that had the wide range of applications that ceramics or silicone had offered Corning in earlier genera-tions. This was the "big megilla" Jamie Houghton was hoping to sponsor, and for a while it looked as though it might just have been discovered.

Placor, a light, rugged material on the boundary between glass and poly-mers, was invented in the laboratories in the 1980s. It appeared to offer degrees of impact and fire resistance that would put fiberglass to shame. The new material looked appropriate for applications in aerospace, auto-motive, lighting, and electronic components, and a pilot plant was con-structed in 1992. Although the material was widely publicized throughout all of the target industries, it had no takers.

Possibly ahead of its time, it was a disappointment to those who had hoped to find the next silicone as a follow-on to fiber optics. The question raised by this apparently fruitless search for another big megilla was whether the ability to be self-sustaining in cyclical innovation, so effective for existing products like Celcor and fiber that were on a fast track, extended to finding altogether new products, or whether very different capabilities were needed. One Corning answer was to find ways to incorporate major new sources of ideas from other parts of the world, in particular, access to fresh sources of absolutely world-class research.

Corning's international presence had been growing significantly ever since the 1960s, and in the late 1980s overseas business accounted for half its revenues. By the early 1990s Corning's structure had come to be known by insiders and outsiders alike as a good example of a global network, a new extended organizational form that closely resembled the web of associations Corning had developed before World War II. This time, however, it was far more international in character, and more technologically ambitious. Joined to this network were organizations of several different types: Corning joint ventures and joint venture partners, subsidiaries, and Corning laboratories (domestic and foreign). All were engaged in the common process of leveraging Corning's technologies.

Joint ventures had traditionally offered a chance to leverage technology for market access and profit in the way Corning had first contrived to use its "associations." But joint ventures had changed for Corning and the nature of their contribution had expanded. Whereas at one time joint ventures were mainly ways of providing Corning with market access for its technologies and sometimes process know-how, as with Owens-Corning and Dow-Corning, now they could also be about gaining complementary technologies. They could be an important way of incorporating Corning technologies into new products for new markets, as with Siecor, or they could be crucial to regaining a competitive foothold in old markets, as with Corning Asahi Video.

By 1992 Corning had seventeen international subsidiaries and thirteen associated companies outside the United States, and they were finding opportunities to do developmental work with many of them. In the same way that Corning had been able to share the cost of the class 3 fiber development with other companies in its network, it looked for other opportunities to shorten the time and decrease the expense of new products in several areas.

Meanwhile, to gain access to the best untapped scientific brainpower available, Corning continued to develop its network of international laboratories. This also allowed the company to take advantage of the smaller, more informal institutional format that it would be hard for Corning to recover at Sullivan Park. In 1992 Corning entered into a relationship with two research institutes in St. Petersburg, Russia, where brilliant scientists who were in some instances world leaders in the theoretical underpinnings of optics and photonics had lost their support after the demise of the Soviet Union. In the latter part of the 1980s Corning's various international laboratories began once again to work together rather than respond solely to the needs of their local operations. Cooperative work could take advantage of special pockets of expertise in each laboratory, as well as their different characters (primarily research oriented, as in Russia, or development oriented, as in Japan).

Outsiders not privy to this technology sharing often asked how Corning's global network differed from a holding company. Considering that major hunks of the company's investment and management attention were still consumed by the consumer and medical testing businesses in the early 1990s, it was a fair question. Corning acknowledged that effective joint ventures were not free; they required relationship building and relationship maintenance at high levels of the organization. And the nature of some joint ventures was changing. As the telecommunications market went global, questions would increasingly be raised about the Siecor alliance, for instance. Would the German Siecor, which produced its own fiber, and the U.S. Siecor, which did not, continue into unavoidable competition? The alliance with Siemens had worked exceedingly well while markets were mainly national in scope, but as that giant telecommunications firm integrated backward into making its own fiber, both Siecors had to restructure to compete.

After Roger Ackerman became chief operating officer in 1991, the answer to the holding company question gradually shifted from a mainly organizational one based on closely maintained relationships between independent entities to one that implied increasing amounts of shared activity. "If we can do it alone we will," was still the standard reply to outsider queries, but Corning was finding ways to gain far more than just income from its network relationships. Corning Asahi Video, for instance, was a chance to make up for the ground that had been lost when Corning's customer base in television had eroded so much that it had stopped investing in television-related technology. The Asahi venture (formed in 1989) brought Corning back into the game with large-screen video. Corning's State College plant, its chief contribution to that partnership, was as good a plant in automation terms as anything Asahi could have accomplished on its own. Likewise, the Samsung Corning joint venture, which Corning had entered into in the 1970s largely to gain revenues for its technology from the giant Korean electronics firm, gave Corning an entree to Asian television and computer markets after most of that global market had left U.S. shores.

Ackerman's new answer to the holding company question, therefore, was not just a matter of investment or payments for technology. Instead, he viewed the desired feature of all the key nodes on the Corning global network as a combination of like values and shared technology. Taken to its logical conclusions, this philosophy suggested a rethinking of the nature of major parts of Corning's business—especially the two that did not match up to these key elements, which were the consumer business and Corning's complex of medical services, now known as Corning Laboratory Services, Inc. (CLSI). The consumer business would take several years of repositioning before it could be sold to the right kind of buyer. CLSI was a more complicated story.

A SECOND CASE IN POINT:
WHY METPATH WAS NOT THE RIGHT PATH, 1986–1995

The medical laboratory business had emerged as a highly profitable subsidiary in the late 1980s. By 1986 MetPath's sales had grown to over a quarter of a billion dollars and its profits had become as important to Corning as any other line of business. Although Roger Ackerman's work had been crucial in stabilizing and streamlining the company, the real boost came as a result of a change in Medicare billing policy. Soon after Ackerman left, the government started paying labs like those run by MetPath directly, rather than via the doctor ordering the test. This elimination of the middleman meant higher fees for the labs and lower costs for Medicare, and "the result," in MetPath chairman Marty Gibson's words, "was just a great run, a great eight years." This source of profit was so important to Corning that in 1988 Gibson argued successfully to have "glass" dropped from the company name, pointing out that a medical company, or "life sciences" as it was coming to be called, had no business being referred to as a glassworks. From then on Corning Glass Works was Corning Incorporated.

Using stock transactions, Corning made over twenty acquisitions to build MetPath into the largest medical testing organization in the world. Under Marty Gibson's leadership, it sought to gain as big a share of this highly profitable pie as rapidly as possible. MetPath was organized into regional laboratories large enough to have economies of scale but local enough to provide rapid turnaround on results. In 1987 and 1990 it acquired two clinical research subsidiaries, Hazelton and Besselaar, to provide clinical research for pharmaceutical companies, and in 1993 it absorbed Damon Corporation to add to its laboratory testing capacity. At that point CLSI accounted for $1.5 billion of sales, a third of Corning's revenues, but the profit picture was already shifting.

Corning's urgency in acquiring and growing MetPath had reflected a sense of the narrow window of opportunity involved in consolidating such an operation. However, the speed with which the company moved meant that it didn't conduct the kind of due diligence in appraising the acquisitions that it would certainly have exercised if these companies had been venture partners. Moreover, the market could not stay so profitable forever. Although changes in Medicare billing in the early 1990s played a role in cutting MetPath's profits, the rise of health maintenance organizations (HMO) was the real culprit. As HMOs began buying testing services in bulk and as their membership grew, so too did their bargaining power. Gibson recalled,

It was the scariest thing I ever saw. We're in New York State on a given test, patient bill $100. That same patient in Baltimore where we're capitated [i.e., working on a per-head basis for HMOs], $1.20. I mean we're not talking from $100 to $80. It's $100 to $1.00. . . . As that managed care grew, our margins just went.[69]

At its peak, MetPath was making 25 percent or more operating margin on sales, and this on over a billion dollars in sales. The HMOs forced that figure down to well under 10 percent. "It went from a great business to a very garden-variety mediocre kind of business," Gibson acknowledged.[70] Moreover it was not Corning's kind of business: the service business required Corning to hire different kinds of people, outsiders who knew the business but were not part of the Corning community. No longer viewed as a growth opportunity for Corning managers and now completely divorced from Corning's technology streams, MetPath became simply an investment.[71]

Gibson was one of the chief proponents of the view that Corning should be a loose holding company; this was a venture-capital conception rather than a value-added conception, and Metpath consequently provided no feedback of useful knowledge to the rest of the company. The medical business was unpopular in other parts of Corning, whose managers noted how practices that were required of most of the company were ignored in the medical division. With the profit gone, the business lost its luster completely. When Roger Ackerman was named COO, putting Gibson out of the running for the top spot, the medical business became an independent subsidiary, its various recent acquisitions grouped into clinical laboratory services Corning Life Sciences, Inc. (CLSI). The decision to spin off the business altogether would have been the logical consequence of Ackerman's redefinition of Corning's core nexus of technology and values, but it was hastened by a Medicare billing scandal that broke in 1993, engulfing MetPath along with its entire industry. It was a costly development for Corning both in money and in reputation. Finding itself under threat of criminal indictment ran counter to Corning's culture and values, for any Corning business. With the laboratory business causing dissension in the management group and affecting morale, the company soon divested the business altogether.[72]

CORNING COMPETES, 1995–1996

Although Corning had achieved a new and improved performance plateau by the early 1990s, it was not impervious to trouble in so large a chunk as CLSI. In 1993, when the company had an off year financially and took a hit in its stock price, top managers decided to deal with the crisis by attempting a Corning version of the restructuring in vogue at the time called "reengineering."[73] But as Jamie Houghton noted, "We didn't call it reengineering. We hadn't engineered the company to start with; why should we reengineer it? We called it Corning Competes, because that was what we needed to be able to do better.[74] In what reminded many people of the first quality push a decade before, the idea was to identify and rethink the company's most critical processes. New forms of information technology offered major productivity gains, but only to those who figured out how to use them strategically. Thus the expected improvement would come in rethinking the way things were done and redeploying people accordingly, instead of laying people off. But massive layoffs had accompanied reengineering at companies across the country, and this prospect caused apprehension at Corning as well.[75] For a company that placed so much emphasis on its people there was an obvious risk of undercutting morale.

The job of leading this effort fell to Roger Ackerman. With the help again of outside consultants, the management group identified the following as its four most important processes: business corporate roles definition, innovation, manufacturing, and purchasing. The name Corning Competes was intended to emphasize its need to be the lowest-cost manufacturer of fiber optics and related technologies even if it could maintain a position of technology leadership. The company's most promising managers were involved in the program teams that resulted.

Because the intent of Corning Competes was primarily to redeploy personnel at the managerial level, the company did not discuss the impending effort with the union. But from the union's point of view, this violated the spirit of the partnership. When their protests highlighted the need for much better communication, Ackerman undertook this himself:

> At that time everybody was reengineering, taking out 10–15,000 people. We never did that. We said 'This is aimed at reducing our cost by taking people from non-value added work. It may change your job by putting you on more value-added things.' That's really what we were doing, and we were helped by the fact that there was growth going on. We did have some reduction (of workforce) but it was done very carefully. We took out a total of

about 700–800 people, salaried employees. But at the same time we also
spent a fair amount of time finding areas for new growth.[76]

The program was judged a success along the usual dimensions. Manufacturing costs were again significantly reduced. The company reduced its
overall costs by $300 million and improved its return on equity by over 3 per-
centage points, an improvement in earnings that continued into 1996. But
more important, the program fueled Corning's efforts to link its technology
base with the company strategy far more carefully than it had been since
the moves to decentralize the company a decade earlier.

Out of Corning Competes emerged not just a redefinition of Corning's
major processes in the four focal areas but some very significant changes in
the way the company did business. One of these was a refinement of the
innovation process: this shifted from a mechanism that served to integrate,
but was aimed at efficient use of technical resources, to a philosophy that
enforced a long-term competitive perspective for all business units. Part of
the shift was to add a requirement for "road mapping," identifying the succession of technical steps that were needed to reach the goals for each business, as well as the money and people needed to get there.

Deep Dive Sessions

Another significant change in the way Corning did business in the 1990s was
the use of intensive off-site strategic planning sessions known as "deep
dives." These were held concurrently at the individual business level to
examine all avenues to significant growth and to allocate resources—not
only the customary financial investment but also the required human and
technical resources. Held every twelve to eighteen months, deep dives kept
the company focused on achieving over 12 percent earnings growth per year
in its portfolio. The point was to integrate R&D into the company in a way
that it had not been integrated since the 1960s, when Amo Houghton and
Bill Armistead met regularly. Not only were each business's R&D spending
plans reviewed and defended in deep dive sessions; for the first time ever,
R&D undertook its own review of the company's entire R&D strategy.

While there were those who grumbled at what they saw as yet another reorganization, Corning Competes laid the groundwork for a new proactive era for Corning technology. For one thing, the restructuring of the technical organization prepared the way for a new generation of management. Dave Duke vice chairman and vice president of research Gerry Meiling, as well as many others who had joined the company in the 1960s, were at the point of retirement. They retired at or before April 1996, when Jamie Houghton also stepped down. When Ackerman moved into the chairman's slot in 1996, he was replaced by two presidents who split Corning's technology-based businesses between them: Norm Garrity, president of Corning Technologies, which included environmental products, specialty materials like ceramics, and specialty polymers and surfaces, and John Loose, president of Corning Communications, which included the fiber business and an emergent opportunity in photonics.

Duke was succeeded as chief technology officer by the far-sighted Skip Deneka, who also became senior vice president. Deneka had long believed in not only preparing for but pushing to bring about rapid generational shifts in businesses. For example, he had been fostering Corning work on photonics—optical electronic components like amplifiers, gain modules, and connectors—for nearly a decade.

Now Deneka would get the opportunity to keep pressing forward with photonics, as well as other new business ideas that he had fostered earlier in his career. Given the large number of retirements that occurred at the time of Corning Competes, it would be up to him to rebuild the research staff at Sullivan Park. In addition, he would have a bigger budget than any of his predecessors, since Ackerman had committed to increasing Corning's research spending from 5 percent to more than 8 percent of sales on a much increased revenue base.

Rather than merely try to respond rapidly to technological trends and customer-articulated needs, Corning was preparing to "turn up the clock speed" for its customers and against its competitors. The objective, once again, was not just to be first to market but to create new businesses and to show customers what might be possible using its new technologies. The company was buoyed in this effort by a new slogan, Growing Corning, which represented aggressive financial goals that could only be achieved by pursuing new high-margin business.

"Growing Corning"

Deneka and his managers were in the middle of replacement hiring when a stategic overview in the telecommunications business resulted in the dramatic shift for Sullivan Park that they had been hoping for. Over dinner after a full day of discussion and debate about telecommunications strategies in the spring of 1997, managers who had just been through the planning session concluded that Corning should invest heavily in a full-scale effort to manufacture photonics components as part of a plan to offer complete optical subsystems. The first move was to put together, effective immediately, a thirty-person core group of developers within Sullivan Park to get the program started and to serve as the nucleus for what would likely grow to three hundred technical staff members dedicated to photonics. With plans afoot to sell the Corning consumer business, as soon as the right arrangement could be made to ensure continuation of the product lines and manufacturing in Corning, New York, many of the people who had spent careers at Corning's Pressware plant producing Corelle were hired to staff the new photonics manufacturing facility.

The old slogan, "Corning Means Research in Glass," was obviously not applicable to this new Corning with its much richer and wider knowledge base, one that embraced ceramics, polymers, and other specialty materials. But in a return to the spirit of that old slogan, Corning was once again actively staking out a high-tech future for itself.

"TECHNOLOGISTS TOGETHER": REMAINING KNOWLEDGE-DRIVEN

It was in the experience of turning waveguides into a huge business that the company discovered clues to its central identity question. Roger Ackerman later recognized this as a key motivational question when he pointed to the potent combination of technology and values as the principal characteristics of a participant on the Corning network. The values to which he referred were the same ones that had motivated a researcher like Harrison Hood when he spoke of being "technologists together" in the 1920s and 1930s. Fifty years later the road to Corning's refound identity was more treacherous. One of its most distinctive traditions, the notion of "patient money," had been questioned and nearly abandoned. Impatient money had led to a rushed marriage with MetPath. Whether Corning's core identity would have long survived further such forays as one of the "world's largest venture capital firms" was anybody's guess. Other elements of the company's identity, as sacred as glass if not as clearly recognized, had also been called into question. Yet, put to the test, Corning's most enduring values proved to be too deeply ingrained to be forgotten, though they could sometimes be ignored.

The marriage of innovation and total quality achieved two important results for Corning. Once matured, these linked disciplines supported the company's regained way of working: relying far less on control than on self-motivated and adaptive behavior. The result was a renaissance in innovative activity in which the entire company—not just Sullivan Park or its research counterparts around the world—could participate, and in which the harvesting of Corning's collective ingenuity became routine. Planar waveguides and photonics, products that required innovation from the factory floor up, showed as clearly as could be that this activity, once so compromised that it had nearly been discarded, was now central to the company's progress.

EPILOGUE

We dedicate this tower today to the tens of thousands of Corning employees active and retired who have contributed to creating the Corning Incorporated of today. All of us working here accept the challenge to carry on the tradition of innovation that has made this company great. I promise you this: like our predecessors in 1896 we will not wait to see what the new century brings—we will do all we can to help shape it.

ROGER ACKERMAN
DEDICATION OF THE LITTLE JOE TOWER, 14 JULY 1999

O N   A   H O T July afternoon in 1999, Roger Ackerman, current chairman of Corning Incorporated joined his predecessor, Jamie Houghton, the mayor of Corning, and a small group of other dignitaries from the company and town to dedicate the Little Joe Tower, a 187-foot-high remnant of Corning's former Main Plant. Still the tallest structure in the city, the tower bore the image of a glassblower in silhouette that had been the logo of Corning when it was still Corning Glass Works.[1] It had been preserved for renovation when the rest of Corning's original plant was dismantled in 1989 to make room for its new headquarters building. It was, said Ackerman, not just a well-loved landmark for the city of Corning but also a potent symbol of the company's early inventiveness. It had originally housed tubing machinery used in the updraw process that Arthur A. Houghton had invented in 1896 with the help of machine designer Charles Githler, one of the company's earliest patented processes.[2]

This symbolic public renewal of the company's commitment to innovation was no mere exercise in nostalgia. The previous few years had seen

Corning place some of its most important bets ever: stripping down to its core technology businesses,[3] doubling the size of Sullivan Park, locating a new photonics plant in the Corning area, and increasing the R&D budget to well over 8 percent of sales. Over the next few months, Corning's quarterly financial results would offer evidence that this commitment was paying off. None of these bets had been risk-free or easy to execute. The free fall of fiber prices during the Southeast Asian financial crisis in 1997 and 1998 in particular had threatened the company's entire growth strategy before the market made a timely recovery.

The technical community had to transform and perform at the same time. Sullivan Park, now only one part of a growing global network of research laboratories, contained more than 60 percent new personnel, some shifted in from other parts of Corning but most newly hired from around the world. The Fontainebleau research center in France had likewise doubled in size. The company's new research center in St. Petersburg, opened in 1998, was the first independent laboratory in Russia to be created by a Western company. It was composed of personnel from two different Russian research centers and employed thirty leading scientists in the fields of optics and photonics.

Assimilating all of these new technical personnel into Corning's core culture, while guarding their freedom to create in their own way, remained an ongoing challenge. The Russian research center in particular, because of unreliable telecommunications with Eastern Europe, had yet to be directly connected to Corning's other laboratories in the way those in Japan (Shizuoka), Massachusetts, New Jersey, and California were. Still, it was possible to foresee a time when all of the laboratories would be connected in real time, sharing urgent projects in a worldwide application of "flexible critical mass."

An even greater challenge lay in consolidating a string of new business acquisitions into the larger Corning organization, a process that was expected to double the company's size between 1998 and 2000. Corning had taken the decisive step of moving beyond optical components to become a supplier of optical subsystems, combining its own proprietary developments in this area with components and intellectual property from a growing list of other companies. To compete with rivals like Lucent Technology (also a major customer), the company could not wait to invent or develop in-house all the elements it needed. By the end of 1999 it had acquired, among others, Oak Industries (a maker of pump lasers) and the Optical Polymer Group of Honeywell, previously of Allied Signal. A key acquisition at this time was British Telecom's Photonics Technology Research Center in Suffolk, England. Skip Deneka described this addition to Corning's portfolio of new businesses as a chance to commercialize new photonics products, as well as a chance to strengthen Corning's next generation research on photonic components and network devices through a research partnership with British Telecom.

A further area of heightened activity for Corning was in its core fiber-optics and cable businesses. Siecor Inc.'s leaders had been warning for years that optical fiber as such, and even most forms of fiber-optic cable, were becoming commodity products. But Corning had introduced a next-generation fiber technology trademarked LEAF (large effective area fiber) to "turn up the clock speed" in this marketplace. LEAF, which was developed by a team of some seventy-five engineers working intensively over a six-month period beginning in September 1997, had already received numerous technical awards. Customers had responded by choosing LEAF for projects like the two-ring 5,400-kilometer European network, a 2 million kilometer U.S. nationwide network, undersea networks, and others in South America and Asia. In the third quarter of 1999 demand for the new fiber had so outstripped capacity that Corning had had to purchase fiber from other suppliers in order to fill its orders.

Corning rushed a new fiber plant in North Carolina into production, but the capacity problem also prompted management to close a deal that had been under discussion for some time: the purchase of its joint venture partner Siemens's portions of Siecor, Inc. and Siecor GMBH along with Siemens's other hardware and equipment interests in fiber-optics technology. This $1.4 billion transaction had the added benefit of resolving the issues that had been developing with Siecor, Inc. as it struggled to compete in a telecommunications industry that was rapidly consolidating on a global basis. As part of the new arrangement the current president and CEO of Siecor, Inc., Sandy Lyons, was named to lead Corning's worldwide cable, hardware, and equipment businesses. These included not only Siecor and the Siemens businesses but also Corning Cables, acquired from BICC Group in early 1999. The Siemens acquisition brought Corning cable and equipment operations in Germany, France, Italy, Turkey, Argentina, and Australia, and led to the establishment of Corning Communications Europe, headquartered in London. It was hoped that these operations together would maintain or increase Corning's massive lead in the world-wide fiber market, already 40 percent market share, compared to Lucent's next largest share of 15 percent: the whole market was projected to double by the year 2003.

Helping to offset the concerns of those who feared a return to the one-product days of television, Corning was gaining an enhanced reputation for itself in several other technology-based growth areas. All of these ultra-high technology areas had previously been small niche products, and some of them had been secret work done only for the government. In 1999, for instance, the twenty-seven-foot diameter Subaru telescope mirror that

The Subaru Mirror is constructed from a mosaic of hexagonal pieces of ultra low expansion glass, each segment able to be individually adjusted by computer controls. After production was completed in 1994 at Corning's Canton Plant and the mirror delivered to Mitsubishi, it would be several more years before the polished mirror could go into service at the Japanese National Astronomical Observatory.

EPILOGUE 445

Corning had supplied to Mitsubishi for the National Astronomical Observatory of Japan came on line. With this installation of the world's largest telescope mirror ever, the ultra-low expansion glass mirrors used for spy satellites were finally brought into the service of the world's astronomers.[4] Completed by Corning's high-security Canton plant in 1994, the Subaru had required several more years of polishing and preparation before it could begin its work. Meanwhile, like the 200-inch Palomar mirror of sixty years before, it had led to other orders for mirrors for the same observatory site, all using the same hexagonal pieces of fused titanium silica bonded together at high temperatures.

Several other significant technology-based products had also recently matured into promising businesses. Out of the blue, though long hoped for, came notice of a sudden upsurge in demand for active matrix liquid crystal display glass. Corning had already spent almost as much money on LCD glass development, its latest use of its fusion glass technology, as it had on waveguides before that business began to pay returns.[5] Now this bet too looked like it would pay off. Japanese television makers indicated their intention to shift all of their new television set production to LCD glass in the first two years of the new century, and several of the leading firms offered to sign long-term contracts. Here too Corning developments had turned up the clock speed on its competitors, introducing a new glass substrate that was both lighter-weight and more rigid than those currently available; a number of competitors had requested licenses for this technology. Corning announced that it would double its LCD capacity by the end of the year 2000, with expanded facilities in Korea and Japan and a new finishing facility in Taiwan.

Advanced Life Sciences, which produced microplates for research in molecular biology, was getting a very encouraging response from its pharmaceutical company customers. Its growing range of tools to support new research techniques for genomics drew on Corning's expertise in polymers, optics, and surface chemistry combined with its capabilities in molecular biology. Corning projected a stream of new products aimed at DNA analysis and drug discovery markets, which were expected to grow to $2–3 billion in the next five years. One of these, a 1,536-well plate used for high throughput screening developed with Pharmacopeaia, Inc. allowed for a sixteen-fold improvement in throughput and a one hundred-fold reduction in reagent consumption compared with the industry standard.

Acquisitions, which had so enlarged Corning Communications, played a role elsewhere as well. In December 1999 Corning announced its acquisition of Optovac from the German company Merck KG. Optovac, located not far from the Canton plant, was a leading supplier of calcium fluoride optics and components for semiconductor manufacture; its purchase helped round out Corning's position as a supplier of optical lithography and laser systems. Meanwhile the company was pushing ahead to bring on line its advanced plant for high-purity fused silica. Located in Charleston, South Carolina, it had been mothballed during the Asian financial crisis of 1997–1998.

In the long-established Celcor environmental business, fresh opportunities were also presenting themselves. The use of microcellular ceramic material by the petrochemical industry promised customers enormous cost savings, and it offered Corning a potential major new growth market. Meanwhile, huge markets were opening for diesel filters; in China Corning broke ground in late 1999 for a large substrate plant to supply the truck market. It also seemed likely that emissions controls, formerly applied only to cars in the United States, might soon be extended to the wildly popular sport utility vehicle category as well; the impact on sales would be enormous.

Even such old-line businesses as ophthalmics, which had been in steady if profitable decline for twenty years, were showing new life in response to new product development. Pollux, a material Corning developed in France as a photochromic opththalmic polymer material, promised to stir up the relatively sleepy market for lenses. It would be given nine months to begin generating cash for the rest of the company with this new technology.

The stock market received the news of Corning's acquisitions and its market prospects with wild enthusiasm. After having driven the company's stock down to a low of $23 in September 1998, when its Asian plans were apparently early casualties of the meltdown of the financial markets in that part of the world, analysts now included Corning in that charmed group of companies viewed as benefiting most from the explosive growth of the Internet, as well as from rapid developments in emerging markets. Company predictions that its stock would rise to around $80 per share based on earnings were surpassed: the stock shot up to a high of $127 in the general 1999 year-end rise of technology stocks. This surge in stock price was a welcome aid in Corning's effort to fill the holes in its optical systems components portfolio, and the company was fully prepared to take advantage of the windfall. But having experienced the fickleness of markets in a similar period in the 1970s, no one at Corning saw the high stock price as something to be relied on. Roger Ackerman's counsel in his frequent communications meetings was "we need to keep our powder dry."[6]

Outside observers could easily have concluded from the reaction of the markets and the financial press that Corning's new opportunities were all the direct result of Ackerman's "Growing Corning" initiative, the work of a few frenzied years. These observers were surprised: *Business Week* remarked on how unlikely it had seemed that Roger Ackerman would make such heavy bets on new technology and go against what it perceived as Corning's traditional structure as a "conglomerate" with a low-tech image.[7] Insiders knew a very different story: far from bucking tradition, Ackerman was reclaiming Corning's core identity as a company focused on technology.

The long view recalled that even the divested consumerware business had been high technology in its day, and every one of the seemingly "new" businesses drew from deep wells of Corning technology and experience. Corning had started an optical components business in Europe as early as the 1980s (though it shuttered it in the early 1990s as a project ahead of its time). The life sciences research substrates revived and recombined Corning's eighty-five-year-old laboratory ware business and the early research work Corning had done in molecular biology. Likewise, the optical lithography business arose out of the company's continued work on high-purity fused silica first begun in the 1930s, while its work in LCD glass could be traced back to fusion glass for architectural panels and photochromic lenses developed at the Avon laboratory, and before that to the fusion process for flat glass developed in the 1960s for automobile windshields. None of these technologies would have been available for rapid exploitation in new markets had they not been nurtured in Corning's technology till, kept in active or near-active status by Corning's judicious use of "patient money."

Nor were the technology-based innovations the only part of the new Corning story that drew heavily on long experience. The ability to build the telecommunications business through friendly acquisition also rested in part on cordial and long-standing relationships with British Telecom, Siemens and BICC, the latter extending back nearly thirty years to the joint development agreements formed to support fiber optics for cable. Likewise, the ability to make long-term deals with Asian companies was partly traceable to the longevity of successful joint ventures like Samsung Corning and Corning Asahi Video.

Although lumped together in the public mind with high-tech companies recently spawned by the Internet, the source of Corning's vitality was quite different, and the issues that remained for it to resolve were likewise of a different stripe. First there was the pressing question of what to do about strategic focus. Should Corning concentrate entirely on telecommunications-related technologies this time or continue to pay the premiums on its traditional insurance policy—investing in research in specialty materials, which was its way of nurturing smaller process options for future growth? Many waited to see whether specialty materials research would lose out completely to the heavy resource demands of the several voracious high-growth businesses, some of them already working toward technology horizons that were ten years off.[8]

While many argued that the practice of concentrating for a time on a few key priorities need not spell the end of specialty materials research, but just defer it for a time, others wanted Corning to heed the stock market's demands for clarity and singleness of purpose and concentrate the corporate research agenda and its capital investment completely on what already seemed like a healthy degree of diversification among several very strong options. These debates seemed certain to continue. For the time being, there was little likelihood that Ackerman or his near colleagues would depart from the company tradition of nurturing future opportunities. Indeed, recent executive promotions seemed to suggest that Corning had settled on its course and intended to consolidate its achievements. The two Corning presidents and co-chief operating officers, John Loose and Norm Garrity, both changed jobs to help with this consolidation. Loose was named Corning's president and chief operating officer, while Garrity became vice chairman in charge of all staffs but the financial staff; Skip Deneka was promoted to executive vice president for science and technology.

Nevertheless the ability to debate these strategic issues openly inside the community was important to Corning's employee formation process, a way of participating in the future that renewed both the people and their commitment. Those new to the company, having joined Corning expecting to do a certain kind of work, needed to know why they might be asked to drop everything to work on projects they had not previously considered in their bailiwick.

Even to accommodate the strategic commitments already made, a new balance point between current needs and future opportunities would have to be found. When would the problem of needing growth suddenly become the problem of managing growth again? How much growth was too much? While Silicon Valley companies worried about the potential dilution of their stock value by the outstanding options issued to their employees, Corning had a different potential dilution issue and it was far harder to measure. In view of the rapidly changing composition of its staffs and the rapid expansion of its many operating sites, it would inevitably reach a point where passing on Corning's inherited organizational skills, its collective memory, and the shared routines that had made it possible to exploit selected new opportunities with lightning speed would no longer be possible. How would leaders know when core capabilities, intangible as they were, were really lost or when interrelationships between companies were stretched beyond resilience? At what point would the increased R&D spending create more opportunities than the company could exploit or even keep alive, with or without venture partners? For Corning, people could not be fungible, any more than they could be up for sale to the highest bidder. Innovation might be termed a business process, but it was still mainly a craft, a craft that survived because of the expertise and commitment of individual men and women, the trust knitting together a network of related companies, and the support of the town of Corning and many other local communities reaching round the world.

NOTES

Chapter 1: Introduction

1. The classic argument along these lines may be found in Alfred D. Chandler, *The Visi-ble Hand: The Managerial Revolution in American Business* (Cambridge: Harvard University Press, 1977). Why this narrative has dominated is discussed by Michael Piore and Charles Sabel in *The Second Industrial Divide: Possibilities for Prosperity*, (New York: Basic, 1984), pp. 29–35.
2. Philip Scranton, *Endless Novelty: Specialty Production and American Industrialization, 1865–1925* (Princeton: Princeton University Press, 1998), pp. 1–24.
3. Works dealing with these matters in their historical context include Louis Galambos and Jane Eliot Sewell, *Networks of Innovation: Vaccine Development at Merck, Sharp and Dohme, and Mulford, 1895–1995* (New York: Cambridge University Press, 1997), who posit long technology-based cycles governing the relations between private sector organizations and public sector governmental and nongovernmental organizations; Margaret B. W. Graham and Bettye H. Pruitt, *R&D for Industry: A Century of Technical Change at Alcoa* (New York: Cambridge University Press, 1990); David A. Hounshell and John Kenly Smith, *Science and Corporate Strategy: DuPont R&D, 1902–1980* (New York: Cambridge University Press, 1988), which, as the name implies, focuses on DuPont laboratories and its relations to DuPont's strategy; David C. Mowery and Nathan Rosenberg, *Paths of Innovation: Technological Change in Twentieth-Century America* (New York: Cambridge University Press, 1999). The institutional focus represented by these books has recently revived among economists interested in business, along with renewed attention to resource-based models of the firm, anchored in Edith Penrose's, *The Theory of the Growth of the Firm*, (1957; reprint, Cambridge: MIT Press, 1980).
4. David A. Hounshell, "The Evolution of Industrial Research," in Richard S. Rosenbloom and Mark Myers, *Engines of Innovation* (Cambridge: Harvard Business School Press, 1995). See also W. Bernard Carlson, *Innovation as a Social Process: Elihu Thompson and the Rise of General Electric, 1870–1900* (New York: Cambridge University Press, 1991); George Wise, "Science at General Electric," *Physics Today* 37, no. 12: 52–61. On changing models of R&D over time, see also Ralph Gomory, "'Technology and Prod-

ucts" and Mark Myers and Richard Rosenbloom, "The New Role of R&D," both in *Engines of Innovation*.

5. Lester Thurow, *The Future of Capitalism: How Today's Economic Forces Shape Tomorrow's World* (New York: William Morrow, 1997), p. 69.

6. Graham and Pruitt, *R&D for Industry*.

7. Robert B. Stobaugh, "A Note on the Use of Alliances," 9-393-029, 8/18/92 (Cambridge: Harvard Business School, 1992), quoting Michael Porter and Mark B. Fuller ("Coalitions and Global Strategy") who see alliances as a move based on weakness. "Alliances as a broad-based strategy will only ensure a company's mediocrity, not its international leadership.... Alliances are best used as a selective tool, employed on a temporary basis or involving noncore activities."

8. David S. Landes, whose classic work on history of technology and the economy in Europe since 1875, *The Unbound Prometheus* (New York: Cambridge University Press, 1968) comments extensively on the different styles of entrepreneurship in Europe and the U.S., communication to M. Graham, 1997.

9. Alanson Houghton, representing the third generation of Houghtons to run the company, left his position as Corning's president to run for congress in 1918, later becoming ambassador to the Weimar Republic and then the Court of St. James. His son Amory served on the War Production Board and became ambassador to France during the Eisenhower administration. Amory's son Amory Jr. (Amo) served five terms in the U.S. House of Representatives after resigning from Corning. Arthur A. Houghton's son Arthur A. Houghton Jr., while he was head of Steuben, became a collector of rare books. Later he gave his collection to several rare book libraries and gave the Houghton Library to Harvard University. He also became head of the Morgan Library in New York City. When he resigned as chairman and CEO of Corning, James R. (Jamie) Houghton became chairman of the board of the Metropolitan Museum of Art in New York City.

10. Amory Houghton speaking to the Corning 1968 Management Conference, April 1968, ARV 27, Corning Incorporated Department of Archives and Records Management, hereafter CIDARM.

11. In the 1960s this reached 50,000 per hour; later the output reached 2,000 bulbs per minute.

12. Words taken from the citation for the National Medal of Technology awarded to Corning as a company in 1996.

Chapter 2

1. According to Donald Stookey, Eugene Sullivan attributed much of Corning's success through the 1930s to its ability to keep its secrets about glass composition. S. Donald Stookey, *Journey to the Center of the Crystal Ball: An Autobiography* (Columbus: American Ceramic Society, Inc. 1985).

2. For a few of the many historical accounts of technology prepared by Corning insiders, see C. J. Phillips, *Glass the Miracle Maker: History, Manufacture, Chemistry, Physical and Chemical Properties, Applications* (New York: Pitman, 1941); R. H. Dalton, "A Century of Chemistry at Corning," TIC R4649 6-25-71; Walter W. Oakley, "Development of Refractory Practices in Corning Glass Works," TIC 8-14-62, Report L121;

"This is Glass" Corning Glass Works, 1957; and Otto Hilbert, Historical Memo on Corning Technology dated 1959–60(?).

3. Roger Ackerman, speech to the International Congress on Glass, San Francisco, July 6, 1998.

Chapter 3

1. Arthur Day to Alanson B. Houghton, 10 April 1911; Houghton Correspondence, CIDARM. For the significance of antitrust legislation and its introduction of uncertainty into lives of large American companies at the turn of the century, see Louis Galambos and Joseph Pratt, *The Rise of the Corporate Commonwealth* (New York: Basic Books, 1991.)

2. Robert Dalton interview; C. J. Parker, "Applied Optics at Corning Glass Works," *Applied Optics,* 7 (May 1968): 735. Material for the general history of industrial research at Corning is to be found primarily in the Hilbert Notebooks and the Technical Staffs files, CIDARM.

3. On Edison and lightbulb making, see G. B. Hollister, "Corning Glass Works"; Robert Friedel, Paul Israel, and Bernard S. Finn, *Edison's Electric Light: Biography of an Invention* (New Brunswick, N.J.: Rutgers University Press, 1985), pp. 162–164.

4. Material on Arthur Day is taken from the following sources: F. W. Preston, "Debt of Glass Technology to Geologists," *Ceramic Bulletin* 44 (1965); J. C. Hostetter, "The Geophysical Laboratory," *Bulletin of the American Ceramic Society* 13 (January 1934); Arthur L. Day, "Developing American Glass," in *American Society for Testing Materials* 36 (1936); C. J. Parker, *Applied Optics at Corning Glass Works*; and Eugene Sullivan, "Arthur Louis Day," *Bulletin of the American Ceramic Society* 20, no.7 (1941): 252–253.

5. The Carnegie Institution, where Arthur Day was employed, had become a powerful force in the national organization of science after the turn of the century. It stood for an interdisciplinary, cooperative approach to the development of science. Day was one of the men who had convinced the Carnegie trustees to make geophysical research one of its core subjects of study. See John W. Servos, "To Explore the Borderland: The Foundation of the Geophysical Laboratory of the Carnegie Institution of Washington," *Historical Studies in the Physical Sciences*, 14 (Washington, 1984) 147–185; John W. Servos in *Chemistry and Modern Society: Historical Essays in Honor of Aaron J. Ihde*, ed. John Parascandola and James C. Whorton (Washington, DC: American Chemical Society, 1983); and John W. Servos, *Physical Chemistry from Ostwald to Pauling: The Making of a Science in America* (Princeton: Princeton University Press, 1990), pp. 231–236; Robert H. Kargon, *The Rise of Robert Millikan: Portrait of a Life in American Science* (Ithaca, N.Y.: Cornell University Press, 1982), pp. 95–98; and Sullivan, "Arthur Louis Day."

6. Another involved outsider after Day was Edward U. Condon, briefly Corning's director of R&D, who was on Corning's payroll for two more decades. A similar function was later performed by W. W. Shaver, head of international research. As a Corning employee toward the end of his career, he was assigned to travel around the world making connections and following up leads with other leading industrial research and academic research departments. When he retired, Gail Smith, another Corning researcher, took over the same function.

7. Robert H. Dalton, "A Century of Chemistry at Corning"; a lecture with slides for internal use, 25 June 1971, pp. 3–4; Corning Technical Staffs Division Library. This source cites the many findings recorded in Amory Houghton's notebooks that were only later rediscovered, presumably owing to the secrecy of the family.

8. Unless otherwise indicated, the following account of the development of railway signal glass draws on papers found in the Railway folder, CIDARM, and the papers of Henry Phelps Gage at Cornell University's Carl A. Kroch Library, Rare and Manuscript Collections (hereafter cited as HPG at Cornell University Archives). Important information concerning technological innovation and American railroads is found in Steven W. Usselman, "Running the Machine: The Management of Technological Innovation on American Railroads, 1860–1910 (Ph.D. diss., University of Delaware, 1985). Detailed discussion of this material can be found in Regina Lee Blaszczyk, "Selling with Science," (one chapter of Ph.D. diss., University of Delaware, 1996); and Regina Lee Blaszczyk, *Imagining Consumers: Design and Innovation from Wedgewood to Corning* (Baltimore: Johns Hopkins University Press, 2000).

9. H. P. Gage, untitled handwritten account of the origins of the optical laboratory, November 18, 1922, HPG at Cornell University Archives.

10. William Churchill to A. B. Houghton, May 15, 1904; HPG, no. 1874, box 13, Cornell University Archives.

11. Blaszczyk, "Selling with Science" pp. 472–473.

12. Servos, *Physical Chemistry from Ostwald to Pauling*, contains a list of forty-four Americans who worked in Ostwald's laboratory at Leipzig before he retired. Among them were some of the luminaries in the development of physical chemistry in the United States, including a Nobel laureate, T. W. Richards of Harvard University, eleven members of the National Academy of Sciences, six presidents of the American Chemical Society, and four recipients, including Sullivan, of the Perkin Medal awarded by the Affiliated Chemical and Electrochemical Societies of America for accomplishments in applied chemistry.

13. Harrison Hood, interview by George Southworth, 9 May 1973, Hood biographical file, CIDARM, describes how the research laboratory evolved informally in the 1920s and beyond, with close involvement by Amory Houghton, Alanson's son.

14. See Leonard S. Reich, *The Making of American Industrial Research: Science and Business at GE and Bell, 1876–1926* (New York: Cambridge University Press, 1985); George Wise, *Willis Whitney, General Electric, and the Origins of U.S. Industrial Research* (New York: Columbia University Press, 1985); W. Bernard Carlson, *Innovation as a Social Process: Elihu Thomson and the Rise of General Electric, 1870–1900* (New York: Cambridge University Press, 1991); on Eastman Kodak, see Reese V. Jenkins, *Images of Enterprise: Technology and the American Photographic Industry, 1839–1925* (Baltimore: Johns Hopkins University Press; 1995) and Jeffrey L. Sturchio, "Experimenting with Research: Keneth Mees, Eastman Kodak, and the Challenge of Diversification" (paper presented at the R&D Pioneers Conference, Wilmington, Delaware, 1985); on research at Du Pont, see David A. Hounshell and John Kenley Smith, *Science and Corporate Strategy: DuPont R&D, 1902–1980* (New York: Cambridge University Press, 1988); and on Alcoa, see Margaret B. W. Graham and Bettye H. Pruitt, *R&D for Industry: A Century of Technical Innovation at Alcoa* (New York: Cambridge University Press, 1990); on Merck, see Louis Galambos with Jane Eliot Sewell, *Networks of Innovation: Vaccine Development at Merck, Sharp and Dohme, and Mulford, 1895–1995* (New York: Cambridge

University Press, 1995). On the different philosophies of industrial research, see Kenneth C. E. Mees, "The Organization of Industrial Research Laboratories," *Science* 43: 763–73; and Mees, *The Organization of Industrial Scientific Research* (New York: McGraw-Hill, 1920); Steven W. Usselman, "From Novelty to Utility: George Westinghouse and the Business of Innovation during the Age of Edison," *Business History Review* 66: 251–304. For a critique of the literature see Michael Aaron Dennis, "Accounting for Research, New Histories of Corporate Laboratories and the Social History of American Science," *Social Studies of Science*, London, Sage 17 (1987), pp. 479–518.

15.   On the growth of American research universities, see Robert L. Geiger, *To Advance Knowledge: The Growth of American Research Universities, 1900–1940* (New York: Oxford University Press, 1986), and Laurence Veysey, *The Emergence of the American University* (Chicago: University of Chicago Press, 1965).

16.   Blaszczyck, "Selling with Science," includes a list of scientific staff at Corning Glass Works who were hired between the 1870s and 1920, table 7.1, pp. 438–439.

17.   See Margaret B. W. Graham, "Lessons from America's Great Experiment," *Across the Board*, May 1987; reprinted as "Another Turning Point for R&D," *McKinsey Quarterly*, Autumn 1987.

18.   Simon Gage's college textbook entitled *The Microscope and Microscopic Methods*, first published in 1881, remained the standard text until well after World War II (17th ed., 1941).

19.   H. P. Gage, "Types of Signal Lenses," *Transactions of Illuminating Engineering Society* 9 (1914): 486–496; and "Colored Glass in Illuminating Engineering," *Transactions of Illuminating Engineering Society* 11 (1916): 1050.

20.   It was also a controversial activity, especially among the specialty manufacturers, who viewed it as a way for powerful customers to enforce fixed prices and also stifle "disruptive" innovation. See Philip Scranton, *Endless Novelty: Specialty Production and American Engineering, 1865–1925* (Princeton: Princeton University Press, 1997).

21.   See Blaszczyk, "Selling with Science." Frederick Winslow Taylor had become well-known in American industry by the turn of the century as a proponent of what was termed "scientific management," a system defining new notions of efficiency, including such tools as time and motion study, which many large manufacturing concerns were adopting, to do away with the system of craft control that had dominated industrial life to that time.

22.   A September 1936 article by H. P. Gage and Norman MacBeth, "Industrial Uses of Daylighting," in *Journal of Illumination* gives examples of critical uses in industry, HPG no. 1874, box 9, Cornell University Archives.

23.   Susannah Phelps Gage to H. P. Gage, 27 April 1913, HPG no. 1874, box 11, Cornell University Archives.

24.   Gage, Report of the Functions of the Optical Laboratory to Falck, 1922, Optical Laboratory Report for 1922, CIDARM.

25.   Gage, Report to Arthur Day, 1921, Reports from the Optical Laboratory, CIDARM.

26.   Eugene Sullivan, "Accomplishments of the Industrial Physicist in the Glass Industry," *Journal of Applied Physics* 8, no. 2 (1937): 122–128, one of many articles written by Corning scientists in various journals to publicize the laboratory's accomplishments after the 200-inch mirror.

27.   This account of the early laboratory draws on interviews conducted in the 1960s and

1970s with Jesse Littleton, Robert Dalton, and Harrison Hood, and the H. P. Gage papers.

28. Blaszczyk, "Selling with Science," pp. 498–500.

29. "Dr. William Churchill suggested the dish be called 'Pie-Right' or 'Py-right'. Someone said, 'No, "Pyrex" sounds better.' The suggestion and its adoption, says Dr. Sullivan, rested on purely euphonious grounds." Otto Hilbert, memo on " 'Pyrex' Trademark," 23 May 1980, p. 1; box 37–2–4, Trademarks folder, CIDARM.

30. Eugene C. Sullivan, "The Many Sidedness of Glass," *Industrial and Engineering Chemistry,* Vol 21, February 1929, p. 177ff.

31. Laboratory Products Growth—Key Events, 1912–1960.

32. Remembered conversation with Harrison Hood, Thomas Carpenter, interview by Margaret Graham, 30 July 1997; WGI Transcripts.

33. Day to A. B. Houghton, February 1917; Houghton correspondence, CIDARM.

34. Ibid.

35. Hood, interview by Southworth, CIDARM.

36. Women were cheaper, as evidenced by memos discussing the cost of setting up a home economics laboratory, which projected a salary of $1,200 for its head. See J. T. Littleton memo, 4 March 1924, unaccessioned material, CIDARM.

37. The actual patents were issued in the name of George S. Fulcher. It was partly because they turned out to infringe some patents issued to Hartford-Empire, which was also working on refractories, that the ensuing joint venture was set up. Historical Memo Notebook, vol. 5, Corhart, n.d. CIDARM. In fact, there was considerable competition between Corhart and Corning around refractories. Walter Oakley, chief engineer, would not buy Corhart refractories, and Corning continued to acquire its own from other sources and make its own pots into the 1950s. Oakley never even visited Corhart until late in 1939, when his visit received notice in Eugene Sullivan's daybook.

38. J. T. Littleton and William Taylor, memo to Eugene Sullivan, January 1938, unaccessioned material, CIDARM.

39. Day, "Developing American Glass"; and Preston, *The Debt of Glass Technology to Geologists.*

40. H. P. Gage, Report on the Optical Department, 1923, CIDARM.

41. Unless otherwise cited, the sources for the following accounts of the home economics department come from the following unaccessioned material in CIDARM: Brief History, Home Economics Department, dated 1974; Lucy Maltby interview, n.d. and "Cooking Up a Double Boiler," Corning Glass Works interoffice memo, October 1951, from Lucy Maltby to consumer products division, design department, and product engineering.

42. Carroll Pursell, "Government and Technology in the Great Depression," *Technology and Culture* 20 (1969): 162–174.

43. This account of Pyrex stovetop developments comes from W. W. Shaver to Dr. G. P. Smith, "Some Corning Developments—1924 to 1972—An Expanded Review," 24 November 1975, unaccessioned materials, CIDARM.

44. Lucy Maltby interview, unaccessioned material, CIDARM.

45. Sullivan, "The Many Sidedness of Glass."

46. Harrison Hood, interview by George Southworth, 1975.

47. Robert Dalton, interview by George Southworth, 1973, biographical files, CIDARM.
48. Sullivan, "The Many Sidedness of Glass," p. 182.

Chapter 4

1. Handwritten notes by H. P. Gage, HPG Cornell University Archives.
2. Letter from David Gray to A. B. Houghton, 23 October 1917, box 4-3-9 Mechanical
     Development folder, CIDARM. Machine development departments had been set up
     much earlier in other industries; see Paul Israel, *From Machine Shop to Industrial Labo-*
     ratory: Telegraphy and the Changing Context of American Invention (Baltimore: Johns
     Hopkins University Press, 1992), pp, 20–23, on the community of mechanical inven-
     tion that developed in the latter part of the nineteenth century. See also W. Bernard
     Carlson, "Building Thomas Edison's Laboratory at West Orange, New Jersey: A Case
     Study in Using Knowledge for Technological Invention, 1886–1888," and Carlson,
     Innovation as a Social Process, History of Technology, 1991, 1-12.
3. See Hugh G. J. Aitken, *Scientific Management in Action: Taylorism at Watertown Arsenal,*
     1908–1915, which summarizes the philosophy of mechanical engineering in the latter
     part of the nineteenth century as found in the papers of the American Society of
     Mechanical Engineers; Aitken also refers to Taylor's part in the development of this
     philosophy.
4. Little Joe was originally a trademark of the MacBeth Evans Company, which Corn-
     ing absorbed in 1936. Significantly, the icon was adopted by Corning as a sign of its
     general attitudes in dealing with other companies.
5. This system was developed by Otto Hilbert when he was treasury director
     (1928–1934), head of the cost department (1934–1937), and then controller for manu-
     facturing reporting to George MacBeth (1937–1940). See box 34-2-3/61, Accounting
     Costs folder, CIDARM for pertinent documents.
6. Arthur Day to A. B. Houghton, 15 November 1910, Houghton Correspondence,
     CIDARM.
7. David A. Hounshell, *From the American System to Mass Production: The Development of*
     Manufacturing Technology in the United States (Baltimore: Johns Hopkins University
     Press, 1984); and Robert Kanigel, *One Best Way: Frederick Winslow Taylor and the Enigma*
     of Efficiency (New York: Viking, 1997). Phil Scranton, in *Endless Novelty,* showed that
     industries that valued novelty, produced low volumes of a product, or redesigned fre-
     quently did not adopt mass production. Corning was somewhere in the middle; its
     product mix included both very high-volume items (e.g., lightbulb envelopes) and
     many products that needed to be flexible to accommodate redesign and alteration.
8. These included Arthur Day, who supervised the effort in its early years, and family
     friend William Sinclaire, as well as the senior machine inventors who did the
     mechanical work. The original shareholders were as follows: A. A. Houghton, 33
     shares; A. B. Houghton 34; Sinclaire, 10; Day, 10; Chamberlin, 5; and Githler, 5. On
     this and other matters concerning the organization of the Empire Machine Com-
     pany, see Alexander Falck, memo prepared for the antitrust investigation, 11 October
     1938, CIDARM.
9. Wellsboro was important in its own right as the first plant in which Corning installed
     a tank melter. Corning had purchased the facility from the Columbia Window Glass

Works in 1916 and rebuilt the extant tank to handle the lime glass that the E machines used. (The lime formula was necessitated in part by wartime difficulties obtaining the ingredients for lead glass and in part by problems encountered trying to develop a refractory that would not dissolve under the attack of lead glass; significantly, Corning shared the patent on this lime glass with GE). Twenty of the E machines were installed, each pair using a tube annealer for its output and producing together about 800 bulbs per hour. This was, for Corning, the state of the art at that time, though no match for the Westlake machine. See G. B. Hollister, *History of Corning*; and Otto Hilbert History Collection, CIDARM, for this and other details.

10.   David E. Gray, Daily Report Diary, file 3 22-5-3, CIDARM.

11.   Quoted in Kris Gable, memo on ribbon machine, Records of Glass Center Project, 1997.

12.   "The Corning Ribbon-Feed Bulb Machine Known as the Corning Machine," p. 88; box 4-3-7, C.G.W.—Machines—Ribbon Machine folder, CIDARM.

13.   O. W. Hilbert, 399—Corning Machine—Ribbon Machine, 23 August 1966, p. 6; box 33-6-01/P6, Ribbon Machine folder, CIDARM.

14.   "The Corning Ribbon-Feed Bulb Machine Known as the Corning Machine," p. 93.

15.   This location was proposed by Woods and Gray, who thought the Ribbon Machine would require a larger melting operation. Memo from W. J. Woods and D. E. Gray to Falck, "Dev. Order #399," 15 September 1925, p. 5; box 33-6-01/P6, Ribbon Machine folder, CIDARM. The cost of installation was estimated at over $231,000, a considerable sum at the time (ibid., p. 6).

16.   These details may be found in O. W. Hilbert, "Conference on Corning Mechanical Development, 27 February 1934," 6 March 1934; box 33-6-01/P6, Ribbon Machine folder, CIDARM; and W. R. Wisner, "Basic Ribbon Mechanical Developments," 23 March 1956, p. 5; box 33-6-01/P6, Ribbon Machine folder, CIDARM.

17.   David Gray to A. B. Houghton, 1916, p. 4; box 33-6-03, Mechanical Development, folder, CIDARM.

18.   David Gray, Daily Report Diary.

19.   In 1940 Sullivan's daybook notes that GE had been withholding some of its findings, and it was agreed to take up the matter with one of its senior executives. This shift toward less openness may have come in response to the antitrust action that the Justice Department was pursuing against the lamp companies and their glass suppliers over the joint process development and patent sharing that had been going on for nearly thirty years. Sullivan daybooks, fragments saved from the 1935 flood, 1926–1940, passim, file 10, 22-5-3, 8 January 1930, CIDARM.

20.   Ibid.

21.   This account of the Production Club is based on collected documents in the Production Club folder, ARV 27, box 34-4-02; G8, CIDARM. It includes newspaper clippings, a copy of *The Cullet*, and a "History of the Production Club, 1920–1940," prepared for a talk by Amory Houghton in 1941.

22.   *The Cullet*, partial copy in Production Club folder.

23.   Anonymous author's memoir about life in Corning during the 1930s, obviously a Steuben designer; CIDARM.

24.   Telegram from G. E. Hale to Arthur Day, J. Hostetter, etc. box 4-4-3, Telescopes folder, CIDARM. This account of Corning's 200-inch mirror project is based on the many internal Corning documents in this box, but especially on George Macauley's

voluminous internal report on the 200-inch mirror project, and his shorter version of this report first delivered to the American Ceramic Society in 1935 and then published in its proceedings. See also Ronald Florence, *The Perfect Machine: Building the Palomar Telescope* (New York: Harper Perennial, 1994).

25. Eugene Clute, "Designing for Construction in Glass—1," *Pencil Points*, November 1932, p. 741.
26. "What Price—Glass Houses," *Glass Industry* 10, no. 11 (1929): 270.
27. John Ely Burchard, "Glass in Modern Housing," p. 379.
28. "A Tower of Glass," *Gaffer*, November 1950, p. 11.
29. "Architectural Photosensitive Glass Program, Sales Plans for 1953–1958," n.d., box 26-3-9, folder 9, CIDARM.
30. The best description of this period may be found in the autobiography of Fred E. Schroeder, pp. 10–12, CIDARM.
31. R. C. Vaughn, 11 April 1931, quoted in O. W. Hilbert memo "Steuben—1924–1933," 1 October 1975, p. 2; box 37-2-4, Steuben folder, CIDARM. See also memo from W. W. Oakley to W. H. Armistead, "Development of Steuben Crystal Glass," 16 March 1966, pp. 1–2; ibid.
32. See "Steuben Glass," in Arthur Houghton, *Remembrances* (privately printed, 1986), pp. 115–124.
33. Autobiography of Fred E. Schroeder, pp. 16–17.
34. Ibid., p. 16. Contrasting views may be found in a memo entitled "Steuben Policy"; box 37-2-4, Steuben folder, CIDARM. Other information on Teague may be found in a memo by O. W. Hilbert, "Steuben—1924–1933," 1 October 1975, p. 3; ibid.
35. Walter Dorwin Teague, "Steuben Policy" (probably a memo to Amory Houghton, 1932); box 37-2-4, Steuben folder, CIDARM.
36. See memo from W. W. Oakley to W. H. Armistead, "Development of Steuben Crystal Glass," 16 March 1966, p. 3; and O. W. Hilbert memo on "Let it Down Easy, Gathering Steuben Glass," 31 May 1979; box 37-2-4, Steuben folder, CIDARM.
37. Untitled memo from George S. to Otto Hilbert, 10 October 1974; box 37-2-4, Steuben folder, CIDARM.
38. The above quotes are from an untitled memo from George S. to Otto Hilbert, 10 October 1974; box 37-2-4, Steuben folder, CIDARM. See also a memo from W. W. Oakley to W. H. Armistead, "Development of Steuben Crystal Glass," 16 March 1966; ibid.
39. See Sally Walker and James Kinnear interviews with Davis Dyer 1998.

Chapter 5

1. See Jeffrey L. Meikle, *American Plastic: A Cultural History* (New Brunswick, N.J.: Rutgers University Press, 1995), pp. 31–45.
2. See John W. Servos in *Physical Chemistry from Ostwald to Pauling* (American Chemical Society, 1983).
3. The term "association" was not unique to Corning. It grew out of the 1920s ideology of the associative state, which historian Louis Galambos has called "a delicate blending of public and voluntary private efforts aimed at solving specific social and economic problems in the society" ("The U.S. Corporate Economy in the Twentieth Century," in *The Cambridge Economic History*). A comprehensive discussion of the

relationship between the problem of monopoly and the associationist philosophy can be found in Ellis Hawley, *The New Deal and the Problem of Monopoly* (Princeton: Princeton University Press, 1966), pp. 36–39. The "association" in Corning's usage was an equity venture set up to take advantage of complementarities between two companies and to promote knowledge sharing between them. Such arrangements were sanctioned by the business-oriented Coolidge administration but rejected as anticompetitive by later administrations.

4.   Earl L. Warrick, *Forty Years of Firsts: The Recollections of a Dow Corning Pioneer* (New York: McGraw-Hill, 1989). Warrick was a senior researcher at Dow-Corning and one of the originators of commercial silicone.

5.   For more on the DuPont history, see David A. Hounshell and John Kenly Smith, *Science and Corporate Strategy: Du Pont R&D, 1902–1980* (New York: Cambridge University Press, 1988).

6.   J. F. Hyde, April interview, 1997. See also "Dr. J. Franklin Hyde," n.d; box 33-6-01, Silicone folder, CIDARM.

7.   Unless otherwise indicated, this account of the invention of silicone draws on a collection of Hyde's own memoirs in "Dr. James Franklin Hyde," n.d. ARV 27, box 34-6-01, Silicone folder; box 34-1-02, Hyde, Dr. J. Franklin folder, CIDARM. It also draws on a series of interviews with Hyde conducted by the Winthrop Group, Inc.(WGI) in 1997 and 1998 on "The Silicones," *Fortune*, May 1947, on Warrick, and *Forty Years of Firsts*.

8.   Statement by Franklin Hyde, n.d., box 34-1-02, Hyde, Dr. J. Franklin folder, CIDARM.

9.   The Mexican Marxist artist Diego Rivera's mural on Rockefeller Center was painted over when it was nearing completion because its portrayal of worker oppression was viewed as too incendiary. By contrast, Rivera's mural for the Detroit Institute of Art, *Detroit Industry*, which was a devastating critique of the assembly line, was allowed to remain although it surprised his patrons, Edsel B. Ford and others. It was later observed that "the annealing problem in making sections for all three of these [glass] panels [i.e., Rockefeller and two other New York City installations] presented problems somewhat similar to those encountered by Corning in making the 200" telescope disk" "Pyrex Panels at Rockefeller Center," 3 April 1958, pp. 2–3; box 37-2-4, Architectural Glass folder, CIDARM.

10. Hyde, interview by M. Graham, January 1997.

11. C. J. Phillips, *Glass the Miracle Maker* (New York: Prentice Hall, 1948).

12. This account appears both in a 28 February 1968 interview with George MacBeth (apparently conducted by Otto Hilbert) and in Sullivan's deposition from the patent interference hearings on Hyde's work. Undated five-page document labeled only "Dr. E. C. Sullivan" in Dr. J. Franklin Hyde folder cited above. See Warrick, *Forty Years of Firsts*, pp. 23–31, which notes that the presentation of two GE papers, one by Rochow and Gilliam, and one by Gilliam, Liebhafsky, and Winslow, caused a stir at Corning, as they both presented findings similar to Hyde's, involving silicone starting materials. Sullivan intervened with his friend William Coolidge of the GE labs, who agreed to hold publication until Hyde was also ready to publish.

13. Hyde, interview by M. Graham, April 1997.

14. Unless otherwise noted, the account of GE's parallel work on silicones that follows is based on a collection of documents found in the Silicone folder, ARV 27, box 33-6-01, P 6; CIDARM, and in the J. Franklin Hyde folder, ARV 27, box 34-1-02; B2, CIDARM. The former includes correspondence between Dow Chemical and Eugene Sullivan

containing their write-up on the silicone sealing compound. It gives a detailed record of the patent applications filed, and of the basis for Corning's claims of priority over General Electric.

15. Eugene G. Rochow, "My Friend Silicone," *Chemtech*, September 1980, describes his version of the story about the disputed work done on silicone at GE. Slayter appears to have been stunned when GE went ahead with research on silicones without telling Corning; he appealed to them, in the interests of fairness, to inform Corning of what they were doing. See also Warrick, *Forty Years of Firsts* and "Dow-Corning," *Fortune*, Sept. 1947.

16. It is not clear how carefully Sullivan supervised this research. He may have felt that the benefits of maximum activity would offset the potential disadvantages of having many institutions with claims. In his daybooks for March 1940 (a rather late date to be inquiring) he noted, "Dr. McGregor will determine at Mellon Institute what rights Corning has in applications of McGregor material which may be developed by Mellon representatives of other companies." According to correspondence with Dow Chemical noted above, it was the habit of Mellon Institute researchers to send reports of their outside contacts to William Shaver at Corning.

17. Acknowledgment published by GE researcher Eugene Rochow in his paper before the American Chemical Society, fall 1940.

18. It appears from the testimony later prepared for Eugene Sullivan at the time of the patent interference hearings that the broadest implications of the silicone discoveries had not fully dawned on Corning's research leadership until GE published its claims. Upon questioning, Sullivan admitted that he had very little to do with research going on in the fiberglass division and that his conversations with Hyde had mostly occurred after 1937 (Sullivan testimony in various papers; box 34-1-02, Hyde, Dr. J. Franklin folder, CIDARM.

19. See papers in box 34-6-2, Sylvania Electric Corp. folder, CIDARM, for the material in this paragraph and the following.

20. Material for this account comes from "Corhart," OH, the Historical Memo Notebook, vol. 5, CIDARM.

21. Walter Oakley, "Development of Refractory Practices in Corning Glass Works," 14 August 1962. By keeping some of their most superior refractories off the market, Corning maintained an advantage over those who could only get the refractories that Corhart produced. See also Wellech correspondence about refractories (CIDARM; also HPG 1945, Cornell University Archives).

22. "Agreement between CGW and Asahi Glass," 25 April 1941, modifying earlier agreement in same folder dated 3 July 1930; box 16-4-02, Corhart folder, CIDARM.

23. Indications of these quarrels are scattered throughout Eugene Sullivan's notebooks in the late 1920s. Sullivan, Falck, and Curtiss all served on Corhart's board, but Falck came to believe that Curtiss was not competent to serve as the liaison to Corhart. During the 1930s the management of Corhart inevitably became mixed up with the problems that were surfacing around Hartford-Empire as the Justice Department decided to investigate and various Corning executives were asked to testify.

24. "Glass Construction Blocks," A. E. Marshall to Houghton, Peden, Cary and Hostetter, 14 March 1931, p. 3; box 33-05-01, Glass Blocks folder, CIDARM.

25. Memo from W. W. Shaver to J. T. Littleton, "Some Notes on the Present Status of Structural Glass in England and the Continent," 13 September 1938; box 33-5-01/P3, Glass Blocks folder, CIDARM.

26. "New Pyrex Construction Unit," *The Glass Industry*, November 1935, p. 344.
27. Memo from W. W. Shaver to G. P. Smith, "Glass Building Blocks," 3 December 1973; box 33-5-01/P3, Glass Blocks folder, CIDARM.
28. Ibid.
29. Memo from A. E. Marshall to Amory Houghton, on "Glass Construction Blocks," 14 March 1931, pp. 4–5; box 33-5-01/P3, Glass Blocks folder, CIDARM.
30. Sales brochure, " 'Pyrex' Glass Construction Unit Manufactured by Corning-Steuben Architectural Division of Corning Glass Works," 1934, p. 1; box 33-5-01/P3, glass blocks folder, CIDARM.
31. Quote from John Ely Burchard, "Glass in Modern Housing," *Glass Industry*, December 1935, p. 380.
32. For more on efforts to promote glass brick in architecture and industrial design, see Jeffrey L. Meikle, *Twentieth Century Limited: Industrial Design in America, 1925–1939* (Philadelphia: Temple University Press, 1979), pp. 117–121.
33. "Pittsburgh-Corning Corporation: A Corporate History," May 21, 1974, [no box] Pittsburgh Corning Corporation: A Corporate History folder, CIDARM.
34. See Games Slayter, draft of article written for *Industrial and Engineering Chemistry*, dated 1958; box 33-5-01, Fiberglas folder, CIDARM. See also "Owens-Corning," *Fortune*, January, 1997.
35. Warrick, *Forty Years of Firsts*, p. 21.
36. See Walter Oakley, "Development of Refractory Practices in Corning Glass"; and Sullivan Day Books, 3 January 1940.
37. Warrick, *Forty Years of Firsts*, p. 35.
38. Specifically, it shipped three different groups of product. Group 1 was phenylsilicon compounds, which included the impregnating compounds for Fiberglas cloth as well as protective coatings for high-temperature enamels and heat-resistant lubricating fluids; group 2 was methyl substitutes, including heat-hardening-type materials used to bond Fiberglas cloth; group 3 included fluids, compounds and rubber, including silicone rubber and various sealing compounds.
39. Note, for instance, the controversy on the Dow-Corning board as late as 1960 as to whether the Durez division of the Hooker Chemical Company should be given a deal to develop the market for a new molding compound; box 17-3-4 folder 12, Directors Meetings Dow-Corning Board pre-1960, CIDARM.
40. Hyde, Dr. J. Franklin folder, CIDARM.
41. Forrest Behm, interview December 1996.
42. The most useful document detailing Corning's nuclear work is W. W. Shaver, "Glasses for Nuclear Applications," 26 June 1961; TIC Report L-63. See also E. U. Condon, handwritten notes on nuclear needs, n.d. (early 1950s?), Edward U. Condon Papers, Glass: Special Glasses for Nuclear Work folder, Collection of the American Philosophical Society; "Corning's Radiation-Shielding-Glasses," sales brochure, n.d. (late 1950s?), pp. 16–17; box 33-6-02 (P5), Radiation Shielding folder, CIDARM.
43. For precise figures, see W. C. Decker memo to Amory Houghton and E. C. Sullivan on contributions by Sylvania and Corning to Atomic Energy Project, 21 August 1956; box 34-6-02 (PL5), Sylvania Electric Company folder, CIDARM. Also, F. A. Bickford, "Atomic Energy: Progress Report for May 1956 on A.E.C. Contract"; J. I. Slaughter, ibid, June 1956; and J. I. Slaughter, ibid., for July 1956, all dated one month subsequent and all TIC Report R-937 (revised as appropriate).

44. See agreement between Corning Glass Works and Sylvania Electric Products, 23 January 1957; Sylvania Corning Corporation binder, CIDARM.

45. See "Visit to Navy Department Bureau of Ships (Lieut. Com. H. G. Rickover)," 7 February 1942; box G9, War Products (Priorities) folder, CIDARM.

46. E. C. Sullivan, "Sylvania," 21 August 1956; box 34-6-02 (PL5), Sylvania Electric Company folder, CIDARM.

47. Memo from W. C. Decker to W. H. Armistead on Corning's potential contribution to atomic energy, 2 May 1956; Sylvania Corning Corporation binder, CIDARM. See also memo from W. C. Decker to W. H. Armistead re Sylvania-Corning situation, 15 April 1959; box 17-3-4, Sylvania-Corning Nuclear Corporation folder, CIDARM.

48. Memo from W. H. Armistead, "Sylvania-Corning," 27 May 1959; box 17-3-4, Sylvania-Corning Nuclear Corporation folder, CIDARM. See also letter from Lee L. Davenport to W. B. Harrison, on Navy fuels, 8 April 1960; box 17-3-4, Sylvania-Corning Nuclear Corporation folder, CIDARM and memo from W. H. Armistead to A. Houghton Jr., "Sylvania-Corning Situation," 7 April 1959; box 17-3-4, Sylvania-Corning Nuclear Corporation folder, CIDARM for a complete analysis of the problem.

49. Garth W. Edwards, "Business Problems in the Commercial Processing and Handling of Fuels," lecture given at the Atomic Industrial Forum Conference, Washington, D.C., 2 November 1959, p. 1; box 17-3-4, Sylvania-Corning Nuclear Corporation folder, CIDARM. This was, in fact, his opening statement.

50. "Sylvania Corning Nuclear Corporation," n.d.; Sylvania Corning Corporation binder, CIDARM.

51. W. B. Harrison to Sylcor board of directors, 29 April 1959, p. 2; box 17-3-4, Sylvania-Corning Nuclear Corporation folder, CIDARM. See also Lee L. Davenport to W. B. Harrison, 8 December 1959, box 17-3-4, Sylvania-Corning Nuclear Corporation folder, CIDARM; and Lee L. Davenport, untitled memo, 10 June 1959; box 17-3-4, Sylvania-Corning Nuclear Corporation folder, CIDARM.

52. "Sylvania-Corning Nuclear Corporation," n.d.; Sylvania Corning Corporation binder, CIDARM. See also letter of resignation from Charles D. LaFollette to Sylcor, 19 April 1960; and Frederick H. Knight to Lee L. Davenport, 7 October 1960; box 17-3-4, Sylvania-Corning Nuclear Corporation folder, CIDARM.

53. CGW press release, 21 April 1960; box 17-3-4, Sylvania-Corning Nuclear Corporation folder, CIDARM.

54. Sylcor informational brochure, n.d. (1958–1959?), p. 3, box PL-5 Associates/Subsidiaries: Sylvania-Corning Nuclear Corporation folder, CIDARM. Interestingly, Sylcor appears never to have offered a glass-based fuel element, despite the fact that glass fibers in particular offered advantages, including "large heat-exchange surface, chemical resistance, thermal shock resistance and refractoriness which ensures working the reactor at temperatures up to 1000°" as well as "simplicity and low cost of manufacture" (K. Lustig, "Nuclear Fuel in the Form of Glass Fiber, *Sklar à keramik* Czechoslovakia, 1959, p. 53). Sylvania had been "working on metallic fuel elements" ("Technology: Their Most Important Product," *Forbes*, 1 February 1962, p. 23) and presumably brought that expertise to the table.

55. See W. C. Decker memo to Amory Houghton and E. C. Sullivan on "Common Areas of Interest with Sylvania," 25 January 1956; box 34-6-02/PL5, Sylvania Electric Company folder, CIDARM.

56. Thomas MacAvoy, interview by M. Graham, 31 July 1997.

57. Batelle Memorial Institute, "A Survey of Opportunities in the Nuclear-Power Industry for the Corning Glass Works," 17 April 1956, pp. 92–94; TIC Report M-44 (Batelle
Report BMI-CGW-608).

58. David Hounshell in his chapter entitled "The Evolution of Industrial Research in the
United States," in *Engines of Innovation*, ed. Richard S. Rosenbloom and William J.
Spencer, points out that antitrust legislation severely limited domestic cooperation in
research for the four decades beginning with World War II. This only changed with
Reagan administration efforts to dismantle much of the more restrictive antitrust
regulation in the 1980s (pp. 41–54).

59. Robert Turissini, interview by WGI, 1997. Turissini was one of Corning's chief managers of international joint ventures in the 1970s.

60. *The Alliance Analyst*, 17 February.

Chapter 6

1. "The United States Government and Corning, 1958–1963–1968," n.d. [September
1963]; box 1-5-2, The United States Government and Corning folder, CIDARM.

2. Blaszczyk, "Selling with Science," pp. 480–488.

3. See Arthur L. Day, "Developing American Glass," Edgar Marburg Lecture presented
to the American Society for Testing Materials, 1 July 1936, Atlantic City, N.J., p. 10;
published in the *Proceedings* of that society. Also C. J. Parker, "Applied Optics at Corning Glass Works," *Applied Optics* 7 (May 1968): 738. For further information on Day
and the geophysical lab, (beyond note 5, chapter 3), see Hatten S. Yoder, "Development and Promotion of the Initial Scientific Program for the Geophysical Laboratory," in *The Earth, the Heavens and the Carnegie Institution of Washington, History of
Geophysics*, vol. 5 (Washington, D.C.: American Geophysical Union, 1994).

4. Arthur L. Day, "Developing American Glass," p. 10.

5. Eugene C. Sullivan, letter to A. B. Houghton, 29 March 1917; box P-4, Optical Glass
folder, CIDARM.

6. John Hutchins, interview, October 1997.

7. Arthur W. Baum, "They Live in a Glass House and Like It," *Saturday Evening Post*, 19
August 1944, p. 26.

8. Many of these employees voluntarily left Corning to take jobs in higher priority sectors. Some did the company a great deal of good by raising awareness about Corning in their new government posts and by sending back useful information.

9. John Munier, interview, March 1997.

10. Chuck Lucy, interview by Alec Shuldiner, October 1998; WGI Transcripts.

11. See O. W. Hilbert, "Priorities: World War II Experience," 24 January 1966 ; box G9,
War Products (Priorities) folder, CIDARM. Also, W. W. Shaver, "Corning Glass
Works Research and Development Projects Actively Connected with the War
Effort," 1945; box 9, War Products (Priorities) folder, CIDARM.

12. See W. W. Shaver, "War Problems for Which Financial Assistance from the Government Might Be Justified," 2 September 1942; box 9, War Products (Priorities) folder,
CIDARM. Examples that were exclusively for the war effort included concrete
coated glass pipe for oil lines, glass bullets for the air corps, and glass containers for
sea mines and depth charges. See also Dr. Robert H. Dalton, interview by Diane
Vote, 11 September 1979.

13. "The Glass Heart of a 'Major Weapon,'" *Gaffer*, September 1945, p. 8.

14. "What Won't They Do Next with Glass?" *Gaffer*, February 1945, p. 4.

15. Munier, interview, March 1997.

16. "The Glass Heart of a 'Major Weapon,' " p. 8. GE, Sylvania, Philco, DuMont, and especially RCA were its main competitors. Note that not all of these plants were necessarily producing CRT bulbs; Corning manufactured a wide range of parts for radar sets.

17. William Decker, "Corning Glass Works and Television," letter to holders of common stock enclosed with stock dividend checks, 28 September 1948, p. 2; box P-8, Television Bulbs folder, CIDARM.

18. "The Glass Heart of a 'Major Weapon,' " p. 8.

19. Dr. John L. Sheldon, "Section A—A History: Corning's Role in the First 101 Years of Television," n.d. (1976?), p. 8; box 12-3-11, Television folder, CIDARM.

20. Memo from E. M. Guyer to O. W. Hilbert, "Electric Sealing—Evolution and Prospect," 15 June 1970; Personal Papers of Augustus Filbert, Television Bulbs folder, CIDARM. It is not clear precisely when Guyer made this leap. He states in an article published in the December 1946 issue of *Electronic Industries* that the "new art of electrical glass working...[is] the result of several years of experiment in the research laboratories of the Corning Glass Works." E. M. Guyer, "HF Glass Working," *Electronic Industries*, December 1946; Personal Papers of Augustus Filbert, Television Bulbs, Guyer folder, CIDARM, suggests that it was a wartime development.

21. The low-temperature melting version was not developed until the late 1950s; for more on this topic, see Thomas H. Briggs, "The Glass Industry," 24 January 1983, pp. 13–14; box P-8, Television Bulbs folder, CIDARM.

22. Dr. John L. Sheldon, "Section A—A History: Corning's Role in the First 101 Years of Television," pp. 8–9.

23. For a more detailed discussion of these early experiments, see C. J. Parker, "Applied Optics at Corning Glass Works," p. 739.

24. R. C. Cleveland, William C. Lewis, and Warren L. Price, "History of the CU Unit Invention and Development"; Personal Papers of Augustus Filbert, Optical Glass folder. DeVoe and company had had help from the Electric Melting Lab. The main people involved were A. A. Erickson (who was in manufacturing), Hicks (before he left for the Manhattan Project), Robert C. Cleveland, and William C. Lewis. See also Charles DeVoe, interview by Diane Vote, 4 October 1979.

25. Otto Hilbert [?]), "Remarks and conversations with Mr. George D. Macbeth," 28 February 1968; box 34-6-3, Parkersburg, WV, 1946–1994 folder, CIDARM.

26. The government instigated the optical glass program in World War I but had not paid for it. "The expenses incurred [in running this program] were covered by CIW [the Carnegie Institution of Washington, where Day worked] and no compensation was ever received for their work." Charles T. Prewitt, *Annual Report of the Director, Geophysical Laboratory, 1988–1989*, CIWGL Papers, no. 2150, p. 194.

27. "Parkersburg," n.d., p. 1; Historical Memo Notebook, vol. 13, Parkersburg section, CIDARM. After the war Corning purchased the plant from the government and converted it to the manufacture of tubing and piping. See also "Gaffer goes to Parkersburg," *Gaffer*, June 1946, melt 4, run 3.

28. This high-tech innovation was paired with the decidedly low-tech "let-'er-down-easy method," which was "fundamental to all of this." C. F. DeVoe, memo to Otto Hilbert, "Optical Glass Devel.," 29 January 1979, p. 2; box P-4, Optical Glass—Folder 1, CIDARM. Pouring the glass into the mold in this "easy" fashion meant filling it at

such a rate and in such a way as to guarantee that the stream of molten glass did not fold in on itself and that air bubbles were not allowed to enter the glass. Another related innovation was the use of full-scale oil modeling, whereby an oil or other fluid, was used to simulate the action of glass being mixed. The results of such tests could then be applied to stirrer design.

29. R. C. Cleveland et al., "History of the CU Unit Invention and Development."
30. An accounting of the four years showed that eighty-eight companies and universities received over $500,000 and over fifty received over $1 million in research support. See Larry Owen, *Business History Review,* "OSRD and the Government," 68(1994): 565-576.
31. The figure is from David Hounshell, "Dupont and the Management of Large-Scale Research and Development, in Peter Galison and Bruce Hevly (eds.), *Big Science: The Growth of Large Scale Research* (Stanford: Stanford University Press, 1992) p. 253.
32. See James Gilbert, *Redeeming Culture,* pp. 38–39; Daniel Kevles, *The Physicists: The History of a Scientific Community in Modern America* (Cambridge: Harvard University Press, 1971) pp. 369-379; and Kevles, "K1S2: Korea, Science, and the State" in Galison, *Big Science,* pp. 312–313.
33. See Edwin Mansfield, *Industrial Research and Technological Innovation,* pp. 10–15, for data on federal research funding by funding agent and performing institution, as well as by allocation among industries.
34. *New York Times,* quoted in Jessica Wang, "Science, Security, and the Cold War: The Case of E.U. Condon," *Isis* 93 (1992).
35. T. Waaland, "Post War Plans," 29 August 1944; box G-8, Postwar Planning folder, CIDARM.
36. See the several documents contained in box G-9, War Production Priorities folder, CIDARM.
37. T. J. Thompson, memo to C. D. LaFollette, "Some Current Aspects of Postwar Business, Technical Products Division," 17 July 1944, p. 4; box G-8, Postwar Planning folder, CIDARM.
38. Box G-8, Postwar Planning folder, p. 1, CIDARM.
39. E. C. Sullivan, no title, 4 May 1951; box G-9, War Production Priorities folder, CIDARM.
40. Box G-8, Postwar Planning folder, CIDARM.
41. T. J. Thompson, "Some Current Aspects of Post-War Business, Technical Products Division," CIDARM.
42. Alan Brinkley, *The End of Reform,* p. 117.
43. Details may be found in Forrest Behm, interview by Davis Dyer, 6 March 1997; WGI Transcripts.
44. Dr. John L. Sheldon, "Section A—A History: Corning's Role in the First 101 Years of Television," p. 8.
45. For a discussion of some of these differences, see L. B. Headrick, unaddressed memo, "Glass Characteristics Required for Cathode-Ray Tubes," 25 August 1944 (revised 12 June 1945 and 25 March 1948); box 17-4-6, Television Glass folder, CIDARM.
46. Sheldon, "Section A—A History," p. 11.
47. Materials on Condon may be found in box 3-3-3/B1, E. U. Condon folder, CIDARM, and in the collections of the American Philosophical Society.
48. Kevles, *The Physicist,* p. 379.

49.   Condon Papers, American Philosophical Society.

50.   Ibid.

51.   The following is based on Chuck Lucy, interview by Davis Dyer, 12 January 1999; and
      Chuck Lucy, interview by Alec Shuldiner, 29 October 1998; WGI Transcripts.

52.   Ibid.

53.   T. Howitt, memo to Amory Houghton Jr. et al., "Dr. Stevenson Visit 9/29/69," 7
      October 1969, p. 3; Technology Staffs folder, CIDARM.

54.   C. B. Wakeman, memo to W. H. Armistead, "Proposal for Corning Growth in Elec-
      tronics," 4 March 1968, p. 1; CIDARM.

55.   See "The United States Government and Corning, 1958–1963–1968."

56.   Thomas MacAvoy, interview by M. Graham, 31 July 1997.

57.   R. C. Cleveland et al., "History of the CU Unit Invention and Development," p. 12.
      On Corning's work in this field in general, see also C. J. Parker, "Applied Optics at
      Corning Glass Works."

58.   Quotations are from Charles D. LaFollette, proposal to air material command,
      "Request for Quotation, Purchase Request 123,855," 24 February 1950, "Outline of
      Optics Research Program"; box P-4, Optical Glass—folder 1, CIDARM. As the above
      suggests, the technical challenge was not size but optical purity. The research pro-
      gram being proposed was "intended to develop methods capable of producing opti-
      cal glass discs up to 36" in diameter and 4" thick," well within the size range of
      previous undertakings. Corning may well have cooperated with German specialists
      in optical glass as part of this program. In a memo from E. C. Leibig to R. Britting-
      ham dated 1 August 1951, Leibig answers a series of questions (earlier posed by Brit-
      tingham), including "If we were to make an agreement [regarding German patents],
      would we send technicians to Germany or would they come here?" Leibig's sug-
      gested answer is "we should send technicians to Germany and also have some Ger-
      mans come over here." However, this same memo indicates that Corning expected
      to improve on the German process, even without the advice of German technicians:
      "Information that we have indicates that the Germans are selling this glass for $14.00
      per pound. We estimate that if our process is successful our costs will be about $6.00
      per pound." E. C. Leibig to R. Brittingham, memo, "Massive Optics," 1 August 1951;
      Historical Memo Notebook, vol. 20, Windows section, CIDARM.

59.   R. C. Cleveland et al., "History of the CU Unit Invention and Development," p. 13.

60.   M. G. Britton, "Development of Manufacturing Process for the Production of High
      Quality Optical Glass," 12 February 1964, p. 31; TIC Report P10-3.

61.   R. C. Cleveland et al., "History of the CU Unit Invention and Development," pp.
      13–14. The research team included DeVoe, Cleveland, and Bill Lewis, as well as Al
      Werner and Hank Hagy, who helped with measurements, and George B. Hares, who
      worked out an appropriate glass composition.

62.   The air force contract stated as its goal the production of "precision optical glass
      blanks... with a degree of perfection which is presently unavailable domestically"
      (C. J. Parker, "Applied Optics at Corning Glass Works," p. 740); technical leadership in
      this field had once again moved abroad.

63.   "Report on Optical and Ophthalmic Glass Operations at Corning Glass Works," 25
      June 1948, chart A; box 34-6-3, Parkersburg WV, 1946–1994 folder, CIDARM.

64.   T. J. Thompson, "Some Current Aspects of Postwar Business, Technical Products
      Division," pp. 4–5.

65. For further details, see William Armistead, interview by M. Graham, 13 May 1997; WGI Transcripts.

66. See S. Donald Stookey, "Modern Glass," *International Science and Technology*, July 1962; and M. G. Britton, "Case History of the Development of PYROCERAM® Brand Glass-Ceramics," 1 February 1966, p. 19; box P-5, Pyroceram folder, CIDARM.

67. Dale A. Noll, "Ceramic Radomes: Materials, Design and Manufacture," n.d. [1967?]; TIC Reprint 002715. An internal document indicated that by the end of 1958 Corning had contributed radomes to the Convair Tartar, Hughes Falcon, and the China Lake missile, and it had filled orders from the Watertown Arsenal, Convair, and the Applied Physical Laboratory (at MIT). See "Pyroceram Confidential News Letter and Product Development News," 1, no. 10 (December 1958): p. 4; box 33-6-02 (P5), Pyroceram Products folder, C/DARM.

68. This data and that found in the following paragraph are derived from a chart put out by the radome department, Technical Products Division in 1963 or 1964 (document attached to Dale A. Noll, "Ceramic Radomes: Materials, Design and Manufacture," TIC Reprint 002715).

69. G. P. Smith, "A History of a Research Project: Glass-Ceramics at Corning Glass Works," 20 June 1975, p. 11; Historical Memo Notebook, vol. 3, Ceramic-Glass section, CIDARM. The announcement was made concurrently with the official opening of the Sullivan labs. (See *Corning Leader* of 23 May 1957 for a number of stories from that day.) At the time, Corning reported having melted experimentally "more than 400 types of Pyroceram [but] only four have been fully investigated and melted in pilot runs to date" ("Corning Introduces Pyroceram: Crystalline Material Formed from Glass," *Glass Industry*, June 1957, p. 332).

70. W. W. Shaver, "Recent Developments in Glass Research," *Symposium on Materials Research Frontiers*, Special Technical Publication, No. 243, American Society for Testing Materials, 1958; TIC Reprints, Shaver file.

71. Waterman presentation to Advertising Managers Bureau of the New York State Dailies, 18 May 1959.

72. See box 17-3-5, Institutional Ads, Corning Ware folder, and Consumer Advertising binders, CIDARM. Journalists took up the cry: "Products of the space age are not limited to Cape Canaveral. The same super-strength ceramic Pyroceram that is used in missile nose cones is appearing in cooking utensils made by Corning Glass Works.... This Corning Ware won't melt, won't crack and won't warp and is guaranteed forever against breakage from temperature extremes" (Marion Fisher Hill, *Cleveland Plain Dealer*, 19 February 1959).

73. H. E. Hagy, "Massive Glass as a Naval Structural Material," 19 August 1969, p. 1; TIC Report L-1009. As Kenneth Pollock noted, "Corning has many years' experience in manufacturing glass and fused silica mirror blanks which weigh many tons" (Kenneth G. Pollock, "Estimates of Present and Future Capabilities for Manufacture of Massive Glass Hull Sections," 4 January 1968, p. 3; TIC Report P-26). These clearly count as massive castings, and experience with them aided Corning in dealing with the problems associated with the cooling of ultra-thick glass pieces; nevertheless, we take the term to apply solely to glass spheres and hemispheres intended for naval applications, and it is so used in most internal documents.

74. Kenneth G. Pollock, "Estimates of Present and Future Capabilities for Manufacture of Massive Glass Hull Sections," 4 January 1968, pp. 23–24; TIC Report P-26. As diffi-

cult as it was to achieve a perfect glass-to-glass seal, it was that much harder to manage a flawless glass-to-metal seal of the sort necessary for the installation of a hatch
or other such hull insert. For an overview of glass-to-metal sealing technology, see
Robert H. Dalton, "How to Design Glass-to-Metal Joints," *Product Engineering* (26
April 1965), pp. 62–71.

75. Kenneth G. Pollock, "Estimates of Present and Future Capabilities," p. 35. One possible answer to the problem of glass's odd fragility was to coat it with a protectant of
some sort: a "coating of acrylic, .016" thick, was applied to four 56" diameter hemispheres for the Naval Undersea Warfare Center at China Lake, California"; results of
this test are not recorded, though there is some indication that earlier such work had
not been fruitful (see Robert H. Dalton, "Recent Developments in Glass," *Journal of
Chemical Education* 40 (February 1963): 103, "through application of this principle [of
applied coatings] we may achieve a worthwhile but not a striking gain [in resistance
to abrasion and overall strength]"). See also H. E. Hagy, "Massive Glass as a Naval
Structural Material," 19 August 1969, pp. 4–5; TIC Report L-1009.

76. Lucy, interview, 29 October 1998; WGI Transcripts.

77. See "The United States Government and Corning, 1958–1963–1968."

78. Jack Hutchins, interview by Davis Dyer, 20 November 1997; WGI Transcripts.

79. Francis Kapper, interview by Alec Shuldiner, 8 August 1997; WGI Transcripts.

80. For a discussion of problems with the concept of spinoff in general, see John A. Alic
et. al., *Beyond Spinoff: Military and Commercial Technologies in a Changing World*
(Boston: Harvard Business School Press, 1992).

81. Amory Houghton to James E. Webb, December 31, 1963; unaccessioned material,
CIDARM.

Chapter 7

1. William Armistead, *The Future of Research (Report to Senior Management)*, 1967; ARV
27, Technical Staffs file, CIDARM.

2. See Margaret B. W. Graham, "Industrial Research in the Age of Big Science," in
Richard S. Rosenbloom, ed. *Research in Technological Innovation* (Greenwich: JAI Press,
1985); Daniel Kevles, *The Physicists*; David Hounshell, "The Evolution of Industrial
Research," in Richard S. Rosenbloom and William Spencer, *Engines of Innovation: U.S.
Industrial Research at the End of an Era* (Cambridge: Harvard Business School Press,
1996), pp. 41–51. Scientists, in particular physicists, had mounted a campaign beginning in the mid-1930s to convince the public, and especially the Washington establishment, that pure science was a necessary pillar of military preparedness and needed
to be funded on that basis. E. U. Condon was a central figure in these debates, believing that science could be relied on to cure all of the world's major problems as long
as it was not taken over completely by the military (E. U. Condon, "Some Thoughts
on Science in the Federal Government," *Physics Today*, vol. 5, No 46–13, April 1952.
Hounshell notes that what made this model especially compelling for leaders of
research-performing companies was that one major prewar avenue to realizing the
benefits from research through technology sharing with other companies had been
foreclosed by the vigorous antitrust campaign begun by the New Deal Justice
Department and continued into the 1970s.

3. See S. Donald Stookey, *Crystal Ball*: pp. 7–12. Unless otherwise indicated, the remain-

der of the sections on Stookey in this chapter are based on this memoir and two interviews with him conducted by Winthrop Group, Inc., one in January 1998 and the other in January 1999.

4. The term "glass technologist" now applied to those who worked on control of melting; earlier it had been used more broadly.

5. Stookey, *Crystal Ball*, pp. 14–16.

6. Quoted in Otto Hilbert, HM, "Television," 17 June 1971, p. 5; box P-8, Television Bulbs folder, CIDARM.

7. See Margaret B. W. Graham, *The Business of Research: RCA and the VideoDisc* (New York: Cambridge University Press, 1986); and "The Threshold of the Information Age" in Alfred D. Chandler and James Cortada, eds., *A Nation Transformed by Information* (New York: Oxford University Press, 2000). See also Hilbert "Television," 1983 HM, unaccessioned material, CIDARM, which cites cost and volumes of radio bulbs sold. These figures did not change much after automation using the Ribbon Machine.

8. Forrest Behm, interview by WGI, 1998.

9. Ibid.

10. The low-temperature melting version was not developed until the late 1950s; for more on this topic, see Thomas H. Briggs, "The Glass Industry," 24 January 1983, pp. 13–14; box P-8, Television Bulbs folder, CIDARM.

11. See several boxes of Dalton correspondence with RCA and other customers in CIDARM.

12. Hilbert, HM "Television," p. 3.

13. John Sheldon, 1954 *Yearly Report*; TIC, research department annual reports, "Sheldon, J. L."

14. Stookey, *Crystal Ball*, p. 17.

15. John Hammond Munier, Annual Report for 1948, Television Summary Report, and interview by WGI, March 1997.

16. See John Hammond Munier, interview by WGI, March 1997; and Howard Kiehl, *Annual Report on Pilot Plant Two Operations*, 1951; TIC, Kiehl Memos and Reports file.

17. Sheldon, *Annual Report* for 1954.

18. Jack Carpenter, interview by WGI, 1997.

19. Large process-oriented companies used pilot plants heavily after the war to continue their process improvement, but they often abandoned work on new materials and new products because introducing them was too disruptive to existing high-volume operations. Graham and Pruitt, *R&D for Industry*, pp. 292–294.

20. William Armistead, interview by WGI, 1997.

21. Condon to Armistead, May 1961 in Condon Papers, American Philosophical Society (hereafter APS).

22. Edwin H. Land, *The Future of Industrial Research* (New York: Standard Oil Development Co., 1945), p. xii.

23. See E. U. Condon, "Acquisition of Property Adjoining the Glass Center," 24 July 1952; and "New Research Center," October 1952, both addressed to Amory Houghton, Condon Papers, APS.

24. Hyde letter, Hyde Correspondence, 1947, unaccessioned material, formerly in TIC files.

25. Specifically these included viscosity, annealing and stress, annealing versus density, light scattering, heat transfer by radiation, viscosity versus electrical resistivity, col-

orants for studying glass structure, small angle scattering, infrared transmittance, and ultraviolet spectrophotometry.

26. Condon to Armistead, 1961 Condon Papers, APS.
27. Frazier continues, "the laboratory supplied several 1,000 pound lots before the responsibility was assumed by a production unit." See also J. F. Frazier, report summarizing color television engineering activities from 1951 to 1957; TIC, "Corning Engineering Research Color Television Bulbs, 1951–1957".
28. Armistead interview, 1998.
29. Amory Houghton, interview by WGI, 1997.
30. Amory Houghton to Armistead, ARV 27, Technical Staffs files, CIDARM.
31. These institutions included Amsterdam, Toronto, Imperial College of London, Cambridge, Durham, Columbia, Colorado, Cornell, Purdue, Rutgers, Harvard, Brown, Michigan, MIT, Penn, Penn State, Rochester, Illinois, RPI, Iowa and Iowa State, Boston University, Ohio State, Louisville, Utah, Wisconsin, and UCLA.
32. E. U. Condon to William Armistead, April 1962; Condon Papers, APS.
33. See the ten-year growth chart in the 1967 *Report of the Technical Advisory Committee* chaired by Condon, Condon Papers, APS.
34. Margaret B. W. Graham, "Industrial R&D in the Age of Big Science."
35. See the *Report of the Technical Advisory Committee*, 1967; Jack Carpenter, interview by WGI, 1998; Howitt, interview by WGI.
36. This was a common philosophy in management circles during the 1960s. RCA's hiring of executives from IBM to manage its strategic new product efforts to a strictly planned timetable, and Alcoa's top level push on its alternative smelting process (ASP) were only two examples of the widely shared belief in top management involvement. See Graham, *RCA and the Video Disc: The Business of Research*, and Graham and Pruitt, *R&D for Industry*.
37. S. Donald Stookey, "Glass Chemistry as I Saw it," *Chemical Technology* 1 (August 1971): 463.
38. Stookey, *Crystal Ball*, p. 21.
39. Quoted in Stookey, *Crystal Ball*, p. 23. Corning later fought one of its most bitter intellectual property battles over this discovery; see chapter 8.
40. Norval Johnston, interview by WGI.
41. See the several hundred inquiries from potential customers about the possible uses of Pyroceram contained in Products "Pyrocerom" folder, CIDARM.
42. John MacDowell, interview by WGI, August 1998. MacDowell, a senior research manager beginning in the 1960s, described it as Corning's corporate tendency in this period to assume on top-down initiative that product development should begin with new materials technology and find a market. This lasted until the Chemcor failure (see below) undermined the broader company's faith in the laboratories.
43. William Armistead, interview by WGI.
44. "Corning FYI: A Special Report on the Chemcor Announcement," Corning Public Relations Department, 21 September 1962; box 7-3-1, Chemcor folder 2, CIDARM. Corning researchers had already announced their findings to the sixth International Glass Congress in Washington, D.C., a couple of months previously. See Joseph S. Olcott, "Chemical Strengthening of Glass," *Science*, 14 June 1963.
45. William H. Armistead, press statement, 18 September 1962, p. 3. See also "Corning Announces New Method for Strengthening Glass Articles," "The Search for Strength in Glass Articles," and statements by William H. Armistead, Joseph F. Olcott, and

Amory Houghton Jr., all dated 18 September 1962 and all box 7-3-1, Chemcor folder 2, CIDARM.

46. Amory Houghton Jr., press statement, 18 September 1962, p. 4; box 7-3-1, Chemcor folder 2, CIDARM.

47. Richard Slawsky, "Makers Seek Use of Miracle Glass," *World-Telegram & Sun*, quoted in "Corning in the News: Chemcor—Early National Press Coverage," 1 October 1962, p. 2; box 7-3-1, Chemcor folder 2, CIDARM.

48. "Typical Chemcor Evaluation By Department," n.d. [early 1963]; box 7-3-1, Chemcor folder 3, CIDARM. See especially M. G. Britton to J. F. Frazier et al. memo, "Proposal for Air Force on CHEMCOR Fiber," 5 March 1963; box 7-3-1, Chemcor folder 3, CIDARM.

49. See "Imagine with Chemcor Glass," Chemcor Products sales brochure, 1968; box 33-5-2, Chemcor 1967-1970 folder, CIDARM. Corning was not the only glass company engaged in work on strengthening techniques. Owens-Illinois developed "Duraglas-treated" containers and PPG had at least two generations of a strengthened flat glass it dubbed "Herculite." See "New View for Glass," *Chemical Week*, 25 July 1964.

50. "Waiting in the Wings: Chemically-Toughened Lenses," *National Safety News*, October 1965, p. 44.

51. See J. J. Domicone, "Safety Windshield Development Program," 8 December 1967; TIC R-3691; and Herbert A. Miska, "Safety Windshield Development Program—A Summary," 24 November 1967; TIC R-3673.

52. See G. Clinton Shay, "History of the Development of Fusion Flat Glass Drawing Process," November 13, 1990, TIC.

53. Joseph T. Littleton, interview by WGI, 28 May 1997. See also Forrest Behm, interview by WGI, 13 May 1997; and Tom Howitt, interview by WGI, 30 July 1997.

54. See W. C. Andrews, "Windshield Sagging Project," *Final Report*, 13 September 1971; TIC E-69-13-5.

55. Memo from C. A. Crawford to G. Bair et al., "Re: MUSCLE Project," 2 January 1962, p. 2; box 7-3-1, Chemcor folder 2, CIDARM.

56. *Advisory Committee Report*, 1967.

57. *Management Conference Proceedings*, 1968.

58. Nine received top priority, including the windshield and the fusion process, three strong glass projects under the code name Hercules, Cercor for automotive heat exchangers in turbine engines, steel refractories, a new kind of glass capacitor, and two new types of building material made of chemically strengthened Pyroceram. To enhance their prospects of success Armistead adopted a technical request system. The hurdle for a new business in an unfamiliar market was to be not just the $1 million projected annual sales expected from specialty glass projects, but $10 million annual sales, supported by a request for technical assistance (RFTA) originating from any of nine eligible divisions.

59. Mal Hunt review document and supporting documentation, 12 November 1963, from Amory Houghton Jr. Technical Staff Files, also Action & Plan for Growth in Electronics, 6 November 1967; memo from Bielawski and Fehlner to Armistead, Riley and Wakeman, Non-technical Issues Encountered during Survey of the Future of Integrated Circuit Technology folder; box 1126, ARV 27, CIDARM.

60. See Signetics brochure "History," n.d. [1969]; box 33-6-02/PL5, Signetics folder, CIDARM.

61. Jack Carpenter, interview by WGI, 30 July 1997.
62. Quoted in "Signetics Shows How in Semiconductors," *Business Week*, 26 July 1969, p. 41.
63. Jack Carpenter, interview by WGI, 30 July 1997.
64. Thomas MacAvoy, interview by WGI, 31 July 1997.
65. Oakes Ames to Houghton and Waterman, memo on Sylvania; and Arthur D. Little report on Sylvania and the structure of the television industry; Box 34-6-02/PL5, Sylvania Electric Company folder, CIDARM .

Chapter 8

1. Amory Houghton, letter of resignation to Donald M. Nelson, chairman, War Production Board, 28 August 1942; box 19-3-06, War Production Board 1943 folder, CIDARM. Houghton joined the WPB in December 1941 (when it was still called the Office of Production Management) as assistant deputy director of the materials division and had been promoted to deputy chief of the Bureau of Industry Branches a couple of months later. As of July 1942 he held one of the top five positions at the WPB. Resignation was not an action to be taken lightly.
2. The 1926 case was *U.S. v. General Electric Co.,* 272 U.S. 476 (1926). It dealt with GE's licensing of Westinghouse for the sale of electric lamps and the use of price-fixing agreements as part of the license contract. For more on the history of antitrust, see James R. Williamson, *Federal Antitrust Policy during the Kennedy-Johnson Years* (Westport, Conn.: Greenwood, 1995); Milton Handler, *Twenty-Five Years of Antitrust: Annual Lectures Delivered before the Association of the Bar of the City of New York,* 2 vols. (New York: Matthew Bender, 1973); Milton Handler, *Antitrust in Transition,* vol. 1 (Ardsley-on-Hudson, N.Y.: Transnational Juris Publications, 1991); Tony Freyer, *Regulating Big Business: Antitrust in Great Britain and America, 1880–1990* (New York: Cambridge University Press, 1992); and E. Thomas Sullivan, ed., *The Political Economy of the Sherman Act: The First One Hundred Years* (New York: Oxford University Press, 1991). Thumbnail sketches of the formation and history of the Glass Trust abound; one of the most accessible is Raymond C. Nordhaus and Edward F. Jurow, *Patent-Antitrust Law* (Chicago: Jural Publishing, 1961), pp. 398–401. The papers related to the *Hartford-Empire* case itself are located primarily in box 34-3-3/G4, Empire Machine Company & 'E' Machine folder 5, CA box 1222, Hartford-Empire Company folder, CIDARM.
3. Hearings before the TNEC, 75th Cong., 3d sess., pt. 2, p. 377 passim. The glass industry had its fair share of attention as well. Bausch & Lomb was held up as a preeminent example of international cartelization for its market-apportioning agreements with Carl Zeiss of Germany, and Owens-Corning Fiberglas was also pilloried.
4. "The Houghtons of Corning," *Fortune* 32 (July 1945): 132.
5. Walton Hamilton, "Antitrust in Action," TNEC Monograph 16 (Washington, D.C.: Government Printing Office, 1940), p. 16.
6. Walton Hamilton et al., "Patents and Free Enterprise," TNEC Monograph 31 (Washington, D.C.: Government Printing Office, 1940), pp. 110–111.
7. A number of other Corning employees, including Alanson Houghton, William Decker, George Hollister, and Glen Cole, were named but dismissed by the Court. See *Final Judgment of the District Court of the United States for the Northern District of Ohio, Western Division, United States of America vs. Hartford-Empire Company, et al.,* 46 F.

Sup. 541, filed 8 October 1942, section 60, p. 48; box 34-3-3/G4, Empire Machine Company & 'E' Machine folder 5, CIDARM.

8. *Final Judgment*, 8 October 1942, sec. 5, p. 8; box 34-3-3/G4, Empire Machine Company & 'E' Machine folder 5, CIDARM.

9. Brief for appellants, *Corning Glass Works et al., v. The United States of America*, 22 September 1943, p. 66; box 34-3-3/G4, Empire Machine Company & 'E' Machine folder 1, CIDARM.

10. George B. Wells, letter to Amory Houghton Jr., 31 August 1942; box 19-3-06, "War Production Board resignation and pertinent letters 1942," CIDARM.

11. M. H. Eisenhart, letter to Amory L. Houghton, 8 September 1942; box 19-3-06, "War Production Board resignation and pertinent letters 1942," CIDARM.

12. Brief for appellants, *Corning Glass Works et al.*, pp. 9–10.

13. Decision of the Supreme Court of the United States, *Hartford-Empire Co., et al. v. United States*, 323 U.S. 386, 8 January 1945.

14. American Enterprise Institute for Public Policy Research, *Antitrust Consent Decrees, 1906–1966: Compendium of Abstracts* (Washington, D.C.: 1968), p. 705.

15. "The Houghtons of Corning," p. 260.

16. Eugene C. Sullivan, "The Place, Magnitude and Character of Research and Technical Development in the Glass Industry and the Need for Patent Protection," 18 October 1939, p. 18; box 34-4/G-7, Patents and Trademarks folder, CIDARM.

17. Ibid., p. 19.

18. Ibid., p. 3.

19. Wherein the defendants were "enjoined from engaging in or participating in practices, contracts, relationships, or understandings, or claiming any rights thereunder, having a tendency to continue or revive any of the aforesaid violations of the Sherman Antitrust Act and the Clayton Act" (Final Judgment of the District Court, sec. 9, p. 10).

20. "The Houghtons of Corning," p. 260.

21. Milton Handler, *Antitrust in Transition*, vol. 1 (Ardsley-on-Hudson, N.Y.: Transnational Juris Publications, 1991), xxiii. The National Association of Manufacturers hailed the eventual outcome of the decision as "perhaps the most important patent case decision in our history" (R. J. Dearman [chairman, NAM Committee on Patents], foreword to George E. Folk, "Patents and the Glass Industry Case," NAM Monograph, 1945, p. 2). The NAM was relieved that the lower court's more draconian judgment had not been upheld. See below.

22. "The settlement follows in broad outline the classic pattern set in other similar cases in the glass industry (Hartford Empire Co.)." "The Impact of Two Historic Antitrust Decrees," *Business Week*, 4 February 1956, p. 26. In order to break the company's hold on the market for tabulating machines and computers, the DOJ insisted that IBM, among other things, begin selling instead of just leasing its products and that it license the relevant patents to all comers under reasonable terms or even, in some cases, royalty-free. In a marked departure from *Hartford-Empire*, the DOJ also got IBM to agree to offer know-how not contained in its patent applications, including direct training of those wishing to engage in the manufacture of tabulating machines.

23. "The Impact of Two Historic Antitrust Decrees," p. 27.

24. Antitrust activity has focused less on abuse of patent monopoly since the 1950s than

it has on other issues, particularly conglomeration. This trend peaked in the Nixon administration's attempts to prevent International Telephone and Telegraph (ITT) from making certain acquisitions. For a history of these cases, see Robert M. Goolrick, *Public Policy Toward Corporate Growth: The ITT Merger Cases* (Port Washington, N.J.: Kennikat, 1978).

25. "The Houghtons of Corning," p. 260.
26. Anchor Hocking Advertisements, *Good Housekeeping*, June and December 1951; CIDARM binder. Anchor Hocking continued to contest Pyrex for market share, though not always on price. In the late 1970s it came out with an amber line of borosilicate ovenware, noting that "if you like Pyrex ware, you'll love Anchor Hocking's Harvest Amber ovenware"; Anchor Hocking Advertisements, CIDARM binder.
27. For examples of these images, see advance proof of advertisement scheduled to appear in various 1971 issues of *Modern Brides, Seventeen,* and *Glamour*; box 17-3-5, Institutional Ads, Corning Ware folder, CIDARM; cover of the 1960 distributor catalog; box 17-3-5, Institutional Ads, Corning Ware folder, CIDARM and advertisement in *The New Orleans Times-Picayune,* 3 April 1959; box 17-3-5, Institutional Ads, Corning Ware folder, CIDARM.
28. September 1964 issue of *Good Housekeeping*; Anchor Hocking Advertisements folder, CIDARM.
29. As noted in G. P. Smith, "A History of a Research Project: Glass-Ceramics," *Glass and Ceramic Bulletin* 23, no. 1 (1976): 15–23: "continuing research at Corning and many other glass laboratories had been on formation of stable glasses *which would not uncontrollably devitrify* [our emphasis]." The mental leap that Stookey and his colleagues had made was to reframe a defect—the tendency of glass to crystallize—into a benefit, a form of innovation that Harrison Hood claimed as Corning's stock in trade.
30. 253 F. Sup. 461 (1966) (*Corning Glass Works v. Anchor Hocking Glass Corp.,* final judgment), p. 465.
31. "Corning Glass' Patent for Pyroceram Upheld by U.S. Appeals Bench," *Wall Street Journal,* 22 March 1967, p. 4.
32. Letter entitled "Possible Litigation" from Philip Churchill (attorney at Fish, Richardson & Neave) to Clarence Patty Jr., 21 February 1968; Executive Papers G 20.2.4, Technical Staffs folder, CIDARM.
33. Memo from C. R. Patty Jr. to Amory Houghton Jr., 2 January 1968; Executive Papers G 20.2.4, Technical Staffs folder, CIDARM.
34. See Regina Blaszczyk, "Selling with Science."
35. Letter to the Honorable Frank E. Moss, p. 353.
36. Norval Johnston, interview by Davis Dyer, 11 December 1998.
37. Voss's new product development reports show that the original product developers knew about the chemical attack problem on glues, but later redesign efforts in service of cost reduction had apparently not had access to, or had at least not taken note of, the original testing data.
38. Thomas MacAvoy, interview by Davis Dyer, July 1998.
39. "Summary of Corning's Percolator Recall," n.d. [c. 1977]; unaccessioned material, CIDARM.
40. McKinsey & Company, "Protecting Research and Development Expenditures in the Years Ahead," letter of transmittal, 15 September 1960; Corning Patent Department, historical file, WCQ—Benchmarking folder.

41. Ibid.

42. Ibid., pp. 1–4.

43. McKinsey & Company, "Protecting Research and Development Expenditures in the Years Ahead," July 1961, p. 2; Corning Patent Department, historical file, WCQ—Benchmarking folder.

44. W. H. Armistead, memo to Amory Houghton Jr. and other Corning executives, "Corning Patent Situation," 19 July 1961, p. 1; Corning Patent Department, historical file, WCQ—Benchmarking folder.

45. George Beall, interview by M. Graham, 28 March 1996.

46. Notation on Clarence Patty, memo to Amory Houghton Jr. and Lee Waterman, 8 July 1964, setting forth a draft that was later reviewed and discussed in a meeting on 9 September 1964; Executive Papers G 20.2.3, Technical Staffs folder, CIDARM.

47. William Armistead, transcript of speech on "Strategy for the 1970s," Corning Management Conference, 23 April 1968, p. 94; Condon Papers, APS.

48. The quotations and outline of material above are taken from Clarence Patty Jr. to Frederick Knight, file memorandum, "Western Electric—Corning Glass Works Patent License Meeting October 7, 1968," 11 October 1968; Executive Papers G 20.2.3, Technical Staffs folder, CIDARM.

49. William Armistead, "Strategy for the 1970s," p. 93.

50. Ibid., pp. 93–94.

51. A comprehensive market study from 1965 makes no mention of telecommunications. See F. B. Leibold Jr., "Fiber Optic Market Study," 22 March 1965; box C.A. 1124, Fiber Optic Market Study folder, CIDARM. American Optical was the only other company that offered products in every major (glass) fiber-optic category. See D. S. Martin to D. L. Dochstader, memo, "Fiber Optics," 26 October 1967; box C.A. 1124, Fiber Optics folder, CIDARM.

52. This account of the origins of Corning's fiber optics business is taken from original reports by William Shaver and Gail Smith of their meetings at the SMTE and the BPO from early 1966 through 1967, first directed to George Bair and then, as word got around, to a long distribution list including the Houghtons, Armistead, and others; see William Shaver and Gail Smith, Period Reports; TIC history files. Further developments discussed below are taken from the following: Chuck Lucy, "Fused Silica and Me," 1998; personal recollections of Chuck Lucy; interviews with Lee Wilson, Chuck Lucy, and Ira C. Magaziner and Mark Patinkin, The Silent War: Inside the Global Business Battles Shaping America's Future (New York: Random House, 1989). Many discussions of the technical issues related to optical waveguides exist; Les C. Gunderson and Donald B. Keck, "Optical Fibers: Where Light Outperforms Electrons," Technology Review 86 (May-June 1983): 3–14, is a good example.

53. Even a glass that does not absorb light will allow it to leak out the sides of the fiber unless the fiber is encased in another substance with a lower index of refraction; this so-called cladding serves as a mirror to reflect the errant light back into the central pathway of the fiber.

54. Don Keck, interview by M. Graham, 17 May 1997; WGI Transcripts.

55. Fran Vorhees, interview by Davis Dyer, November 1997; WGI Transcripts.

56. John Hutchins, interview by Davis Dyer, 20 November 1997; WGI Transcripts.

57. They were BICC and Plessey (British telecoms equipment suppliers), Siemens (the German electronics giant), CGE and the Telecoms Ministry in France, Pirelli and the

Telecoms Ministry in Italy, and Furakawa and Nippon Telephone and Telegraph in Japan.

58. Lee Wilson, interview by M. Graham, 27–28 November 1997; WGI Transcripts.

59. Ibid.

60. L. C. Gunderson, "A Case History of The Optical Waveguide Project at Corning Glass Works," n.d. [1980], p. 6; unaccessioned material, CIDARM.

61. Amory Houghton Jr., quoted in "The Trials Of Amory Houghton Jr.," *Forbes*, 1 August 1977, p. 37.

62. According to Al Michaelsen (explanation to the authors in March 1999), Furakawa, the Japanese joint development partner, opted not to take the license to Corning's know-how that its funding guaranteed it in order to avoid the secrecy provisions that would have entailed. Furakawa chose instead to pursue its own technological regime in its production of fiber-optic materials.

63. Lee Wilson, interview by M. Graham, 27–28 November 1997.

64. Ibid.

65. Ibid.

66. This decision was appealed by Corning but upheld by the Court of Appeals for the Federal Circuit. *Corning Glass Works v. U.S. International Trade Commission* 799 F.2d 1559, 1562, 1572 (230 USPQ 822, 831) (Fed. Cir. 1986).

67. "Corning Glass Wins Patent Case against Sumitomo," *Wall Street Journal*, 14 October 1987, p. 16; for more on the case, see *Corning Glass v. Sumitomo Electric* decision (5 USPQ24).

68. Ibid.

69. Alfred L. Michaelsen to W. C. Ughetta, memo, "Van Campbell's Requested 'Mission Statement,' " 5 June 1985; Corning Patent Department, historical file, WCQ—Benchmarking folder.

70. "The 'Right' Type of People" [memo on hiring for the patent department], 17 October 1985, pp. 2–3; Corning Patent Department, historical file, WCQ—Benchmarking folder.

71. W. C. Ughetta, presentation to the management committee, "Summary of Issue to be Resolved," 17 October 1985, p. 2; Corning Patent Department, historical file, WCQ—Benchmarking folder.

72. J. F. Hyde, letter to Prof. Howard W. Post of University of Buffalo, 27 June 1947; TIC files.

73. Thomas H. Briggs, "The Glass Industry," 24 January 1983, box P8, television bulbs folder, CIDARM.

74. N. A., "The CGW Patent Department—A Change in Orientation," 1984 Corning Patent Department, historical file, "WCQ—Benchmarking" folder.

75. Ed Grainger, Plant Engineer from Martinsburg describes how information about process improvements circulated among Corning plants during his career beginning in 1966 and ending in the 1990s. Grainger himself took expertise from working with chemical strengthening of windshield glass, a product failure, to Martinsburg, where it became part of Martinsburg's very successful Corning Ware production process. Later he was encouraged to travel to other Corning plants to share what Martinsburg had discovered with them. Interview with Davis Dyer, September, 1998.

76. According to John Fanale, the experienced plant manager who turned around RCA's glass plant in Circleville, Indiana, and made it profitable, RCA was at the point of

admitting defeat in its glassmaking endeavors because its engineers refused to listen
to the glassmakers they had hired from Owens Illinois and Corning. The glassmakers
were demonstrating outside the plant with placards that read: "Corning's Way,
Owens-Illinois's Way, RCA's Way—What About Our Way?" Interview with M. Graham, October, 1999.

Chapter 9

1. This widespread dilemma was recognized in the 1970s by numerous commentators,
    but one of its best summaries came in the 1989 publication of an MIT study on the
    pervasive productivity problems of American industry entitled *Made in America:
    Regaining the Productive Edge*, by Michael Dertouzos et al. By the time this book was
    published, the problems involved were widely understood, but no other work high-
    lighted so clearly the systemic nature of the problems, shared by all sectors of the
    economy—industry, government, and academia.
2. Gibson joked that he had learned so little about the controller's job that when they
    closed the books his role was literally to slam a book shut in a small ceremony in the
    plant vestibule. See Martin Gibson interview, February 1999 and Van Campbell inter-
    view, February 1999.
3. See "The 1967 Market for Fused Quartz, Fused Silica and Vycor" by J. A. Busick, mar-
    ket planning department, March 29, 1968; Box C.A. 1124, CIDARM.
4. The Houghton family still reported close to 20 percent ownership of the company's
    stock at the end of the 1960s, a share that diminished gradually during the next sev-
    eral decades.
5. RCA's purchase of such nontechnology based companies as Banquet Foods, Hertz
    Car Rental, and Coronet Carpet had outraged many of its shareholders and demor-
    alized its first-rate electronics research laboratory; Graham, *The Business of Research*.
6. Martin Gibson, interview by Davis Dyer, February 1999.
7. "History of Television Business" memo, 1971, spells out the decline in revenues and
    the fear of Zenith now also threatening to integrate backward. When the television
    bulb business hit its lowest ebb in 1975, sales went to flat zero for six weeks and earn-
    ings fell 75 percent, or barely 2 percent of sales. The number of domestic customers
    Corning could supply went from twenty-eight to five. For ensuing morale issues, see
    video taped discussion between Amo Houghton and Bill Decker, 1975.
8. See Capital Crunch meeting files: consultations with key consultants over the out-
    look for capital availability, ARV 27, CIDARM, and Amo Houghton, April 1968, Man-
    agement Conference. It should be noted that the decade of 1972–1982 was the only
    down decade the US stock market has ever had.
9. On pollution control initiatives, see David Leibson, interview by Davis Dyer, 9 Feb-
    ruary 1999; *Corning and the Environment*, brochure, May 1981; unaccessioned material,
    CIDARM. Joe Rothermel, interview by M. Graham, 15 May 1999.
10. See W.C.D., memo, "Gas," 9 November 1939; box 33-5-01/P3, Glass Manufacturing
    Fuels folder, CIDARM.
11. Allan Cors, interview by Davis Dyer, 13 May 1999.
12. Minutes of Strategic Management Conference, 1968.
13. William Armistead, memo on the future of research, October 1968. This entire sec-
    tion draws on the same Armistead memo.

14. The managerial responses are all found in the same file, collected by Amory Houghton Jr., Ray Voss, memo on general managers' briefing, October 1968; and William Decker in brief cover note on the Armistead memo, 1968; Armistead memo on line managers' deficits; Voss memo on general managers; Dawson post mortem on Signetics; Littleton's post mortem for the windshield project and on the growth problem; Technical Staffs Files, ARV 27, CIDARM.

15. Norm Garrity interview, February 1999, cites, for instance, Leibson's decision to assign him to Charleroi for hot glass experience, as a characteristic career development decision.

16. Leibson interview, February 1999.

17. William Armistead, interview by M. Graham, 13 May 1997. The problem of very demanding, very complicated proprietary processes such as the one invented for Corelle was not Corning's alone at this period. As David Mowery and Nathan Rosenberg point out in *Paths of Innovation,* it was a kind of "Dreadnought" problem that many corporate technical organizations encountered when they pushed proprietary processes rather than maintain balanced development of both products and processes. RCA's elaborate and demanding electron beam recording approach, for instance, intended to keep licensees dependent on its superior technology and to repel recording pirates, was a burden on its own videodisc manufacturing capability (Graham, *RCA and the Video Disc*).

18. RKC, "Corelle and the Impossible Dreams of Jim Giffen," 10 June 1996 and "Laminated Sheet," n.d. [1970s] Glass Innovation Center, Hub Machine/Corelle.

19. Opal glasses, like glass ceramics, crystallize partially when properly heat treated. But unlike glass ceramics, they are relatively soft and thus of limited use even where opacity is required.

20. William Armistead, interview by M. Graham, 13 May 1997.

21. For more on the precise nature of that challenge and its solution, see William H. Dumbaugh, "Laminated Glass," in *Engineered Materials Handbook,* vol. 4, *Ceramics and Glasses* (Materials Park, Ohio: ASM International, 1992).

22. David Leibson, 1998 interview. Corning Z Glass, a Harvard Business School case, offers a disguised account of product introduction, where a similar craft-oriented plant manager resembles Giffen, and Dave Leibson and his group are the process-oriented tiger team.

23. Rumrill-Hoyt, Inc., "Preliminary Merchandising Plan, Corelle Livingware Introduction, 1968," 22 November 1967, p. 4; and "Recommendation for Names for Corning's New Hercules Product," 24 May 1967, p. 4; box C.A. 1124, Miscellaneous (Corelle Livingware) folder, CIDARM.

24. For Corelle Livingware, see "Laminated Sheet," n.d. [1970s]; Glass Innovation Center, Hub Machine/Corelle "The Corelle Livingware Story," 20 September 1978, p. 4; Glass Innovation Center, Hub Machine/Corelle. MacAvoy objectives package 1971–76, Planning Assumptions; and for market share *Forbes,* August 1, 1977, p. 32.

25. This technology came to Corning (as well as to many other U.S. glass manufacturers) via Preston Laboratories, a small consulting lab run by a British scientist who argued that glass should be melted in giant cylinders, with the heat being applied electrically within the batch and new batch materials added at the top in such a manner and amount as to blanket the molten glass with a solid layer of unmelted material. Jack Hutchins regarded Vermel as one of the contributing inventions to

Corelle; see J. R. Hutchins, interview by Davis Dyer, 10 November 1998; WGI Transcripts.

26. For Corelle outcomes and consequences, see Headlines in a Hurry, 29 February 1984; box 33-5-01/P3, Corelle folder, CIDARM. Jim Scott interview, April 1999; and RKC, "Corelle and the Impossible Dreams of Jim Giffen," 10 June 1996; Glass Innovation Center, Hub Machine/Corelle. Problems with Corelle in Europe were both process and product oriented. The price in that market would have to be so high that Corelle could not compete with low-cost earthenware.

27. William H. Dumbaugh Jr. et al., "Method for Making Multi-Layer Laminated Bodies," U.S. Patent 3,737,294, awarded 5 June 1973; MacAvoy, "Technology to Be Utilized," handwritten in July 1971 objectives. He noted, "Very tricky: cost—$3–4 million minimum."

28. See "Marketing Myopia," an article in the *Harvard Business Review* by Theodore Levitt, Professor of Marketing. Corning was traditionally at odds with such views. Amory Houghton Jr. generally listed shareholders behind employees, customers, community as stakeholders in the business.

29. MacAvoy interview, December 1998.

30. Ibid.

31. These effects were such common consequences of productivity programs that two well-known professors at the Harvard Business School, Robert Hayes and Bill Abernathy, gained notoriety for their *Harvard Business Review* article entitled "Managing our way to Economic Doctrine" which pointed out that financially based management techniques produced short-term thinking. They maintained that American companies were undercutting their own ability to invest for the long term, especially in manufacturing. See also William J. Abernathy and Kim Clark, *The Productivity Dilemma* (New York: Basic 1983).

32. According to John MacDowell, a long-time senior research manager, these businesses had had very little contact with research since the early 1960s or before, so they had stopped renewing themselves even before the strategic matrix introduced the idea of cash cows.

33. See MacAvoy's 1971 personal objectives document as president. He has decided to deemphasize new technology in favor of technologies already available.

34. MacAvoy, interview by Davis Dyer, 10 July 1998.

35. See Suresh T. Gulati, "Ceramic Catalyst Supports for Gasoline Fuel," draft, 29 November 1995, p. 2; Augustus Filbert Personal Papers; MacAvoy, interview by Davis Dyer, 10 July 1998.

36. For Cercor, see *Facts about Cercor,* Cellular Materials brochure, 1958; Glass Innovation Center, Glass-Ceramics-Pyroceram/Visions folder; Gail P. Smith, "Cercor: The Development of a Product," *Research/Development Magazine,* November 1963; "The Beginning of the Catalytic Converter," n.d.; Historical Memo Notebook, vol. 3, Ceramic-Glass, CIDARM; and Suresh T. Gulati, "Ceramic Catalyst Supports for Gasoline Fuel," p. 5.

37. Dave Duke, interview by Davis Dyer, 18 April 1997.

38. Thomas MacAvoy, interview by Davis Dyer, 10 July 1998.

39. For Celcor research, see R. D. Bagley et al., "Extruded Cordierite Substrates for Automotive Emissions Control," 18 June 1996; TIC report L-4438 MAN. See also Gulati interview; MacDowell interview; Hutchins interview.

40. Dave Duke, interview by Davis Dyer, 18 April 1997.
41. Charles (Skip) Deneka, interview by M. Graham, 10 December 1998.
42. Dave Duke, interview by Davis Dyer, 18 April 1997.
43. Richard Dulude, interview by Davis Dyer, April 1999.
44. Ben Dobbin, "Corning's Smog Busters," *Corning Leader*, 25 April 1994, p. 2A.
45. MacAvoy, interview by M. Graham, 22 January 1997.
46. MacAvoy, interview by Davis Dyer, 10 July 1998.
47. Hutchins, interview by Davis Dyer.
48. Lucy Interview.
49. Hutchins interview, and Amory Houghton Jr. interview.
50. Dave Duke, interview by Davis Dyer: "We were sucking up resources and engineers."
51. Gibson, interview by Davis Dyer, 1999.
52. See Robert Maurer "Optical Fibers—Past Present and Future Historical Development," 9 September 1985, TIC LZ763. The remaining discussion of Waveguide research comes from interviews with Chuck Lucy, Bob Maurer, Don Keck, Pete Schueltz and Fred Quan. See also Joe Morone, *Winning in High Tech Markets*, pp. 147–155; and Ira Magaziner and Mark Patinkin, *The Silent War*.
53. Bob Maurer, interview by M. Graham, 1998. See also Lee Wilson interview with M. Graham, Nov. 1997, and Lucy interview.
54. BCG also concluded that Corning should only produce boules, the first stage of optical fiber, leaving the later and more profitable stages of production to others.
55. Jeffrey Hecht, *The City of Light* (New York: Oxford University Press, 1998). Hecht covers the entire industry in an extremely informative history.
56. Gitimoy Kar interview, 1998. Kar's team chose to run both IV and OV until OV could be fully commercial so they could begin selling some fiber in the open market.
57. Dave Duke, interview by Davis Dyer, 1997.
58. Deneka interview, 1998.
59. MacDowell and Keck interviews.
60. Dave Duke interview.
61. Joe Hicks interview, 1998. This account of the early Siecor joint venture draws on interviews with Hicks, Dawson, and Wilson.
62. Dawson, interview by Davis Dyer, 1998.
63. Ibid.
64. This account of laboratory morale draws on interviews with Howard Weetall, Jack Hutchins, John MacDowell, Harmon Garfinkel, and Pete Schultz.
65. Ralph Messing, *Biotechnology Patent Digest*, p. 1968.
66. MacAvoy, interview by M. Graham.
67. Joe Littleton study of innovation, from his personal files, dated 1974.
68. J. R. Houghton, interview by M. Graham, 1997.
69. This account of the Avon Laboratory draws on interviews with André Andreu, Jacques Lemoine, and Chuck Wakeman.
70. International R&D, WHA 2/1/73. Copy bound with Jacques Lemoine OPCOM Review, 13 May 1993.
71. See Armistead memo dated 2/5/73 copied in Jacques Lemoine's presentation to the operating committee on the history of the Avon laboratory, his personal copy dated 5 May, 1993.
72. Lemoine, OPCOM review.

73. Wakeman interview, August 1997; John Dunphy interview, March 1996; Lemoine interview, August 1998.

74. André Andreu, interview by M. Graham, August 1997.

75. Filbert interview, July 1997.

76. Jack Hutchins, interview by Davis Dyer, 20 November 1997.

77. This was characteristic of the unusual degree of freedom Corning researchers enjoyed in the mid-1960s. Many like Weetall, MacDowell, and Keck, tell of trying out projects that their bosses did not ordain or in some instances that their bosses did not even approve.

78. Augustus Filbert, interview by M. Graham, 1997.

79. Hutchins, interview by Davis Dyer, 20 November 1997.

80. See "Medfield's Innovative Instrument-Makers," *Gaffer*, October 1967.

81. Marty Gibson, interview by M. Graham, 30 April 1997.

82. See Corning Medical brochure, n.d. [1976]; box 34-6-3/PL4, Medfield, MA, 1967–1985 folder, CIDARM; and Alan F. Donnelly, Corning press release, "Corning Establishes Worldwide Medical Group," [August] 1975; box 1-5-2, Corning LARC System folder, CIDARM.

83. Dick Dulude, interview by Davis Dyer, 21 September 1998.

84. See Alan F. Donnelly, draft for press release, "New Instruments Automate Last Routine Manual Chore in Hematology Laboratories," n.d. [previous to August 1975]; box 1-5-2, Corning LARC System folder, CIDARM.

85. Harmon Garfinkel, interview by M. Graham, 30 April 1997.

86. Charles Wakeman, interview by M. Graham, 11 July 1997.

87. Marty Gibson, interview by M. Graham, 30 April 1997.

88. Jack Hutchins, interview by Davis Dyer, 20 November 1997.

89. J. C. Littleton, interview, 20 December 1972, pp. 19–20; unaccessioned material, CIDARM.

90. Ibid., pp. 18–19.

91. Marty Gibson, interview by M. Graham, 30 April 1997.

92. Jamie Houghton, strategic analysis and tactical plan through 1985, dated 1982— Houghton Personal Files.

93. MacAvoy interview. Amory Houghton became convinced of the economic inevitability of this move because Sylvania had managed to acquire ribbon machine technology, undercutting the last advantage Corning had in this business.

94. See Morone, *Winning in High Tech Markets*, p. 142. MacAvoy had been determined to use every possible tool available to focus. Not surprisingly, some of the tools pushed the company in the opposite direction.

Chapter 10

1. *Financial World*, May 19, 1987 referred to this as "a bewildering variety of businesses." Such expressions of bewilderment from financial analysts became a larger and larger factor in the thinking of company leadership from this time on. See also case prepared for in-house use, "Case A: The Corning Growth Experience," 1995.

2. Houghton recovered and continued as chairman until April of 1996.

3. The notion of institutionalizing innovation goes back to the 1970s when Texas

Instruments adopted a much studied and much admired stage-gate process which
was largely a process for resource allocation among competing project opportunities.
See Marian Jellinek. *Institutionalizing Innovation: A Study of Organizational Learning
Systems*, 1979. Based on fieldwork at Texas instruments, Jellinek's work was one of
the earliest items in the literature on organizational learning, and documents Pat
Haggerty's approach to integrating planning for new products into the regular business activities of the firm.

4. Corning strategy characterized by Ackerman in the first annual report signed by him
    as chairman (1996).
5. Corning Glass Works *Annual Report* for 1982, issued in February, 1983.
6. James R. Houghton, "The Role of Technology in Restructuring a Company,"
    Research Management, November/December, 1983, pp. 9–16.
7. J. R. Houghton, June 9, 1999. Note that this was interpreted in absolute terms. In real
    dollar terms as well as in percent of sales, Corning's investment in R&D had
    decreased since the 1960s.
8. Ibid.
9. "Corning's Class Act," *Business Week*, 13 May, 1991, pp. 68–76.
10. J. R. Houghton, interview by WGI, 9 June, 1999.
11. A widely shared assessment of the qualities of the two men, best articulated by Mar-
    tin Gibson in 1999 interview with Davis Dyer.
12. At first only a few companies strove to compete with the Japanese. See David T.
    Kearns and David A. Nadler, *Prophets in the Dark: How Xerox Reinvented itself and Beat
    Back the Japanese*, 1995; for Corning's story, see Ira Magaziner and Mark Patinkin,
    Silent War: Inside the Global Business Battle Shaping America's Future (New York: Ran-
    dom House, 1989).
13. See Corning's "blue book," in-house publication.
14. See "CGW, Swiss Firm Completes Forming of New Company," *Corning Leader*, 18
    July 1985, p. 2A.
15. J. R. Houghton interview by M. Graham, June 9, 1999 characterized the Ciba-
    Corning relationship as a case of a very good relationship, but with diverging inter-
    ests on the part of the principals. See also Joseph Morone, *Winning in High Tech
    Markets*.
16. Howard Weetall, interview by M. Graham, February 1999.
17. Gitimoy Kar interview 1998.
18. Marty Gibson interview, 1998.
19. Norm Garrity interview cites both the unexpected creativity showed by aluminum
    when it was threatened and the insistence of the "IBMs of this world" to have some-
    thing really cheap. "We were way ahead of the curve," says Garrity.
20. T. Kozlowski interview by Margaret Graham and Kathleen McDermott, March 1996.
    For a comprehensive treatment of quality as understood at the time, see David
    Garvin, *Managing Quality: The Strategic and Competitive Edge*, and William E. Cole. *The
    Economics of Total Quality Management* (New York: Oxford University Press, 1989).
21. MacAvoy, interview by M. Graham, 1998.
22. "Corning's Class Act."
23. For this account of Corning's quality program, see interviews with Forrest Behm,
    James R. Houghton, Thomas MacAvoy, and Norman Garrity.

24. J. R. Houghton, "Six Strategies" speech to the Charlotte Chamber of Commerce, 19 January, 1994.
25. See also *Fortune*, "The Seven Keys to Business Leadership" (Reprint).
26. McKinsey Consulting Company, *Report on Patent Department*, 1973.
27. Presentation by Al Michaelsen to the Management Committee, 1985, internal patent department document.
28. For quality in research, T. Kozlowski interview 1996, Charles Craig interview 1999, Eve Menger interview 1999, A. Filbert interview.
29. Corning's Quality organization was dismantled as part of Corning Competes, a reengineering effort launched in 1993 and completed in 1994, described below.
30. Norm Garrity, interview with Davis Dyer, 1999.
31. David Nadler, quoted in *Enterprise Magazine*, Cover story, 1992, noted that Corning is unusual in not falling into the uniformity trap.
32. J. R. Houghton, "Diversity at Corning," speech delivered at Owens-Corning, Quebec, 7 January, 1994.
33. "Corning's Class Act."
34. J. R. Houghton, History Advisory Committee minutes, April 1999.
35. MacAvoy, interview with M. Graham, 1998.
36. Lester Thurow, National Public Television Commentaries in the 1980s and Thurow, *Head to Head: The Coming Economic Battle among Japan, Europe, and America* (1993).
37. See Margaret B. W. Graham, "The Current Transformation of Corporate Research," Special Issue of *Technology in Society*, Pergamon Press, 1986.
38. For organizational shifts in R&D, see Jacques Lemoine interview, and Op Com presentation.
39. J. R. Houghton strategy documents, personal papers.
40. Clarence Patty interview, 1997, reflected that 1983–84 marked what he believed was a turning point in Corning's patent policy.
41. *Technology Assessment and Strategy* document, 1983, MacAvoy personal papers.
42. For the innovation task force, see interviews with Marie McKee, John Dunphy, Tom MacAvoy, Charles Craig, and the Program of the Innovation Conference, 1986.
43. McKee interview, 1988.
44. MacAvoy speech given at the innovation conference, 1986.
45. Charles Craig interview, August, 1999.
46. Kozlowski interview, 1996.
47. As described by Robert Burgelman, *Inside Corporate Innovation: Strategy, Structure and Managerial Skills* (New York: Free Press, 1988).
48. Interview with Fred Quan.
49. Kozlowski interview, 1996, and Craig, 1999.
50. As mentioned in Chapter 1, numerous accounts of Corning innovations have been written throughout Corning's history. Inventors Wellech, Stookey, DeVoe, Shay, and many others have written their own accounts of important inventions. Histories and historical presentations have been prepared for internal use in most generations. Slide shows by Robert Dalton, "The History of Chemical Research at Corning," and John Hammond Munier, "A Perspective on the Role of Research, Development, and Engineering in the Corning Glass Worlds, The First Hundred Years," 30 September, 1976, TIC L1842, were used repeatedly in the Technical Center for internal and external communications meetings. In the 1970s Amory Houghton Jr. himself conducted

videotaped interviews with numerous key people to preserve a personal record of key aspects of Corning's experience.

51. Eve Menger interview; Menger was one of the few technical people hired into Corning from the outside during this period. According to Menger, one reason the policy of concentration of force was so effective was that it involved "repotting" people. In Corning's culture it was understood that people who were asked to retrain in a new discipline needed time and support to make the shift. The shift having been made, they could add a vital cross-disciplinary perspective to an urgent project that enhanced problem-solving. Another important factor in the success of this practice was that many people, not just one or two, were involved at a time.

52. Garrity interview.

53. FMC Corp, for instance, started a similar plant in Aiken, South Carolina, though it was a non-union plant. General Motors adopted similar principles in its "greenfield" start-up of the Saturn Division in Spring Valley, Tennessee.

54. Garrity interview. See also "A New Breed on the Line," *Washington Post*, 2 August, 1992.

55. On the evolution of the fiber optics industry generally at this time, see Hecht, *City of Light*. On Corning specifically, see Morone, *Competing*; Magaziner and Patinkin, *Silent War*.

56. The Northeast Corridor System project was AT&T's attempt to modernize its existing Boston to Washington system, which was particularly overloaded and antiquated at the time, using optical fibers.

57. Jeffrey Hecht, *City of Light*, pp. 196–197.

58. Duke interview.

59. Dawson interview.

60. Joseph Hicks interview by Davis Dyer—the original projections for Siecor envisioned a niche company with sales of $50 million in the 1990s, its primary rationale to gain market access and customer understanding for Corning.

61. Dawson, interview by M. Graham, February 1997.

62. Hicks interview.

63. *Financial World*, 19 May 1987.

64. Hicks interview.

65. Hecht, *The City of Light*, pp. 229–230.

66. In the late 1980s a typical cable contained 48–96 fibers.

67. Kar interview.

68. Ibid.

69. Gibson, interview by Davis Dyer, 8 February 1999.

70. Ibid.

71. J. R. Houghton interview with Davis Dyer, May 1999.

72. Dave Duke and Howard Weetall in interviews stress that the medical business in general did not share Corning's norms and values, which was uncomfortable for many people who joined it from Corning.

73. Champy et al., *Reengineering*.

74. J.R. Houghton interview.

75. A popular parody of Corning's reengineering efforts was "Corning Deletes."

76. Roger Ackerman interview, 1998.

Epilogue

1. Significantly, Little Joe was an inherited logo belonging first to MacBeth Evans, which merged with Corning in 1936. Adopting the other company's logo was typical of Corning's respect for the heritage of the companies with which it was connected.

2. See p. 83.

3. This was accomplished by divesting both the $2.1 billion clinical lab testing unit and the $675 million consumer housewares business (the latter was originally priced at just under $1 billion, but that deal with AEA Investors—which was relying on large Asian sales to make the acquisition work—fell through and Bordon, a KKR company, got it at a significantly lower price). After these divestitures Corning was slimmed down to a $3.5 billion company employing about 18,000 people.

4. "Building the World's Largest Telescope Mirror: How Clarkson Alumni at Corning Incorporated Triumphed through Teamwork," *Clarkson Magazine,* June 1994, pp. 22–27.

5. Statement made by Norm Garrity, executive vice president, Corning Technologies, in a communications meeting held at Sullivan Park in October 1999.

6. Roger Ackerman, internal corporate communications video, October 1999.

7. "Has Corning Won Its High-Tech Bet? After Trashing the Stock, Wall Street Sees a Net Play," *Business Week,* 5 April 1999.

8. These issues were raised by Garrity at the communications meeting cited above. Shortly afterward he and his counterpart in Corning Communications, John Loose, changed jobs to help with this task of strategic focusing. Loose became president and chief operating officer, and Garrity became vice chairman in charge of staffs with special emphasis on balancing the current and future needs of Corning's businesses for technical resources.

INDEX

277; *Fortune* magazine on, 292; increases research budgets, 71; serves on War Production Board, 178, 280, 285, 452n9; at U.S. Mission for Economic Affairs, London, 179; views nuclear fuels as growth opportunity, 168; and Walter Bedell Smith, 168, 179; and Walter Dorwin Teague, 120

Houghton, Arthur Jr. *(1906–1990)*, 372–373; and antitrust suits, 283–284; and libraries, 452n9; and Steuben glass, 118–119, 120, 121

Houghton, Arthur Sr. *(1866–1928)*: becomes Corning president, 63; and Empire Machine Company (1909), 90, 457n8; and knowledge-based strategy, 34, 81; and railroad signal lens color problem, 38; and research, 36–37, 41, 65, 89–90; and support for mechanization, 80; and updraw process, 82, 84*i*, 441

Houghton, Charles *(1846–1897)*, 10, 36–37
Houghton family, 9*i*, 250, 290, 393, 395
Houghton, James R. *(1936–)*, 373*i*; adopts total quality management, 401–402; chief executive (1983–1996), 9; and corporate strategy, 387; and cultural diversity, 407; and high-technology strategy, 422; and innovation process, 414; on innovation *vs.* quality, 408; and investment in optical waveguides, 423; and management by team, 397; and Metropolitan Museum of Art, 452n9; and research funding, 395, 409; and research portfolio, 395; succession planning for, 393

Houghton Park, 250
House of Glass, 114
House Un-American Activities Committee, 200
housewares. *See* cookware; Pyrex
Howitt, Tom, 255
Hub Machine, 214, 258, 339, 340*i*, 342
Huber, Cathryn, 57*i*
Hudson, Bill, 397, 419
Hunt, Mal, 217, 269–271
hurricane Agnes flood, 15, 332–333
Hutchins, Jack: and Avon laboratory, 375; and biological research, 378; and dual career ladder, 371; on fiber optics attenu-

ation announcement, 315–316; on Genencor, 381–382; and layoffs, 348; and research portfolio, 395

Hyde, J. Franklin: and architectural glass, 132–133; career at Corning, 73, 128, 134, 159; and David Gray, 133; and fiberglass, 133–134, 152, 154; on industrial research climate, 161, 245–246, 325; joins Dow-Corning, 159; joins Owens-Corning Fiberglas, 134; and Mellon Institute, 134, 136; patents, 137, 159, 292; and plastics research, 127; and research model, 223; and silicone research, 75, 129–130, 135, 137; and vapor deposition process, 6, 130–132; World War II research projects, 159

Hygrade Lamp Company, 142. *See also* Sylvania

identity, corporate, 17, 393, 439, 441, 447
Illuminating Engineering Society, 47
immobilized enzymes, 6, 378–379, 380
Industrial and Engineering Chemistry, 76
industrial management, science of, 100
information control, 75, 139
initial stock offering, 13, 290
innovation: process, 408, 413, 415–422, 437; *vs.* productivity, 392; task force, 410–411
Innovation Conference, 414–416
intellectual property: Alfred L. Michaelsen on, 323; and antitrust, 191, 289, 290–291; costs of managing, 299; Federal funding and, 179–180; lessons from Dow-Corning experience, 161; and military contracts, 174, 205, 217–218; neglected, 301; and optical waveguides, 308, 317–324; reactive approach to managing, 279, 280; as strategic asset, 3–4, 325; technique for protection of, 189; trademarks, 292. *See also* knowledge-based strategy; patents
international laboratories, 410, 432, 442
international markets, 334
International Telephone and Telegraph. *See* ITT
internship program, 253